the ART and SCIENCE of TAKING to the WOODS

the ART and SCIENCE of TAKING to the WOODS

C.B. COLBY & BRADFORD ANGIER

illustrated by ARTHUR J. ANDERSON

STACKPOLE BOOKS

THE ART AND SCIENCE OF TAKING TO THE WOODS

Standard Book Number: 8117-0109-3
Library of Congress Catalog Card Number: 71-100344

Printed in U.S.A.

For the Camp Fire Club of America and its members, who have done so much for conservation since it was founded back in 1897, and particularly for its Committee on Conservation of Forests and Wildlife formed in 1909.

Contents

PART THREE   LEARNING THE TRICKS OF THE CAMPING CRAFT

CONTENTS

PART FOUR BEING SET FOR THE NEXT TIME

PART ONE

GETTING READY
TO TAKE OFF

1

What Kind of Camping for You?

EVERY NOW AND THEN SOMEONE INQUIRES HOW BEST HE CAN TAKE to the woods. This is a loaded question. There are numerous types of camping and camp vehicles, each having its pros and cons. Too, many variables involve the new woodsman himself—age, budget, driving experience, vacation preference, and so on. So recommending one type of camping over another can be quite a gamble. Fortunately, however, an outdoorsman can tailor his sport to fit his income, age, and interests. Here's how.

For the hale and hearty there is backpack camping, and done right, there's nothing to it. For the family and for groups, there are tents, folding tent trailers, travel trailers, campers mounted on the beds of pickup trucks, and mobile-home vans. Let us present the good and bad points of each of these ways of taking to the woods and let you decide which best fits your needs.

For those who plan one-night stands, the wheeled vehicles are more convenient than a tent, with the better bets being the pickup camper, the travel trailer, and the motor van. These vehicles involve no pitching, dismantling, or, in case it storms, the packing of wet canvas.

Although convenient, the tent trailer—a small, two-wheeled trailer to which a tent is affixed—requires some erecting, dismantling, and repacking. If extra rooms are used, these also must be detached and repacked before the trip can be resumed. Some traveling campers prefer to use station wagons, sleeping in the vehicles during overnight stops and saving tent pitching for longer stays.

Tents have many advantages for the beginning camper. Compared to other types of shelters, they are inexpensive. They need not be towed or maneuvered into position, and they are comfortable except during extreme weather conditions. Tents can be carried to and erected in places that are not accessible to a driven or towed vehicle.

The lightweight tents can be backpacked. They can be pitched in a few minutes. Yet at minimum cost they afford protection from storms, insects, and snakes. When pitched on a platform such as are now found in many campgrounds, and protected by a fly, larger models provide extremely comfortable and durable summer homes.

Tents can be bought in so many sizes, materials, and designs that nearly any preference can be satisfied and a group of almost any size accommodated. Tents of good quality, given reasonable care, will last for years. Another great advantage is that they can be stored in attic, closet, basement, or garage when not in use.

On the other hand, tents do have their drawbacks. They require an area that is fairly smooth and level. They must be put up and taken down. They are subject to damage from sparks, little animals such as mice and chipmunks, sharp objects, and an assortment of other things. If they are packed away when damp, tents may mildew, although many of the modern fabrics have been treated against this hazard.

But tents have been in use since about 1000 B.C., and in spite of all their shortcomings, they are still the preferred shelter of the great preponderance of people who spend their spare time out of doors.

Tent trailers are roomy, affording off-the-ground living and sleeping for as many as a half-dozen campers. They have numerous built-in conveniences, including stoves, iceboxes, sinks, and in some cases even toilets, plus zip-on rooms and plenty of storage space. The beds are large and even come with mattresses.

The ground on which a tent trailer is parked does not have to be smooth or level. If necessary, the contrivance can be moved into position by hand. These advantages also make it a simple matter to park a tent trailer in your yard or driveway unless this practice is prohibited by local zoning laws.

The disadvantages of tent trailers include their initial expense, several times that of a tent of comparable size plus accessories, and the fact that they are not allowed on some parkways. Such trailers must have a license, and the user must learn how to maneuver them.

Travel trailers of almost any towable size boast far more conveniences than do the tent trailers. These niceties include hot and cold running water, refreshing showers, and even electric lights. Travel trailers require no erection, of course. They can be warm and comfortable in any type of weather, many of them being in permanent use in Alaska and other cold country. When in place they can be connected to the electricity, running water, and sewer facilities that are available today in many trailer grounds.

The average passenger car can tow one of the smaller travel trailers easily and with little loss of gasoline mileage. And once you've arrived at the camping spot with the trailer, you can disconnect the car and use it for sightseeing and other purposes, an advantage not to be had with pickup campers and motor vans. Travel trailers need but little maintenance, and they come in numerous sizes in a wide choice of designs.

Disadvantages accrue, too, with the use of travel trailers, however. Like tent trailers, they are banned from some parkways and in some areas may not be parked in yards or driveways. If the trailer uses bottled gas for stoves and other appliances, it may be prohibited from passing through some tunnels. The expense of a travel trailer can be a high hurdle, also. These trailers must be licensed. Maneuvering them takes some practice. Much to the regret of the younger members of the family, no one may ride in a trailer while it is being towed along a highway.

In addition to being easier to maneuver and park, pickup campers have several advantages over a trailer. They are ideal for many hunters and fishermen in that, because of the rugged construction of the pickup truck on which the camper body is mounted, they can be driven into country that can't be reached by a towed vehicle or even a low-riding passenger car. They usually cost no more than a good travel trailer, whose convenience they practically duplicate. Riders are allowed in the living quarters of the camper while it is en route, and when it arrives at the campground it can be connected to electricity, water, and sewer system.

The expense of the pickup camper is foremost among its disadvantages, although this cost may be spread out if you have a genuine use for the truck once the camper body is taken off. Again, local laws may prevent the parking of such vehicles in yards and driveways, as well as keep them from certain parkways and tunnels.

Unfortunately, once the pickup camper is parked at a campsite, the truck cannot be used by itself for side trips as can the vehicle towing a travel trailer. It is true that some camper bodies can be removed from the trucks and stored on jacks. However, this chore is not recommended for the casual camper.

The motor van is the most luxurious of all mobile living arrangements. Such land yachts boast all the conveniences of a large travel trailer. Yet they are commonly classified as pleasure vehicles, opening parkways to them that are closed to trailers and campers. Vans handle well. They may, of course, be ridden in while on the go. Finally, a van can really be a home on wheels, affording shower, toilet, running water, closets, double beds, electricity, and other features.

Its high cost and the fact that it has virtually no use other than as a mobile home are foremost among a van's disadvantages. Too, vans bearing propane gas tanks may be turned away from tunnels. Finally, the van owner requires another vehicle for general transportation.

If you decide on one of the towed units, either a tent trailer or a travel trailer, remember that you'll need special hitches on your car, extra insurance, provision for lights on the trailer, and a special license for the latter. On the other hand, taking to the highway with a trailer embodies no special skills, although you'll find that you require more room to pass and a longer time to stop. However, backing a trailer takes practice. Speed limits for trailers are sometimes lower than for automobiles.

Driving either a pickup camper or a motor van is less demanding, although at first you'll feel as if you're driving an apartment house while sitting in the lobby. You may find that these rigs will tend to wander somewhat more than a car does. Too, until you get accustomed to the extra weight and bulk, high winds will probably give you a few uncertain minutes. If you are an experienced driver, though, you should have little difficulty.

Choosing the unit that is best for you depends to a large extent upon the sort of camping vacation you are planning. If it is to be a leisurely sojourn in one or two particular regions, a tent, tent trailer, or small travel trailer will be ideal. Any of these can be left at the campground while you use your automobile.

If you plan to keep on the go, a pickup camper or motor van will be more convenient. There will be little vehicle maneuvering with either of these rigs, and it won't be necessary to erect a tent or strike camp. Regardless of weather or extreme temperatures, they will be snug. For those aiming at the rough hinterlands, the pickup with its truck power will be ideal.

Motor vans and large travel trailers are at their best on fine highways leading to well-appointed campgrounds that have facilities for parking and servicing such rigs.

If you're really going to get away from it all, to go to the other extreme, the best bet by far will be a lightweight tent. One of these can be backpacked so comfortably that you can hike almost anywhere with home conveniently on your back.

Tenters still greatly outnumber campers who use wheeled units, and for a good reason. Tents are by far the most economical shelters. They come in almost unlimited variety. Finally, innumerable outdoorsmen feel that tenting is the only true way to take to the woods.

Tents can be transported with a minimum of difficulty in a trunk, on a roof rack, or just behind the front seat. You can take them into the most primitive of the farther places on your back. They can be hung from trees, pitched with external or internal frames, or erected on fiber glass ribs in the shape of an igloo. There are even tents with hollow ribs that you inflate to erect. Tents come in sizes for lone individuals, for pairs, and for entire families. Some have built-in rooms. Most these days are equipped with sewn-in floors and with complete screening, so that they are about as comfortable in moderate weather as any wheeled rig.

If you are not certain whether or not you'll take to the outdoor life, try a tent. It will give you an opportunity to test your likes at a most moderate expenditure. The more affluent, the older, and the less adventurous might well try a tent trailer, travel trailer, pickup camper, or motor van. If you're not sure about any of these, rent one at first.

It comes down to this. The kind of camping that's best for you is the one that gives the most pleasure and relaxation for a price you can afford. By balancing the pros and cons detailed in this chapter and matching them with your special desires and needs, you're almost certain to come up with a form of camping that will lift you out of yourself.

2

Taking to the Woods
for Economy

THERE COMES A TIME EVERY YEAR WHEN THE FAMILY BEGINS TO consider the annual question, "Where shall we go for our vacation?" The companion query, of course, is, "What will it cost?" The answer to this usually has a great deal to do with the response to question number one. A family may have to do some serious planning before it can decide upon a vacation that will be enjoyable for all hands, at a price everyone can afford.

There is, however, one type of group vacation that's both inexpensive and popular—a camping trip. In other words, taking to the woods may be the answer to your vacation problem.

From an economy angle, a camping trip is away ahead of most other types of vacations. For example, let's compare the cost of a tent trip with that of traveling with motel stops or a sojourn at a resort hotel.

Say a family of four goes on a ten-day vacation, stopping either at motels or a resort hotel. They will probably need two rooms unless the youngsters are very small. This can run about $30 a night or $300 for ten days. Restaurant meals will come to about $20 a day for the four for three meals; another $200 for the ten days. Add one more $50 for extra expenses such as tips, snacks, special clothing, and shoes, and they will have spent over $500. Another thing? A vacation at a resort calls for more and better clothing than does a camping trip.

By contrast, a camping vacation for this same family of four can cost less than $380 the first year, while future vacations will take only a small fraction of this because the "accommodation" will already have been paid for.

A good 10 x 12 cottage-type tent, or a similar one to hold four outdoors folk, will cost about $100. This will have screened windows and doors as well as a sewn-in floor. Air mattresses will run about $25, cots $20, and four good sleeping bags with three pounds of insulation apiece a total of $80. A gasoline or propane two-burner stove will cost about $20 and a lantern using the same fuel a similar amount. An icebox may cost $12, and a set of folding table and stools will run to $22.

14

Add a 9 x 9 fly for both shady and rain-free eating for about $20. This comes to a grand total of some $320 for all lodgings, and you'll be going first class. Camp meals will run as little as $6 a day for the three meals for four campers. Add this $60 to the cost of the gear, and you'll have an initial expense of $380 for food and lodgings.

Of course, you can eliminate the table, stools, and eating fly, and buy less expensive sleeping bags, cutting the cost, but we'd suggest getting the best sleeping bags your budget can stand. They will last for years with good care and will be important to your comfort from the very first night.

You can supplement the above outfit by using such things as cooking utensils and flashlights from home at no added expense. And, depending upon the locale, you can really rough it and cook over an open campfire if you prefer.

If you can't decide which tent to buy or what additional gear is necessary, you may be able to rent them from an outfitter for this first trip and then decide later what to own. The above outfit can be rented, item for item, ten days for about $75. If you decide to leave out the cots, eating fly, and table and chairs, the rig will rent for about $55. Adding in meals at the same $60, the whole trip outside of travel expenses and personal gear you may buy could cost less than $150, even with all the items listed.

Many would-be campers ask about campground fees and other such expenses. Privately owned campgrounds, run as business ventures, usually charge $1 to $3 a night per family, sometimes offering special weekly rates. Often this fee includes firewood, hot showers, and use of recreation rooms and laundromats. At other campgrounds where the site rates are low, you may have to buy such necessities as firewood for about $.50 for a large bundle or $.25 for a bushel basket of slab wood.

None of our large national parks charge for camping other than the small park entrance fee which may be $1 or $2, and there is no charge for any camping in our national forests. There you'll have to fetch your own firewood and provide your own entertainment. State parks generally make a small charge, and ordinarily it's for an entire family. In a very few campgrounds under certain conditions no open fires are permitted, one reason why it's good to have some sort of stove along. Even with campground fees, your trip will be inexpensive.

One other detail that makes camping vacations economical is the fact that almost any type of clothing may be worn. Most families take along one respectable outfit apiece to wear for church, when having an occasional meal at a restaurant, or for staying overnight at a motel for a hot bath. But for most camping, any rough, comfortable duds will be fine.

If there are just two of you and you'd like to take a hiking vacation by yourself, the journey will cost even less. The tent will be much smaller or eliminated entirely by use of a shelter tarp. You'll get along without a lantern, icebox, big stove, table and chairs, and eating tarp, so your outfit will run well under $100. And for many years after the initial expense, your lodgings will be free.

Some individuals who have never camped ask, "But what can you do?" To those who have enjoyed the pleasures of camping, this is a funny question, for there are innumerable things to do, and all at little or no expense. There is often fine fishing, boating, hiking, and mountain climbing. Camera addicts will have a ball on any camping trip. Many campgrounds, particularly in state and national parks, have trained lecturers who give interesting talks on nature, geology, and local history.

Numerous camping areas have boats and canoes to rent and evening campfires with impromptu entertainment and sing-alongs. Riding horses are frequently available. There may be swings, seesaws, horseshoe pitching, and ball fields for the youngsters. Some campgrounds have libraries for those who'd like to relax and read. There may be a small zoo or museum.

Many campgrounds are within a short drive of some natural wonder, historic site, or a settlement where movies are shown. Or if you'd like to shut things off and recharge your personal batteries, there's no happier place to loaf than on an air mattress under a shady tree by a stream or lake.

If you are wondering how you can take to the woods near some particular spot you'd like to visit, a good way to start is to go to the local gas station and get maps of the area in question. Check the map to see what symbol indicates a campground and look for those near where you wish to go. Chances are you'll find one.

If none is shown on the service-station maps, write to the conservation department of the state you plan to visit and ask for such campground information. These departments, located in the state capitals, frequently publish lists of even privately owned campgrounds within their jurisdictions.

Or write to the National Park Service, Department of the Interior, Washington, D.C. 20240, as well as to the Forest Service, Department of Agriculture, Washington, D.C. 20523 for their lists of campgrounds. These two services supervise thousands of camping sites, and they'll all be free. There are also many campground guides on the market which include federal, state, and individually owned camping sites.

If you'd like to try stop-and-go camping, using your outdoor outfit instead of tarrying at motels and hotels, take maps, guides, and booklets and try to lay out a route that will provide a campground to stay at each night. Suppose you find an area where there seems to be no campground. Then it's frequently possible to arrange with a local farmer to camp overnight on his property, perhaps offering him a small fee if he seems hesitant. If you do get such permission, be sure to leave the site as clean as it was before you stayed there, if not cleaner.

Numerous campers who travel across the country carry food for breakfasts and dinners but stop for lunch in restaurants. Others prefer to break camp in the darkness, stop for breakfast at the first promising restaurant, and then enjoy a leisurely day with a picnic lunch beside the road and a dinner that evening in the relaxation of camp. It's up to you, but if you do break camp early, remember other campers may still be sleeping.

Carrying a small icebox will keep perishables in fine shape between meals, and if you're lucky, you can replenish your ice supply along the way. Just watch for "Ice for Sale" signs. If the icebox still has plenty of ice when you come to one, but you'll probably need some in a few hours, it's not a bad idea to buy ice on the spot and put pieces in plastic bags or covered pots. Even wrapping a block in newspapers or ponchos will save most of it.

Camping provides an inexpensive introduction to the outdoors and permits many a family to take vacations near scenic beauty, historical sites, and other places they might never be able to visit under other circumstances. At the same time, many families who could afford more expensive vacations prefer to take to the woods with a tent for sheer enjoyment.

If economy is a vital consideration in your vacation plans, give serious thought to a camping trip. The youngsters will enjoy every minute of it, the lady of the household will find that the leisurely pace of camping makes even household chores a pleasure, and the men in the family will find a lot of new interests together. The fun is there, the new friends are there, and the fresh new sights and sounds and relaxation are there. What may be even more of a pleasant surprise, the price is right.

3

Preplanning
Pays Premiums

TRIPS WHEN YOU TAKE TO THE WOODS SPONTANEOUSLY ARE OFTEN fun and generally work out well despite forgotten can openers, raingear, that telephoto lens, and other assorted items left behind in the rush to get started. However, long trips to campsites, extended one-spot camping vacations, and long journeys with overnight tenting stops turn out more satisfactorily if some advance planning is done.

Planning does more to insure that you will get a greater amount of pleasure out of your camping than you had imagined. It will pay big dividends in advance fun, later memories, photographs, and adventure. We're not talking just about what to take, where to go, or what to eat. Instead, let's consider how to decide where to go, when to start, and how to get more from the journey.

Most camping trips hinge on when you can get away, and this in turn may depend on school vacations or on occupational vacation schedules. You may be limited to weekend trips, a four-day weekend, or you may be fortunate enough to have several weeks off. Time will determine whether or not you stay close to home or venture farther afield. With today's highways and automobiles, the family can camp a few hundred miles from home even on just a long weekend.

Why not get out a map and draw a 150-mile circle around your home town. How much of that country within the circle have you visited, and how many campgrounds can you locate within the region? Likely you'll find hundreds of miles of roads you've never been on and many historical landmarks you've never seen.

If camping is merely a by-product of a hunting or fishing trek, when you go will be governed by the open seasons. On the other hand, if the main reason for the journey is to camp, it is well to make the most of the traveling as well as the actual tenting. For tenderfeet, almost any pleasant campground will be a treat. If you're a veteran, perhaps a change of season will be in order.

Do you live far inland? Then why not make a trip this season to see the ocean, the wild shorelines, and the sweeping dunes? If you have been going to the beach for many seasons, then the smell of tall spruce and the strange wild screech of high winds above

17

timberline may stir new ideas of what taking to the woods can be like. Mountain men may find the prairie vastnesses impressive, while the flatlanders may discover among the roads that wind through the peaks a new and exciting experience.

If you've never been across our borders, why not try Canada or even Mexico? If you dwell in the East, give some thought to a camping trip to Canada's New Brunswick, Nova Scotia, Prince Edward Island, Cape Breton, and even wild Newfoundland. Those who live in the Midwest or the Far West can drive to the Dominion's vast wheatlands or its pristine northwestern provinces.

In many parts of our country you can get in both mountain and seashore camping in a single trip. Every state has dozens of scenic, historic, and scientific points of interest ranging from mines and meteorite craters to ghost towns, waterfalls, and battlefields. Not all are in every state, of course, but scanning a map of almost any state will reveal numerous points of interest to mark down on your preplanned route.

Before backing out of the driveway, look over the mapped area on the route to your campground and the territory around where you will erect a shelter. There may be a dozen spots you'd like to visit. If you expect to be in one place for a week or so, you'll have ample time to travel from your camp to see still more. If your journey is to be nomadic, plan your path among campgrounds close to points of interest.

If you have a hobby, a camping vacation will be a grand way to further it. If it's photography, there is hardly an area on the continent that does not offer outstanding scenery and unusual opportunities to use photo equipment. If your hobby is mineralogy, there are canyons, fossils, lava beds, stone mountains, old mines, and placer deposits of everything from diamonds to jade from one end of the land to the other. Marshlands, migratory routes, and wilderness nesting grounds for the bird watchers in your party will keep all binoculars occupied. If your avocation is history, why not visit the many battlefields, war memorials, and historic restorations found in almost every state?

There must be many parts of our country that you have promised yourself or the youngsters that you would someday visit. Including such localities in a camping trip is a pleasurable and inexpensive way to keep that promise. There are the famed cliff dwellings in our national parks and monuments for the budding archeologists, plus vast and mysterious natural caves in some of these same regions.

And if you have ever dreamed it would be fun to try out one of the many long trails, such as the East's famed Appalachian Trail or the West's star-scouring Pacific Crest Trail, why not make it a reality this season? Many of these great trails cross and recross fine highways; so you can hike over as much or as little as you desire.

One of the most productive ways to plan an engrossing and pleasantly educational sojourn is to assemble maps of the states through which you will drive and camp, plus a detailed guidebook of the campsites in those states. Most maps compiled by state recreation, park, and conservation departments not only indicate points of special interest but state-operated campgrounds as well. These maps, along with those from the National Park Service, Department of the Interior, Washington, D. C. 20240, offer many such route choices.

If you can arrange it, you may enjoy an early spring or late fall camping trip. While most public campgrounds stay open until October or year-around, they are generally free of the hordes of campers after Labor Day or whenever schools generally open. If your small fry's school starts classes a few days later, you may be able to get in some fine uncrowded camping days.

If you can take your vacation anytime, why not go as soon as the local schools have

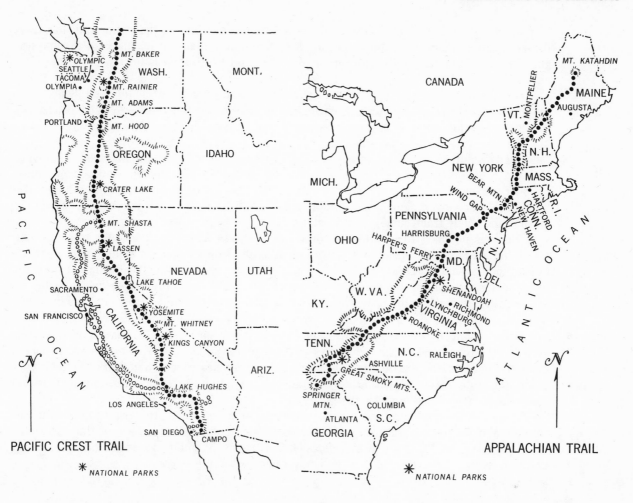

closed? Then you'll have an opportunity to tent during the cooler spring weeks before the summer heat and before the crush begins to tax campground capacities. If your schools close in midweek, leaving then will be even better, for traffic will be relatively light and the chances of locating a good site will be better.

A camping sojourn should be interesting and leisurely. Unless you have to be at a particular spot at a definite time, why not combine the journey with exploring off-the-highway roads instead of sticking to the main thoroughfares? There are usually some excellent roads parallel to main turnpikes, and many of them offer more scenic views, less traffic, and greater numbers of restaurants, motels, and service stations than superhighways.

If you have to travel with another car, you may be interested in an experiment the Colbys tried recently. The family bought a set of small walkie-talkies for under $50 to use in the local volunteer fire department, and tried them out between moving cars on the highway to test their efficiency. The experiment turned into quite an affair. True, the noise of the engines caused some interference, but with the small antennae out a window it was possible to talk clearly when the cars were half a mile apart or more.

On the open road, to indicate a desire to talk to the other car, the driver of the lead car would blink his tail or brake lights three times, and if the driver of the following car wanted to talk, he'd toot his horn three times. This saved keeping the sets on all the time. It was handy to confer on them when to stop for lunch and so on. It also kept the passengers from being bored, and in an emergency it would have been handy to alert the other automobile.

One other thing the authors have learned over the years, often the hard way, is to try to plan a trip so as not to pass through any large cities between 4 and 7 P.M. During these hours many offices and factories close, and the traffic is often extremely heavy.

Another small point that may very well make your camping trip more pleasant is to take along fishing gear. If you are passing near a famous fishing lake or stream, try your luck. A 2- or 3-day nonresident fishing license is usually inexpensive, and if you are in no hurry to move on, stop over a day or so and invest in such a license and some relaxation. Licenses are generally obtainable from tackle stores, town clerks, hardware stores, and even from some service stations.

There is no need to mention planning for highway safety by checking your car and trailer for worn tires, burned-out tail- or headlights, cracked hose connections, or whatever. When towing a trailer, check the route you have selected for two things, especially in or near metropolitan areas. First, trailers of any type are banned from many parkways in the East, especially in the New York area. Campers are also banned from similar highways.

Campers and trailers are banned from numerous tunnels if they are equipped with appliances using bottled gas, such as gas carried in pressure tanks outside the vehicle. In case of fire or collision, such tanks can be potential bombs. All such vehicles must detour. The penalties for violations of such ordinances are severe. It's wise to check your proposed route to see if you will run into such a situation. Incidentally, this does not apply to camp lanterns and stoves.

Planning the next camping trip so you can get more out of the traveling, as well as the actual camping, will return more for your investment. If all members of the party pool their interests, hobbies, and preferences and a trip is planned to accommodate as many of these as possible, the vacation will pay dividends for everyone.

4

Camping in Canada

THOSE OF YOU WHO'D LIKE TO COMBINE A BIT OF FOREIGN TRAVEL with camping can easily do so by setting sights for Canada. Our vast northern neighbor, surpassed in land area among the nations of the world only by the U.S.S.R., can boast of magnificent scenery, numerous splendid campgrounds, and a sort of built-in welcome mat.

The Dominion's national parks alone include more than 75 beautiful campgrounds, many of which can accommodate more than 500 tents. These camping areas are equipped with many of the finest accommodations available anywhere. They have playgrounds for the youngsters, hot and cold water, and nearby groceries. Most of them also have fishing, boating, and swimming. Other remoter camp areas are more isolated, for those who want to get off by themselves.

Canada's provincial parks offer hundreds more campgrounds in often spectacular surroundings. As for the tremendous areas of the country's North, these contain more wilderness than will probably ever be camped in, but they often necessitate special transportation and guides.

Canadian camping conditions in general are similar to those here south of the border. Possible exceptions are the local regulations, weather that is apt to be chillier later in the spring and earlier in the autumn, and the fact that in such a province as Quebec you may find your tenting neighbors talking French more often than English. All these factors can add up to making a camping vacation more interesting.

Canadian roads are good, the campgrounds adequately marked, and the supervisory personnel at the parks mighty congenial, helpful, and eager to make you feel at home. You can get explicitly illustrated booklets, free for the asking, on every part of the country. These list campgrounds, facilities, and various sorts of helpful information. The major sources for these publications are the local travel departments in the provincial capitals and the Canadian Government Travel Bureau in Ottawa, Ontario, which will put you in touch with any local bodies of interest.

Campgrounds in some areas are especially numerous, as for instance in western Canada just east of notable Jasper National Park, which straddles the border between

Alberta and British Columbia. Between the two northern cities of Calgary and Edmonton, northeast of the Park, there are twenty-eight campsites within a sixty-mile radius, almost all on water and on improved roads.

From the Great Lakes eastward, the Dominion has many clusters of campgrounds. Along the rugged coasts of Quebec, New Brunswick, Nova Scotia, Prince Edward Island, and even Newfoundland there are campsites. In fact, here's a vast region just made for camping, yet few U.S. campers have tried it. The Maritimes offer spectacular scenery, foreign attractiveness, top hunting and fishing if you're interested, and superb camping facilities. They also proffer some of the pleasantest camping neighbors you'll find on this continent.

Not to be missed is a trip around the breathtaking Cabot Trail, which circles the cliffs of Nova Scotia's Cape Breton Island. On its big loop around this sea-girt arm, the Cabot Trail is dignified by wild scenery, rugged cliffs, fine roads, many sight-seeing turnoffs, and numerous lovely campgrounds. Camera fans will never forget the spuming surf, crags, rolling moors, replicas of Scottish shepherd huts, and generally photogenic countryside in every direction. Many of the camps are in areas of the wildest scenery.

Most of the motoring in the Maritime Provinces and its neighboring country is fine if you stick to roads indicated by red lines on the maps. On roads shown as blue, fine blue, or dotted lines, you may expect almost anything. Many of these are dusty in the extreme, slippery when wet, and may ride like a washboard. The speed limit is 60 m.p.h. on most roads, which, when they are the main thoroughfares, are wide, well marked, and well paved. The Cabot Trail itself is especially well surfaced, marked, and graded. By the way, when you see a reduced-speed sign on any of these roads, it's wise to obey promptly. There's generally a potent reason for such markings.

One of the loveliest spots in this general area is Gaspesian Park on the Gaspé Peninsula at the mouth of the historic St. Lawrence River in Quebec. Then there's Newfoundland, where the coastline is wild and weird but the fishing terrific. For those who don't like snakes, incidentally, Newfoundland is said to be completely snake-free, and we've never seen one there ourselves.

Nearer to the central United States, Ontario offers some exceptional camping facilities. Its great Algonquin Provincial Park, covering 3,750 square miles, affords camping and canoeing on no less than 2,100 lakes. Canadian Route 60 takes a 30-mile loop through the Park. From this highway you can reach out into many areas for real wilderness camping or take advantage of the six public campgrounds along the main route. Besides these half-dozen improved areas with their many facilities, there are several designed for group camping by Boy Scouts, Girl Scouts, and similar groups.

If you're interested in melding camping and canoeing, there's ample opportunity here to do so, either with a guide or on your own. These canoe trips can be booked for a day, a week, or longer. If you like, you can rent complete outfits, including food and canoes, for as long as desired.

Those venturing off the beaten path into this Canadian wilderness must have a forest travel permit, obtainable from park gates, park offices, and at other convenient places in the park. Such a permit entitles its holder to camp in the wilderness. It also advises officials approximately where he'll be in case of emergency. These permits must be carried by any party in the wilderness, particularly during the forest-fire season, from the first of April through October.

Entering Algonquin Park, you pay a small fee to use the park facilities. The fee is about 50 cents a day, or you may buy a season pass for $2 which is good in other provincial parks as well during the year. There are also small charges for camping at regular campsites. Food is available, and so is ice, at Portage Store and Lake of Two Rivers. You can obtain gasoline, maps, and numerous other camping needs at several spots.

The Park's deer and bears will contribute to your entertainment. The deer are quite tame and may be fed with caution, although you should be careful not to make any sudden motions near them. Children prone to make abrupt movements, especially infants, should not be permitted to approach them. Too, do not stoop down in front of any deer, as this invites a charge.

The bears should be left strictly alone. They should never be approached or fed, as they are not tame and can be dangerous, especially a sow with cubs. Bears may appear anywhere, but they will usually not bother you if you do not alarm or annoy them. Do not throw anything, even food, at them, or attempt to frighten them by charging them on foot. They could turn the tables on you. This advice on bears, incidentally, no matter how many times you may see it safely violated, applies everywhere on this continent.

Ontario is well prepared to handle visiting campers. In addition to the excellent campsites in Algonquin Provincial Park, there are numerous others. All in all, the central Canadian province has more than 260 campsites with a wide spectrum of facilities. An excellent free booklet describing all these may be obtained by writing the Department of Travel and Publicity, Toronto 5, Ontario.

One detail noticeable in Canada is that usually camping is not allowed in picnic areas. Neither is picnicking allowed in regular campgrounds. Generally, at the approaches of a campground there is a green and white sign that tells you, "Camping, 1,000 feet ahead." Then at the entrance there is a polished wooden sign with the name of the campground on it. Check in with the official on duty, and he will assist you in selecting a tent site. If you have firearms with you, have them checked, as they're not permitted in park and many other campgrounds.

The farther west you travel in the Dominion—and now that the Trans-Canada Highway is completed, such a trip is a genuine pleasure—the more national parks there are. Manitoba, at Riding Mountain, has one of more than 1,000 square miles with several well-furnished campgrounds. Saskatchewan has seven camps in Prince Albert National Park.

In Alberta you find plenty of public campgrounds not only along the thoroughfares but also in the four great national parks: Jasper, Banff, Waterton Lakes, and Wood Buffalo. Although this last, far to the north, is beyond the reach of the average outdoorsman, the three others are reached by excellent roads and provide hundreds of campsites.

In Canada as elsewhere, most park campgrounds have tables, fireplaces, parking spurs, garbage bins, and frequently free firewood and even tent poles. On the other hand, good drinking water is not always available, although many sites either have fine piped water or pure water from streams, wells, and springs. If you are ever in doubt anywhere, boil water for five minutes and let it cool for drinking. Or use the water-purification tablets discussed in Chapter 32. Unless traveling on a forest travel permit, you are usually requested to camp only in designated areas, and this has its advantages. In such regions the water is generally pure, and there's firewood and other conveniences.

If no ready-cut firewood is at hand, be sure to use either standing dead timber or down timber, or break out the handy camp stove. Keep your fires small, never leave them unattended, and be certain they're dead out when you leave no matter where you camp. Leave your campsite as neat as you found it, neater if possible.

Camping conditions in Canada are generally excellent. About the only things you may have to complain about are swarms of black flies that appear in June and early July. These winged biters, also found in many northern sections of the United States, can be a source of considerable annoyance if you don't have adequate protection. Use plenty of insect repellent during the day, preferably a type containing N, N-diethyl-toluamide, which will be specified on the label, and you'll be all right. For the nights, make sure your tent has finely meshed screening. Mosquitoes may also be abundant.

The equipment needed for a Canadian camping trip is generally the same as for camping elsewhere, but make certain that plenty of warm duds are packed for the evenings. If your equipment requires special fuel or parts, better tote your own supply. However, such ordinary components as propane-gas cylinders can be purchased in most sporting-goods and hardware stores, and of course a luring assortment of fishing tackle can be had near water areas.

On a first trip above the border, a few things may be surprising. For example, the tank of your car and boat motor will hold fewer gallons. The reason for this is that the imperial gallon dispensed in Canada is about one-fifth larger than the U.S. gallon, so be sure your tank will hold what you request the attendant to put in.

Prices for different articles may vary, and it's a good idea to have some Canadian money as well as American. In most stores and other establishments near the border or main highways, U.S. currency will be accepted without question and the prevalent premium paid. But in some remote areas far from the border Canadian money may be needed for everything. You can change your money at a local bank before leaving or when approaching the port of entry.

Crossing the border into Canada is no problem, although numerous American campers have hesitated to take to the Canadian woods because they think it is. If you keep a few points in mind, you'll be through the port of entry in a matter of minutes.

A detailed and interesting booklet called *Canada Border Crossing Information* is free for the asking from the Canadian Government Travel Bureau, Ottawa, although you really don't need such circumstantial information under ordinary conditions. Just make sure that you carry some paper indicating that you are a U.S. citizen. No passport is required. If you are a naturalized citizen, you should have your naturalization certificate with you. You'll need such identification in order to get back into the States after your visit, and it will serve to prove your identity while you're in the Dominion.

Your driver's license is good in Canada, and there is ordinarily no fee for your vehicle or trailer. However, if you are driving any sort of a truck to which a cabin is attached for camping, you will have to pay a truck license fee when entering Ontario. This does not apply to camping trailers, just to trucks. It is charged because some states in this country require a fee for trucks from Ontario. Check with the Canadian Government Travel Bureau, Ottawa, Ontario, before you drive your pickup camper over the border. These Ontario truck plates cost about $20, and a violation may cost you up to $30 or so.

Your camping gear may be taken into Canada without fee or trouble, but you should have a list of the make, model, and number of all cameras, rifles, and motors, so they may be registered with a minimum of difficulty. Such registration enables you to get your gear out of Canada without fuss when it's time to re-enter.

If you have a camera, you're allowed to carry into Canada up to six rolls of film and a dozen flashbulbs per person. You may, however, buy such standard items in Canada without any difficulty.

If you plan to fish on your Canadian camping trip, naturally you'll need nonresident fishing licenses. Check with the port of entry officials, and you can probably purchase them right there or later from park personnel. Hunting licenses are handled the same way. Pistols, revolvers, and automatic (not including autoloading) rifles are not permitted in Canada. Fifty rounds of ammunition per individual are permitted free of duty. However, an entry permit for firearms and fishing tackle does not entail permission to hunt or fish without the proper licenses.

Automobiles are admitted under a traveler's vehicle permit for six months of touring without payment of tax. This permit can be extended by mail if you decide to stay longer. You must have your vehicle registration with you. If the car does not belong to you, you must have a letter from the legal owner giving you permission to drive it. The same is true of motorcycles and bicycles.

If the family pup is along, you must have a certificate from a licensed veterinarian of the United States or Canada indicating that the animal has been vaccinated against rabies during the preceding twelve months. Such a certificate should contain a recognizable description of the dog and give the date of vaccination. Cats may be carried into Canada without such a certificate provided you don't take them into a Canadian national park. In national parks west of Ontario, the rabies certificate is required of both dogs and cats. Both must be registered at the entrance to any of the national parks.

Upon re-entry into the United States, you'll be questioned about your place of birth and may be required to show the proof mentioned earlier.

For something fresh in camping, try being a foreigner for a change. Visit the Dominion of Canada and find out for yourself how enjoyable camping up under the northern lights can be. The scenery is often noteworthy, the campers friendlier perhaps than those you're accustomed to, and the park officials mighty helpful. Campfire smoke takes on an added vigor, and the grub tastes at least as fine as it does back home. We think you'll like it.

5

Alaskan Camping Is Different

TO OUTSIDERS FROM THE LOWER 48, ALASKA OFFERS FANTASTIC scenery, especially friendly people, wild roads, glaciers, and wildlife, plus some astonishing statistics. It also offers exciting camping for those who go properly equipped to take to the woods, are able to fend for themselves if they have to, and are not expecting too much in the way of camping conveniences.

For years, particularly since the building of the epic Alaska Highway, we've been getting questions about the present forty-ninth state. As a result, both the Colbys and the Angiers took off for this tremendous wilderness a few months ago to re-examine the northwestern corner of the continent as a whole and to investigate its camping opportunities and handicaps.

If you look at a map of Alaska, you will see that the state's entire highway system is found in the general Anchorage-to-Fairbanks area. This section is but a very small portion of the entire state, most of which is unreachable except by air or, in some cases, water. Even Juneau, the capital, which the Angiers visited again and where they picked up Publicity Director Mike Miller of the Alaska Travel Bureau for a few highly informative days, down on the panhandle hundreds of miles from the main portion, is inaccessible by any road. The only ways to get there are by boat or aircraft.

General road conditions in Alaska are excellent. There are, however, several short but interesting exceptions, among them the old portion of the Sterling Highway along which several campgrounds are located, the Denali Highway from Paxson to Cantwell, and roads in Mount McKinley National Park. Most other Alaska roads are two-way blacktop, well marked and maintained. True, you may note the lack of stout fences on some of the high corners, but after a few miles you don't even miss these.

The way to travel-camp in Alaska is with the pickup camper. About 90 percent of all Alaskan campers use this type of recreational vehicle, while about 8 percent employ some sort of towed trailer, hardtops being in the majority, or travel home.

Tenting, so popular to the south in Canada and the contiguous United States, is almost unheard of in Alaska. Exceptions are to be found among the Indians and Eskimos, backpackers, hunters, and to a lesser extent fishermen far from more substantial shelter, and a few very hardy souls who wheel up the Alaska Highway with tents in their cars.

Campgrounds in Alaska, with a few very welcome exceptions, usually consist of merely a turnoff into a gravel-surface and generally not-too-level area containing a few picnic tables and benches and the inevitable oil drums for rubbish. There is no area set apart for tenters, with level spots for tents, and it is almost impossible to drive stakes into the ground in most places.

Potable water is rarely available, there is seldom any shelter from the often-high winds, and sanitary facilities are few and far between. These shortcomings are especially evident in numerous areas in which the lack of motels and other hostelries makes camping a necessity.

The lack of drinkable water is one of the most important factors contributing to the popularity of pickup campers, travel trailers, and mobile homes in Alaska, where, incidentally, you can rent them. Most of the state's campgrounds are far from any piping. The drilling of wells is difficult, and most of the streams that flow past campgrounds are unsuitable for use as a potable water supply. These streams originate in or are fed by glaciers and are laden with glacial silt. Their water looks milky and is undrinkable.

Most camping vehicles have their own water supply. But campers using tents must search for a source of drinking water—gas station, private home, or clear brook—and chances are that such a source will be miles from a campground. Of course, the stream water can be boiled or treated with purification tablets. In fact, water-purification instructions, discussed in Chapter 32, are posted at the entrance to most Alaska campgrounds.

Other factors that promote the use of recreational vehicles in Alaska are frequent rains, low temperatures, high winds, lack of firewood, and animal intruders. Even enthusiastic tenters feel a lot more secure in a pickup camper, for instance, than with only a piece of canvas between them and what Alaska has to offer in the way of wind, weather, and wildlife. A hardtop tent trailer or a mobile home is as pleasant at night as the pickup, but you can run into some situations in which towing a trailer can be pretty frustrating.

Camping in a tent in bear country, and practically all Alaska can be considered this, has its hazards. Too, wind is no small factor in discouraging the use of tents in Alaska. On the treeless portions of the state such as along the Denali Highway and the vast tundra areas, high winds can flatten a tent in a hurry. You'll see many an Indian tent guyed down with enough rope to moor a dirigible, and come upon others blown flat while their owners have been away hunting or berrying.

Precautions are necessary for users of camping vehicles, too. Be sure the rig's water tank is full, the propane supply is adequate, and the fuel tank level is kept as near the top as possible. Service stations are far from numerous, and many of them do not sell propane or ice.

The best way for a camper to see Alaska, unless he is determined to drive there in a camping vehicle or car, is to fly to Anchorage or some other sizable city, either from his home or from the end of the picturesque ferry service in Skagway, then to rent a pickup camper. That way you'll save many days of travel and avoid having to take along a mountain of gear.

Rental travel-camping vehicles come equipped with sleeping bags or bedding, cooking utensils, dishes, cutlery, and tools. All you'll need are camera, binoculars, fishing or hunting gear or both, rough wear, and perhaps a fairly dressy outfit in case you decide to socialize. However, city getup isn't really necessary. You'll see many a traveler, right off the trail, enter a restaurant, drop his pack and rifle or rod, and pick up a menu without getting a second glance from the other diners. Informality is the rule in Alaska, and it is most refreshing.

To be specific about what gear to take, we'd suggest both lightweight and warm duds. Summer temperatures can vary—and quickly, particularly at sundown—from the 90's to the low 40's. During the summer it is often cold enough to see your breath some mornings inside a camper. On the other hand, lighting one burner of the gas stove will warm the unit in minutes.

Bring along raingear, waterproof boots, and a wide-brim hat of some sort. Inexpensive plastic parkas with hoods and matching pants, plus lightweight pullover rubber boots, are fine for travelers. The plastic parka will come in handy not only during sudden showers, but also when the wind picks up and the sun goes down. Worn over a wool sweater or jacket, the parkas are easy to move around in, even when you hike up glaciers.

By all means, take along camera and plenty of film. Make room for a telephoto lens, if you can come by one, for it will enable you to take close-ups of wildlife, glaciers, and other distant and interesting subjects. Binoculars will perform the same service, and if you are a marksman or big-game hunter, take along your spotting scope even though you plan no shooting. Often a "white stone" on a faraway high slope turns out to be a goat or Dall sheep.

Take plenty of clothing changes, for laundromats are few and widely separated, and many of the streams are unfit for washing, thanks to the milky glacial silt known as "rock flows." Insect repellents are a must during mosquito and fly seasons.

You've never driven a pickup camper? Don't worry, for after a few miles you'll be as confident behind the wheel of such a rig as you are in your own automobile. A little careful driving at first, common sense, and an awareness of road conditions will enable you to go safely even on high mountain roads.

Here are a few other suggestions for the first-time camper driver: Put all movable objects including luggage on the floor or in a securable closet or cupboard. Remove and store the stove grills, or use clips to keep them in place and prevent their rattling. Turn off the propane gas at the tank while traveling. To avoid flooding in your living quarters, be sure the cap on the water tank is tight. Check it after wheeling over especially rough roads. Take along extra gaslight mantles, and have flashlights at hand for after-dark tire changes or other repairs.

Speaking of tires, there is one good way to avoid tire trouble when traveling such gravel highways as the Denali Highway or the greater part of the Canadian portion of the Alaska Highway. Keep your speed below 35 miles an hour, except perhaps where the roadbed is especially smooth.

On such gravel roads it is also good practice to slow down when another vehicle approaches, particularly when the second vehicle is traveling at high speed. If you are also driving fast, gravel thrown by the other rig's wheels can damage your vehicle. Many experienced Alaskan campers, as well as those along the way north in British Columbia and the Yukon, protect against flying gravel by covering their headlights with cardboard or tape for daytime traveling, and they often cover the over-cab windows with sheets of cardboard or light plywood.

On steep grades, use lower gears instead of brakes. Keep your speed down if it is very windy, and slow down at once if any unusual sway is evident.

Refill the gas tank when it gets down toward the halfway mark, and check your oil at every stop. See to this yourself, as not all stations in the Far North do this automatically. Check your propane tank every few days, and be on the lookout for a service station that carries propane. Many Alaskan campers take along ten extra gallons of gasoline and a couple of extra quarts of oil just in case.

If you ever have serious trouble on an Alaskan highway, unless you know where you are, don't try to walk to the nearest house or service station. You may be in for a marathon hike. Instead, wait for the next passing vehicle and ask its occupants for a ride or request them to send back help. The great majority of Alaskan motorists still have the helping-hand attitude of the pioneers and will gladly come to your rescue in any way they can—quite a refreshing change from the attitude on highways in the lower 48.

Just for fun you may care to take along a pair of small inexpensive walkie-talkies for use when two of you are fishing or exploring in different spots or when one of you stays in the rig. These are also ideal for talking from the cab to the camper unit and vice versa, even while en route.

If you are planning to take to the woods in Alaska and it will be your first experience with renting a rig, it's a good idea to check out the following items:

Try to be sure, by inquiring at a garage if necessary, that the camper unit is not too heavy for the type of wheels that the truck has. The combination of rough roads and a too-heavy load can split a wheel, even a steel one.

Check to see whether the rig has enough propane, fresh water, and utensils, and be sure that the mounted tires and the spare are in excellent shape. The cupboard doors should stay shut, any detachable table's latching arrangement should be in working order, and the rig should have at least basic tools including jack and handle, X wrench for tire lugs, screwdriver, pliers, and perhaps a hatchet or ax.

Another handy tool is a small shovel for use in garbage disposal and safely extinguishing campfires. The shovel can also be used to dig a small depression into which a wheel can be driven in order to tilt the unit so that the icebox will drain outside rather than inside the camper. Another way to tilt the rig for drainage is to run one wheel up onto a ramp made by laying one end of a plank on a small log.

The first-time driver of a pickup camper must remember that this rig stands a lot higher than an automobile does. So he should keep an eye out for low-hanging signs and overhanging roofs around gas stations and for low branches in campgrounds. Such caution soon becomes second nature.

The cost of renting a pickup camper usually runs from about $25 a day on up, the exact figure depending on the size of the rig. In many cases, this figure is the entire cost, there being no additional charge for mileage. You will have to buy only gasoline, propane, ice, and grub. The rigs are well covered by insurance for both owner and driver, and, generally speaking, they are well maintained and equipped. Your state driver's license is honored in Alaska.

There are several guidebooks on Alaska camping. The best one, *Alaska Recreation Guide,* is published by the state itself and is available through the understanding and prompt Alaska Travel Division, Pouch E, Juneau, Alaska 99801. It is packed with useful information on camping in general, campsites, and highways. The affable Mike Miller, energetic publicity director for this division of the Alaska Department of Economic Development, can fill you in on any details not covered by the guidebook.

For the sake of clarity, it might be well to point out that some of the descriptions of campgrounds in the state-published guidebook may be misinterpreted by campers who are familiar with guidebook descriptions of campground facilities in the lower 48. For example, down here "25 camping units" usually means 25 tent or trailer sites containing fireplaces, firewood, running water, and perhaps a store, flush toilets, and other conveniences. In Alaska that description may merely indicate room for that number of vehicles alongside a road, or it may mean an area set apart from the highway and containing 25 tables and an equal number of refuse cans. On the other hand, it may mean a well-established campground with a water supply and pit privies.

Drinking water is so rarely found in Alaska campgrounds that if a site has this facility, the Alaska guidebook will say so. In the contiguous 48 states potable water is available at almost all campgrounds, and so the guidebooks rarely mention it.

There is much to see and explore in Alaska, a state so vast that even if it were cut in half, Texas would be no more than the third largest state. And travel-camping is, for those who like the outdoors, the finest way to see it.

An adventure—that's the only way to describe a camping trip to Alaska, whether it is in a tent, trailer, or pickup camper! Alaska still reeks of frontier days, with its gold rushes, dog sleds, totem poles, and glaciers. You become more than just familiar with the all-important bush pilot, the delicious king crabs, and the spectacular scenery.

Being in Alaska means that you have left the "lower 48," as Alaskans refer to the rest of the United States except Hawaii, and that you are what the residents call an outsider. Not that you are treated like an outsider by any means, for nowhere will you meet friendlier people, enjoy finer hospitality and courtesy, and experience more frontier-style neighborliness than in Alaska's hotels and campgrounds and even while out on the tundra with a flat tire.

Perhaps as the state's population increases this frontier spirit will disappear. But for some time to come an Alaskan camping trip will be a heartwarming experience as well as an eye-filling adventure. Just driving from one campground to another is an event, for each section of Alaska has its own attractions, including interesting terrain and fantastic scenery. The backdrop changes almost with the mile.

Not all Alaska is mountains and glaciers. In fact, portions of the vast Gulkana River Basin—viewable from the Glenn, Denali, and Richardson highways—are reminiscent of the prairies in the western part of the contiguous states. Everything in Alaska is vast—flatlands, icefields, forests, and mountain ranges. And you can see unbelievably far in the clear air. For example, from Anchorage on a clear day Mounts Foraker and McKinley almost 150 miles to the north are plainly visible.

Alaska is a state in which the nearest filling station or house may be three hours of fast driving away; a state whose capital, Juneau, is farther from Dutch Harbor in the Aleutian Islands than the Colby home in Briarcliff Manor, New York, is from Omaha, Nebraska. As Mike Miller's state camping brochures say, Alaska is the world's largest campground!

Certainly, camping is the best way to enjoy the romance of Alaska, and in numerous areas it is the only way to see the countryside. And even if you prefer not to fly, you can get to Alaska, or reach home from there, without having to drive many hundreds of miles on the Alaska Highway. How? By boarding one of the luxurious Alaska state ferries, which sail between Seattle and various Alaskan cities.

Many campers drive their rigs aboard one of the ferries in Seattle and sail to Haines, Alaska, where they pick up the Haines cutoff road, which joins the Alaska Highway at Haines Junction in the Yukon. Other campers drive all the way to Alaska and then board a ferry for the return trip. The cruise from Haines to Seattle takes an unforgettable three days and four nights.

Ferry fares depend on the size of your vehicle and the kind of stateroom you prefer. The vehicle fare for the Haines-to-Seattle trip, for example, is $97.50 at this writing for rigs up to ten feet long and $195.25 for vehicles ten to twenty feet long. Passenger fare for the trip is $54.50 per person. Ferry reservations should be made well in advance of your journey.

For schedules and all other information on this ferry trip down the smooth and spectacular Inland Passage from Haines to Juneau, Sitka, and Ketchikan, to name a few of the interesting stops along the way, write to Mike Miller, Publicity Director, Travel Division, Pouch E, Juneau, Alaska 99801. He can also supply you with maps and a plenitude of other colorful material.

If you spend a couple of hours poring over such tantalizing reading matter, you will understand why we can't wait to get back to Alaska. There is so much you don't see even on a dozen trips and so many things you want to see again.

6

Pros and Cons of Tents

WHAT KINDS OF CAMPERS PREFER TENTS TO HARDTOP SHELTERS ON wheels? They are the young people, the economy-minded newly married, the backpackers, and the pack train campers. They are the canoe-trip enthusiasts and the explorers of the white spaces on the maps. They are the Boy Scouts, the Girl Scouts, the Camp Fire Girls, and the young folks of the American Youth Hostels. They are the individuals who want to get away from city living and take to the woods under canvas, next to nature, as did the pioneers and the old-time woodsmen.

Outside-Frame Cottage Tent

Tenters, generally, do not care for one-night stands in crowded campgrounds along main highways. They select campsites away from the main traffic arteries; places where they can spend enough time to enjoy the local wildlife, find where the fish are lurking, and soak up the scenery. They prefer not having to strike camp at sunup, hurry on, and set up again at another campground come sundown.

The desire for high mobility is one reason for the preponderance of recreational vehicles in the big, bustling campgrounds along our main highways. Tenters aren't so much in evidence because they are away from where the action is—in smaller campgrounds removed from traffic or at least away from the commotion of transient campers in larger campgrounds.

Tenters aren't antisocial. In fact, they are among the friendliest of outdoorsmen. It's just that they like to get away from the sight and sound of transportation. They are apt to compare wildlife they've seen, fish they've caught, and pictures they have taken, while vehicle users are discussing miles per gallon, highway conditions, and the type of bathroom in their coach. Among the millions of outdoor-minded Americans, there are more tenters today than ever there were.

There are a few general considerations that should be kept in mind when selecting a tent. For instance, round tents pose some problems on how to place your sleeping bags or cots. Outside-frame tents, which are not as rigid as those with interior frames, are easier to pitch and a lot cooler to erect in hot weather. On the other hand, outside storm flaps on windows may give more protection against driving rains than inside flaps, but you may have to dash outside in a sudden storm to close them. While sewn-in floors help to keep out snakes and insects, they have to be swept frequently, and they must be placed on sites that are relatively smooth and free from sharp stones, roots, and similar cloth-floor hazards.

Small tents are easier to pack or handle and erect, but they can become exceedingly confining during a long rainy spell. Fiber glass rods will not buckle or corrode, but they are heavier than those made of aluminum. The so-called wing-type tents that have a large, over-hanging top forming an awning and big, screened windows are cool and roomy, but if one of the four stakes that hold them up comes loose, the whole tent may fall down. It's wise to double-guy these models. Tents of lightweight materials are easy to fold compactly but offer less protection in high winds and bad storms. Those without frames are easy to pack but require some improvisation once you reach your site.

If you have already been camping, you likely have some definite ideas on the good and bad points of any model of tent, but perhaps you are looking for a new and better type. If you have not been camping or haven't had an opportunity to look over the many models available, it might help if we discussed the pros and cons of various tents. Let's consider some basic types, starting with the small backpacking sizes and working up to the largest ones that are functional for family camping.

One thing is certain. The $40 tent of today is a far better buy than the $150 one of a few years ago. The modern tent lasts longer, thanks to better waterproofing, rot- and mildew-resistant fabrics, aluminum frames, and stronger screening and zippers. Even some of today's economy models will last for a quarter-century or longer with a minimum of care and repair.

The pup tent of World War I, still popular with Boy Scout troops and as a backyard play tent, has undergone some changes over the years, and all for the better. The original tent was an unsatisfactory affair, merely a piece of canvas stretched over a low ridgepole and staked down at the corners. Later, a closed-in end was added which gave some protection in wet weather but also trapped a plentiful horde of insects. The original pup tents were made in two pieces known as shelter halves. Each piece was carried by one individual, and they were buttoned together to form a two-man tent at night. These tents were lightweight and could be pitched with either poles or ropes or propped up on rifles if poles were hard to locate.

These days the so-called pup tents come with many improvements. They have sewn-in floors, screened doors with storm flaps, outside aluminum frames, and they arrive in different sizes. They are still one-man or two-man tents, however, designed strictly as overnight shelters. They are lightweight, compact, and easy to put up. Their chief drawback is that they lack room for more than one camper with a lot of gear or for two men with a minimum of equipment.

For one-night stops they are fine, but they aren't very functional for rainy-weather use, as usually you can neither sit nor stand in them. Unless you are backpacking alone, you'll probably be better satisfied with a slightly larger tent, such as the miner or mountain tent.

These tents are similar to the pup tent, but they have one end that is much higher, six feet or more, so that you can stand to dress and occasionally stretch during a stay inside in wet weather. While heavier to carry than pup tents, they are still in the lightweight class. They come with screened door and window and usually a sewn-in floor. The window is generally at the back for cross ventilation.

Some mountain tents have a raised roof that forms a higher wedge shape, and these provide even more roominess. Some have guys attached to the center or the sides that pull out and give more room close to the floor. Most of these shelters can be suspended from overhead branches or from a rope lined between trees, a definite pro if you wish to save weight.

The old familiar wall tent, in which many of us experienced our first taste of camping, is still sold in several sizes, all with the same inconveniences of the original models and with what few good points they did have. They are inexpensive, many of them being available as army surplus. To erect them, you need only two upright poles, a ridgepole, guy ropes, and pegs. There their good points seem to end.

Wall tents generally have no windows, no screens at the end doors, and no floors. The walls are invariably so low that the only walking area, except in the larger sizes, is in the center under the ridgepole. One end pole is right in the middle of the doorway. The door flaps, ordinarily tied together with tapes, leave numerous openings for insects and, when closed, make the interior hot and dark. In some models, the side walls can be rolled up and tied, making for better ventilation, certainly, but letting in the bugs. The frames are generally of squared hardwood, heavy and difficult to pack or carry. Unless you are dedicated to this old tent, you'll probably prefer to consider a more modern type of shelter.

The Baker, Whelen, or lean-to tent is inexpensive, easy to erect, and usually has a fine, full-front-width awning which can be closed over the door, or at least slanted downward, in bad weather. Unfortunately, most of these have no windows; so when the cover is all the way down in bad weather, it is dark and stuffy inside. On the other hand, this is really a forest tent, to be enjoyed with a friendly campfire in front. It can generally be so located that, with the awning angled downward, heat will be radiated inside and weather eliminated.

In addition, one model has a screened front as well as the awning, a rear screened window, and a sewn-in floor. The rear window also has a storm flap. This is a fine, modernized version of the old lean-to tent, but it still has limited walking space because of its sloping roof and is pretty dark inside when the front is lowered. One of us has rigged his with transparent plastic curtains across the door. Now he can leave the awning up for protection in a driving rain and still have light inside. Being able to leave the awning up in rainy weather no matter how open the locality is where you're camped is useful since you can keep firewood dry under it, store an outboard boat or motor, and even use the closed space as garage for

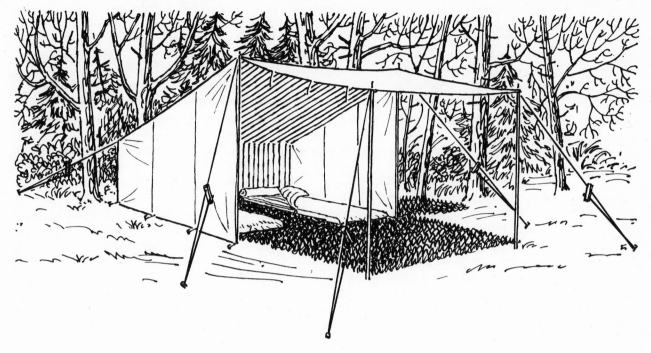

Baker Tent

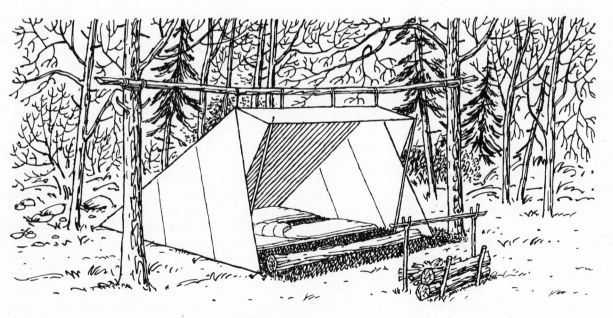

Whelen Tent

one of the small cars.

The long-popular umbrella tent, both the square floor models and those having one or two side rooms for family use, now comes with an outside aluminum frame instead of the old, heavy, inside frame made of steel. These are rugged tents, and generally they are fitted with two or more screened windows with storm flaps and a sewn-in floor. It's sweltering work to erect those that have an inside frame. The tents have a pretty good walking area since the walls are well up from the floor.

Because the umbrella tent's front awning also serves as a storm flap for the door, it's neither very long nor wide, and because most of the door is covered by screening, the flap normally must be dropped in bad weather. You can beat this cycle by covering your door with plastic screening. The erection of an umbrella tent ordinarily takes more than one man, but once it is up it makes an excellent shelter.

Some models have a storm hood that, covering the entire top of the tent, is useful on cooler summer days and insures better protection during heavy downpours. Large umbrella tents may weigh up to some 85 pounds, and toting one can be a problem when you must park your car some distance from the campsite. If your outdoor party includes a couple of men, on the other hand, these tents are fine in spite of the weight and the time it takes to pitch the larger sizes.

Some umbrella tents are made with an opening in the wall opposite the door so that a station wagon can be backed right under a flap. This enables you to pass back and forth between tent and wagon under cover. Some igloo-shaped, self-supporting tents also have this feature.

There are some bad points to this sort of construction, however. It is nigh impossible to make the connection between the tent and the tailgate of your wagon insectproof, and it is frequently hard to come by a site where the tent and wagon can be arranged so that this connection can be used as designed. If you back the station wagon onto the campsite, the front of the tent, opposite the connecting tunnel, will often face away from the site's most-used area. If you drive front first onto the site, often on a small turnout spur from the road, and then connect the tent to your wagon, the tent is pitched between the vehicle and the thoroughfare. In this situation, you generally can't use your wagon unless you remove the tent.

About the only ideal site for such a tent is a beach where the doorway can be put up facing the water and the wagon backed up to the other side of the tent and connected to the tunnel. You'll have to keep in mind to unhitch the tunnel from the tailgate should you decide to travel to town for supplies.

Some tents have built-in fiber glass frames or aluminum tubing under tension to hold the tent erect and the floor out taut. There are also tents held up by inflated tubing. All such tents make excellent overnight shelters. They can be moved about when erected to take advantage of a vagrant breeze that will cool the interior, or the door can be turned away from a high wind or nearing storm. If you decide that the ground under the tent is too rough for comfort, you can shift the tent to a smoother area without taking it down. These tents are easily assembled and erected and stand high winds surprisingly well. They are often, not always, expensive but well worth the price.

As a rule, however, the igloo-shaped tents do not have very good windows. Even in the larger sizes, the windows are small and high in the walls. Because of the shape of this sort of tent, the door is narrow, and because of that, the storm flap provides a very small awning. This can be a bother if you desire good protection over the open door. Too, the narrow door can prove troublesome when you're moving in and out with bulky gear.

The cottage type of tent with vertical sides and high eaves has many advantages. They boast large windows with storm flaps, sewn-in floors, and plenty of walk-around roominess. The bad points include the time required to pitch them, the number of poles and guys which may run up to ten or so, the lack of a good awning over the door, and the large area of smooth ground needed for pitching.

One model seems to have overcome most of these disadvantages except for the size of ground area required. It has an outside aluminum frame, big picture windows all around, and a spacious awning over one whole side where the door is located. This tent is also so designed that there is no pole in the center of the doorway, as there is in many cottage tents.

Many cottage tents weigh up to eighty pounds, but when erected, they make livable shelters for a long stay. They have enough room for rainy-day activities indoors and even for the use of double-decked bunks.

Weigh the advantages against the disadvantages when selecting a tent. Consider such factors as the amount of room required for the shelter, the type of ground on which you will be likely to pitch it most of the time, the availability of material with which to make a frame if the tent does not come with one, the tent's weight, and the work that it takes to erect it.

Rocky, uneven areas are fine for a small tent, but they can become frustrating if you try to pitch a big one requiring a lot of level ground. A site above treeline may be fine for a tent that has its own frame, but it's impossible for a tent designed to be supported from an overhead branch or rope or from a pole frame cut on the spot. Sandy soil makes for smooth tent floors, but it can be a difficult place on which to pitch a big tent requiring many pegs and guy ropes. Here a tent with a self-supporting frame is great, as it is where rocky ground makes stake-driving a nightmare.

Careful assessment of a tent's features and serious consideration of its pros and cons before purchase can do a lot to prevent later disappointment. The type of camping you plan to do, the type of vehicle you expect to travel in, the number in your average party, and the sort of terrain where you plan to camp should all be considered. Bad characteristics may turn out to be good ones for another camper with a different kind of journey in mind.

About a million tents were sold in 1968 at a cost of some $70 million. An estimated 8 to 10 million tents—almost ten times the number of wheeled vacation rigs—are used annually in the United States. Can anyone doubt tenting's popularity?

Yesterday's tents were drab, heavy, and difficult to erect, partly because of heavy wooden or steel frames. They were hot in summer, didn't keep out insects, and had inadequate windows and doors. Even so, they got millions of campers to take to the woods.

Today's tents are made in bright colors and are sometimes even striped, weigh but a fraction of what their predecessors did, have fully screened doors and windows, sewn-in floors, and zippers instead of tie tapes. And they go up in the time it formerly took to cut the poles.

There are as many styles and types of tents today as there are campers' tastes. In one outfitter's catalog alone we counted nearly 70 different units—from a tiny plastic tent that can be carried in a pocket to a 10-person model with several rooms. Between these extremes are 2- and 3-man tents made of canvas, plastic, and nylon; cottage tents; and tents with inside frames, outside frames, and frames that can be blown up by mouth or a hand pump. Some tents can be mounted atop a car or over its trunk, while others can be hung from trees or attached to the rear of a station wagon. Modern Omars are continually coming up with new ideas that make tenting more attractive, comfortable, and economical.

Many camping families now use more than one tent during a vacation. They utilize one for the adults and another for the small fry who want to be on their own. Some families even put up a third tent—for dressing, as a toilet tent, or for the storage of luggage and other gear.

One subtle indication that tents are more popular than ever is their availability from sources that didn't carry such equipment a few years ago. Formerly, tents were available only through sporting-goods dealers, camp outfitters, and big mail-order houses. Today you can find them in department stores, in discount houses, and in many trading-stamp outlets.

Like the boatman who starts with a canoe or rowboat and progresses to bigger and plusher craft, many campers begin with a tent and go on to a tent trailer, pickup camper, or maybe even to a magnificent motor coach. But many of these campers wind up back under canvas again—for the sheer fun of it and to recapture the true meaning of taking to the woods.

Is tenting becoming a thing of the past? Not by a long shot! You can bet your last tent peg that as long as there is an outdoors to get next to, millions of people are going to take to it in the most pleasant and economical way—under canvas.

7

Quality Back of Beyond

YOU SELDOM SAVE WEIGHT BY BUYING A "BARGAIN." THE ARTICLE IS likely to be bulkier, too. The safest procedure when you're outfitting to take to the woods, where you'll want to be entirely self-reliant and independent of the towns, is to buy only the best quality. The big exception is in the case of growing children.

If you're not sure you'll like camping, then borrow or rent what you can, instead of buying shoddy, which will never be satisfactory. On the other hand, this doesn't mean the highest priced article. The safest procedure until you're experienced is to trade only at reputable stores.

Anyone who's taking to the woods for the first time finds a bewildering array of equipment to entice him. Most items in this dazzling assortment of gear come in a variety of grades, with prices to match. Unfortunately, the new camper is often faced with the problem of separating the quality merchandise from that which, despite often fancy prices, is shoddy. There is also the problem of knowing which of two similarly priced items will provide long life and continuing satisfaction.

Although it is generally true that one gets what he pays for, sometimes the costlier outdoor items are no better than the less expensive articles. In fact, some inexpensive pieces are actually superior to the so-called luxury models.

The majority of manufacturers in the expanding camping market are reliable and put out first-rate products. However, there is growing evidence that, as always, a few quick-buck operators are starting to jump on the camping bandwagon with gear that is flashy and attractive but of inferior quality. While the warning "Let the buyer beware" still holds true, there are nevertheless many ways to spot good design and high quality in camping equipment regardless of the price tag.

In sleeping bags, for example, the marks of high quality include honest measurements. Look for bags that are of generous cut. A skimpy sleeping bag can be frustrating, particularly for a big person, and it soon wears out at the points of stress. A regular size bag should measure at least 33 by 75 inches, and a so-called king-size bag should be at least 39 by 82 inches. The increasingly popular double bags, which sleep two persons, should be 50 by 74 inches or larger.

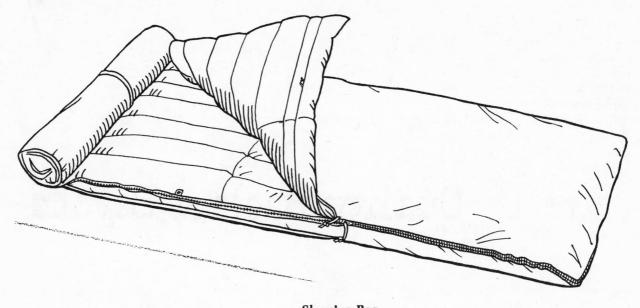

Sleeping Bag

Insulation is another mark of sleeping-bag quality. If the bag is advertised as down-filled, be sure that the filling really is down and not just feathers. All reliable brands of sleeping bags have a tag that confirms what the filling is: new goose or duck down, re-processed down, synthetic fibers, or whatever. Examine the tag before you make your purchase.

Thickness with lightness means better insulation. New goose down is the best of all insulative materials, one ounce of it insulating about 500 cubic inches. Goose down springs back resiliently after being compressed and so provides air spaces for heat retention. New duck down is almost as functional. Dacron 88, a man-made fiber developed specially for sleeping bags, is used in most high-quality robes that do not have down as a filling.

Some of the really cheap bags use insulation that is scarcely better than old rags. If the tag on the bag does not satisfactorily describe the insulation material, and if the seller will not do so, buy something else.

In first-rate bags, the insulation is either bonded to the covering material or affixed to it with a minimum of stitching. The more such stitching a bag shows, the more thin spots it is bound to have. Cheaper bags often utilize very elaborate stitching patterns to discourage second-rate insulation from shifting and balling up.

Fine-quality sleeping bags also have large, heavy-duty zippers with two-way pull tabs or reasonably spaced snaps. Insulation strips protect the occupant from contact with the metal. These insulation strips also help prevent cold air from entering the garment through the zippers or between the snaps, and they keep warmth inside.

Sleeping-bag liners should be of high-quality material, often flannel, that is colorfast. If the lining is of pile, this should be nonallergenic to prevent all-night sniffles and watery eyes. A good nylon lining is comfortable, quickly warming to body temperature, and it permits easy movements and is long-wearing. The nylon should be porous enough to permit "breathing."

A pillow or the lack of one is no indication of a sleeping bag's quality. Many expensive bags are pillowless.

Interested in a mummy-type sleeping bag? Then check the zipper. It should be long enough so that you can get in and out of the bag easily, of course, but it should also enable the bag's being turned inside out for airing. The hood should be large and free enough so that it can be drawn about the head, leaving only the face exposed, when the temperature plummets.

Be certain that there is no rubber or plastic in a sleeping bag, whatever its type. The dry cleaning of bags having these materials is difficult if not impossible. In cold weather plastic or rubber may stiffen or crack. More importantly, an impervious covering on a sleeping bag will retain body moisture, and you'll be miserably, and in cold weather dangerously, damp in short order.

Air mattresses, another most important item of camping gear, come in two materials, plastic and rubberized fabric. The plastic pieces are the less expensive, and some of them

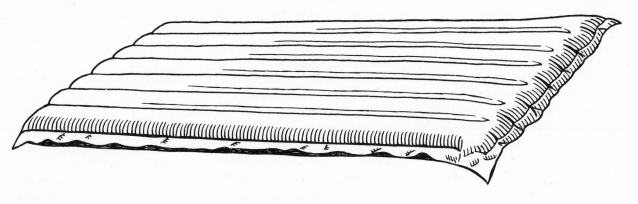

Air Mattress

are excellent. Unfortunately, however, plastic mattresses puncture all too easily. Repairs, although simple enough, are a nuisance, especially in the middle of the night. If you decide on saving money with a plastic mattress, look for a heavy-duty one, and try to ascertain if the material will stiffen, as some do, in frosty weather. These plastic types are easily damaged by sparks and by sharp objects, and their seams if skimpy may let go with a whoosh.

Rubberized-fabric mattresses will last for decades. They are a bit harder to blow up, but this is little problem, especially if you use something like the soft bulb pumps which can be worked with hand or foot and pack safely in the sleeping gear itself. Once inflated, such a mattress will hold for weeks without refilling. The material can be patched very easily and durably.

Air mattresses, whose material should be of uniform thickness with plenty of lap at the seams, should have sturdy metal valves that are screwed tight rather than being closed with the rubber or plastic plugs that are so prone to pop out when the sleeper shifts suddenly.

Another point to keep an eye on is the size of a mattress when it is inflated. Both plastic and rubberized-fabric air mattresses always look longer and wider when flat, some losing as much as three inches in both width and length when inflated. Actually, design varies. Generally the boxed and tufted varieties come in rubberized fabric and are more expensive, but the best of these more than compensate for this drawback by comfort and durability. The tubular types are usually made of plastic.

The mattress may or may not have a pillow, those with separate valves being the more convenient, especially when a sleeper likes a soft surface beneath him except at the head. If weight is a problem, you can buy a short mattress that will cushion the vulnerable shoulders and hips, leaving the legs and feet to be provided for otherwise, perhaps by a few evergreen boughs.

The same hunt for signs of high quality should be continued when you buy a tent. Look for shelters with reputable brand names, and then check for the fabric. The water-proofing in high-quality tents does not rub off. The wax fillers used to waterproof cheaper tents do. The tent fabric should be of uniform thickness. The stoutly sewn seams should be turned over on themselves like interlocking U's instead of being just lapped together once and stitched. The former so-called lap-felled seams withstand far greater strain. They also shed water better and longer than do the simpler seams. Heavy stitching thread is used in good tentage, and the sewing is straight and uniform, with no loose ends dangling.

Tent corners, as well as those of tarpaulins and dining flies, should be ruggedly re-inforced. Grommets are best set well back from the edge of the material, securely fastened, and stoutly reinforced. Stake loops or ties should be well sewn and strong.

If the tent has a sewn-in floor, check this for tears in fabric or for blisters and bubbles if plastic-coated, and make certain that the flooring is not full of wrinkles where it meets the tent walls. Some new tents have the waterproof flooring carried up the sides for several inches, for drier interiors.

A tent's door and window screens should be of fiber glass, with a mesh fine enough to keep out the smallest insects that might bother you, such as the nefarious no-see-ums often so active at dusk and at dawn. Storm flaps should be zippered and should entirely cover the respective opening. Unless you are going to use your tent in the Far North or in alpine country where zippers might freeze, storm doors should be zipper-closed rather than tape-tied for better protection in high winds and driving rains. Knotted ties may either come loose in gusts or become hard to loosen when the need arises. Tying a small stick in the knot will help. Pull out the stick and the knot will be loosened. Tent zippers should, of course, be strong, rustproof, and well sewn into the material.

The majority of modern tent frames are made of tubular aluminum instead of the old-fashioned wood or heavy steel. Most uprights either telescope into position or come in sections that can be fitted together at the campsite. If you're interested in the sectional type, be sure that the components fit together properly and that the locking devices really hold the sections together rigidly. In any event, once you've decided upon a tent, you'll do well to erect it at home before going on that first memorable camping trip. That way, you can wet the fabric down with the hose for shrinkage, and you can make sure that all parts are there and that they fit.

If your interest lies in a backpacking tent that uses poles, make certain that the pole sections are small enough so that, when stowed in the tent bag or rolled up with the fabric, they make a compact package. Too, beware of splintery, weakly joined poles that come with some of the cheaper backpacking tents. In this connection, the small tents with inflatable ribs are certainly worthy of consideration.

The weight of tent fabrics varies. It is not necessarily a measure of quality unless extra weight is added by the cheap, waxy waterproofing considered earlier. If the tent fabric feels waxy, rub it briskly with your handkerchief. If some of the color comes off, the waterproofing may rub off so readily during ordinary use that the tent will soon leak.

Nylon tents, even the most expensive, are hard to waterproof against heavy rains inasmuch as the material will not shrink tight when wet. Stitch holes in the seams are particularly likely to leak, even in the finest-quality nylon tents. Such a tent is so light, however, that you can usually manage to carry a lightweight plastic tarp to toss over it in bad weather or, better, pitch such a tent under a protective fly. Most top-grade nylon tents, in any event, boast a double roof.

What about guy ropes? No matter what the tent, these should be good and long rather than on the skimpy side, and they should be made of a good material. The rope diameter should be substantial enough to hold the tent securely. Depending on the size of the tent, a diameter of 3/8 or 1/2 inch is usually sufficient.

Stakes should be either high-impact plastic or rustproof metal, and they should be long enough to go into the ground securely. The wooden stakes often supplied with cheaper tents are apt to split when being hammered in, and they are relatively heavy. Another disadvantage is that they retain moisture and so should not be packed with the tent, a separate waterproof bag usually being required. Plastic or metal stakes, on the other hand, can be wiped clean and dry before packing. Of course, if you're traveling in sheer wilderness and going as light as possible, you may choose to cut your stakes on the spot.

When buying leather shoulder straps, belts, tie straps, and such, make sure that the material is really leather and not some inferior substitute. In a pinch, you can usually tell by the smell. Make certain, too, if you can, that the leather is oil-tanned to prevent cracking. The leather should be of even thickness, and both sides should be firm and smooth, not fuzzy. Thin or limber areas denote poor leather or bad tanning. Incidentally, you have to be extra careful when buying leather "bargains" in Mexico, as Mexican leather is rarely oil-tanned.

If the leather is outfitted with buckles, these should be solid brass rather than brass-plated, or they should have a plating that will not rust. Solid-brass fittings are often stamped as such. Nickel silver is good, too.

In the field of camp axes, hatchets, saws, sheath knives, and such, get the best you can afford. Look for reputable trade names and good materials. Select tools, as much as possible, that have good steel and sensible handles.

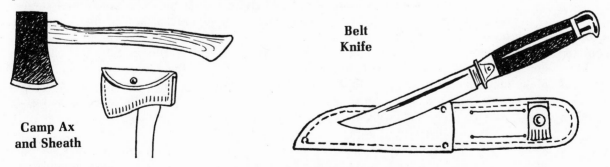

Camp Ax
and Sheath

Belt
Knife

For instance, avoid a flashy belt knife with a 7- or 8-inch handle and a fancy sheath. The days of Jim Bowie are long gone; so stick to the more functional sizes. The longest of the several belt knives that one of us owns has a 6-inch blade, the shortest of them being half that long. His all-time favorite has a 4-inch cutting edge that, kept sharp, can help build a snug lean-to or skin a moose. The other of us prefers a handmade Randall 6-inch blade that is the only knife with which he has ever been able to skin an entire big grizzly without stopping to resharpen. It is likewise excellent for fuzz sticks, emergency shelters, and other wilderness chores.

Carbon-steel blades are going to discolor after being in contact with meat, but this won't affect their utility. Stainless-steel blades look fine but are difficult to resharpen once they've lost their keen factory edges. Campers need a blade that can be made keen with a few strokes on a hone. Incidentally, unless such a hone comes with the knife, perhaps in a special pocket in the sheath, purchase a small carborundum and use it often.

A knife that's going to be used for general camp chores should have a blade of fairly heavy steel, one that you cannot bend. This blade should have a fairly straight cutting edge and a curve at its tip. If you'll be skinning a lot of game, perhaps even running a small trapline throughout the winter, get a blade with a more curved tip and a shorter straight edge.

Beware of knives with fancy handles. Select one with a simple handle of real antler, laminated leather discs, or good wood. Be leery of small handles, as they soon become uncomfortable. And shy away from those with oddly shaped bumps or finger grips unless the handle is made to order to fit. Be certain that the blade and handle are securely bonded and that the latter fits your hand comfortably.

Good knives seldom come with cheap sheaths, and you can often tell a knife's quality by this accouterment. The sheath should be made of heavy oil-tanned leather with stoutly sewn or leather-laced edges. The sheaths of some of the very best knives have a tough fiber liner and a leather keep lock which snaps into place over the knife handle.

Some knives of good quality have a belt loop that goes over the belt and back down, where it is sewn or riveted to the sheath. Other good knives have sheaths employing belt slots. This latter arrangement is adequate if the leather in which the slots are cut is heavy and if the slots are long and wide enough to accommodate a heavy belt; the only kind you should be wearing in the wilderness where, on occasion, it may have to perform emergency duty. Each such belt slot should have a round hole at each end to prevent its tearing. The user of such a sheath, whatever its belt-holding arrangement, should be able to tilt the knife so that he can sit down comfortably.

Sheaths for axes and hatchets should completely cover the blade if not the complete head, and the leather should be particularly thick, tough, and well sewn or riveted.

The wood in ax handles should be straight-grained, smooth to the touch, and stained or waxed, never painted. Paint may conceal splinters or cracks, and in any event it is tough on the user's sliding hand.

Checking the Hang of an Ax and Alignment of Blade to Handle

Know how to check the hang of an ax? Hold the head toward you, with the blade up, and sight along the edge. The blade edge should align with the center line of the handle. Make sure that the wedges in the front of the ax handle are well set and that the wood about them is not cracked. The wooden helve should fit snugly into the opening in the ax head, with no spaces showing between wood and steel.

Camp saws, even the folding variety, should have comfortable handles. The teeth should be of the crosscut type, well spaced, and with a good wide set that will not bind in green or damp wood. The saw should be designed so that the blade can be kept taut. Even then, warm it before using it in subzero weather, or the steel may snap. This also applies to hatchets and axes in extremely cold weather. Warm heads before chopping. Once chopping has begun, they stay warm.

Camp iceboxes should have adequate carrying handles that won't pinch your hands. The interior corners should be rounded for easy cleaning. The drain spigot, recessed into the outside of the box and thus protected, should be set low enough to permit complete draining. Latches should be mechanical rather than magnetic and designed so that they can be opened with one hand. Magnetic latches may pop open unexpectedly, although opening them when you want to get in often requires two hands, a shortcoming inasmuch as the user is often carrying something.

A tray or rack to keep vulnerable foods out of the melted ice at the bottom of the box is a must. Icebox hinges should be strong and attached securely, and the cover should be airtight. All metal parts of the box should, of course, be rustproof. The lightweight foam-plastic containers make good, inexpensive iceboxes. Make sure, however, that handles and latches are strong and securely attached and that there are no punctures in the material. Other marks of quality here include thick foam-plastic, nonrusting metal fittings, and rounded interior corners.

A number of good camp lanterns are available. Try to be sure that the one you pick has a handle long enough not to be affected by the heat from the mantle. The base of the fuel tank should be broad enough to prevent the lantern's tipping over. The globes should be pyrex or some other heat-resistant glass, and they should be easy to remove for cleaning and for the replacing of mantles. Finally, a camp lantern's fuel-pumping mechanism should work smoothly and easily.

Good camp stoves are designed so that the grill can be removed for easy cleaning of the stove interior. Windscreens should be sufficiently heavy that they do not bend easily. All knobs, and this applies to lanterns as well, should be easy to grasp and turn. All flexible gas tubing should be smooth and flawless where it joins the metal fittings. Check all screw threads to make sure that they are coarse enough to prevent cross-threading and that they have not been damaged during assembly.

There is considerable question about army and navy surplus. Many of these items, including shovels, picks, and metal containers should be all right, if not too rugged for the use you intend, if they are genuine surplus and not cheap imitations. However, such surplus may date far back, and any leather or fabric items that old may have deteriorated considerably. You can test leather items by bending them sharply. If cracks appear, the leather is dry, dead, and probably useless.

An item's G.I. color does not mean that it is genuine surplus. Check instead for a contractor's number from the service for which the item was made. Surplus gear may seem to be a great bargain, but if there's doubt about such items, you'll be far better off to avoid them. Too, as far as real wilderness use is concerned, surplus is apt to be too heavy.

By following the preceding tips, you should be able to assemble a good-quality camping outfit that will give you years of pleasure and service. In general, you should do all right if you stick with well-advertised brands, buy from a reliable outfitter, and check each item carefully. One thing more. Beware of the hard-sell salesman who acts and sounds as if he has never been closer to the woods than his own backyard.

Camp Lantern

8

Clothes to Take
to the Woods in

WHAT SORT OF CLOTHES YOU TAKE TO THE WOODS IN CAN HAVE considerable bearing on your comfort, health, and safety. They may also save you a lot of money over just a few years if you choose them with care.

Clothes for the bush should be selected with an eye to the weather expected, the season, and the kind of camping you're headed for. Real backcountry duds for roughing it would look almost as out of place in a civilized cottage-colony camp as the cottage garb would appear in the deep woods. However, wearing the latter in the wilderness could be downright dangerous, especially so far from any clothing store that might help you to rectify your mistakes.

Outdoor clothing should be comfortable, durable, and functional. It needn't be the very best or the most expensive. But it should very definitely be the best you can afford. The two exceptions to this are for growing children and for individuals who aren't sure they're going to like camping.

Otherwise, you'll do best to pick such clothes, as they will last longer, look better for a longer period, feel better, and come back from washing or cleaning in better condition. Good-quality outdoor garb should be of comfortable, full cut, practical design, and sturdy material throughout. The seams should be conscientiously turned and sewn, reinforced at strain points, and practically shrinkproof. Buttons should be sewn on to stay. Any zippers should be rugged and smooth-running. Color should, of course, be fast.

A telltale mark of quality, particularly noticeable with shirts, is that the material is matched at seams, pockets, and cuffs unless, of course, it is deliberately mismatched for effect. Good shirts also have long tails to keep them inside the trousers when you're exerting yourself. Good trousers have extra material at the seams and wherever else you'll need freedom of action. Pockets should be deep, strongly sewn, and of heavy pocket duck. Back trouser pockets should be button flapped. Too, both of us personally like our shirt pockets buttoned down with a stanch flap that'll keep often vital necessities from falling out when we bend forward.

Take along at least one complete underwear change even in cold weather, and keep one set washed, for perspiration-soaked inner clothing won't keep you as warm and comfortable as clean wear will.

Socks should be woolen even in summertime, for such material squeezes air in and out of your footwear with every step, cushions your feet, washes easily, and dries quickly. Too, it is warm and comfortable even when wet. Be sure, though, that such socks are neither too long nor too short. If they're long, they may wrinkle and cause blisters and chafing. If they're short, they'll rapidly wear out in the heel and big-toe areas.

Before you take to the woods, wash all new socks to test for shrinkage and to remove possible excess dye. If all-wool socks adversely affect your feet, wear a thin pair of cotton, silk, or lisle socks inside them.

It's unfortunately true that wool socks wear out more quickly than cotton or part-cotton, so if you don't have the equipment or skill to darn them smoothly, take several pair. Three pair should do for a two-week jaunt, or four for a month if you wash them frequently.

If the weather is cold and the size of your footwear, as it should, permits, wear two pair of wool socks for more warmth or a heavy woolen pair with heavy cotton socks inside. Both pair should extend above your boots to cushion the tops of these against your leg.

As for trousers, there, too, weather will have a bearing. For summer warmth use such materials as poplin, blue denim, duck, sailcloth, or gabardine—especially tight, hard, light woolen gabardine. Blue jeans are fine if you like them, but don't make the mistake of buying the tight western style unless you plan to spend most of your time in the saddle. They're too confining for on-foot camping and hiking. On the other hand, well-made and rivet-enforced loose blue jeans are generally good all-around camping trousers.

Army-type suntans are also good, as are several other summer-weight khaki trousers. Many wash easily and can be adequately pressed by stretching them tightly over a line or spreading them out smoothly on a warm sunny ledge or along the bottom of a canoe. If you're hunting, look for fabrics that are soft and quiet. Steer clear of corduroy since it's noisy, takes a long time to dry after a wetting, and usually ends up stiff. Don't forget that wool is quieter in the woods and sheds water better than the cottons. All in all, though, comfortable clothing that will stand rough wear is about all you'll need for warm-weather camping.

Cold weather calls for heavier materials, and there are many good outdoor trousers of wool and wool-and-cotton, some quilted and lined for additional warmth. A few have knitted cuffs for tucking into socks or boot tops, or maybe you'll prefer breeches.

Ski-type trousers, on the other hand, are generally too tight for comfortable wear in the woods, although their under-arch loops are a convenience for keeping your trousers down inside your boots, a role in which breeches with their laced legs excel. If there is much snow, hard-finish woolens will shed it.

Whether light or heavy, trousers to take to the woods in should not have upturned cuffs—another vote, incidentally, for breeches, especially in weather during which you'll be wearing 8-inch or so boots. Cuffs catch dirt, leaves, bugs, and even sparks from a campfire, and they can trip you dangerously by suddenly snagging on roots, low branch stubs, and rocks.

Either suspenders or belt are fine for keeping up your trousers, or you can wear both. Suspenders leave the vulnerable middle of the body free of binding, and if you wear a belt for a knife and other such accessories, they will put their weight on the shoulders rather than on your less adaptable hips. The best are the heavy galluses type, available from outdoor outfitters. Wear a substantial belt, with a good solid buckle, that in an emergency can be used for other purposes.

Woolen shirts are good the year around. Cotton flannel also is effective for cool evenings and for days when insects are biting, as well as protection from the wind under a tightly woven outer jacket. Cotton shirts are standard in mild weather. We like those with long sleeves which can be rolled during hot hours and then shoved down again in cool spells or when insects are blackening the air. You can also buy, or have made from your trophies, buckskin shirts that will wear well for years. These are warm, windproof and insectproof, although they may wet through quickly unless specially treated by the manufacturer.

Two lightweight woolen shirts, or a cotton shirt with a heavy woolen shirt over it, are good for warmth on chilly evenings. Should you get wet, the wool will keep you snug. Some like a shirt that goes over the head and is operated by some three buttons at the neck. More adaptable, though, is the type that buttons all the way down the front and can be worn open like a jacket. During hot weather, too, you'll be cooler if the tails dangle free.

If you're interested in getting through the woods unobtrusively and in seeing game, pick clothing of dark or neutral colors. Dark browns, grays, forest greens, and dark plaids are good. Those just interested in camping who like bright colors, or hunters who should have protection, will find almost any color in plaids and solids. Incidentally, the fluorescent orange shades stand out more vividly than the old reds, and yet are just as invisible to wildlife.

Sweaters can be practical and comfortable. They range from fine lightweight models to beautiful and wildly patterned Indian sweaters made of native wools. The latter are warm but expensive. Loosely woven or knitted sweaters are troublesome if the country is at all bushy, their loops catching on branch stubs, but they can be worn under a thin windbreaker.

Windbreakers of tightly woven materials to wear over sweaters, sweat shirts, or even heavy wool shirts are well worth considering even for summer camping. These should have strong zippers, ample pockets, and plenty of room for shoulder swing. It's a particular boon if they have been treated with some functional waterproofing compound. Both of us have old, closely woven, windproof, and nearly waterproof jackets with four big pockets that have been ideal for many seasons. These are known as "bush jackets" and can be worn with or without belts. They are also known as "safari jackets"; some have bi-swing shoulders.

For very cold weather, there are many varieties of net, synthetically insulated, and down-filled underwear. Unless you plan to camp in really extreme weather or at exceptionally high altitudes, the insulated suits are ample. The heavier of these, worn under woolens, will keep a reasonably active man warm in temperatures sixty degrees below freezing and not overheat him enough so that he'll dangerously perspire, either. You can also buy insulated socks and mittens. They are quilted and filled with good synthetic, easily laundered fillers, boasting up to about 70 percent of the insulation of genuine down.

In cold weather, too, you'll need a parka or mackinaw. A bountifully pocketed model of the latter is the more functional in moderate climates because it can be worn open or partially open. But in the Far North we like the parka because the hood holds in body heat and keeps the neck warm even when it is not worn over the head, a boon when you're hunting and want to hear all that's going on in the surrounding wilderness.

Many kinds of raingear are on the market, ranging from inexpensive ponchos to suits consisting of jacket and pants, whose cost depends on individual quality, materials, and details. One of the newer jackets being offered for sale is made of treated nylon that, although completely waterproof, permits body moisture to escape through the fabric, eliminating the moisture which collects across the shoulders of many rain suits. Others have double material over the shoulders with a net vent under the outer layer for ventilation.

Hats are a matter of personal preference. One of us never wears one except when a storm drives through the wilderness, then pulls one of the softer felts, the popular Maine guide hat, out of a pack or pocket. The other of us prefers a battered, old western hat. Most men like a comfortable hat or cap when in the woods, and a broad-brimmed hat protects the face from sun, glare, branches, and helps to prevent chapped lips. These hats also shelter the face and neck from rain and sleet. If need be, a good, big felt hat can be used as a bucket and for swatting flies and fanning the fire. Soft roll-up cloth hats are convenient and last for years, and even an old baseball or G.I. cap will do. A New Brunswick guide we knew wore an old beret, and this came in handy when it came time to handle the boiling tea pail at noon. A soft beret or cap can also be worn under a rain hood for warmth.

It's a fact that if you've trouble with cold feet, the difficulty can often be corrected by covering your head, and for sleeping outdoors many campers like to wear a knitted toque or sailor's watch cap. Some prefer to sleep in one of the three major styles of hooded sweat shirts: with zippered front, full pullovers, and pullovers with a short buttoned opening at the throat. You can beat the cold problem in some bags by pulling the extending lining or the actual top of the bag over the head. But don't make the mistake of breathing in the bag, or the moisture from your breath will gradually and steadily diminish its insulative qualities.

Though we've been considering this woods gear with men primarily in mind, the suggestions are also suitable for the ladies and the youngsters. Our wives, both veteran campers, suggest that the ladies dress in such tried and true camping duds as blue jeans, divided skirts, culottes, and slacks, with perhaps a cotton dress taken along just in case you hit civilization now and then. Women and girls have a wide variety of colorful materials to choose from. Jackets are usually made from blue denim, chino, and similar tightly woven fabrics, and many are treated with waterproofing.

Those of the feminine sector who can wear slacks will find many designed with the outdoor woman in mind. They are well cut and full enough for comfort, and they have well-stitched seams and reliable zippers and buttons. Tightly fitting stretch pants are available in blue denim and khaki, both practical colors for camping. Ski clothes, when they are comfortable for walking, are comely and functional in the bush.

For fairly cold weather, women are finding that the Viyella-type underwear, made with two layers, is fine under slacks. For colder days, there are many kinds of quilted and insulated underwear, including sleek and attractive coats and jackets which can be worn either beneath the clothing or as outerwear.

Regular outer jackets for women come in many styles and colors. Some are just windbreakers, while others resemble men's safari jackets, fine when worn over a lightweight sweater. These jackets are usually cut full and are very comfortable. There are many woolen jackets in bright plaids, some of them intended for evening wear. If these woolen jackets bother your neck, wear a scarf or ascot.

Like most women, our wives hate hats in camp. Both take along several big, bright scarves to tie over their heads in windy or cold weather. Don't forget one of those small folding rain hoods for sudden showers. These hoods, which can be carried in a pocket, are handy if you do not like hooded raingear or rain hats. There are also several soft, fabric hats which can be rolled up and tucked away when not in use. They are particularly comfortable when the sun is bright.

There are many fleece-lined vests, jerkins, half-length, three-quarter length, and full-length coats made of various fabrics from lightweight, high-count materials to sheepskin and Hudson's Bay Company blanket cloth. There are women's buckskin garments, as well; all in all a wide choice. Many of these garments come in cheerfully bright colors.

Rain suits in feminine sizes are available, but if you can't find them, boys' suits are suitable for small women. Perhaps you'll like a compact storm suit with a hood.

If you have youngsters along, changes in the weather can make considerable difference in their activities. Remember that children are usually warmer than adults, so don't load them up with more clothing than they need just because you are cold. As the explorer Vilhjalmur Stefansson used to tell us, a sweater is what a mother puts on her child when the mother is cold.

If the weather is warm, you can't beat chino pants, jeans, and short-sleeved shirts or blouses for children. Long pants will save wear and tear on small knees and ankles, as well as keep insect bites to a minimum. If the children are really small, dress them in brightly colored shirts and head coverings so you can spot them around a campground or in the woods. With their love of adventure and exploring, children can disappear in seconds.

In the evening, long-sleeved shirts, jackets, or sweaters will baffle insects and keep out dampness. Lightweight sweat shirts are fine for this, and they are easy to wash. Many youngsters like to sleep in hooded sweat shirts and even sweat pants, as they are fleece-lined, instead of pajamas, but take the latter along if they will make the small fry happier and easier to get to bed.

Have some sort of rainwear handy for the boys and girls, since they may want to go outside even when it's storming. Rain suits, ponchos, and slickers plus rubber boots and rain hats will keep the youngsters dry, busy, and out of your hair on wet days.

Sneakers are good camping footwear for children. The rubber soles make them ideal for climbing, and if they have ankle-high tops, they will prevent scuffed ankles. Rubber boots, or boots with rubber bottoms and leather tops, are good for bad weather. A pair of moccasins will make campfire watching more comfortable.

If your youngsters sunburn easily, broad-brimmed hats and baseball caps will protect their eyes and faces from bad burns. If the days turn cold, a knitted toque or beanie will keep your child's head warm.

Cold weather also calls for warm sleeping gear for the youngsters. Sleeping suits with attached feet are good, or the children can wear clean, dry socks to bed. Some camping mothers put the juveniles into tights before letting them crawl into the sleeping bags.

One subject that always starts an argument around a campfire is outdoor boots and shoes. Every outdoorsman has his own theories. A wide variety of footgear is available for those who take to the woods, and your choice will depend a lot upon weather and terrain. There are so many types, heights, sole designs, and sole materials that you can always find something you like.

Some footwear is pretty fair for all-around use, and some has specific uses. The main things to consider when buying outdoor boots are when and how you'll use them. The material of which they're made will have a great bearing on how successful they will be, no matter how much you pay for them. Besides the soles, there are three basic kinds of boot and shoe material: canvas, rubber, and leather. Sometimes they're combined.

Canvas, of course, is the lightest and cheapest. It will allow your feet to breathe in hot weather, and it's quick to dry. On the other hand, it's not waterproof, will wear through rather quickly, and is not warm in cold weather. Canvas-topped sneaker-type shoes are adequate for pleasant-weather outdoor wear, and they'll even do for hiking along something like the Appalachian Trail if you have replacements handy. Sneakers are especially good for youngsters who will probably outgrow a pair in a season, even if they don't outwear them. For summer camping, sneaks are light on your feet and cool in hot weather. The rubber soles give fine traction for general walking. Many campers will wear nothing else.

Sneakers or the like are often a must around boats. They're also good on beaches, even if the low-side models pick up part of the terrain with every step. They are fine for climbing seashore rocks and ledges and, because sneakers dry rapidly, many campers like to wear an old pair while wading and looking for shells. The surplus, high-sided jungle boots, if you can still find a pair, are particularly good for this.

Be sure to buy canvas shoes wide enough and long enough, or you'll soon find your big toe wearing holes. Sneakers with rubber toe caps resist this boring from within, incidentally. For general outdoor and camping wear, ankle-high sneakers are the more functional.

Rubber as a boot and shoe material is waterproof, warm in cold weather if the article is insulated and roomy, and under normal conditions will wear well. But it's heavy, hot in warm weather, and as the material doesn't breathe, will cause sweating.

Rubber shoes and boots are ideal for one thing: wet going. You can't beat them for getting around in wet morning grass or boggy ground, during a downpour, or when there's snow. Insulated rubber boots are warm and waterproof for extremely wet, cold weather, even though they may be somewhat heavy and bulky.

Any boot worn in cold going should be of loose fit, never tight. The air space between boot and sock and around your foot will act as insulation, letting your feet move freely and thus helping circulation. Boots keep your feet warm not only by keeping cold air out but also by keeping warm air in. Air space inside the boot will make this two-way operation work better.

One disadvantage of insulated rubber boots is that if you snag the outside layer of rubber, water may get into the insulation. If this happens, you will have trouble getting all the moisture out. In this case, roll and squeeze the wetness toward the puncture until no more comes out. Then, if the hole is large enough, prop it open with a bit of toothpick or twig and let it air. Don't patch such a tear until all possible moisture has been removed. Then a simple rubber-tube patch will do the trick.

Some rubber boots have felt insulation. These are fine while dry. If you perspire heavily or get water into them, they will become soggy and should be dried before you don them again.

Insulated rubber boots of any type are fine for cold-weather camping, sitting on a deer stand, and using anywhere a complete waterproof covering is important. You can't beat them for dry feet when it's wet outside.

Leather is the best all-around material for boots and shoes, as has been proved by their many centuries of use for footgear. Its only enemy is really wet weather. But with preparations now on the market, even that bugaboo can be combated pretty well. Leather is pliable, lets your feet breathe through it, and wears well under most conditions.

Regardless of trade names, most boot leathers are cowhide or horsehide. Both make fine footwear so long as they are well tanned and are free from weak spots. There are some sportsmen's shoes that are built from genuine elk, moose, deer, and bull hides, but these are exceptions. They seem to wear no better than good honest cowhide.

You'd do well to be wary of black or exceptionally dark-colored footwear. Dyes can cover up thin, thick, brittle, and rough spots so that you may not notice them when making your purchase. Watch out, too, for Mexican leather, which is sometimes poorly tanned. Good leather looks good, feels good, and has a well-oiled smell.

Leather footwear is never completely waterproof without some sort of dressing or greasing. There are silicone processes that greatly increase the water-repellent qualities of leather when combined with a composition sole that's welded to seal the bond between sole and upper. A good grade of boot grease will do much to keep your feet dry when it is applied to leather uppers, but nothing much can be done to waterproof a leather sole.

Good leather boots allow your feet to breathe in hot weather, yet when worn with thick wool socks are warm in cool weather. Don't buy boots with too-high tops. Leather, unlike rubber, will sag, so high tops may form uncomfortable wrinkles and folds about your ankles and heels. Then there's the added expense and the extra weight, the latter being of considerable moment, considering how many times you'll be picking up and laying down each foot during a day in the bush. Unless you need very high boots for support, an 8- or 10-inch top will be as high as you'll ever need. Higher boots for snake country are an exception.

Whether your boots or shoes are all-leather, all-rubber, or half-and-half, be sure they're large enough to be worn with heavy socks. When you stand your weight may be on both feet, but when you walk it's on one foot and then the other. This extra weight causes your feet to elongate and spread, particularly if you're carrying a pack or heavy gear. Veteran campers often make sure they have something heavy in their hands when they stand on one foot for measurement at the shoe store. Don't forget, either, that your feet will swell with exertion, and be sure to get your wilderness footwear at least one full size longer and one full size wider than what takes you comfortably along city pavements.

Never go into the woods with new shoes that haven't been broken in. Soft leather shoes and boots may be worn around home for a few days to break them in, but heavier boots sometimes require more radical treatment. One way to get a good fit is to put them over whatever socks you'll wear, stand in water until they're well soaked, and then walk in them until dry.

The all-leather boot is about the best choice for warm weather. Even during fairly cold weather they'll do fine if you wear warm socks. Just be sure the boots are large enough for air space and socks without crowding. For damp or rainy weather, keep your boot tops greased or sprayed with silicone dressing.

One of the best yet cheapest all-around roughing shoes is the old-time army shoe on a Munson last, with the smooth side of the leather inside. It doesn't look like much but is extremely comfortable when broken in and will wear well. The smooth leather interior prevents chafing, and the box toe gives plenty of walking room. Another similar type of high shoe has a top of rough-finish leather and a sole of crepe rubber. These are very comfortable and will take a good many scrapes and bangs. They do wet through rather easily, though, and take a comparatively long time to dry. But for dry-weather hiking, they're fine.

Many types of so-called engineer boots, with medium to high tops, have an ankle strap to keep them snug, and some have a top strap. A lot of these boots are pretty glamorous but will do well for camping unless you have a lot of walking to do. Then they're apt to work up and down in the heel. Too, the high tops are hot in summer. If you are in snake country, though, the higher top models are safest.

One famous boot of this type has been a standard with snake hunters for several decades. One of us has had a pair for more than twenty-five years, and except for a new set of heels about ten years ago and some repairs where an Airedale cut her teeth on the back seams, they're still intact with the original soles. They're fine over and under long trousers and will protect your legs and ankles from briers, wet grass, and snags. The only drawbacks are that the ankle strap occasionally catches on vines and brambles and that the boots are quite warm in hot weather.

For footwear that uses a combination of materials, the most popular and practical is the leather-topped rubbers that originated in Maine. With leather tops well greased, these boots will do in almost any weather but the wettest. They're fine for snow, and even in slush they perform well. We've both used them many years for hunting, snowshoeing, tracking in the deep snow, and almost every sort of winter outdoor wear. They have advantages over either all-rubber or all-leather boots.

The rubber bottoms keep the feet dry. The soft leather tops, available in various heights, are flexible and yet, with easily applied dressing, will keep feet and legs snug. The foot section is broad and roomy, so you can wear plenty of socks. If you don't take too long, you can wade through water almost to the boot tops without getting wet. Many like to wear these boots with socks long enough to turn down over the knotted laces. With rawhide laces tied with a square knot, and their ends tucked back down inside the boot top and covered with such turned-down socks, the boots are practically snagproof.

Leather-topped Rubber Boot

When you treat the tops of such boots, be sure that the grease or other waterproofing is of a type that won't injure the rubber of the bottoms. These boots will even be agreeable for warm-weather wear if you lace them loosely so that air squishes in and out with each step. With two pair of warm socks inside they will do for all but the most extreme weather and the deepest snow, especially if you get a pair of warm, preferably arch-supporting innersoles.

The soles of any outdoor footwear should be selected with safety in mind, for you're apt to be alone and on your own at least part of the time in the bush. Plain leather soles and heels can become extremely slippery on such common things as dry pine needles and leaves, frosty grass, and wet surfaces. Even on dry, crumbly trails such as you find in high country, and when the going is steep, smooth leather soles and heels can be a hazard. Too, they wet through quickly in ordinary damp travel, making them even more of a danger.

A crepe rubber or composition sole is better, especially if it has a molded tread. A nonslip pattern on rubber soles is important, one should never forget, for there are few things slipperier than smooth, wet rubber. If you are a leather-sole advocate, at least use rubber or composition heels with good nonskid characteristics. They will absorb walking shock, too, while helping to prevent skidding and slipping.

Some outdoorsmen prefer a straight-bottom, or platform, sole, while others insist on a heel. We both happen to like a heel for mountain climbing. For general wear, however, a platform sole is fine. A heel helps you to hold back when coming down a grade, but it also picks up a lot of mud. One solution here is to select a heel that slants upward and forward on its front edge. The slope won't pick up much forest litter or mud, and what it does will drop off.

If you plan backpacking or hunting, sure-footedness will be all-important. Slipperiness is bad enough at any time. But when you're carrying a heavy pack or loaded firearm it can be downright dangerous.

As far as boot fastenings are concerned, the simpler they are the better. Laces should be strong and either braided or of rawhide. Plastic laces are too slippery to be generally satisfactory at this writing, although improvements are coming along all the time. Braided laces should be heavy enough to stand strong pulling, snagging, and friction from brush. The tips are one place where plastic excels. Metal tips often pull off. In an emergency, it may be well to remember that frayed ends can be covered with a bit of evergreen pitch and formed into a point.

Zippers save time, but they can go wrong a long way from a replacement. Zippers also can leak in really wet weather. The best of them are fine on jackets, but on boots you'll do well to keep away from them. Some heavy flying boots are made with zippers, but these were designed for sitting rather than rough walking.

Some outdoorsmen argue for eyelets on boot tops, while others swear by hooks. A satisfactory compromise is a combination; eyelets over the instep where the laces are almost never removed, and hooks at the top where you unlace them most often. Rawhide laces fill in the eyelets so that there's little danger of their snagging. Buckles at the top of boots may look dashing, but they're prone to sag and, at best, we can see no need for them.

As for overboots, overshoes, and waders, there are several fine types that can add to your pleasure when you take to the woods. For those not planning to do a lot of deep-water fishing with chest-high waders, hip-length rubber boots will be the most that will be needed for walking in deep wet grass or during wet weather. Some low waders and boots come in soft, pliable rubber that can be pulled right on over regular footwear. They have tough, cleated soles, yet can be rolled and carried in a rubber envelope inside a pocket. There are several calf-high boots of this material that are fine for braving early-morning wet grass, crossing boggy areas, and fording creeks.

Cowboy boots are suitable for riding a horse or appearing an inch or two taller. But the toes are ordinarily too pointed and the heels too high for comfortable walking for any distance. The high heels pitch you forward. Then the tight, pointed toes make you miserable, for your toes cannot spread to support your weight. About the best shoe for both riding and walking is a standard leather boot with about an 8- to 10-inch top and moderate heels. These do well in the stirrups and are fine on the ground.

Then there are hobnail boots. These are fine for mountain climbing and for getting over rough, rocky terrain where the danger of slipping is ever present. But for general camp and outdoor wear they're too heavy, too hard on tent floors, often too stiff to be comfortable, and they can ruin a boat. You'll be well advised to leave them to mountaineers.

Caring for outdoor footwear is, like so many other things about taking to the woods, mostly a matter of common sense. Keep the gear cleaned of tar, pitch, and caked-on mud. Keep the leather portions either well greased and pliable or well sprayed with waterproofing. Keep the groove between the sole and the uppers clean and greased. Check for seams that may be pulling loose, and repair them before they let go.

When you get your boots soaked, dry them slowly; never in a hurry. One way to help this along is by filling them with warm, never hot, pebbles or sand, or by stuffing them with tissue to absorb the moisture. In any event, let them dry slowly in a warm place, but never near an open fire or they'll harden and shrink. Here's one thing to note well. Even the top interior of a hot tent is too warm.

Keep rubber boots and soles away from grease, as this may injure the material. Keep the cleats or tread brushed or picked clean, so that you'll have some protection in slippery going. When hiking in snow, check occasionally to see that the cleats remain open.

No matter what type of footwear you buy, get the very best you can afford. This practice will pay off in long wear and comfort, and with all camping clothes, as well. There is no substitute for quality, especially when you're by yourself back of beyond.

9

Be Ready for Rain

INTO THE LIFE OF EVERYONE WHO TAKES TO THE WOODS SOME RAIN must fall, and for the tent camper such moisture presents special problems. Owners of mobile homes have no great difficulty in wet weather, but possessors of folding tent trailers are only slightly better off than the tent camper. Damp weather can be a disheartening experience or a truly pleasant phase of camping, depending on how you prepare for it. Some of our most rousing days in the wilderness have been in the rain.

Readying for a wetproof camping trip is not expensive and requires only a few extra items of gear. First, the main shelter, probably a tent, should be leakproof. Second, the work area, likely the space beneath a fly, should be dry. Third, your rain garb should be adequate for protection as you move outside the tent and work area, and ponchos, raincoats, hats, and boots should be waterproof. Finally, you should be equipped with suitable protective covering for your personal gear.

The fabric of both conventional tents and folding tent trailers should be of good quality, made by a reputable concern. Suitable material will withstand a downpour as long as is necessary. The seams should be lap-felled, reinforced, and well stitched. Roof and walls should be designed to shed a maximum of rainwater speedily, and they should have no wrinkles, pockets, and depressions in which fluid can collect.

A good rain shelter should have a sewn-in floor to protect the interior from seepage under the walls. Doors and windows should have zippered storm flaps for complete closure in heavy rains. Good window closures are especially important when the sides of the tent are slanted rather than vertical. Small awnings over the windows will help to keep out moisture, and an awning over the door will enable you to leave and enter without being accompanied by a downpour.

One factor to consider before buying a tent is that in wet weather you and your family will be spending more time than usual inside. Unless you're backpacking and must weigh every ounce, get a somewhat larger tent than is required for minimum shelter, particularly if there are youngsters in the group. Nothing can make camping more frustrating than a small tent full of damp, restless youngsters with nothing to do.

56

Even lightweight tents will shelter you in heavy rain if they are pitched correctly and made of good materials. Make as sure as possible that nothing rubs against the tent fabric during a rain. In wet weather move cots, duffle bags, and other items away from the sides and avoid coming in contact with the tent fabric, for a leak will likely develop where you touch it.

All tent materials of natural fibers will absorb water during a rain. The individual threads swell, causing the woven area to shrink. This action closes the tiny openings in the weave and makes the material watertight. New tents should be soaked down and dried out before they are taken on that first trip to assure water repellency. If you have the room, set the tent up in the backyard and wet it down with a hose. Or, depending on the climate, leave it up for several nights so that night dampness can help set the weave.

Even a good tent will admit some light spray during a storm unless the weave has shrunk tight and sometimes even then. Unless damp weather precedes the storm to shrink the weave, this action takes place during every rain, for the material dries afterward and the fabric once more becomes porous. This shrinkage, although only slight, is potent. Unless you allow for it, stakes may be pulled out, seams ripped, and grommets torn from the material.

Whenever the weather turns damp or rainy, therefore, allow for this shrinkage. If the tent has an outside frame, it will be good to shorten the poles slightly. The idea is to let the tent sag a bit so that the fabric can shrink without damage. Guy ropes—unless plastic —shrink, too, so loosen them also.

If you are utilizing a folding tent trailer with rooms attached that need stakes, poles, and guys, loosen them. For no matter how long they are used, canvas and hemp will always shrink when they become wet. Slacking off the lines takes only a moment and can save valuable equipment.

Numerous types of flies have a rope sewn into the edge for added strength. Sometimes this border will shrink more than the material, and sagging will result. If a border-reinforcing line gives you this problem, replace it with a plastic rope or simply eliminate it.

If a tent or fly starts to hold a pool of water, do not raise it with anything of small diameter to dump the puddle. Instead, swathe your hand in a jacket and raise the pocket of fluid gently so that a leak will not develop at the area of contact. Lowering the fly or tent frame may increase the pitch so that the puddle will run off naturally, which will be even better.

The tighter the weave, the less water can penetrate and the more nearly waterproof the fabric will be. Canvas, of course, is made of cotton, as is duck. Even materials with such fancy names as balloon silk and Egyptian cotton are still made of cotton, although the finer grades are fashioned of long-fiber, high-quality threads. Good-quality cotton tents last many years with good care. Cheap tents stand up a much shorter time. The best stratagem is to buy a tent of the best quality you can afford.

If you are backpacking, weight and bulk come to be mighty important, but a properly designed lightweight tent can be entirely satisfactory if the material is tightly woven and adequately treated. A lightweight tent requires a steep roof and should be pitched so the material is smooth and taut. Lightweight canvas of about eight ounces per square yard makes a good tent for backpackers, while a 10- or 12-ounce canvas provides a more durable tent, suitable for those who travel by automobile, boat, or packhorse.

Thin cotton fabrics need some sort of waterproofing if they are to withstand a heavy downpour. Waterproofing is generally applied by the manufacturer. Such a tent, well waterproofed by the maker, will likely do for several seasons. When it starts to leak, you can renew the treatment yourself.

Some waterproofing consists of a paraffin solution colored to match the material, while others depend on an oil base. Both do a good job, although the paraffin treatment tends to make the material somewhat stiffer. On the other hand, an oil-base treatment is more likely to let color rub off on hats and jackets when you brush against the sides of your shelter. Both oil and paraffin waterproofing may be highly flammable unless some sort of fireproofing has been added. If a manufacturer claims his tents are 100 percent fireproof, ask for a sample swatch and test it with a match.

If your tent is an old one that's starting to leak in a few places rather than generally, these weak spots can be waterproofed quite easily and quickly with a stick of paraffin. A block of canning paraffin may be bought at a hardware or grocery store for a few cents and merely rubbed into both sides of the leaking area. Or you can buy a camper's pushup stick of no-drip wax made for this identical purpose.

It's sound procedure to have another individual go inside the tent and push up slightly under the leaky spot with some smooth surface such as a pot bottom or smooth piece of wood. This not only marks the leak so that you can locate it from the outside, but you can also press the wax more firmly into the material as you rub.

If the tent is a battered old veteran that leaks in many spots, your best bet will be to waterproof the entire thing. If the material is torn as well, patch all holes first. Patch material should be approximately the same weight fabric as that of the gear you're fixing. After the edges of the tear have been sewn together to prevent extension of the damage, cement a patch over the tear. Patches should be round so that there are no corners to catch and lift. Each patch should extend at least an inch beyond the tear in all directions. Canvas patches in various-size assortments and tubes of canvas cement are available inexpensively.

Waterproofing a complete tent may sound like quite a project, but actually it's not too difficult. Several good waterproofing compounds are on the market that can either be brushed onto the material or sprayed from pressure cans. Some of these compounds include mildew and rot inhibitors.

Many prefer the paint-on solutions for a really durable job. When you use this method, the material is saturated thoroughly with the solution, almost as it would be if you dipped the tent into it. On the other hand, the spray solutions aren't so messy to use, and a can may be carried along on a trip for treating small leaks as they appear.

A tent that is to be treated for waterproofing can either be spread flat on a table or lawn and painted or sprayed, or erected tautly and painted or sprayed like a small cottage. Many campers prefer having their tent pitched, feeling they're less apt to miss places. In any event, be sure to give the floor and roof especially heavy treatment. They come in contact with the most water. Remember that the floor may actually rest in moisture long after a storm passes.

If you'd like to treat a tent or tarpaulin with a good and proved homemade waterproofing solution, the job can be accomplished without too much difficulty. One of the best homemade solutions is simple to make and easy to apply. Just drop some blocks of canning paraffin into a gallon or two of white gasoline and let them stand for a few days or until as much paraffin as possible has been dissolved. The blocks may be eaten away entirely, or there may be nothing left but some thin, pock-marked paraffin wafers. About a pound of paraffin in a gallon of white gasoline is the right ratio, and you can shave the paraffin with a knife to speed up dissolving.

Take this saturated solution outdoors and—keeping all cigarettes, sparks, and open flames well away—paint it onto the tent or tarp. Use a clean, rather stiff brush, and work the liquid well into the material, particularly on roof, floor, and seams. The fluid will soak into the material and the gasoline will evaporate, leaving a coating of paraffin throughout the fibers. This treatment does not make the fabric too stiff, although it may stiffen slightly and shrink a bit as it dries. You can even use this solution on your convertible's top, and it will certainly make it waterproof. The white paraffin doesn't rub off much, and the color of the tent is not greatly changed, perhaps becoming a little darker.

If you prefer to use some solvent other than gasoline, you can substitute either turpentine or benzene. But remember that these, too, are very flammable, so use extreme care.

Probably the simplest of all home waterproofing methods is to rub block paraffin onto the material, section by section, as it's spread out on a smooth, hard surface. Once this is done, use a warm, not hot, iron to set the paraffin into the weave.

Nylon tents are generally waterproof, but because the material does not shrink when wet, moisture occasionally enters through the needle holes in the seams. Such needle holes and seams can be waterproofed with a liquid sealer that can be painted over the stitching, a job that should be done before a trip. There rarely is time to apply the sealer when rain threatens.

An extra fly or a sheet of plastic material spread or pitched over a tent makes it drier and easier to pack after a long rain.

Speaking of flies, one pitched over the eating or working area enables your party to spend considerable time outside the tent despite rain. It will also protect gear and wood. A 10 x 10-foot fly will cover an 8 x 10-foot area when pitched, two feet being lost to the roof slant. It is especially important to remember this when procuring a fly to cover a specific area of a tent of a certain size.

A fly over the work area is fine. If possible, pitch another fly from your tent entrance to the work area. Then you can move back and forth under cover.

Often plastic sheeting or lightweight tarpaulins can be used in many ways. Attach the edges to tents or fly roofs with clip-on clothespins. Plastic sheeting can be clipped to screened eating shelters to keep out the rain, and edges of tarps spread over food can be clipped down to prevent their blowing. Passageways can be made with tarpaulins and clip-type clothespins.

During the days before sewn-in floors, it was standard procedure to trench a tent. This consisted of digging a small ditch beneath the bottom of the tent walls and then draining off the lowest corner with a shorter ditch. Today with sewn-in floors and widespread regulations against trenching, this practice is seldom seen. Besides, in the forest, moisture generally sinks quickly beneath the leaves and other litter. Trenching sometimes causes erosion. If it is permitted and necessary, however, one of those little surplus trench shovels is ideal for the job.

Despite care, tents are prone to become accidentally torn, punctured, or burned. In rainy weather, holes are inconvenient, especially if the damage is in the roof or high on a wall. To be ready for any such damage, bring along a few patches or a piece of similar tent material, shears, and a tube of canvas cement. If you want to be really safe, add to this repair kit a few yards of heavy carpet thread, several needles of the correct size, and a thimble.

Sew the edges of a cut or tear together. Then, using cement, apply a patch. Add a duplicate patch to the other side of the fabric for additional strength. If you have no implements for sewing, or if the damage is a burned hole whose edges can't be brought together, use one patch outside and another inside.

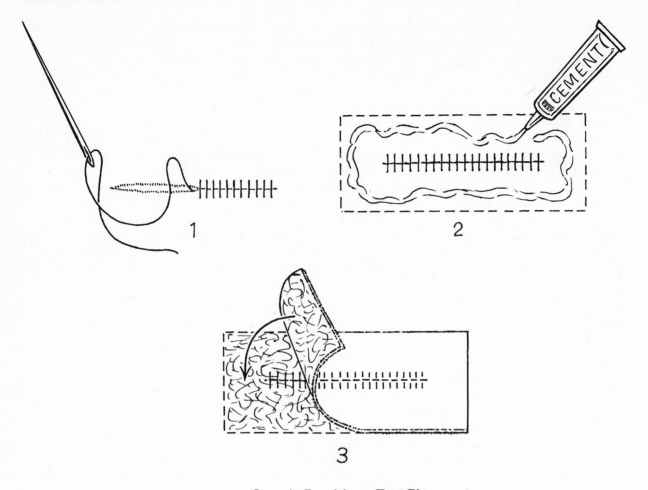

Steps in Repairing a Tent Rip

The edges of a patch should extend beyond the hole as much as an inch all around if possible, and the patch should be well cemented to keep water from working underneath along the upper edges. Properly applied patches will last for years. If the hole is small, adhesive plastic will seal it temporarily, or you can buy sticks of wax with which to rub a section to seal any small drip opening in a seam or canvas.

Some campers advocate pitching a tent under trees when possible, thereby using their foliage for added protection. But these same guardians will allow water to drip on your site long after the rain has ceased, and their shade will prevent the sun from drying out the tent and gear later. It is often possible, however, to erect a tent not far from trees so that you achieve both the protection of tree foliage during the storm and the heat of the sun afterward.

Rain suits and ponchos will protect you as you move about away from shelter. The former will provide the better protection, and you can don either or both halves and use the hood or not, as you see fit. Many prefer an old hat instead of the hood unless the storm is a driving one. Then the hood protects the back of the neck better than a hat.

If you are not using the hood in a rain, turn it inside out and roll it up behind your neck so that it doesn't collect a quart or two of water. An inexpensive plastic rain suit costs in the neighborhood of $5. The cost is about double that for a heavy-duty one of rubberized fabric. Ponchos cost less, and a poncho has other handy uses; as a small tarp, as an emergency shelter in a sudden storm, and as a windscreen. But the sides may slap open when you wear it, and it can shed water down your trousers, front, and back.

If you consider a hat stifling, about the best sort of wet weather headgear is either a fisherman's rain hat with a short brim in front and a wider one behind, or a western-type hat with a wide brim all around. The western hat is fine for bright days as well as wet ones. With a bit of extra waterproofing, it will take quite a storm in stride.

For treating clothes to shed water, one of the excellent spray-can waterproofing mixtures on the market will do a very good job, quickly and easily. These can be used on backpacks, by the way, in addition to shirts, trousers, jackets, and hats. Don't get too much in one spot. Instead, give the article a good general spraying and then rub it with the hand or a rag sprayed with the solution. If at all possible, let the item dry overnight before using it. Don't spray too heavily on a felt hat, or it may stiffen. Remember, a material must breathe, or body moisture will condense inside and make it clammy.

Too many campers when waterproofing treat their jackets and hats but overlook their trousers. Pants come in for plenty of dampness when you walk through wet grass or other vegetation and when a poncho drips on them. Give extra attention to the front of your trousers, especially the knees, and to the seat. Such treatment may prevent a chill when you've been kneeling or sitting on damp ground.

These commercial spray-on mixtures can also be used on leather shoes, and there are several types of oil or silicon boot mixtures. If your footwear is of all-leather construction, you can do a good job of waterproofing with the dubbing or neat's-foot oil obtainable from a shoe store or outfitter.

If your boots or shoepacs are part leather and part rubber, keep oil and similar waterproofing away from the latter as they may damage it. Rub waterproofing well into seams and into leather tongues, a spot often overlooked when waterproofing boots. On footwear with all-leather soles, run the waterproofing well into the groove between sole and uppers. All waterproofing of boots will have to be renewed from time to time; so when you take to the woods, it's smart to carry a small can or jar of whatever you use.

Such leather goods as pack straps, creel handles, rifle slings, handgun holsters, knife sheaths, camera and binocular straps and cases, and rifle scabbards and cases should be protected from moisture with a suitable dressing. With some of these, such as sheaths and scabbards, be sure not to make the leather too soft.

Treating your gear to shed water will not only protect it from rot and mildew in addition to moisture, but it will make your camping trip a lot more comfortable. This is particularly true if you camp near water or high in the mountains where clouds are apt to settle down over your camp. Such protection is surely recommended when you are camping by boat or canoe. A little waterproofing in the right places ahead of time can make a lot of difference in how a camping trip turns out.

Even if you have a fine tent, some of your outfit may need extra protection from rain and moisture. There doesn't seem to be anything better than plastic bags of assorted sizes. You can place dry items in these bags, expel the air, and seal them with an adhesive tape to keep everything dry, and you can always see the contents. Such items as firearms, camera, and binoculars should be well protected.

Painters' plastic drop cloths, handy and inexpensive, are fine for throwing over food, equipment, and even a tent itself in wet weather. They can also be used for windscreens and as coverings for walkways. Many other uses will come to mind if you have a few on hand. These huge sheets tear quite readily if abused, but they are still convenient to have along.

When bringing handguns that you do not plan to use for some time, give them long-term protection with a plastic pouch that contains a built-in chemical which prevents rust as long as the pouch is sealed. These pouches are large enough for most handguns. If you carry a firearm in a case lined with foam rubber, check it frequently in damp weather. Foam rubber may hold moisture. These are still fine cases, but it is always a good idea to check for moisture occasionally, especially near salt water.

A bracing campfire adds much to the cheerfulness of a damp camp, but often a fire is not only hard to start but difficult to keep going. Even the best firewood is hard to ignite and keep burning if it has been subjected to a long and soaking rain, especially if the moisture is freezing as it falls. Keep your spare logs under a tarp or even in your

How to Protect Firewood from Rain

tent if there is room. A bundle of really dry sticks will be enough to get the campfire started. Then you can add damp wood, which will steam dry and crackle away.

Wet weather in camp doesn't need to be a gloomy affair. With a good-size tent, some paperback books, a deck of cards, and familiar games for the small fry, you may even achieve the real rest that taking to the woods is supposed to provide.

10

Taking a Tool Kit to the Woods

SOONER OR LATER, EVERY CAMPER MUST BECOME A REPAIRMAN, builder, or inventor to take care of an emergency back of beyond. Making renovations and improvising gadgets are part of the fun of taking to the woods.

Although facts of space and weight will drastically limit what can be carried, you can with a little planning tote along the wherewithal for a considerable assortment of emergency projects. You'll be able to complete a lot of minor repairs to tents, tools, fishing gear, and other equipment. You can even fashion a few camp conveniences.

Over years of camping, we've used small tool kits for many wild and weird purposes. Likely you have said, "Now if I just had a bit of wire, a nail, a paper clip, or a rubber band, I could fix it." Why not include such items in your camping tool kit?

A camping tool kit might contain any of the following: nails, small oil can, copper wire, pliers, screwdriver, paper clips, small file, small shears, assorted rubber bands, butcher twine, tube of cement, liquid metal, old toothpaste tubes for melting as solder and using with evergreen pitch as flux, small saw, friction tape, and transparent adhesive tape. With close packing, most of these will fit into a cigar box or surplus first aid pouch.

What you take or omit depends upon how long and isolated your camping trip will be and on how much you can carry. It's a good idea to keep a list of what you needed or used on previous trips and to gauge your current kit from that.

The tools in the kit have many obvious uses. Pliers can cut wire and fishhooks, turn small nuts, and serve as a miniature vise. We both like small pliers having jaws that move in a parallel manner rather than at an angle. This makes them easier to use as a wrench. Such pliers also have wire-cutting jaws that are mighty handy.

A set of small screwdrivers will help in taking care of fishing reels and other mechanical gear. We both picked up a set of nesting screwdrivers a few years ago, the smallest blade of which is small enough for our sunglasses. Such a set is inexpensive and often includes an awl blade.

A flat file about six inches long will be handy for sharpening axes and badly nicked knives, as well as for putting a point on nails and sharpening metal tent stakes. For finer work, you can take along a small whetstone, fine on one side and coarse on the other, but the small file alone will do a pretty effective job on edged tools. The file can also be used with flint or quartz to start a fire in an emergency, and one never can tell when one of these is going to arise. A wooden handle can be attached in camp to protect your hand.

The small shears, which you may borrow from your first aid kit, will be helpful in making patches for torn canvas, trimming broken fingernails, or as a drill for making holes in leather or soft wood. Use one of the pointed blades as a drill by rotating it so that the cutting edge does the work.

Some campers also carry a pair of small tweezers. We both have these in our first aid kits. They're fine for holding small screws until they can be started. They're also excellent for removing splinters, perhaps with the aid of a magnifying glass, and you'll find other employments for them, too. Incidentally, just because the items in a repair kit are small, they need not be cheap. As with everything you lug into the farther places, get the best you can afford.

The other items mentioned will have numerous uses, some obvious and some not. Nails can be utilized not only as fasteners but also as emergency fishing sinkers. A nail can be held with the pliers and heated in the campfire, then used to burn holes in leather or wood or for making the wooden handles of tools. They can be used as pins to hold canvas bundled together or to repair ripped tents. As nails, they will help make camp furniture, construct lean-tos, and fabricate racks for clothing and utensils. About three dozen 3-inch nails with good heads will do. Even half a dozen can be a great help. In a pinch, you could even use nails with sharpened points to tip spears and arrows for survival equipment.

Soft copper wire will serve many emergency purposes. It can be used to lace broken packsack straps and belts after you have punched or burned holes in the leather with a nail. It will lace torn canvas. Wire can also be used to wrap such items as cracked ax handles, paddles, oars, and tent poles. It can be used to suspend food out of the reach of small animals, as it's too slippery for them to climb, and they can't easily bite through it. It can be used as a shoelace or a clothespin. It will wrap a split fishing rod, and a small loop will serve as a line guide. We once replaced a lost tip guide with such a loop, and it lasted the entire season.

Copper wire also comes in handy for repairing a split pack basket or for safely hanging a hot lantern from a branch. You can use it to hold on a searingly hot pot lid or to suspend and rotate meat over a fire. It will help you fashion camp furniture and to make small utensils of bark, punching holes in this with a nail first and then lacing among them with the soft flexible substance. If your electric-lantern wire breaks, you can rewire it. A cross stick plus a length of copper wire makes an excellent fish stringer.

Paper clips are another handy item for your tool kit. They can be linked together to form a reasonably strong chain, bent to make small hasps or bindings on boxes, or straightened and used as probes to clean appliance tubes. You can even use paper clips as lightweight sinkers. One of us attached a paper clip to the end of his spin-casting line between fishing sessions to keep this from slipping back into the reel housing. If you accidentally pull a drawstring from the neck of a duffle bag or from your pajamas, a paper clip can help you replace it. Just attach the end of the drawstring to the clip and work this through the cord tube with your fingers, pulling the string along with it.

Rubber bands will prove answers to a lot of camping problems. Use them to hold waxed paper or foil over opened food containers. A rubber band will grip a bunch of nails in a compact bundle. Rubber bands can be used to keep your tent door snugly closed if there's no zipper. Just close the door by pinning rubber bands across the opening. Then when you want to sneak in without being accompanied by too many insects, just stretch the opening. The bands will close it quickly and firmly behind you.

You can also use rubber bands to keep the lid of your creel snugly closed without locking it. Then you can lift it enough to slide in a fish, and the bands will close it tightly again. If you have to resort to survival methods, rubber bands when doubled will make a pretty fair slingshot, effective on birds, all of which are edible. If insects are cantankerous, use rubber bands to snug down the cuffs on your shirt and trousers, making it harder for the winged biters to reach your hide.

A strip of red rubber band will make an emergency worm for fishing. Use rubber bands to keep cutlery from rattling and moccasins snug. They can keep paper towels from unwrapping and, coiled around a cake of camp soap, prevent this from slipping out of your hand when you're down by the lake.

If you expect to be away from civilization for some days, a small tube of strong, quickly drying cement and perhaps one of liquid aluminum or steel will be handy. The cement will repair fishing rods, cracked paddles and oars which should be well wrapped with copper wire afterwards, tent poles, and in an emergency even broken glasses. By the way, if you depend on glasses, always carry a spare pair.

Liquid metal, which hardens in the air, can be used to repair leaking fuel tanks, broken metal items, and even to make sinkers. To fashion the latter, mold the paste into the proper shape, poke a small twig through it before it hardens to make a hole for the line, or insert a copper-wire loop before the metal hardens. Such solidified metal can be filed smooth with the little file in your outfit.

A small oil can with a screw top to prevent leaking is handy for loosening tight bolts, nuts, and valves and for keeping rod ferrules from sticking. A light wiping with an oily cloth will keep flashlight caps from sticking or corroding. Wipe your edged tools with oil in wet weather. Dampness makes fire lighting tricky, but a few squirts of oil on kindling will start a fire quickly when the usual methods don't work.

The roll of transparent adhesive tape will be handy in many ways. One friend of ours stripped the threads on the cover of his spin-casting reel and repaired it with a strip of this tape. Tape can also be used as a guard on fishhook barbs, to hold covers on opened containers, and for sealing small openings in milk cans. It can also be pressed into service to hold bandages in place in an emergency and to repair small broken gadgets. A strip over your rifle or pistol muzzle will keep out dirt and snow, but remove before firing. A strip around an adjustable rear sight may keep it from injury or prevent a change of setting. Friction tape is useful for heavier work, as for repairing the handles of broken axes and other tools.

Butcher twine can be used to repair torn material, hang up gear, tie objects together, serve as wicking in kerosene stoves and lanterns, and, when greased, to act as packing for leaking joints in gasoline stoves and motors.

When you take to the woods, all you really need are a few simple tools, some odds and ends of repair material, and a bit of ingenuity to keep your outfit in working order. Tailor your tool kit to your individual needs. Each trip will add ideas that can improve your future journeys into the woods.

11

Packing Makes Perfect

WHEN YOU TAKE TO THE WOODS, KNOWING HOW TO TRANSPORT your equipment safely and conveniently can go a long way towards making your trip successful. Most of us these days travel to the jumping-off place in a motor vehicle, and the proper packing of your sedan or station wagon will do much to make the journey pleasant and the task of unpacking more convenient.

Safety is the prime factor to be considered in the loading of any vehicle with several hundred pounds of heavy and often sharp-cornered gear. Such heavy items as stoves, fuel containers, and iceboxes should be located so that they do not affect the balance of your vehicle—perhaps equipped for the trip with extra springs—and cannot shift enough to endanger the occupants. Too, you'll want everything conveniently arranged so that plenty of room will be left for the passengers to ride comfortably. A well-packed car or station wagon makes for an enjoyable ride and avoids waste motion, inconvenience, and frustrations at every stop.

The safety factor is particularly critical when such loads are to be packed on the outside of your vehicle in some type of roof or trunk carrier. The location and security of external carriers are very important.

Too, stow heavy gear as low in the vehicle, and as close to its center of gravity, as possible. If you are traveling with a station wagon, place heavy items close to the rear of the back seat. If there are no extra passengers, it may prove worthwhile to remove this second seat even though it ordinarily folds down flat. The amount of extra space thus gained can be amazing. In any event, pack progressively lighter items in place as you work toward the tailgate.

Such a loading system will keep the rear of the vehicle from sinking low over the wheels and so will reduce the chance of the tailpipe's or muffler's banging the ground when you wheel over rough back roads or roller coaster up abrupt grades. The system also reduces the possibility of side sway occasioned by too much weight in the rear. It makes jacking up the rear wheels when and if necessary a lot easier. Incidentally, keep that spare tire where you can get at it in a hurry.

Keeping all heavy items low in the body affords not only better weight distribution but, in the case of high items, also better visibility through the inside rearview mirror. Any vehicle used for such camping loads should also be outfitted with an outside rearview mirror, preferably one on each side so that you can swing more safely into a right-hand lane.

If you are using a sedan rather than a station wagon, the loading space includes the trunk, the rear seat, which may also be removed, and possibly a roof rack. Use the car's interior and the forward part of the trunk for heavier items. Save the roof rack for bulkier but lighter gear such as lightweight tents, sleeping bags, and aluminum camp furniture.

Be sure to place your possessions so that none of the items will continually squeak, thump, or rattle during the drive. Nothing is more nerve-racking on a long trip than such background commotion. Pack soft items such as towels or paper napkins around anything that might sound off en route. Paperback books, so welcome around a campfire, are also good buffers.

If you are using a sedan, be sure to secure the trunk lid firmly. A heavy load and a bumpy road are a combination that can pop open a closed but unlocked trunk lid, possibly strewing a trail of camping gear for some distance before the misfortune is discovered. Locking your trunk is a particularly good habit in bear country such as Yellowstone Park, where the critters know every trick for getting trunk lids open.

Never place anything but soft items on the shelf below a sedan's rear window. During sudden stops, occasionally unavoidable if you are to keep from colliding with animals, such things as camera, binoculars, firearms, and pressurized cans of liquid can become high-speed projectiles aimed at the heads of passengers and driver. Furthermore, placing such items there, or atop the dashboard, exposes them to extreme heat which can ruin film, affect lens settings, etc. Incidentally, packsacks with frame backs provide substantial guards between the rear of the vehicle and the front.

If you carry such expensive possessions as camera and binoculars atop the dashboard, any swerve can send them sliding. It could be disastrous to reach for a plummeting camera while steering around a hairpin curve on a mountain road. If you understandably want such items to be nearby, keep them on the front seat or let the passenger hold them.

Camera equipment, binoculars, handguns, and the like should be protected by plastic bags if the backcountry route you plan to follow may be dusty. Don't think that all this dust will be to the rear. Some if it will be kicked up underneath your own vehicle, plus that raised by those ahead, and sucked into your car even if all the windows are shut. This is especially true on such a wilderness road as the great Alaska Highway, where dust during the dry months is so heavy that you'll likely be driving with the lights on even at midday. Just a few grains of dust can scratch lens and damage the working parts of camera, binoculars, and fine weapons. By the way, an icebox is a practical place to stow film.

All firearms should, of course, be unloaded and broken down or cased while you're en route. Some provinces and states are mighty particular about the transportation of weapons of any kind, especially handguns. Check the law and be certain.

Such items as emergency flares, first aid kits, and fire extinguishers should be carried under the front seat, if there is a place for them there, where they'll be immediately available. However, put them on the passenger's side so that, if they slide forward, the passenger can easily retrieve them and they won't be so likely to lodge under the driver's foot pedals.

Roof racks can be handy. If you are using one, make certain that it is firmly fastened

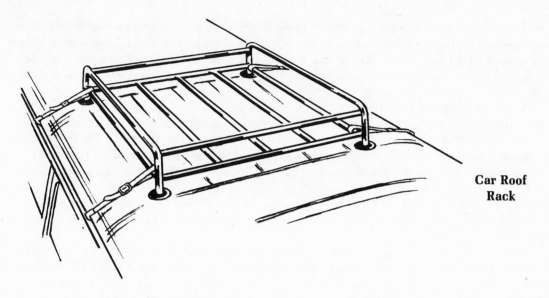

**Car Roof
Rack**

with gutter straps and suction cups. Locate it well forward on the roof, over the vehicle's center of gravity. If you graduate to two roof racks, place the higher one in front so that it can help protect the lower one and its cargo from wind, dust, and rain.

Available elastic shock-cord grips, stretched over a bulging cargo and hooked to the frame of the rack, are excellent for lashing down gear. Thin plastic sheets are too fragile to protect equipment from high winds or pelting rain. Use a sturdy tarpaulin. If your roof rack has a zipper-closed cover, be sure to check the zipper frequently, especially after using it. If you have a place to attach it, a good way to make sure that the zipper stays shut is with one of those little padlocks with a combination lock.

If your roof rack is metal-enclosed and has doors with locks, better check these, too, before and during the journey.

To pack successfully, the initial trick is to keep the gear within reasonable bounds. Start with a list of everything you'd like to take if you had the room, having the fun of mentally living through a few days in camp. Include items that may be difficult to obtain in the area where you plan to stay.

When you begin to whittle this initial list down to practical size, remember that if you take things that will serve two or more needs, so much the better. For instance, soft paper towels in a roll will serve as napkins, covers for open food, and so on. If both your camp stove and lantern work on white gasoline, each can be refueled from the same can. If your stove burns bottled gas, a lantern using the same fuel will permit using the same sort of tanks on both.

If your tent has a screened porch, it won't be necessary to carry a screened fly for the eating area. A boot for your station wagon can eliminate the need for a tent, although a small one may still be handy for storing paraphernalia while you sleep in the wagon. If you take cots, you can do away with air mattresses, or vice versa, unless you prefer both. You'll find many similar ways to eliminate and double up to save space and cut down on weight.

Once you've pared the list as much as seems possible, assemble everything a day or so before the departure date. Then actually pack it in your car. This will indicate how much stuff you must eliminate beyond the supposedly rock-bottom list. It's only in the packing that you'll learn the final answer about what you can and can't take. Too, a lot of gear just won't fit where you planned to put it, and so things must be shifted to make room. It may take an hour or more to fit everything in its ideal place where it will ride well, be handy when needed, and can be repacked conveniently.

Incidentally, before you begin stowing gear into your car or wagon, it will be a sound maneuver to take out the spare tire, jack, lug wrench, and road flares. The space they leave can be filled with belongings you won't need on the road. Then, as packing nears completion, place the spare tire and related equipment where you can get at them readily in case a tire lets you down. Include a couple of broad, husky wooden wedges with which to block the wheels when shifting a tire or parking on a grade.

Keep possessions as much as possible in units or containers. For example, a wooden box about 3 feet long and 1 1/2 feet wide and deep will hold stoves, lanterns, flashlight, and camp ax. All you'll have to do when you reach a campsite after dark is haul out this box, and you'll have all the basic items for pitching camp and getting supper after dark. The cooking gear can all ride together in a packsack. The perishable food, of course, will be in the icebox, while the rest can be in pasteboard boxes.

Speaking of perishables, you may find ice almost impossible to get at most campsites. Then never pass up a chance to replenish your supply even if you still have some left. Better take along a large plastic dishpan or a canvas basket or folding bucket in which to carry extra ice wrapped in newspapers. Admittedly, it will melt faster outside the icebox than it will when in, but when the block in the box has melted partway down you'll probably have some left in the pan or pail with which to replenish it. Just don't forget to empty the water periodically from the spare ice carrier so that it won't slop over on sudden stops.

Box for Camp Equipment

Ice containers and water jugs should be kept out of the sun as much as possible, of course. Even then, water jugs generally won't keep water cool for more than a few hours unless you start off with about 75 percent ice or really chill the jug to begin with. A good system, whenever you can manage it, is to fill a wide-mouthed jug all the way to the top with ice cubes, then fill in the spaces with cold water.

Whenever it is possible, it's a good idea to freeze clean milk cartons full of water for use in the icebox. When this frozen liquid melts, you at least have some cold fresh water to drink, and the water isn't slushing around in the bottom of the box.

On an extended camping trip especially, it is important to keep things in the same places every time you pack and unpack. Then when you want anything, it is reasonably easy to find it without too much effort. Gear such as jackets, coats, and rain clothing can be placed on top of the load so long as there's no danger that they'll blow out the back or obstruct your vision. If you are a fisherman, better keep a small box of your favorite lures or flies handy. Too, pack one of your rods atop the load or attach it to car eaves so it will be available when you come to an enticing pool.

Sharp equipment such as saws, axes, and shovels, as well as tent pegs and spiked poles, should be packed so that they won't cut or puncture other gear as the load shifts. It's smart to stow them securely, with the blades or spikes pointing toward the rear in case of a sudden stop.

The convenience accruing from smart packing will be evident again when you arrive at the campsite. A general rule is to put in last what you will wish to bring out first, be it a tent for shelter, a tarpaulin for protection, or grub for a quick meal.

Let's assume that food will be your first concern at the campsite. Since food and stove are heavy items, it's advantageous to keep the former in small batches so that only a small container or two need be taken out at a time. This approach is easier than having to remove a huge, heavily packed, unwieldy kitchen unit containing everything.

An umbrella may seem out of place on a camping trip, but an old one can come in plenty handy for unloading in the rain. A lightweight tarp or a large sheet of plastic, stowed in a handy place, can be used to keep unloaded gear dry until you can get it inside the tent.

If you will be using a folding table, stow that in a handy spot, too. If the ground is wet at the unloading place, pile your gear on the table. And if you arrive after dark in ordinary weather, the table is a good spot to put a lantern that will throw some light on the operation. Or maybe a spotlight, or one of those little lights that plug into the dashboard lighter, can be used for that purpose.

Should your plans include stopping at a motel, pack a small bag with the few items you'll need during the stop. Then you won't have to unload a whole suitcase or duffle bag to get at your pajamas, toothbrush, and razor.

It pays to be space-conscious. If you try to use all the space available, you'll be astounded at the amount of gear that can be taken along on a camping trip. Numerous tiny spaces are always available for those little items that can add fun and convenience to a vacation.

For example, an extra pair of boots can be filled with a small flashlight, waterproofed matches, extra batteries, sheath knife, and paper napkins. The spaces in your gasoline or propane stove can hold a small roll of paper towels, washcloths, or a box of matches wrapped in foil for safety. You might even put a candle or some flashlight batteries in the hollow center of a paper towel roll.

The space under or behind your spare tire may be big enough for a few handfuls of dry kindling, a tool or two, a coil of clothesline, or a sheathed hatchet. The hollow globes of camp lanterns will hold extra mantles, a few matches, or similar tiny items, but be certain that none of them touch the fragile mantle. If you are carrying many canned goods, you'll find that odd cans can be inserted almost anywhere. The same goes for those books and magazines you never seem to find time enough to read in the city.

Air mattresses can be rolled, not folded, inside your sleeping bags or tucked into the back corners of an enclosed cartop carrier, the type that has sloping sides.

The crease between the back and bottom cushions of your car's front seat—which is often full of old wrappers, match packs, and an occasional lost coin—may be just the place to stow an emergency flare. With many cars, a flare can be easily rolled into this crease, removable with a finger in an instant. Such flares, which burn for some fifteen minutes, can be used as emergency lights, to start a balky fire, or for the original purpose of warning traffic of an accident. They are available at auto supply and hardware stores.

So use planning and imagination when packing your car. The wrong kind of loading can mean broken springs, overheated tires, hot engines, and long, slow grinds up steep grades, besides being pretty rough on brakes on mountain roads and in sudden stops. On the other hand, a wisely packed vehicle is worth its weight in safety and convenience, both on the road and later at the campsite.

12

Dry Run

WHEN ONE OF US RAN A TV SHOW FOR YOUNGSTERS, WE ALWAYS had what we called a walk-through before going on the air. Everyone literally walked through whatever he was going to do on the show, so the director could see if the cameras were always where they were supposed to be. Often they weren't, but with this prior information they could be so located before we went on the air.

Campers might take a tip from this technique and have a walk-through or dry run before taking to the woods to be sure they have everything they need and that it all will work. It's best to find out in advance what's missing and what won't function. The time for such discoveries is not when you start to pitch your canvas in the wilderness. A good checkup will forestall a lot of inconvenience.

If there is room in your backyard, garage, or even living room, give your tent a thorough test. If it has been rolled up in the attic or basement, open it all the way to make sure there are no mice nests, collections of seeds, or chewed holes in it. No matter how well you may have packed it, or how often you have inspected it during the winter, you may find that mice have moved in and chewed a hole in the material. The best way to inspect a tent is to pitch it, then go over everything carefully.

If the tent has holes, patch them with similar material, using either waterproof glue or small stitches. Waterproof the patch and seams afterward with paraffin or spray waterproofing. Check all seams to see if they need restitching or reinforcing. Look over the grommets.

Make sure that the tent has enough stakes and guy ropes, plus a spare of each. Think it over and be as certain as possible that the system you're using guarantees that pegs, poles, and guy ropes will arrive at the campsite along with the tent.

Look for holes in the tent's door and window netting. Make sure that the zippers on doors and windows run easily and are well attached. If the linkage meshes or disengages with difficulty, apply a bit of stick lubricant. Check the tapes on window curtains, doors, and awnings to see that they aren't pulling loose.

Don't neglect to look over your tent poles. If they are aluminum, make sure they are not bent or dented and that the end caps are in place. If one of these is missing, the pole end may cut tent floors and such. A rubber crutch tip from the dime store often makes a suitable replacement. If the poles are steel, look for rust or chipped paint. Sand down such areas and touch them up with paint.

You may care to paint the poles of all your flies and tents either light yellow or white. They'll then be easier to find if you set up after dark or strike camp before dawn, and you'll also be less likely to run into them at night. They'll probably be easier to find even in daylight, too. One of us once lost a green steel tent pole off the top of his station wagon while passing a cornfield, and he had the devil's own time locating it among the green corn.

Check wooden tent stakes for splitting and metal stakes for bent or dulled points. Paint the tops white so you won't trip over them at night. Keep stakes in a bag. They're less apt to damage tent fabric this way, and if you have one, you'll have them all.

Go over your camp stove to determine if the valves turn easily by hand. Beware of using pliers on such valves. You may break plastic knobs or damage metal ones. If a valve turns with difficulty, apply a bit of penetrating oil to the stem and allow it to work into and loosen the threads.

If your stove runs on gasoline and requires a pressure pump, see that the latter operates smoothly. A few drops of oil dropped into the hole so marked will keep the plunger washer soft and the pump functioning. Check the stove by filling and running it. If it burns smoothly, you can be sure that fuel lines are not blocked and tiny jets clogged. Gasoline left in a tank over the winter may become gummy and choke lines and jets, so if you didn't clean out your tank before storing the outfit, you may have a messy job getting the stove into shape now.

If your stove burns propane, be sure the fuel tanks are full or nearly so before starting the journey. Propane burns brightly right up to almost the last of the gas, and during the winter the tanks may have leaked a trifle, further reducing the supply left from last year. Nearly empty tanks are light in weight compared to full tanks. Compare them with the tanks in a store. If theirs are much heavier, better take along some. Examine any flexible gas lines to make certain that the rubber isn't cut, badly worn, or loosely fitting at terminals. If the lines appear at all faulty, replace them. Leaking gas can be dangerous.

Lanterns should be gone over carefully. Look for leaks, broken mantles, and dirty globes. Gasoline lanterns should be inspected for leaky pumps. Oil these where indicated, as you do the pump on a gasoline stove. Incidentally, it's a good idea to drain your lanterns before storage, then to place them in a handy box or paper bag over the winter to block dust.

Examine electric lanterns and flashlights for burned-out bulbs, exhausted batteries, corroded terminals, and loose wires. If you carry a spare bulb, make sure it is still good. While you're at it, clean lenses and polish reflectors.

Unroll your air mattresses and blow them up, leaving them that way overnight to see if they hold air. If you have separate air pillows, include these, too. If the mattresses have been folded since last year, instead of being partially inflated and rolled as is preferable, leaks may have developed along the creases. If a mattress goes down overnight, first check the valve. If that appears to be all right and doesn't bubble under water, blow the mattress up hard and immerse it part by part in the bathtub, putting additional pressure on all portions until you find the leak.

Even a tiny leak will let you down overnight. Repair any, therefore, with suitable patches and cement, being sure the former are large enough to cover the holes and ex-

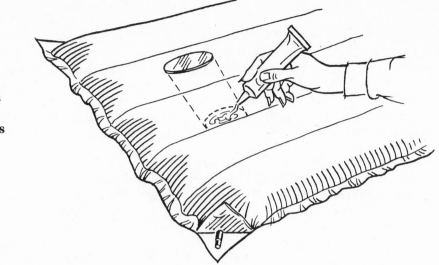

**Repairing a
Leak in an
Air Mattress**

tend a generous margin beyond on all sides.

Get out your sleeping bags, unzip them, and look them over. Mice sometimes work their way into the middle of a bag, too, even when it's rolled. Check the zippers to make sure they are running smoothly and are not catching in the material. A bit of stick lubricant, not oil, will help smooth them out. If you haven't been using a bag liner, this might be the year to begin. Such a liner saves the inside of the bag and makes it quite a bit warmer.

Test the tightness of wooden hatchet and ax handles. One way to do this is to hold the tool by the end of its handle, with the head hanging down. Note where the head is on the handle. Then pound on the end of the handle. If the head moves up on the handle, things are too loose for safety.

Then, using the method just described and trying not to pound on the tool's head while resting its handle on the floor, drive the handle as far as possible into the head. Drive the wedge or wedges in front of the head in farther and, if necessary, add another. A 6-inch band of bright color painted onto the handle of the ax or hatchet near its end will make the tool easier to spot in the woods.

Go over leather sheaths. If there are loose stitches or rivets, have a local shoemaker repair them. Or do it yourself, perhaps buying for about $1.50 a sturdy stitching awl for the purpose. Sharpen all tools before putting them away again and lightly oil them to prevent rust.

An icebox that has been closed for months should be aired. The hinges should be lightly oiled, and the catch should be examined to make sure it is still keeping the lid tightly closed. Check the water plug to find out if the cap is snug and the opening free of obstructions. Touch up any scraped or chipped paint. If you have one of the ultralight boxes of plastic foam, look it over for leaks and be certain to check whether or not the handles are still tight.

Does your auto-top rack need paint, replaced straps, or new suction caps? Suction caps that have been bent all winter will be difficult to stick to your car roof. And if you've bought a new automobile since last season, try your rack in advance for size. Sometimes a

**Testing the
Tightness of an
Ax Handle
and Resetting Head**

73

new roof design or decorative grooves will make an old reliable top carrier impossible to use. Don't wait until the morning you pack for the expedition to find this out.

If you've packed a lot of camping gear away in boxes—such as soap, towels, lightweight tarps, rope, small tools, mittens, clotheslines, folding buckets, and cooking utensils—check them over to see what's in which box and in what sort of condition everything is.

How well stocked is your first aid kit? You may have used some items and neglected to replenish them. Vials or tubes may have leaked. Sterile packets may have become torn. Medicines may have become outdated. It's worth the time to check all these things and where necessary to restock with fresh supplies. Don't skimp on drugs. A lifetime of research has gone into them, and there's absolutely no substitute for them when they're needed.

If you use such things as folding chairs, tables, and cots, make sure their seams are not torn and that the material has not dried or rotted. A few drops of oil on the joints of such conveniences makes them work considerably easier.

As soon as everything is in order, it's not as ridiculous as it may sound to have the family walk through a camp-pitching rehearsal. You may be surprised how many details you've forgotten. Keep a list. Before the camp has been entirely pitched, at least mentally, the length of the list will probably be a shock. Such missing items as clothesline, shaving gear, games for the youngsters, a stake for the pet, plenty of towels, plastic throw material in case of wet weather, water buckets, and pads to put under the tent poles to save the floor should all be jotted down so that you won't forget them later.

There's one thing more. If your trip is planned for the near future, it may be a valuable part of your dry run to rehearse packing the automobile before the day you plan to go. You've no doubt added new items to your camping outfit, and the small fry have grown.

A lot of tears and trouble may be avoided if it's at rehearsal time that you discover you just don't have room for some items. Perhaps an autotop rack, or even two, will solve your problems. But if you wait until the day you plan to start, you may not be able to get one in time. For less confusion, both plan and pack ahead of time.

Even old-timers, who travel light, will probably admit that a dry run has its advantages. You'll find it interesting as you walk through a camping trip ahead of time to find out what you've forgotten from your last one. On the other hand, you'll discover it satisfying to take stock of the good ideas that you are able to remember. And don't forget those lists. Besides, at least one-third of the fun of taking to the woods is in the anticipation.

PART TWO

CHOOSING WHERE
AND HOW TO GO

13

Cycle Camping

CYCLE CAMPING IS BECOMING INCREASINGLY POPULAR WITH MANY youngsters and not a few adults. It offers plenty of good, all-around exercise, some leisurely looks at slow-moving scenery, and a change in camping routine.

Covering country by bicycle, you'll glimpse many sights you'd have missed from your car. As in canoeing, by taking it easy the first day or so, your muscles will be spared much misery. The youngsters, as you'll regretfully learn, probably won't even need that brief a breaking-in period.

A husky youngster can pedal more than forty miles a day if roads and weather cooperate. Even an aging parent can manage twenty miles or more if he takes it easy. The secret is to set your own pace and enjoy the trip.

Where shade is scarce, cover most of your daily distance before the sun soars too high. Stop early if you find a good spot, and get plenty of rest before the next day's pedaling. If you know where you are going to camp and can settle in there in the twilight or after dark, rest during the hottest portion of the day and go on during the cool evening. When traveling after dark, though, be sure each bike has an adequate headlight and taillight or reflector. Wear light-colored outer clothing.

Journeys of 100 miles or so are not unusual for cycle campers once they get into shape. Even longer trips can be made if the terrain is favorable and the pace leisurely. Some of those who take to the woods by bicycle go over the proposed route by car to locate camping spots and get advance permission to tent. Such an approach sidesteps a lot of worry and possible difficulty. Don't think that traversing the route by automobile will spoil it for a bicycle trip. Scenery never looks the same from over handlebars as it does from behind a steering wheel.

One agreeable way to plan such a camping trip is to obtain a large-scale map and plot a route along back roads. Your aim shouldn't be to make time, but rather to see country and enjoy yourself. The back roads will take you away from heavy traffic and into picturesque regions.

Some parties arrange to ride their bikes to a distant spot and then take the train back

home, shipping their cycles in the baggage car. Others plan to pedal around a big circle, coming back to the beginning point by a different route.

No matter what type of open highway you travel, keep single file and stay to one side. Switching back and forth, even on a country lane, can be disconcerting to drivers and dangerous to cyclists. You'll be astonished at how fast "slow" vehicular traffic seems to proceed when you're pushing pedals instead of an accelerator.

Don't exhaust yourself attempting to pedal up steep grades unless your bike is geared for hill climbing and the roadbed is good. It's easier otherwise to get off, push, and stretch your legs. In rolling down long or steep hills, don't make the mistake of letting the machine get out of control because of the unaccustomed weight of camping gear.

It will be more difficult than usual to stop quickly, and your coaster brake may become unduly hot. Stop occasionally on exceptionally long grades and let it cool. Watch out for stretches of sand and loose gravel and keep an eye open for holes or washouts. Such hazards can easily throw a heavily loaded bicycle. And don't forget: your wheels are supported by wire spokes, not pressed steel as in a car's.

If your journey is to be over dusty byways, bring along a rag for cleaning exposed moving parts and an oil can for lubricating them. Keep rag and oil in a plastic bag to prevent their dirtying other parts of your outfit.

About the only tool you'll require is an adjustable wrench or one of those universal tools sold at bike stores that fits almost everything. A tire-repair kit and pump may afford added peace of mind.

In planning what to bring, you'll be governed largely by the length of the trip, the method of carrying your gear, and how often you'll pass through towns. There'll be no need to tote much food if you can buy it along the way. Use the space instead for items important to your comfort and purchase food from day to day as needed. Many bike campers prepare only their breakfasts and lunches, sitting down to their big meal of the day at roadside cafes. It's all a matter of personal choice.

If you're going around the course first by automobile, why not borrow a trick from backpacking and cache food and other necessities where you'll need them along the route?

As for packing, the main thing to remember is that your outfit should be carried on the bicycle, not on your back. A backpack soon becomes uncomfortable, as well as causing uncertainty in balance. Too, its extra weight may lead to chafing from the saddle.

Use a pack to hold your gear if you like, but strap it to the back wheel rack. Either that, or hang one on either side for better balance. Some cycling stores sell panniers that hang from the rear wheel rack, and some campers build plywood boxes that they fasten to this rack with bolts and wing nuts. You can build such containers functionally of outdoor plywood and fit them with hinged tops, painting them inside and out to match the bike and to make them waterproof.

In a front basket, where they'll be available in a hurry, you can tote such items as lunches, canteens, raingear, and first aid kit. Certain pieces of gear can be affixed to the crossbar of boys' bikes, but keep any such bundles narrow so that you won't have to ride bowlegged. Roll all externally attached gear in waterproof material to protect it from the weather. A pair of rubbers or a set of those stretchy rubber boots into which trousers can be tucked is handy, too.

Many touring campers strongly recommend toe clips for pedals so that not only will the feet be held securely to these levers, but also the upcoming pedal can be lifted for additional power. This can make a surprising difference in climbing or when a burst of speed is called for.

As for camping gear, one of the handiest gadgets is a small gasoline or alcohol pocket stove. In a camping spot where there is either no firewood or no open fires are permitted, you can still have a hot meal with a minimum of difficulty. Carry a small can of extra fuel, too. These tiny stoves come in many styles, but all weigh less than two pounds. They are inexpensive. For instance, you can buy a small stove using a popular brand of canned heat for less than a dollar, complete with a can of fuel. This model folds flat and weighs about ten ounces new.

A sleeping bag designed for the weather expected will take up less room and be far more comfortable than the same amount of warmth in blankets. A bag with two pounds of insulation will do pretty well for summer cycle camping, while one with three or four pounds will keep you warm in spring or fall. Such a bag can be tightly rolled and strapped to the back rack or handlebars. Web straps of various lengths, incidentally, will be of great value in attaching your outfit.

If you have a small lightweight tent, be sure to take it along. If not, carry a lightweight tarp or some large sheets of plastic. In a sudden shower, you can make a pretty snug tent of either a tarpaulin or plastic sheeting, using your standing bike as a ridgepole.

Clothing should be rugged and comfortable for the long hours of pedaling. Shorts may be fine, but watch out for sunburned knees and thighs. Lightweight trousers are almost as cool as shorts, are more comfortable at night and in cool weather, and give better protection from sunburn and dust. Just be sure the legs can't flap dangerously close to sprocket or chain. If they do, wear bicycle clips or roll the legs above the danger area. Cuffs are a bother for numerous reasons.

If you wear hats, a broad-brimmed one will keep your head cool while protecting the back of your neck from both sunburn and rain. Sunglasses (get good ones) will guard your eyes from sun and dust. A warm jacket for evening and for damp weather will be welcome. A poncho with a hood is ideal if you have to keep going in the wet to reach shelter.

Take along extra underwear and socks. Choose soft, absorbent materials. Pedaling can be hot work. Personal items will include jackknife, flashlight, insect repellent, matches in a waterproof container, and toilet articles.

As for individual cooking and eating gear, a small frypan, preferably with a folding handle, stew pot, cup, bowl, plate, fork, spoon, and perhaps a knife, unless you're using a pocket blade, will be sufficient. If you prefer a group kit, there are numerous fine ones from which to choose. Instant coffee will eliminate lugging a coffeepot along, although you can brew the regular kind handily in your stew pot. In any event, a cream substitute, plus sugar if you use it, will dress up the taste.

Canned goods can be carried more easily by cyclists than by backpackers. So you can have canned meats, soups, and stews. Possibly fresh vegetables, milk, meat, and eggs may be bought along the route. In other words, don't carry more food than is needed.

Here are a few tips on getting your bicycle ready for the trip. The saddle should be just high enough so that when the pedal is at the base of its stroke, your knee will be slightly bent. This will afford more power and prevent sawing back and forth across the saddle. The saddle should never be tipped forward on a long trip. If it is, you'll be forever battling to stay back on it, and much of your weight will be supported by your arms instead of by your pelvic bones on the saddle.

Keep the saddle level or tipped slightly back. Avoid too much backward tilt, though. If your arms become tired or your back lame, it's a sign the saddle is not at the correct angle. A few miles will tell. Never have the handlebars and seat adjusted so that you assume a bent-over racing appearance. It may look jaunty, but it's far too tiring for the average bike tourist.

Speaking of racing, don't try to break any records on a bicycle camping trip. It's like canoeing. Take it easy, and if you reach a good camping spot before the intended stopping time, don't insist upon pushing on. Park where you are and enjoy it.

Be sure to carry an accurate, up-to-date map. One may be particularly valuable when you encounter a road that proves bad for cycling. Then try a different road. It may even be far better than the original selection. As you travel, ask about road conditions ahead, not for automobiles but for bicycles.

While touring country roads, you may run into dogs that don't like bikes. As a kid on a rural paper route in New Hampshire, one of us carried a water pistol full of ammonia

**Water Pistol for
Keeping Dogs Away
with Ammonia**

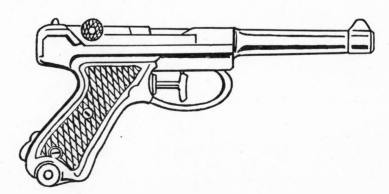

water, which worked like a charm. One snootful, and the pup lost interest in the skinny legs and wasn't damaged himself.

A veteran rural mail carrier told us that the best defense against such a dog is to get down on one knee and call him to you. It sounded like suicide, but once in desperation we tried it. The rambunctious pup slid to a stop, then retreated swiftly behind the house. As long as he was wanted, he desired no part of the kid or his bicycle.

When making camp, there are a few special things to keep in mind. If you enter upon any private lands, be sure to close all gates you may pass through so no livestock can stray out. Be very careful of open fires. Check with local authorities to see if an open-fire permit is needed. If it is, get it before building a fire. If you've been unable to locate the owner of the land, and he shows up and asks that you leave, do so at once. If you're polite, he may change his mind and stay for a cup of coffee instead. It has happened.

When your bike is not in use, stand it up where it'll be out of the way. This is particularly important after dark. Cover the machine with some sort of waterproof material to protect it from dampness.

During the last few years a new breed of bike—the off-highway motor bike—has been introduced to sportsmen. These vehicles are small, particularly rugged, and easy to ride. They're generally powered with little five-horsepower gasoline motors and have an extremely low gear ratio so that they have slow speed and tremendous power for climbing. They can do about 18 m.p.h. on the highway, give some 200 miles on the gallon, and ascend a 45 percent grade over rough ground, brush, and rocks.

These little two-wheelers can carry up to 250 pounds, plus the rider, so you can get plenty of camping equipment on one. Special highway sprockets are available for some models so that you can buzz along at up to 45 m.p.h. Naturally, you must comply with state motor vehicle regulations before you take one of these rigs onto a public highway. If you think you're too old to use an ordinary bike on a camping trip, or if you want to get off the beaten path and make your own trails, perhaps one of these gas-powered mountain goats will tickle you.

Whether you ride a leg-powered or gasoline-propelled two-wheeler, you may enjoy taking to the woods by cycle this summer. Get out a map and look for the fine-line and dotted roads. Set your course by the back byways and enjoy camping adventure.

14

Scooter Camping

THERE IS MORE THAN ONE WAY TO TAKE TO THE WOODS. DURING THE past few years, a new kind of camping and outdoor recreation has been opened by an odd-looking vehicle—the trail scooter. Initially popular in the West, this small, unstreamlined, and briskly popping contraption soon began working its way east.

A trail scooter is simply one of those low-speed, low-geared, two-wheel vehicles powered by a small gasoline engine of low horsepower. The wheels are generally small, measuring less than eighteen inches in diameter, and the tires have knobby or tractor-type treads for rough going. These scooters weigh about 150 pounds, and the wide tread distributes the weight so that they seldom leave a deep mark, even on a finely manicured lawn.

Trail scooters should not be confused with the streamlined highway scooters that are outfitted with lights, fancy springs, and highway tires, and which zip along at normal highway speeds. Trail scooters are designed for off-highway travel, mountain climbing, and packing heavy loads up and down rough terrain.

There is normally no shifting of gears, just a centrifugal clutch that lowers the gear ratio as you give it more power. This affords maximum power with a minimum of motor effort. But naturally beyond a certain point your speed decreases as the power increases, and you just can't go any faster.

When taken to the woods, these trail scooters are in their element and are nearly unstoppable, clambering up and down 45-degree grades, climbing over downed logs, and fording shallow streams with even more alacrity than a good pack mule. They chug easily through underbrush, tall timber, mountain meadows, and open sagebrush country, carrying several hundred pounds of camping gear or other cargo.

For the camper who can't hike the way he used to and still wants to get away from civilization, they're a real boon. With perhaps the scooter's handlebars folded flat, he can tote the rig in the back of his station wagon. At the end of the highway, he can take off on scooter power, exploring and camping.

Trail scooters are outfitted with both rear-end and front-end wheel brakes. Anyone who can ride a bike, and some who can't, can safely navigate one of these little contrap-

tions after a bit of instruction. A hunter with a scooter can lug out a 200-pound buck single-handed. Out West these scooters are used to herd cattle, check fences, explore, carry supplies to fire towers, and generally act as sort of a combined saddle and packhorse.

There isn't too much flat area for loads on the back of a scooter. With a little imagination and a lot of web strapping, though, you can carry everything needed. A tightly rolled sleeping bag with air mattress and shelter tarp enclosed can be stowed behind the seat, and a duffle bag or large rucksack filled with grub can be fastened behind that.

A couple of surplus musette bags affixed to the sides of the frame will tote numerous small items within easy reach. Regular saddlebags make ideal side bags for scooters, or you can make your own from heavy canvas. Just be certain that no ropes or straps hang anywhere near moving belts or chains.

We've discovered that 6-foot web straps are more functional than rope for attaching gear to the back rack. However, we'd suggest taking along some fifteen feet of sash or parachute cord for adding extra items or for pitching a shelter tarp. Many scooter way-farers take along a pup tent, mountain tent, or plastic sheeting for a shelter. Others carry large rubber ponchos to be used either for rainwear or as a shelter.

If the prospect is for really wet weather, bring along a pair of pull-on rubber boots and perhaps a plastic two-piece hooded rain suit. Such a combination is excellent for hustling through wet brush and dew-soaked grass. A wide-brimmed hat will protect your face from low branches and the back of your neck from rain or snow.

Since weight is scarcely any problem in scooter camping, you can bring along a small gasoline or alcohol stove and a candle lantern or small kerosene or gasoline lantern. When heading for a region where water is questionable, you can carry your own supply.

These little scooters are so simple to operate and so ruggedly constructed that you'll need few tools on a camping trip. We carry a small S-wrench so that if the belt drive gets too loose, we can shove the motor forward to tighten it. We also bring along a pair of slip-jaw pliers and a short-handled screwdriver to fit the scooter's machine screws. Regular gasoline is fine, and one filling of oil will do for the season.

A clear-plastic bicycle or motorcycle cover, unless you can find one especially made for your machine, will protect an idle scooter from showers and dew. Such a covering can also shelter a few sticks of firewood and some kindling, or even some of your camping outfit. You can even sit under one of these covers yourself when caught in a sudden downpour with no time to pitch a tent. It works fine.

If trees are scarce at the campsite, set the scooter on its stand on firm level ground, tie a tarp to the top of the machine, and stake out the corners to make a sleeping shelter.

Sleeping Shelter Made with Tarp and Scooter

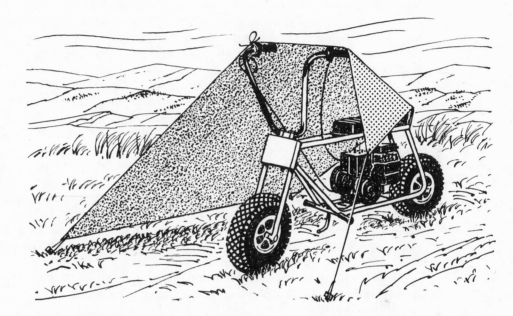

It won't be spacious, but at least you'll be sheltered. Too, the end of the tarp will keep the scooter seat dry. Be sure, of course, to keep the campfire and any other open fires well away from the bivouac. The machine does burn gasoline, and leaks are possible.

Although a trail scooter opens up a variety of wilderness possibilities, don't make the mistake of thinking that it's like sitting in an easy chair. Taking to the woods in a scooter can be enough exercise and adventure for even the most blasé soldier of fortune. If you're new to trailer-scooter camping, perhaps a few words of caution are in order. We learned some of them the hard way.

There seem to be three stages a scooter rider goes through. There's a sort of fearful period during which he'll ride his scooter only on smooth, level ground. Then after discovering a few tricks and a lot of confidence, he'll tackle anything and even go out of his way to find the wildest possible terrain. Finally after a few scares, a tumble or two, and a lot of pleasant mileage, he knows where he can travel in safety and does so, using the scooter to hightail to his destination in comfort. All three stages can be interesting, but the last is the best for scooter camping.

While learning to handle a trail scooter, it's a good idea not to tackle difficult terrain until your control reactions are automatic. Tooling around trees and over rocks is apt to lead to the unexpected. If your control of the vehicle is automatic, you'll avoid a lot of rough riding and be able to keep looking ahead to pick the best path.

Traveling on a scooter is a lot like riding a horse. In going uphill, lean forward to keep the center of gravity forward. When coming downhill, lean back and let the compression of the engine act as a brake. If the scooter seems to be turning the engine too fast on a long downgrade, open the throttle a bit so that the engine will again begin holding the machine back, or use the brakes.

In traversing ledges, lean a trifle to the uphill side to keep the front wheel from turning downhill and picking up speed. The same applies to crossing any steep terrain. When you come to a fallen log that you can't ride over easily, approach it slowly and lift the front wheel a bit with the handlebars while moving the rear wheel closer. When the rear wheel touches the log, bring your weight off the seat, gun the motor carefully, and the rear wheel should climb the log. If instead it just bumps and then begins to dig in, better lift it over or find a way around. If the country becomes too rough, get off, and using the throttle to keep the machine moving, walk alongside it.

Before crossing a stream, check for depth and particularly for any deep holes. A trail scooter will take a woodsman across almost any brook if the bottom is hard or gravelly and the water not too deep. Check the manufacturer's instructions, and start your experimenting in shallow water. Keep the water below the carburetor and wiring, and if the engine is hot, below the engine itself.

When you come on small downed branches, try to meet them at right angles with the front wheel even if you have to turn this momentarily. This prevents the front wheel from suddenly swerving to one side. The rear wheel can pass over at any angle. Small round stones are another hazard to your front wheel, so keep a firm hold on the handlebars. The wheels will firmly grip almost any surface except gravel, loose shale, and snow. Go slowly over these surfaces and you'll be all right. Keep an eye open, too, for wet leaves, slick rocks, and powdery sand.

One obstruction that will stop a trail scooter is soft mud. But the vehicle's light weight permits lifting it out of a mudhole and locating a way around.

When traveling through low brush or heavy grass, keep your feet well back on the pedals. Otherwise, you might catch the toe of a boot on a projection below the pedal and bend your foot down and back painfully. As far as that goes, even when the going seems perfectly smooth, remain alert. Watch for anything low ahead, and go through any low branches by leaning over the handlebars and keeping your head down to protect your eyes. Also watch out for low fences and especially electrified fences.

Taking to the woods with a trail scooter can be full of adventure, but check first to make sure that scooters are allowed where you'd like to ride. Check with responsible authorities about entering doubtful lands. If it is all right to travel there, be sure you use courtesy when you meet others.

Keep away from pack trains if at all possible. If you can't bypass them, shut off your motor and wait until they are well beyond you before starting up again. Trail horses and mules are all too apt to be spooky in the presence of a scooter, even when it is parked.

Bypass domestic animals if they seem nervous, and in any event throttle down and work your way past them slowly, making as little commotion as possible. Give hunters a wide berth. If you yourself are hunting, remember that any laws about shooting from a vehicle also apply to scooter riders. It can be dangerous as well as illegal. Use your machine to get into game country. Then have the fun of stalking and shooting on foot.

When riding over wilderness slopes, don't go straight up and down. Instead, slant across slopes. This not only will help prevent erosion from starting along your tread marks, but it will also make the ride a lot easier on the scooter and your own carcass. Leave any gates as you find them. If they were shut, be sure to reshut them.

It's poor policy to smoke as you ride. A branch may flick sparks from a cigarette, pipe, or cigar, and start a fire long after you've passed by. Incidentally, trail scooters are ideal for toting pump cans or "Indian tanks" into hard-to-reach regions for fighting blazes. Just make sure that no one ever has to fight a fire started by you.

Taking to the tall timber with a trail scooter can be a new adventure for both tyro and veteran campers of all ages. For the young and venturesome it can mean getting into regions beyond the end of roads, exploring areas where few individuals have been before, and taking along plenty of gear and grub to make a long stay possible.

For the older camper, it can mean an easy and comfortable way to travel off the beaten path with his outfit, still getting away from it all and not arriving in camp too winded and too bushed to enjoy himself. Once you've had the chance to try one of these little two-wheeled contraptions, likely as not you'll itch to load it with your personal outfit and head off the highway.

15

Camping with a Boat

WANT A REAL CHANGE OF PACE IN CAMPING? THEN TRY TAKING TO the woods with a boat for your next trip—not a cruise in a big craft with bunks, galley, head, and all the comforts of home, but a camping trip with a small boat. You can do it with any small outboard-powered runabout, rowboat, canoe, or a collapsible craft. All you need is a seaworthy craft of adequate size, some imagination, a few items of camping equipment, and a spirit of adventure.

It's not even necessary to own a boat if rentals are available. More and more boating enthusiasts are becoming interested in camping, and at least as many campers are discovering they can use small boats to reach isolated campgrounds. To the boater, camping means he can cruise farther and not have to hunt for a commercial resort to stay ashore at night. It cuts down the cost of a long cruise and makes a shorter one more fun. To the camper who has never traveled along the wooded shoreline of a lake or river in a small boat, such an experience can make a camping trip something special.

Naturally, the size of the camping party will be governed by the size of the boat used and the size of the outfit carried. If the party is too large for a single craft, two or even three boats will make for more safety, more space for gear, and more relaxation along the way.

Almost any kind of small boat will do for such a trip, from a collapsible boat carried in your car to an outboard-powered craft trailered behind your automobile. We've used all types of boats, and it's actually a matter of preference which to take, depending on how many individuals are going, the duration of the trip, and the amount of gear it'll take to keep you going.

If the journey will include open, possibly rough water, or an extended travel plan, consider a powered craft designed for big water, for you will have to carry extra fuel as well as camp gear. Rough water can eat up fuel and time. If your idea is to meander down a smooth river or explore a lake, a rowboat, skiff, or johnboat with a 3- to 10-h.p. motor will be fine.

Even a canoe will take you there and back with safety and comfort in fairly calm water.

Canoes are far safer than many have been led to believe, and with good distribution of weight and passengers they are about as safe as any other type of craft. By the way, especially when you have power on another craft, it's convenient to tow a canoe.

The natural way is to attach a line to the bow. The trouble is that, even with a perspiring steersman in the stern, the canoe haws all over the place. The solution? Loop a line around the body of the canoe, at right angles to its length, roughly two feet from the tip of the bow. Fasten the tow rope to this belly line under the center of the keel. Then,

How to Keep a Towed Canoe from Digging Bow into Wake

loaded so that the bow rides slightly high, the canoe will skim gracefully and arrowlike after the towing boat without additional steering of any kind.

Folding-type and rubber craft are better suited for exploring wilderness lakes and waterways where any sort of boat must be packed in with your camping outfit. They're best suited for a one- or two-man trip where rough going is anticipated.

If you plan to camp ashore as boat campers generally do, take along either a small lightweight tent or use the boat as a shelter. If the route includes an area where the shorelines are low and easy for beaching a boat, you may care to try some boat-tarp combination shelters. On the other hand, if the shores will be muddy or steep and rocky, it will be easier to take along a tent or use the boat as a campsite.

Many boat campers have discovered that the average small boat can be made into a snug and comfortable camp with the aid of a few odds and ends and a little ingenuity. We saw an adroit idea recently. A rowboat owner had rigged up a camp right in his boat. He had made a folding platform from three 6-foot boards hinged together like a folding screen. When not in shelter use, this was utilized as a floor in the bottom of the boat.

At night, he unfolded it and placed it across the rear and center seats of his boat. On this, he put up a two-man pup tent complete with screened doors and sewn-in floor. He placed his air mattress and sleeping bag in the tent and was cozy as could be. When it rained, he just took his gear in with him and rode out the rain dry.

One of us has had fun with a similar rig in his own take-down rowboat. This happens to be an almost extinct fiber glass and wooden affair made by Ed Link of Link Trainer fame and no longer built. The center seat can be removed, so it makes a fine little camp. We use two inverted "V" frames of 36 x 2 x 3/4-inch wood, held together at one end with a two-inch bolt and wing nut. There is a choice of three holes two inches apart so that the height of the ridge can be varied as liked. The "V" frames have been stained dark red to prevent their warping after wetting.

When ready for the night, we set up the two frames, one by the front seat and the other by the back seat, and then run a line over them. This line, sashcord or clothesline size, is started from an eye ring in the bow, run over the top of the first frame, down the other side, up through the crotch, back over the top, and on to the aft frame. We run it over the top of that, down through the crotch, up over the top again, and then down to an eye ring on the stern, where it is tied off. This not only keeps the two frames steady, but it serves as a ridgepole as well.

A couple of lightweight tarps are spread over the line between the frames and down over the gunwales. To fasten the tarp ends taut and yet allow some emergency play in case of wind, small rocks tied to two-foot cords are attached to the grommets in the tarp corners. Each stone weighs about the same as a small brick, and the ropes permit the stones to hang under water. This not only keeps the canvas tight, but adds stability to the boat. By removing the center seat, we thus have a snug shelter with plenty of room for sleeping gear.

This setup could be used with a canoe as well if the frame were lighter and lower. If you try this with a rowboat, as we have, remove the oarlocks since they might rip or puncture the tarp where it passes over them. You could use a rigid pole for the ridge, of course, but they are hard to find when you want one and would be difficult to carry. The rope does just as well if kept taut, and it can be used as a clothesline when not in use as a ridge.

Don't try to spend a night on open water in such an affair. Anchored close to shore in a sheltered cove or tied up near the beach, however, it makes a fine place to sleep.

For boat camping, no more gear is needed than what you likely already have for camping ashore, with the possible exception of a lightweight tent. Do not use a gasoline-powered stove on the boat. Propane and alcohol stoves are fine for boats. Water will extinguish alcohol flames, but water on a gasoline fire merely spreads it. Use a gas or alcohol stove, or go ashore for your cooking, as you probably will, anyway.

One handy item for boat camping is a supply of waterproof plastic bags with rubber bands to seal them. These should be used to cover such things as film, camera, firearms, some types of food, spare clothing, binoculars, and so forth. Once in these waterproof bags, the items can be stored in conventional duffle bags or wherever you plan to stow them.

Some lash their key equipment to a seat, thwart, or gunwale. Others feel that if the boat is lost, they'll then lose everything; so they keep their gear untethered, the idea being that some items will be salvageable. It's a matter of preference and would depend largely on the body of water you're boating. On a small river, for instance, we'd lash. If air is trapped in the plastic bags, many items will float.

Even a small boat will carry an amazing amount of cargo if this is well distributed, balanced, and kept low. A 16-foot aluminum canoe, for example, will carry about half a ton of passengers and cargo. Keep the heavy items in the bottom of the craft and evenly distributed from side to side of the center line.

Bulky items can be put on top, if light, but still try for a low silhouette. Use duckboards or some other type of platform in the bottom of the boat in case of accumulating rain, spray, or small leaks. A layer of small branches or boughs will do for a grid if nothing else is handy. Then place a waterproof tarp down before you load and bring the sides up around the gear.

A small plywood or plastic box attached to the gunwale with hooks or small "C" clamps is handy for keeping such possessions as camera, film, and binoculars within reach whether you're rowing, paddling, or running on an outboard.

Speaking of outboards, many are now using small motors on canoes, both conventional and square-stern models. The former will take up to a 3-h.p. motor on a side bracket quite safely. The latter in the 16-, 18-, and 20-foot lengths will accept even larger motors. Using an outboard with a canoe permits either steering with the motor itself or setting it straight ahead and using a paddle for a rudder. With the paddle on the opposite side from the motor, the balance is better. There are now several sizes of electric outboard motors that will run for many hours on a 12-volt car battery; they are excellent for canoes.

With canoes, folding-type boats, and rubber craft, distribution and balance of weight and passengers is all-important. Keep the load low and well balanced as you add the various items. If you are to paddle alone, load so that the bow is a bit higher than the stern.

In windy weather, shift the load so that the bow is a trifle lower than the stern to prevent the craft from weathercocking or swinging with the wind. Any incoming rain generally means wind, so prepare for it by either heading for the nearest shore or not starting out if you haven't left shore. No matter what the weather outlook, it is far safer to go farther and keep close to shore than to strike out across a windy expanse of open water.

Boatmen taking up boat-camping probably know about trailering, launching, safety afloat, and boat handling. Those taking up boating in connection with camping, however, before starting on an extended trip should try to take one of the courses in small-craft handling offered by the U.S. Power Squadrons or the Red Cross. It will pay off in water safety and peace of mind.

Regardless of your skill with a boat, if there are youngsters along, be sure each one has an approved life preserver of his own and wears it whenever the boat is underway. Even if your small fry can paddle pretty well in the local pool or swimming hole, the sudden shock of being dumped overboard can scare a small passenger right out of any sketchy ability to keep afloat. Besides, it may take a while to reach him. A life preserver can keep such a dunking from becoming a tragedy.

As for special clothing for boat camping, about all that is required is some raingear. This can come in handy even on sunny days if the water is choppy and you are likely to catch some spray. Sneakers or rubber-soled shoes are a must for boat use, and rubbers are handy if there is likely to be water in the bottom of the craft.

It's also wise to take along a bailing can, and big sponge as well, to keep the bottom of the boat as dry as possible. A broad-brimmed hat or cap, sunglasses, and suntan lotion can also prove to be highly valuable, for reflected glare from the water on a sunny day can be murder if you have to sail into it for a long spell.

Food for a boat-camping trip may be a bit more complicated than for a vehicle camping jaunt, due to a lack of space as well as the fact that you can't drop in at a local store as easily as when you're on the road. In areas where boating is popular, many marinas either carry staples or can tell you where they can be obtained nearby. If possible, check with others who have cruised the same route and know where the food stops are.

Fortunately, unlike a backpacking vacation, you can carry many food items, even heavy ones, in a boat. If your craft is large enough, even an ice chest will be no problem. Meals and cooking must be tailored to the size of the boat and what it can carry, of course, but there's such a wide variety of food now in the stores that actually the sky is nearly the limit. Incidentally, burlap bags are handy things in which to store canned foods. But be sure to code the contents on each can with scratches or fingernail polish in case the labels soak off, as they always seem to do on any trips that we take.

If your boat has a folding canvas top and possibly side curtains, you may decide to stay afloat for meals as well as for sleeping. In that case, some sort of folding table or shelf will be needed for the stove and dishes. Some boaters have solved this problem with a wooden chest which holds cooking gear and serves as a table as well. It can also be used as a seat. Small folding webtop stools take up little room and are far better than nothing to sit on, whether aboard or ashore. They sell for under $2, weigh about two pounds, and will hold a 200-pounder.

Almost every state conservation department, as well as the National Park Service, has maps showing good waters for both camping and boating, with moorings, campgrounds, and portages marked. If there are boat enthusiasts or a local boating club in your area, talk with its members and ask their advice.

Many United States and Canadian lakes have shoreline campgrounds for such sojourns, and maps of their vicinities show these. Maps put out by the various big oil companies, especially those handling marine fuels, often show waterways suitable for boat camping. Local filling station owners will tell you the addresses of oil company travel information bureaus.

If you have never combined boating with camping and have been sticking to the trails and highways to get from campsite to campsite, you'll find that boating and camping go together like ham and eggs.

16

Taking to the Woods in a Canoe

WATER BOILS UP IN A FURY OF WHITE AIR BUBBLES, THE LITTLE suction holes twirling like dervishes, as you dig energetic holes in the stream with your glistening paddle. The slim craft trembles under the power of the strokes. You take advantage of a slant of current, then an eddy, in pulling beyond a spray-drenched boulder.

The rush of water hurtles you on to a leap in space over an area of cataracts, then to weave in a controlled plunge through broken rapids. It's like this all day, with ensuing silences of quiet pools, until you pull ashore to boil the noonday kettle, ten feet tall.

A canoe affords one of the most exciting, least expensive, and surpassingly pleasant ways of taking to the woods. Even comparative greenhorns can pack up to 800 pounds of crew and cargo into an 18-foot aluminum craft weighing no more than an easily portaged 75 pounds. This way two 150-pound paddlers can carry 500 pounds of grub and gear, more than enough for a memorable two weeks in the wildernesses of this continent anywhere.

Two of the most relaxing outdoor pastimes are camping and canoeing. Maybe you have camped along a lake or stream or on an ocean beach, listened to the soft, intrusive sounds of nature getting ready for bed, and longed to explore farther down the alluring shoreline. Or maybe you've paddled silently along a wooded shore, listening to that same music and thinking how enjoyable it would be to linger awhile and explore.

Then why not combine camping and canoeing and more than double your pleasure? Loading outdoor gear into a canvas or aluminum craft and heading off into the woods, or even along the quiet shores of a familiar stream or lake, can lend a completely new dimension to exploring the outdoors.

Canoe camping requires very little more effort, and many times considerably less, than does car camping. And a canoe can carry far more gear much easier than a backpacker can. As a matter of fact, even a 16-foot canoe, with a width of at least 33 inches and a depth of at least a foot, will accommodate two campers, an adequate outfit, and two weeks' provisions very nicely, at the same time not floating too deeply in the water.

Those of you who have never taken a canoe camping trip might like to begin planning

one now. Such a venture can be different, not at all costly, and a lot of fun. It can be a small tour of a local lake's shoreline, a trip down a friendly and familiar river you've never actually cruised before, or an expedition into the northern wilds with guides, portages, big game, and perhaps some genuine adventure.

First, though, let's rid ourselves of some of the traditional myths about the perils of canoes and canoeing. The use of a canoe is by no means limited to experts. Thousands of youngsters go canoeing every summer while at camps. And many other individuals with a minimum of boating experience go on canoe trips into sheer wilderness without mishap.

Even a tyro should be able, with a little care, to handle a canoe well enough to take a camping trip, particularly if the craft is properly loaded with plenty of gear. A well-loaded canoe can ride out really rough water as safely as a flat-bottomed rowboat.

There are numerous sizes and styles of canoes, from the little 13-foot "pumpkinseed" models to 22-foot freight canoes that can safely handle three-quarters of a ton. Canoe weight depends not only on whether aluminum, fiber glass, canvas over wood, or some other material is used, but also on the thickness of the substance and on what fittings round out the job. Generally, canoes sold today have flotation compartments that prevent their sinking even if swamped. So if you get dunked, hang onto the canoe, and grab the paddle, too, if you can.

For a one-man trip, a 15-foot canoe with a 34-inch beam (width across the widest part), a wide flattish bottom, and blunt ends will be about right. A 16-footer with a slightly wider beam will be better for a two-man cruise. If there are to be three men or a youngster along, plus heavy gear, an 18- to 20-foot craft will be the thing to use.

One of us has covered some rough water in Hudson Bay, near the mouth of the Churchill River, in a 20-foot freight canoe powered with an outboard while hunting white whales. Even in rough water, this 20-footer proved safe and seaworthy despite fast runs and quick turns in a variety of wave conditions. Such a craft in ordinary waters would be safe and reliable with almost any load it could carry.

Aluminum canoes are rugged and relatively light but somewhat difficult to patch permanently. Canvas-covered canoes are stronger than they look, and the fabric is simple to patch. Fiber glass craft are exceptionally tough and, like aluminum canoes, are extremely safe if equipped with foam flotation units. Wooden canoes, of course, have natural buoyancy.

Canoes of average length, 16 feet, can carry nearly half a ton of crew and cargo safely, provided the load is kept low and evenly distributed for balance. They cost, depending upon construction and size, up to around $350. But you can rent canoes, too.

In fact, you can plan a real cruise into unfamiliar territory under the direction of some professional canoe-trip outfitter and have little to worry about or to provide for yourself. These outfitters furnish everything from canoe and paddles to the cooking equipment, sleeping gear, tents, axes, and the like, all for about $5 a day or less per person if there are two or more in the party.

Such a trip makes an inexpensive vacation and one which can be a rewarding experience, safe for the whole family, and a real test of your woodcraft. For a veteran camper with no previous experience in water travel, it can be another new and challenging event. For a tenderfoot with but a few close-to-home camping excursions under his belt, a canoe camping trip with his entire household can provide a lot of safe excitement.

It is important, particularly if you expect to run any rough water, to load a canoe so that the weight is midway between bow and stern and as close to the craft's center line as possible. The only exception to this rule applies to paddling alone. Then arrange the weight so that the bow rides slightly higher than the stern. This exception does not apply, however, if you expect to be bucking a strong crosswind. If so, use the dead-center loading system to keep the craft from weathercocking downwind.

Too many new canoeists toss in their outfit helter-skelter and then paddle from a sitting position. Sitting is fine for just drifting along, seeing the sights, or perhaps fishing or hunting. For serious paddling, however, the semikneeling position is far better.

Position yourself so that your flanks rest against, rather than on, the front edge of the seat. Your knees should be spread apart, close to the sides of the craft and resting on pads of some sort. Incidentally, rubber gardening pads are fine for this purpose. If you get cramped in that position, kneel on one knee and extend the other leg out straight. If there are two paddlers, one can kneel and the other sit from time to time to give the kneeler's muscles a rest.

When in open water and the going is very rough and choppy, head into the waves. If things get too hairy, get as low in the craft as possible, lying down if necessary, and let the wind drift you to safety. Keep an empty tin can and a large sponge handy for bailing in case you do ship water or splash a lot aboard with the paddles.

Anyone who can't swim should wear a life jacket. In fact, this isn't a bad idea for everyone at all times, especially as these days good flotation jackets are available in a number of nonbulky designs resembling the regular outdoor jackets on the market.

Plastic bags are a boon to the canoeing camper. Gear such as cameras, binoculars, pocket stoves, and some food items can be packed in small plastic bags, the tops of which can be knotted or closed with elastic bands. Larger items, even tents and sleeping bags, will fit into the huge plastic bags now available. It's a good idea to extend this plastic-bag protection even to vulnerable contents of your pockets such as wallets and papers. These containers protect gear from dampness, and they can also keep things together in a way that'll make loading and unloading easier.

If some of your outfit is too bulky to be put into waterproof containers, cover it with a tarpaulin and lash it down securely. A burlap sack is a handy container for cans. Try to avoid piling the gear any higher than the gunwales or thwarts.

Lashing the cargo to the thwarts or gunwales has two advantages. It keeps the load from shifting, and in case of a tipover it keeps the cargo with the canoe. Air trapped in the plastic containers and in the gear generally makes an upset canoe float higher, and a high-floating canoe is easy to get ashore, either with help from the wind or with the crew swimming it ahead of them.

Some canoeists attach the paddle to a thwart with a long thong so that the paddle won't float away in an upset, and this is a good idea, particularly in white water. If otherwise you suddenly find yourself in the water and the paddle is more than a swimming stroke or two away, head for the canoe first. A canoe without a paddle is a lot more safe than a paddle without a canoe. Again, it makes good sense to wear a life jacket, and children and nonswimmers should be made to do so.

A too-long paddle is awkward to use because the canoer's hands must be placed so far apart. A too-short paddle wastes energy and may force the paddler to place his lower hand down where the blade begins, thus getting an uncomfortable grip.

One way to be sure that a paddle fits you is to stand with it upright in front of you. A stern paddle should reach from the ground to your nose; for bow use, to your chin. Select a medium-wide rather than a very wide blade, and get a spare.

Learn as soon as possible, when paddling alone for the first time, to keep a straight course without changing sides nearly every stroke. Begin on whichever side seems handiest for you. Reach well ahead to start the stroke. Then angle the blade a bit in drawing it back. The inside edge should lead, with just enough angle to offset the natural tendency of the bow to be shoved to the opposite side from which you're paddling. If necessary, give the paddle even more of a twist before completing the stroke. All this works out a lot more easily than it can be described.

Another way to keep straight is to end each stroke with an outward push of the blade. Again, personal experimentation is the key. If you overdo the final lunge and the bow is pulled too far to the side opposite your stroke, another pull or two with the blade held straight will get the canoe back on course. Again, it's all easier to do than to describe.

When you have mastered the technique from one side, it's a simple matter to shift sides. You'll want to do this periodically, in any event, if only to rest your sinews.

Get in the habit of leaning well forward. The arms may be kept straight, although some bend the upper arm a trifle. Short, rather swift strokes are more effective than long, slow ones for covering country. Short, choppy strokes are not only less tiring, but they maintain a canoe's momentum better, especially if you're paddling against wind or current.

With two paddlers, the more experienced individual should be in the stern, where his strokes will offset those of the outdoorsman in the bow. Working on opposite sides will pretty much keep the canoe on a straight course, although it will be up to the stern paddler to steer. Whenever the paddler in the bow wants to shift sides, the individual in the stern should follow suit.

With the bow paddler maintaining even, regular strokes, the stern paddler often will find himself taking advantage of the momentum by finishing his strokes with the paddle held as a rudder. This way, with the blade at right angles to the current, it will be a simple matter to steer the canoe smoothly either right or left.

When you are paddling in the bow, don't try to steer unless you suddenly glimpse an obstruction and have no time to warn the stern paddler, who does the steering under ordinary conditions. Just maintain a good steady stroke and let the stern man steer as he paddles.

If you are canoeing on a large body of water or in an area where squalls are prone to come up unexpectedly, keep fairly close to shore. Your trip may take longer, but if the canoe does swamp, you'll be able to get to shore in a hurry.

Another big advantage of staying close to shore is the possibility of seeing wildlife. We have both thrilled to unexpected sights of deer, moose, bear, lynx, beaver, mink, otter, raccoon, and assorted water birds along the shores of a hundred waterways. A canoe's silence enables its passengers to see and hear much that a power boatman never dreams is close.

One more advantage of sticking close to shore is ease in locating a campsite for the evening. Try to pick a level, raised spot with a good clear-cut shoreline rather than a marshy edge. This will allow you to come up alongside, step out onto dry land, and unload from the side of the canoe rather than inconveniently over one end.

In any event, if you are paddling alone, don't run the bow far up on shore and then try to get out by walking forward over the cargo. Aside from possible damage to the spine of the canoe, such a craft with its bow resting on shore and the rest of the hull in the water is apt to tip easily. Instead, come up parallel to the shore and step out. Then move the canoe nearer for unloading.

Tie up your craft securely, or when it's empty pull it entirely ashore and turn it over. Unneeded gear can be kept dry by stowing it beneath the overturned canoe.

Matter of fact, if you want to travel really light, leave the tent at home and sleep under the overturned canoe, perhaps with a tarpaulin spread over it for added shelter. You can make a fine two-man shelter by propping up one side of the canoe and staking an edge of the tarp behind the canoe and the other in front of it. Other solutions will come to mind, mostly depending on the size of the tarp being carried and on the kind of country, inasmuch as this will figure in how easily you can prop up the craft in different positions, high enough to get the thwarts out of the way.

If you have a long way to go on fairly calm water, you may care to try sailing a canoe or a pair of them. Lashing two canoes together will make an untippable catamaran that sails along nicely. If the two craft are of the same size, form your catamaran by running a stout green, not dry and brittle, pole from the bow thwart of one to the bow thwart of the other and lashing this pole down. Run another pole between the stern thwarts.

The bows of the craft should be about four feet apart and the sterns a couple of feet farther from each other. This helps to keep the catamaran on a straight course and will also aid in preventing water from piling up between the two canoes.

A sail can be fashioned by lashing a tarp, blanket, or poncho to two upright green poles in the bows. These poles can either be tied in position or, if you have a crew of four, held upright between the knees of the two bow men. A rope from the top of each mast to a rear thwart will help keep the sail steady. The stern men steer the craft with paddles, a soul-stirring job with a brisk wind blowing and flattening waves by slicing their tops into your faces.

If you and a partner are alone in a single canoe, why not try sailing as we both used to do on Lake Winnipesaukee in New Hampshire. The man in the bow holds up the sail; a blanket or something similar lashed to two light poles. If the wind is steady, he holds the poles well apart to make the sail wide. If the breezes become gusty, he moves the poles closer together to make the sail smaller. In an emergency he can simply turn the whole thing loose, to be picked up afterwards. You'll be astounded at how swiftly a loaded canoe can traverse a couple of miles of water with such a Rube Goldberg rig.

Don't try sailing or even paddling if a bad storm threatens. If you simply must leave a stopover spot, such as an island, under such drastic conditions, you may want to improvise a sea anchor. This simple device will keep the craft headed straight downwind in spite of waves that might otherwise buffet the canoe about and make steerage difficult or even impossible. Even with a sea anchor, though, it is best to paddle fast enough to give the craft a workable degree of steerage.

A sea anchor can be made from any good-size pail or bucket having a stout handle. A

**Improvised Sea Anchor
to Keep Canoe Heading
into Wind**

folding canvas camp bucket or one of the large plastic containers will work fine. Tie one end of a 15-foot length of stout line to the pail's handle and knot the other end to the middle of about 8 feet of similar line. The ends of this latter, shorter rope should be tied to the opposite sides of a rear-seat support.

When the pail is in the water, its dragging force will be exerted on the underside of the canoe at keel line. In potentially dangerous open water, such as Great Slave Lake, it is sound practice to have such a yoke rigged ahead of time and cached under a rear seat.

A sea anchor even has a fringe benefit. If the craft swamps and you go over the side, the anchor will retard the canoe's drift, enabling you to swim to the safe buoyancy more quickly.

What about the outfit you should take along on a canoeing vacation? Be sure to have an extra paddle, a good ax, and preferably some such saw as the handy Swede saw, waterproof matches, raingear, first aid kit, plenty of grub for those ravenous appetites, and of course comfortable and serviceable clothes.

Make your first trip fairly short and sans portages if possible. You can spend ten unforgettable days covering only ten miles of waterways, camping and fishing as you go, and have a vacation that'll remain delightfully in your memory for the rest of your life. Of course, you can paddle more, camp less, and cover a lot of territory. Either way can be enjoyable, but on a long cruise, be sure of transportation back to the starting point unless you plan a round trip.

The procedure we've found most soul-satisfying is to leave our car and paraphernalia of civilization at a railroad river town, board the upriver train with our canoe and outfit, arrange for the train to stop at some advantageous spot such as a bridge, and then paddle back to the original town at our leisure.

When taking to the woods in wild country, be sure to let someone know where you're going, when you'll be back, and about where you plan to camp. In parts of Canada a travel permit is needed to enter the wilderness, and woe betide you if you're caught without one. This permit simply means that you've listed with the Mounties or other authorities the names of those in the party, the route, and the time you expect to be in the bush. It's just common sense to let responsible individuals know where you can be found in case of emergency.

If you're interested in a real but safe wilderness canoe journey, look over the ads in outdoor magazines for the names and addresses of some of the outfitters specializing in this sort of family expedition. Or figure out a cruise of your own. One that caught our fancy a few years ago started in New York and ended in Nome, Alaska.

On the other hand, if you wish to try a journey closer to home and perhaps along familiar waterways, such a jaunt should be even less expensive and in many ways just as much fun. Pick a river which has a minimum of falls and rapids to portage around and no settlements along its banks. Or settle on a big pond or lake away from populated areas, where there will be a minimum of cottages and boat traffic, and explore its shores.

Get a map of the waterway and study it for possible camping sites, adventure spots, or fishing regions. The Geodetic Survey maps are excellent for such use. Too, many state park agencies and conservation services publish fine maps of connected rivers, lake chains, and other canoe routes, as well as special campgrounds for canoeists. A local canoe or boat club should be able to point your prow toward some rousing canoe-camping country.

Don't plan to cover many miles the first day. Paddle along slowly, enjoying the scenery and the fun of silently snooping along the shoreline.

When you go ashore to pitch camp in back country, you may have to protect your paddles from porcupines. They love the salt left by sweaty hands. Wash each paddle grip and shaft with soap to remove this. Wash off the ax handle as well, for a porky can ruin either in a single night.

If your canoe is canvas-covered, check it for damage and repair any small rips or snags before taking off again the next morning. You should carry a small tube of canoe glue, as well as bits of canvas for making repairs.

If the cut or rip is a small one, cut off the loose threads about the opening with a knife. Separate the canvas from the wood for about an inch all around the break, and then put a well-glued cloth patch under the torn material with the wet glue next to the wood. Press the torn canvas down on it, holding the opening together firmly. Another patch may be added outside the tear until you get to where you can paint the damaged spot with good canoe paint to seal it.

If you have no repair canvas, almost any tightly woven material such as part of the flap of a duffle bag will do in a pinch. Lacking glue, you can use spruce sap. Dig some of the hardened pitch off the tree with a knife, melt it over a fire, being careful as it is extremely flammable, and use it as you would the glue. If it hardens while being applied, smooth it into place with the bottom of a hot frypan.

Fiber glass canoes require a special patch kit which may be purchased from the dealer along with the boat. Outfitters usually supply a repair kit with the crafts they rent. Learn how to use the kit before an emergency arises.

To assure the safety of your trip, all you have to remember are a few simple rules. Don't overload your craft with either gear or passengers. Keep cargo and human weight low in the canoe. Take an extra paddle, although in a pinch you can whittle one as we've done. Don't cross broad areas of water if the wind is blowing or a storm approaching. If the canoe upsets, stay with it because it will float. Preferably, wear a flotation jacket or some such device. Don't drop sharp or heavy objects into the canoe, and never jump in it.

If you want a different vacation, begin now to think about a canoe-camping trip for the next warm weather. It can be fun—the planning, the actual going, and the remembering.

More and more campers are shunning crowded public campgrounds in favor of more isolated vacation areas. These individuals are seeking quiet, solitude, and the chance to observe and enjoy nature as it really is. And many of them are finding that canoe-camping fulfills all these desires.

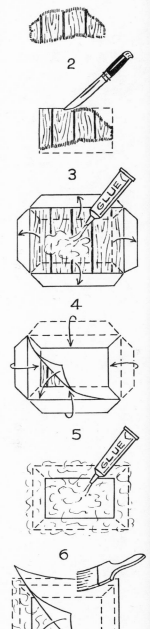

Steps in Repairing Rip in Canvas-covered Canoe

17

Camping on Wheels

MANY CAMPERS STILL PACK TENT AND GEAR INTO THE FAMILY CAR and hit the road for the backcountry with the wife and youngsters, and many still back-pack their outfit or carry it in a canoe on a wilderness camping trip. To us, such trips are taking to the woods at its best.

Times change, however, and many individuals now use camping vehicles that provide as much luxury as the campers enjoy at home. Such sybaritic living, to many tenters, is not camping. But modern camping vehicles have encouraged millions of people to take long, outdoor, sightseeing trips. We're all in favor of that, no matter how swank the vehicle and whether the trip is called camping, touring, or mobiling.

What kind of folks prefer hardtop trailers, pickup campers, and luxurious motor homes? Generally, they are older outdoorsmen who can afford these expensive vehicles, those who want as many conveniences as feasible, and those who would rather be on the road than pitching camp and staying out.

The comfort and conveniences of recreational vehicles have made it possible for millions of Americans to travel-camp in downright luxury. Many veteran sportsmen prefer these vehicles to tents, where roads permit, for such rigs allow them to break camp and move on quickly, and with a minimum of bother, to happier hunting grounds or to a better pool down the road.

Each type of travel unit has certain advantages and disadvantages. Before you spend any money on one, let's consider a few.

For instance, an individual who lives in the country might prefer a camper unit mounted on a pickup truck. Such a camper is removable, and the truck can then be used for farm work. On the other hand, a city dweller would likely have no use for the truck except when he took to the woods, and local ordinances may prohibit storing the truck in the driveway.

In selecting a camping vehicle, consider the number of people in your group and their ages, where and how you expect to camp and travel, whether you'll stay for a long time becoming acquainted with one neck of the woods or decide on one-night stops, whether

Pickup Camper

you'll want to camp in much the same way every year, and whether you'll use the vehicle a great deal or keep it stored much of the time.

The covered wagons are rolling again, but these are the kind filled with thousands of Americans seeking camping fun and adventure. Whether it's called station wagon, suburban, ranch wagon, Beverly body, or by any other name, the modern version of the old Conestoga wagon is playing a big part in getting people to take to the woods.

The station wagon is especially suited to camping, since it may be used for sleeping and has a large carrying capacity that makes it possible to take along many items that would be hard to handle in a regular sedan or convertible. Those who have wagons and don't use them for camping decidedly should try it, and those who like camping and are thinking of buying a new car should consider a station wagon's advantages.

Wagon manufacturers are considering the outdoorsman more and more when designing their products, and camping-gear designers are making their wares more and more with wagon campers in mind. As a result, the wagon owner has a head start toward camping economy, comfort, and convenience.

Station wagons adapt themselves very easily to camping. With a minimum of added equipment, they can provide transportation, bedroom or tent, dining room, and storeroom, all in one. And with some of the newer items they can be made even more efficient. Take the bedroom phase, for instance. If you don't care to pitch a tent for an overnight stop, the wagon will serve as one, as thousands who spend all their camping nights in their wagons have discovered. Two or even three individuals can bed down comfortably in most of them.

There are several types of pneumatic or quilted pads which fill the entire back of a wagon, converting it into a large double bed. These tailored pads may be purchased for most makes and models. Not only fine for sleeping, they also provide a safe, cushioned play pen for the small fry. Those who prefer not to invest in such an overall pad can use two air mattresses side by side, or buy two small single mattresses that can be joined with snaps. One of the real advantages of station-wagon camping is not having to reach a campsite early to pitch a tent. And if it's raining or snowing, the advantage is doubled and redoubled.

Station-wagon sleeping generally requires some sort of screens in the windows to keep out insects. These may be secured from camping outfitters, or can easily be fashioned from a few yards of fine-mesh material. Drape about a square yard of this between frame and door. Fasten the bottom edge of the screening to the door with short pieces of tape, sealing it. You can then still roll the glass up and down from inside without disturbing the screening. By screening one front-seat window this way and one back-seat door on the opposite side, you'll have cross ventilation, yet still be able to enter or leave the wagon through the unscreened doors.

To make screened doors that you can open and shut, cut a piece of material slightly larger than the glass area and attach it with strips of tape around the opening, making sure you can still open and close the glass. Commercial screens generally permit the doors to be worked with the screens in place, but they may not fit any new car you may buy.

A canvas boot is available that slips over the tailgate and covers all the windows right up to the front seat. This unit has a screened window at the back which has a storm cover. For further privacy from the front, string a line inside from one clothes hook to the other and hang a blanket over it. Several types of shorter boots may be had which just enclose the rear opening of the wagon. These are available for all models and have screened windows.

Another pleasant aspect of wagon camping is that electric lights go on at the touch of a finger on the dome light, or you can use a smaller light on an extension cord from the lighter plug. This outlet can also be utilized to heat water for instant drinks in case you wake up to rain and would like some coffee, tea, or cocoa without trying to get a stove or fire started. If the morning is really disagreeable, you can dress, climb into the front seat, and drive to town for a spot of breakfast without having to get out in the weather.

When you wish to sleep in the wagon bed, what do you do with the gear there? Some merely take it out of the wagon, pile it on or under a picnic table, and throw a tarp over it. Others move it to the front seat or lodge it under the opened tailgate out of possible rain. Those who use a small dressing tent can store extra gear there during the night. Some use one or two auto-top carriers for the purpose.

Outdoorsmen who like tenting with their wagon camping, or have a family that needs more room, will discover that the tent makers have them in mind. There are several tents that incorporate a wagon into their designs. One has a back tent wall that opens up to enclose the open tail of a wagon so that campers can climb in and out without leaving cover.

Campers who want to use their car can leave the tent pitched just by unhooking the tent wall from their vehicle. It drops to become the fourth wall of the tent and away they go. Another covering is similar to a lean-to tent, with the front canopy attached to the side of the wagon's roof so that, again, there's cover between car and tent.

Still another tent is mounted atop a wagon, so two youngsters or adults can sleep on the roof and two more in the wagon bed. A really swank two-story affair is mounted on the wagon top, extends out and down to make a dressing room, and then hitches to the sides of the wagon to provide an all-enclosed, double-decked unit for the whole family.

The main drawback to such an arrangement is that it's impossible to use the car while camp is pitched. However, it makes a fine long-stay home, and it's exceptionally well engineered.

A station wagon can tote a tremendous amount of bulky gear. It can carry dinghy-size boats, all assembled, without the use of auto-top carriers. Outboard motors, stove, and such luxurious camping items as folding tables, chairs, and playpens, tent poles, and complete kitchen units can be carried with ease. Many who take to the woods in boats carry their craft inside the wagon, all packed with camping gear so that they just slide the boat out with all the paraphernalia in it. This is one way of solving the problem of where to store gear while sleeping in the bed.

As with any packing, the things you want first should be packed last in the wagon, so you can get at them first on arrival. If you're to erect a tent the first night, pack it close to the tailgate along with poles, stakes, ax, ditching shovel perhaps, and anything else needed. If your initial night will be in a motel, pack overnight necessities in a small bag you can keep handy. The same goes for lunches, cold drinks, or icebox if you plan to snack while on the go.

If youngsters are a part of the party, you may care to arrange the load to shape a napping area. Stow hard and bulky objects along one side of the wagon bed and pile such things as sleeping bags, blankets, and tents along the other, as flat and level as possible. The small fry can stretch out for a snooze on the softer materials. An auto-top carrier will be an aid in keeping many of the bulkier and hard-to-pack items out of the interior.

The long, flattish top of the station wagon is generally well braced for supporting such top carriers, as well as boat carriers, sleeping tents, and similar loads. Some campers latch on two carriers, one behind the other. One may be used for books, magazines, games, dry kindling, a bag of charcoal, and similar odds and ends. These top loads have little or no effect on driving characteristics. It's no wonder that American campers by the thousands are taking to the modern versions of the Conestoga wagon of pioneer days.

Station-wagon camping does, however, have disadvantages. As already considered, campers who wish to sleep in the wagon may have to unload it. The standard station wagon does not have built-in cooking or sanitary provisions, so campground facilities must be used. If you use a tent, it may be necessary to stow it soaking wet after a storm. Although there's more room for camping gear than in an ordinary automobile, storage space is still limited to the wagon bed, top carriers, and the space around the passengers.

Camping trailers, those small folding units that open into a tent, free more space for passengers in a vehicle. These trailers are increasingly popular for many reasons. They're easily towed, even with a compact car, and they are highly maneuverable. They can go anywhere a car can go except where towed vehicles are prohibited. They can be moved short distances by one or two individuals.

The folding unit provides sleeping accommodations for four or more campers on good beds, and these trailers generally have ample storage room for most of your gear. The folding tents are simple to erect, and uneven ground makes no difference as the whole unit can be leveled with adjustable corner supports. Camping trailers can be parked in a backyard, a wide driveway, or a turnabout. Maintenance expense is low, and the trailer places very little load on the towing vehicle. Too, these shelters can be used when separated from the vehicle used to tow them.

Disadvantages? Driving speeds must be lowered when you're towing one of these camping trailers, and you must learn to maneuver them in traffic and when parking. If the ground is uneven, as it may be at the campground, such managing is sometimes difficult. Of course, the tent must be unfolded and erected upon arrival at the site. You cannot tow a boat behind one of these trailers, although a few are big enough so that a small craft can be carried on top.

A flat tire can be a problem if there is no space for the trailer, and certain highways are closed to trailers when there are high winds. In some areas, even these comparatively small trailers may not be parked in private driveways or yards. Extra rooms may be added if the party is large, but since even the basic unit opens up to two or three times the folded size, some tent sites are not large enough. You may be obliged to pitch in an area reserved for a large vehicle, and usually such areas are less picturesque. A trailer license is required as well as a hitch and connections.

There are several makes of compact camping vans, but all of them are basically similar. Inasmuch as there is no trailer, these vans are highly maneuverable, and passengers can use the interior space while on the road. The roof can be used for a boat or for additional carriers if need be. A single insurance policy and license covers the whole rig, and no hitches or connections are required. There's usually sleeping room for four adults and from two to four youngsters, depending on their ages. Many vans are fitted with toilets, small sinks, and storage units for clothing.

On the debit side, these small vans provide only limited room for those spending much time in them during bad weather. Head room is rather low, though some of these vans have extension roofs that do provide a little more height when they are elevated. If more

Camping Van with Extension Roof

space is required, extension rooms can be added, but then the vehicle cannot be moved until they are detached. Once a camping interior has been installed in a van, the usefulness of the vehicle for hauling and other purposes becomes limited.

Travel trailers are trailers that are completely self-contained although they are towed by another vehicle. They are fairly maneuverable on all but the roughest roads. Driver and passengers can travel in comfort in the towing vehicle, with all gear stowed in the large trailer. Once the latter has been parked and leveled, the towing vehicle can be unhitched and used separately. These trailers are weatherproof, and they can be heated.

Travel Trailer

They're often equipped with toilet, hot running water, electricity, shower, stove, and sink. Generally, there's plenty of storage room for clothing and extra gear. Four to six people can bunk in most of these trailers. Tourists with small children, as well as elderly individuals who like to travel with all the conveniences, many times prefer this type of trailer.

The travel trailers do, however, have certain disadvantages, including the fact that they can cost as much as $6,000 or more. They require hookups to water, electricity, and sewage lines, as well as to gas lines if that fuel is used. Not every campground has all these connections, and if they do, the areas set aside for trailers of this size frequently lack shade or privacy.

These large trailers are not permitted on certain parkways, and they are prohibited in certain tunnels. Unhitching and maneuvering may be difficult for the uninitiated, and toll charges are high. In wooded regions, low branches present a problem, although more and more campgrounds are trimming trees so that large trailers can pass easily underneath. Generally, the law forbids riding in these trailers when they're on the road.

Camping units mounted on the chassis of a pickup truck or in the pickup's body are popular. Some of these units have a sleeping extension over the truck's cab. These camping vehicles are maneuverable even on rough roads, and passengers may ride in the living space. There's often communication between the driver and passengers, through an opening in the back of the truck cab by inexpensive two-way radio, or by means of an electronic intercom unit. Inasmuch as the entire rig is self-contained, there's no gear to pack up if you want to drive off somewhere.

Inasmuch as the truck is more powerful than a car, pulling a boat trailer is no problem. With some pickup-camper models, too, a boat can be carried on the roof. The camping unit may be removable, permitting you to use the truck separately. Generally, the units are equipped with beds for at least four, sink, stove, closets, and toilet. A variety of interior details and equipment is available.

These pickup campers are banned from some parkways, and from all tunnels if there is cooking or heating gas aboard. Higher tolls are sometimes charged for these vehicles. Since many of them are quite tall, low branches may be a problem. If the camper body is removed so that the truck can be used separately, passengers are obliged to crowd into the cab or ride in the back regardless of the weather.

Numerous women do not care to ride in a truck under any circumstances, so the truck is often not useful as a second car for the family. As considered earlier, the parking problem with a truck can be difficult to solve. These units cost as much as $5,500 and more. For campers who have no other use for a truck, that's a large investment. The length of the truck limits the size of the camper body. Finally, all highway rules and regulations applying to trucks are in force with pickup campers.

For those who like to travel but are not too keen on tenting, there's the travel coach—a complete, small home on a truck chassis or a specially built chassis that's easier to drive.

Travel Coach

They cost as much as $12,000. These outfits are classed as pleasure vehicles, so they can be used on many parkways that refuse towed vehicles, house trailers, tent trailers, and pickup-camper units. They are maneuverable on highways and secondary roads, and they can be driven at highway speeds as they are not classed as trucks. They sleep as many as eight. Many types of interior layouts are available, with sinks, fans, stoves, good beds, dining nooks that make up into additional beds, picture windows, carpets, toilets, air conditioning, full-length mirrors, and plenty of storage room.

On the other side of the coin, such units are not too serviceable on backcountry roads, and most of them cannot be taken through tunnels as they carry propane gas cylinders for heating and cooking, plus lighting in some instances. A completely electrified model eludes this restriction, but none of these large vehicles are permitted on some roads because of their weight. Usually they cannot be used to tow a trailer. Expert maintenance is required. Too, it may be difficult to find a place where the toilet tanks can be emptied, although this is always a problem with built-in sanitary equipment.

Before selecting a camping vehicle, try to discuss the different types with those who own or use them. Consider, too, that a detriment to one individual may be an asset to another. For example, many do not like to tow anything behind a car or station wagon, while others can give good arguments in rebuttal. Some outdoorsmen like to park the living unit and use the towing vehicle for side trips, although others see no advantage to this arrangement. Talking to those who have had firsthand experience will help you make the right decision.

18

Everything on Your Back

EVEN IN THIS AGE OF SPACE SHIPS AND NUCLEAR POWER, MORE OF the world's tonnage is carried on men's backs than by all mechanical means combined. In other words, backpacking is still the world's No. 1 way of moving things, and campers contribute no small portion to this globe-wide mode of transportation.

In Europe particularly, backpack campers of many ages are a common sight, and along the two great hiking trails of the United States—the Appalachian and the Pacific Crest routes, with their many segments and tributaries—you can literally see hikers from eight to eighty years old. Outside of this, however, in the United States it is usually the younger campers who strap on their packs and take to the woods.

If you want to take to the wilderness without benefit of car, station wagon, trail scooter, wagon, horse, or even canoe, backpacking is not an unpleasant choice. We've both lugged our camping gear many miles, and there's nothing quite so satisfying to a rabid camper as to know that he got to where he is by shank's mare with all his necessities on his back. In fact, one of us has written an entire book on the subject: Bradford Angier's *Home in Your Pack*, published by The Stackpole Company.

Backpacking isn't for the soft city camper or any camper who is out of condition, for it's rugged exercise. It's true, though, that by taking it easy during the early stages anyone in good health can work himself into condition as he travels. Too, with some care in selecting the pack itself, even an inexperienced woodsman can comfortably tote sufficient gear and grub into the bush for a weekend sojourn.

Much depends upon selecting a proper pack. That, in turn, depends to some extent upon how long you plan to be gone and what, therefore, is needed. To carry only food for a weekend, a lightweight tent, and summer sleeping bag, a fairly simple knapsack will do, with the bulkier items lashed over the top. For a longer trip, the larger capacity of a packframe will be required. Unless you're in good condition, avoid heavy loads until you get in shape to carry them without danger of a strain or injury.

The modern pack of the right sort is cleverly designed for backpacking and is made from fine, lightweight materials. When we were small fry, we did our backpacking with homemade packs designed from an old pair of trousers or a gunny sack. Such improvisations serve a lot of junior woodsmen back of beyond without benefit of scientific engineering, space-age materials, and hard-to-find spending money. Nowadays, you can select from among perhaps three dozen types, sizes, and styles of backpacking gear.

However, only three types are suitable for serious backpacking vacations: the frame pack, the packboard, and the pack basket. Of these, the frame pack is the most convenient.

The frame packs, which have some sort of comfortable metal frame to keep the pack itself away from your back, range in price from about $6 to more than $30, depending on make, design, size, and the complexity and quality of their many possible details. They've been used by famous expeditions around the globe and can be had in almost any shape—triangular, rectangular, or square.

The metal frame, in keeping the bag portion upright, rigid, and away from the body, makes a frame pack cool to carry and prevents hard items from digging into your hide. The lower part of the frame, often buckled into place around the waist, is curved to fit your waist or hips, preventing the pack from shifting from side to side during a climb.

Many of these frame packs have external pockets for small items. Such a pack is excellent for a trip of any duration where lightness and convenience are desired. Look for good materials, long closing flaps with straps long enough to reach the buckles no matter how loaded the pack may be, stoutly sewn seams, and nonrusting hardware. Make sure the shoulder straps are wide, padded, and of some nonrolling material, good honest leather still being the best. Nothing can ruin a backpacking vacation quicker than shoulder straps that become ropelike and cut into your flesh.

The canvas should be of heavy material, say 13 to 15 ounces to the square yard. It should be tightly woven. If it's not sufficiently water-repellent, spray it with some of the good preparations on the market. Some of these packs have a double or reinforced bottom.

The packboard or bare packframe has been used for centuries to carry bulky objects over long distances. Trappers have used them in the north country for lugging traps and carrying out pelts. Big-game hunters have borne out trophy heads and hides with their help, and with them rangers have toted everything from two-way radios to fire-fighting equipment.

The modern packframe may be of seasoned wood or lightweight metal tubing. Sometimes the hollow tubing is cleverly used to hold liquid fuel for a camp stove, fishing line and hooks, or a vital supply of matches. There's even a type of packframe, made in a small California factory we toured recently, that has a lightweight extension at the bottom that converts into a comfortable, low camp chair. Modern packframes come in both adult and juvenile sizes.

Many packframes have sacks that are designed to slip over them for carrying equipment enclosed and protected. Others, such as the Trapper Nelson packboard, are used by simply strapping the gear in a tarpaulin and lashing it onto the frame itself. Certain of the packframes and packboards can be used either way.

A pack basket is usually made of white-ash splints about an inch wide, woven into a large, sturdy basket about 18 inches high with a top opening of about 14 by 11 inches. The bottom of a pack basket is slightly larger than the top. These baskets come in several sizes, with even small ones for the youngsters. The rugged canvas hood for wet weather fits loosely, so if the gear emerges above the rim, the hood will still fit the basket.

We've used many types of packs, and the pack basket is one of our favorites. Granted, it can't be folded and stowed away neatly. It's heavier than most canvas packs, weighing about six pounds empty. It doesn't normally boast pockets. On the other hand, it will com-

Frame Pack

Packboard

fortably tote hard and off-shaped items as easily as it will a week's supply of bread. It stands up on the ground and is not easily tipped.

It can be used as a storage container in camp and later at home. When a family's youngsters are small, many ride miles on a parent's back in such a basket, although there are special packs built for just this purpose, too. Pack baskets range from about $6 to around $10. Their wooden splints are usually left in their natural whiteness, but they can be stained if you like. A good coat of marine varnish will keep a basket in condition for years.

Some canoe campers line pack baskets with plastic bags or sheeting before stowing their gear. Rigged this way, a pack basket will float high and dry in case of a dunking. Other campers buy packsacks large enough to hold one of these baskets and thus enjoy the advantages of both, including outside pockets. Others design and attach pockets to the basket hood.

Pack Basket

Don't try to lug more than 25 to 35 pounds except for short distances unless you're an experienced and conditioned backpacker. In spite of some military practices, a pack of 60 pounds or more is not a normal load for a human being. Carrying heavy loads on your back can be dangerous, too, if you're out of condition. Start easy, walk slowly, and climb surefootedly regardless of your age and health. You're out for a good time.

A tip? A pair of soft shoulder-strap pads, costing from about $.50 to some $2, can

Shoulder-Strap Pads

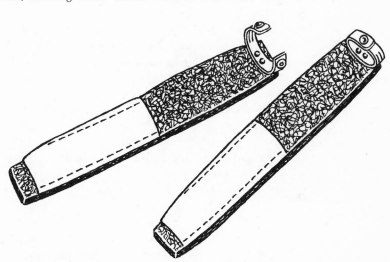

make all the difference when it comes to comfort. Use them to avoid chafing. A substitute? Handkerchiefs or gloves shoved between strap and shoulder.

If you plan on a backpacking vacation in the season ahead, get in condition during the intervening months. Plan the equipment list with an eye to compactness and lightness, and select a pack best suited to your trip and gear. Then take it easy. Backpack camping—with your pockets and belts free of a lot of heavy items and your hands ready for shooting, picture taking, or climbing—will be an enjoyable experience.

Backpack camping is the kind of topic that immediately starts outdoorsmen arguing across the campfire. Some are completely against it, while others would go on no other kind of a camping jaunt. Best way to decide is to try it for yourself. Perhaps we'll be able to help smooth the trail for you with a few suggestions.

The footwear, where the hiker and trail meet, is of primary consideration. Rubber-soled, heelless, canvas-topped sneakers are good on dry rocks but may be slippery when the going gets wet. Too, the lack of heels offers little grip in going downgrade and in traversing a pebbled or a crumbly surface. Sneakers are also likely to get soggy in wet weather and, unless they can be dried in the sun within a few hours, are clammy to wear. Furthermore, sneakers give less ankle protection than many like on uneven ground, and they cause excessive perspiration. On the other hand, they're light, comfortable, and comparatively inexpensive. They're especially popular in the East.

The proven favorites among many trail veterans, particularly in the West, are the special boots stocked by the big catalog-issuing sporting goods dealers for the express purpose of hiking. Equipped with the best of rubber lug soles, they provide good traction and long wear. They are safe, comfortable, and quiet, but not inexpensive. With reasonable care they are good for years, however, especially as they can be handily resoled.

If your sporting goods dealer cannot readily obtain these for you, it is practical to order them by mail, as a proper fit is guaranteed. To measure your feet, put on the socks you intend to don on the trek. Then stand on a large sheet of paper, distributing your weight equally on both feet. Holding a pencil vertically, clearly mark the outlines of each foot. Send these outlines to the outfitter, along with a notation of the length and width of your regular dress shoes.

Always break in a new pair of boots before heading down the trail, and wear two pairs of socks. You may like a thin, smooth pair next to your feet, and a heavier woolen pair over them. Take two extra pairs of each type and change frequently, keeping one set always washed and perhaps drying on the outside of your pack. If your boots are old, make sure that they have good soles, sound heels, and no ripped stitches.

Choice of clothing will depend upon where, when, and how long you'll be on the trail. You will need a couple of sets of underwear, at least. Trousers should be cuffless, have deep pockets, and permit easy movement. The two hip pockets should have buttoned flaps. A watch pocket is handy for compass or other small articles such as a pocketknife.

You'll appreciate a flannel shirt. Carry an extra one to serve as a sweater or for a change now and then. One cotton-flannel shirt and one wool shirt make a functional combination. It's a good idea to steer clear of short-sleeved shirts, as you may prefer long sleeves during cool evenings and if the insects are bad. You can always roll up long sleeves.

If the weather may be cold, take along a closely woven windbreaker jacket and a sweater to wear under it. Then you can put on various combinations of shirts, sweater, and windbreaker to suit the climate. Outer jackets should be water-repellent, as well as loose enough to wear over sweater and shirts. Knitted jacket cuffs have a lot going for them. They're warm, for one thing, and they also help keep insects from going up your sleeves.

For raingear you can pack along a lightweight plastic poncho with attached hood in country without brush. More substantial are a wide-brimmed felt hat and a regular rubber poncho with the hole in the middle. The rubber poncho will double as a ground cloth and a windbreak, as well as protect you and your pack from rain during the hike.

For headgear, a soft felt model with a wide brim is good to shield your eyes and protect your neck from sunburn and soaking. A lightweight felt hat will keep your head cool because of the air space under the crown, as well as warmer on a cold day for the same reason. If you insist on a cloth hat or cap, be sure to get one with a leather rather than a cloth sweatband. There's nothing clammier than one of the latter when it's soaked with perspiration from hiking.

One of the so-called 1 1/2-gallon western hats is fine and will give satisfactory, long service. Such a hat can be used for many purposes in addition to a head covering. You can carry water in it in a pinch, fan the starting campfire with it, and use it to hold personal belongings while you sleep. If the nights will be cold and your sleeping bag has no flannel flap, take along a lightweight knitted toque to sleep in.

When it comes to sleeping gear and weather protection, again there are violent, good-natured arguments among veteran outdoorsmen. Some say by all means save the weight of an air mattress but carry sleeping bags. Others demand blankets and an air mattress. Some want lightweight tents. Others go for a tarpaulin over a rope.

Probably the soundest advice is to personally weigh the merits of each item, then make up your own list. If, for example, you don't believe an air mattress is necessary, try sleeping on the rug beside your bed some night. We're betting you'll climb into bed before dawn. An air mattress helps provide vital rest during a strenuous backpacking trip, and that's important. If you still want to keep weight to a minimum, take a 3/4-length air mattress and strew a few boughs beneath your feet.

Sleeping bags are superior to the same weight of blankets on the trail. They pack well, are warm, and you can't easily kick your feet out at the bottom. The most popular models for hikers are the weight-saving mummy types, with about two pounds of down or one of the synthetic fillers. Down provides the most warmth for its weight when termperatures dip, but it's also the most expensive. With a little more weight to carry, the best of the new synthetics can do just as good a job. By the way, it's a good idea to use a lightweight rubber or plastic ground cloth, or your poncho, under the sleeping bag, as dampness considerably decreases its heat-conserving abilities.

There are also many types of rectangular sleeping bags which are light enough to carry for long distances on your back. These have their own particular advantages, including the fact that they can be opened wide for easy airing, something that should be done periodically to increase warmth and buoyancy. Too, they afford more sleeping space. Some of these bags can be zippered together for two people, if desired. Rectangular bags come in numerous weights and materials, are easier to roll and pack than blankets, and afford far better protection.

No matter who wins the blankets versus sleeping bag argument, a tent is a sound precaution for additional nighttime protection, especially if the weather may be bad or if you plan to be in one place for more than a night. All backpacking tents have a couple of characteristics in common. They have to be light and compact to carry. Beyond that, what you pick will depend on individual preference, what you have in mind to pay, the kind of country to be covered, and the percentage of weight you choose to concentrate on shelter.

There is plenty of choice, varying from crawl-in tents weighing about two pounds and costing around $25 to small, light, somewhat more spacious one-man tents weighing closer to three pounds and costing about twice as much. When two outdoorsmen are hiking together, they can get a tent big enough for both and divide the weight, although not necessarily the tentage, between them. This ratio of weight per hiker continues in the trail models of the larger tents. Some big enough to sleep four, complete with pole assemblies for use above timberline, weigh only twelve pounds, which is still three pounds per camper.

Many backpack campers prefer a lightweight tarpaulin to a tent, hanging it over a rope or propping it up with poles to form a shelter. Tarps fold compactly and have many uses. On the other hand, they offer no protection against insects without the addition of mosquito bars, and they don't provide the shelter a tent can in severe weather.

A compromise? Plastic tubing, available at outfitters, that is put up by running a rope

Lightweight Tarpaulin Shelter

through it to serve as a ridge and tieing this several feet high between two trees. No pegs are necessary, the weight of the occupant anchoring the tube. Such tubing can also be obtained in longer lengths, so that one camper can sleep at each open end, if you wish.

For cooking utensils, you can get along with the minimum or be as fancy as packing limitations allow. The least you'll need is one frypan and one cooking pot. Then each individual will need a plate, cup, fork, and spoon. Most campers carry a small knife which will cut food and spread jam as well as anything else. Plastic cups are better than aluminum,

Shelter of Plastic Tubing

while stainless steel is best of all. A number of companies make nesting cooking and eating outfits in various sizes with sufficient equipment for all.

There are also several extremely tiny stoves, any of which can come in handy in the mountains above timberline, on a wet day anywhere, and for those times when you want to cook a bite without later having to find water to douse the campfire. For example, we have a little alcohol-burning pocket stove, about two inches high and three inches across, that will boil water in some five minutes and start eggs and bacon sizzling in a hurry. It weighs about half a pound, costs around $2.25, and can't explode or leak.

We have another tiny stove that costs about $10, but has a small tank for the alcohol, a fine jet burner, and will cook things very fast. This model folds compactly and weighs two pounds. The smaller one will burn for an hour on one-third pint of alcohol, and the larger for three hours on half a pint.

Meals on a hiking vacation will depend on personal preferences. The best way to go about deciding on a menu is to get together with your party members, count up the required meals, for the breakfasts put down such items as bacon, eggs, and dried fruit, and so on, and then add everything up.

For lunches, if you plan to be on the trail at midday, consider bread for sandwiches and fillers such as cheese, peanut butter, deviled meats, jams, and the like. Small boxes of raisins do well for dessert, and plain dried fruits are good to munch on, too. We generally like to relax around a small campfire at noon, boil water for tea, and toast sandwiches on forked green sticks.

For the big meal of the day, at night, plan on canned meats, stews, and perhaps fresh fish if tempting lakes and brooks are nearby, plus bread or rolls and fruit for dessert. Dehydrated foods, discussed elsewhere in this book, will spare you from packing considerable weight.

Dried fruits and vegetables, which are not always as tasty as the canned types, save a great deal in weight and bulk. Such staples as fast-cooking rice are tasty, lightweight, and easy to prepare. Instant oatmeal, ready to eat when mixed with a bit of hot water in a bowl, provides a substantial breakfast and is easy to carry.

Sugar is important on a backpacking trip, for you need energy. Honey, jams, and jellies are alternatives. Be sure to take along some such form of quick energy. Chemical sweeteners contribute none of this. Bouillon cubes, also short on energy and nourishment, make appetizing drinks for a change or can be used as a meal-starting soup. If you want to carry fresh eggs, which will keep for upwards of a week, an aluminum egg carrier is available that will tote four eggs in safety. Or, handier still, settle for powdered whole egg.

Backpack camping, especially with a companion or two along, can be a lot of fun. It's not as satisfactory in every respect for family camping as car or station-wagon camping, although all over the country toddlers and oldsters are taking to it happily. But healthy adults and teen-agers may find it mighty pleasant. It leaves a lot of hustle and bustle and expense behind. There's no other kind of outdoor vacation that can compare to these backpacking jaunts, none that can take you so close to peace and utter freedom.

19

Shoestring Camping

A FEW CAMPFIRES AGO SOME FRIENDS AND WE WERE TALKING ABOUT how we used to take to the woods as kids, not just regular camps but off by ourselves in twos and threes for an overnight trip or a weekend in the tall timber. It brought back memories and a lot of laughs. We also realized anew that camping on a shoestring can be a lot of fun.

We used to take to the bush with an old blanket that had seen warmer days, some sort of sheet or big pieces of oilcloth for a tent, a kerosene lantern, matches for a wood fire or a can of solidified alcohol for cooking, and an ancient hatchet. We also toted along a frypan, a covered pot, a tin cup, and a stalwart looking hunting knife which was generally a battered kitchen refugee, in a homemade sheath of old shoetop leather we'd stitched with rawhide and a sharp nail.

Despite our pinched equipment, we had some tremendous times and thus began our love affair with the woods and fields that has carried the two of us for over half a century.

The more we talked about those economy-class tenting trips that night, with flames lifting from fresh fuel as we shoved the unburned spokes of the wheellike fire into the glowing embers, the more interested we became in just how inexpensively a camping outfit could be assembled with today's soaring prices. Most of us can't quite make it a $10 tenting trip, but with some imagination and a few items from home you can do pretty well for about $15. You'll have a lot of fun assembling such an outfit and using it, too.

Such gear would include a shelter of plastic sheeting, a two-burner canned heat stove, a camp lantern, a hatchet, an icebox in case you'll be traveling by car, and an air mattress. Other items from home would round out the outfit. While this setup is designed for the lone camper, for just a bit more it can serve for several individuals. The only added expense would be for air mattresses for the additional campers.

By poring over the camping catalogs, you'll be amazed at what can be gotten together for a very few dollars. The first thing to consider is some sort of shelter, and there is an inexpensive solution. Several companies make transparent sheeting of tough plastic for painters' drop cloths, covering for stored automobiles, winter protection for shrubbery, and similar uses. These sheets are light and waterproof. The 9 x 12 rectangles sell for about $.50 each, and three can be used to make a pretty rugged shelter, dining fly, or tent, provided you add a light frame of saplings, some line, and a bit of thought.

The material can be angled over a line and guyed out to make a king-size pup tent. Raised higher, a plastic sheet will serve as a dining fly. A good-size lean-to can be formed

Shelter of Transparent Plastic Sheeting

by spreading plastic sheeting over a light frame of saplings. Use the material doubled for a stronger shelter. This way, too, if there is a puncture through both thicknesses, you can reverse one of the sheets so that the hole will be covered by an intact portion of the other sheet.

When knotting guys to the corners of this material, fold the corner over, bunch the fold, and then tie cord around the corner between the bunched material and the main area. Do not expect a cord looped through a hole in such material to hold without tearing. Small tears can be patched with transparent mending tape, paper masking tape, or adhesive tape from the medicine kit.

When you have covered the sapling frame with plastic sheeting, being careful not to tear or puncture it on sharp branch stubs, place a few light branches over it to help hold it in place and prevent it from ballooning in the breeze. If you have an old bed sheet or any large piece of fabric, put this over the shelter frame under the plastic for additional strength.

A few extra sheets of this inexpensive plastic will come in handy as covers for food, ground cloths, or catch basins for soft rainwater. And they make fine emergency ponchos for resisting the elements, a good reason for carrying one compactly folded in a breast pocket when traveling in the bush.

Include in your shoestring outfit a ball of stout twine or light nylon cord. About fifty feet of the latter with a 550-pound breaking strength will cost about $1. Twine is much less expensive but not as strong.

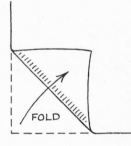

FOLD

Knotting Guy to Corner of Plastic Sheeting

113

Once you are all set for shelter, you'll want to consider an inexpensive stove unless, of course, all the cooking will be done over an open fire. An open fire will save a couple of dollars, but in many localities the convenience of an economy stove will make this expense worthwhile.

For about $2 you can buy a two-burner canned-heat stove that folds flat for transporting. This uses small cans of solidified alcohol which cannot explode or spill, yet can be started easily, then extinguished by merely replacing the top of the can. The fuel sells for only a few cents a can, depending on size, and is completely safe to carry. While not as hot as the more expensive gasoline, propane, and L/P stoves, these tiny units can take care of a fine meal, heat water, or keep foods hot on your table until you're ready.

As for a camp light, unless you plan extensive reading or such, the small kerosene lanterns are excellent. These come in two sizes, one being about nine inches high exclusive of handle and the other being about a foot high. The small one burns for some eighteen hours with one filling of kerosene and sells for under $2, while the larger model, costing about a dollar more, will run thirty hours and give more light. Either lantern is fine for camp and gives enough illumination for most camp chores, especially when supplemented with a bright campfire. They make fine all-night lights, too.

You likely have some flashlights around the house. Take one or two along.

For building a shelter, chopping firewood, or driving stakes, you will need a hatchet. A hatchet is less expensive than a long-handle ax and is adequate for an economy outfit. You can buy a cheap one for as little as $2 with a sheath, and this will be heavy enough for simple camping. The best hatchets cost more like $6, but cheaper models will do all right except for chopping heavy logs. Keep any hatchet sharp for safe, easy cutting.

When backpacking, naturally you won't bother with an icebox. But when traveling to your destination on wheels, some sort of icebox for food perishables will be a handy thing for more than just an overnight stay. For an inexpensive camping outfit you can buy a pressed-styrofoam cooler that keeps food very well and costs as little as $2.

One of these, plus a ten-pound block of ice, should keep all perishables for a weekend or even longer. Although these iceboxes are not comparable with metal or plastic ice chests that sell for many times this economy price, they are exceptionally lightweight and with care will last for several seasons of enjoyable camping.

About the only sleeping gear the economy-minded camper needs to spend money for is an inexpensive air mattress. If the weather is mild, just a blanket or two or an old comforter will do. You should have a soft mattress, though. The toughest old woodsmen we know all do, and one is well worth the price.

There are many comfortable plastic air mattresses on the market that sell for as little as $2, and you can't invest that sum any better for sleeping ease. These are not as durable as the expensive rubberized-fabric mattresses, but with care they'll do well for many a trip. They will last longer, by the way, if you make sure that the ground under them is free from sharp stones, root stubs, and pointed twigs. Many mattresses come with built-in pillows for added comfort.

You can borrow your cooking utensils from home, saving that expense. Minimum equipment includes a frypan, a covered pot for heating water, soups, and stews, and a coffeepot if you don't use one of the instant beverages. Paper cups and plates are fine for a camping weekend and save washing, or if you have some old crockery or aluminum plates, take them along instead.

Eating gear can be kept to a minimum. Take a knife, fork, and spoon, preferably light stainless steel, for each person plus a large serving spoon and a spatula. The spatula is fine for turning pancakes, hamburgers, bacon, fish, or toast in a frypan and also for fanning a stubborn campfire into life if there is no wind.

If you already have a jackknife, take it along by all means for cutting meat, cord, or wood, or bring a sharp kitchen knife for the same purpose. A serviceable sheath for a kitchen knife can be made out of cardboard and some sticky tape. This will protect the blade when the knife is not being used.

In the absence of some screening to close the doors of your tent or the front of your shelter during warm weather, some insect repellent will be needed. Nylon mosquito netting comes to about $.75 a square yard, but a few yards will make your night more comfortable by keeping out most of the insects you attract. Attach the netting to the plastic material with either some adhesive tape or a few spring-clip clothespins.

To sum up, it is possible to assemble inexpensively quite a complete camping outfit for an overnight or longer trip to the woods. All that's needed in addition to the items outlined is food for the journey. Because you have to eat no matter where you are, this should not be included in the list of projected expenses.

Campers who decide to try taking to the woods on a shoestring and find that it is fun, even with economy-type gear, can always improve the outfit and keep the original items as backup items for the better outfit.

Get a real tent first, then a stove or lantern, and keep the folding stove to heat things on the table or for toast. The original little lantern can furnish extra light in case the better one should ever fail to operate. The inexpensive icebox will be fine for the small fry's supply of soft drinks or for extra milk, or it can be used as a storage bin for foods so that small animals can't get at them.

When you buy better air mattresses, the plastic ones are fine as beach toys, for sunning, or for use as backrests. They'll also serve as spares when you have visitors or an extra youngster who wants to come along.

All in all, this shoestring camping outfit can provide a great deal of pleasure for many trips, and most of the items that make it up will last for years. If the weather is good and you're stimulated with a spirit of fun and adventure, this sort of economy outfit may bring even more pleasure than a really plush outfit.

A good many expert campers began their experiences in the woods and fields with such an outfit, and now they look back upon these times as some of the most satisfying they've ever experienced. An investment of about $15 could do the same for you.

20

Camp and Hunt Here

HUNTERS WHO LIKE TO CAMP DURING THEIR AUTUMN TRIPS, AS WELL as those campers who like to hunt varmints during the warm months, are often hard-pressed to combine the two sports. Use of firearms is forbidden in our national park lands, as it commonly is in state parks and near privately owned public campgrounds. The possible exceptions are the places where public rifle ranges are included in the recreational areas.

Not a few sportsmen have discovered that the perfect answer to the problem of combining hunting and camping lies in our national forests. Here, in contrast with our national-parks policy, hunting is encouraged under the multiple-use management system. Hunting in the national forests, on the other hand, is subject to the license fees, seasons, special-permit laws, and other regulations of the states in which the land lies. A hunter should become familiar with the state rules before hunting in a national forest.

The more than 181 million acres of our national forests provide habitat for actual millions of game animals and game birds. The former include moose, antelope, elk, mountain sheep, mountain goats, and javelinas, as well as whitetail, mule, and blacktail deer and black, grizzly, and Alaska brown bears. Predators include lynxes, bobcats, cougars, coyotes, foxes, and assorted smaller species. The game birds include wild turkeys, ruffed grouse, blue grouse, Franklin grouse, geese, and many species of duck.

Many of these varieties can be found in a single national forest, as, for example, Shoshone National Forest near Cody, Wyoming. This wilderness of nearly 2,250,000 acres offers the following game hunting: moose, deer, elk, mountain sheep, antelope, black and grizzly bears, and numerous species of game birds.

Other western national forests offer excitingly comparable lists of game for the hunter-camper. Eastern and southern national forests contain game typical of their areas of the country. Not only are the trophies here, but some of the finest fishing waters of the nation glitter within the boundaries of the national forests, along with spectacular wilderness, scenery, and privacy.

You may camp and hunt in season anywhere in our national forests except for a few spots that may be closed because of fire hazard or other temporary circumstances. Too,

116

some state and federal game refuges are within the national-forest boundaries, and of course there is no hunting within such preserves.

There are 154 national forests and 18 national grasslands administered by the Forest Service of the U.S. Department of Agriculture. The camping sites therein are especially noted for their privacy. They are generally separated by 100 feet, with plenty of shrubs and trees between. In some regions, open-field camps are to be found. Whenever possible, however, privacy is planned as part of the lure of national-forest camping. It's easy to get there, too, as a great many of our major highways pass through one or more national forests.

If you are attracted by backcountry camping, consider the 83 wilderness areas in our national forests. These embrace more than 41,000,000 acres and include some of the wildest scenery this side of the moon. No permanent roads cross these wilderness areas, and no vehicles except fire-fighting equipment are allowed within the boundaries. Trails are few, and they're for hikers and horses only. Rarely are there established camping sites or shelters within these areas, and you'll have to pack in all your gear and food to explore them. They remain real wilderness.

The regular season in national-forest camping areas extends from May 30 through Labor Day weekend, although some areas in the South are open all year. Nevertheless, even following the regular season when water is shut off and flush toilets are locked, you may still camp in established campgrounds, using fireplaces and tent sites.

No reservations are required at any time of the year, and almost all national-forest campgrounds are free. Where there is a charge, for special equipment and services, it is very minimal. In a few popular areas, the stay is limited to two weeks. But ordinarily, and of course at all times outside the regular campgrounds, your vacation is unlimited.

Small trailers are permitted at most national-forest campgrounds. However, there are no water, electrical, or sewage connections for trailers, and no waste water may be dumped upon the ground. Remember that these are national forests, not national parks, so facilities aren't fancy. Tables, benches, and fireplaces are yours for the using at most sites, and campfires may be built with permit in almost any part of our national forests except when the hazard is great.

You should check with the ranger for fire permits. At many of the campgrounds cut firewood is available. If it's not, you can rustle your own. It's permissible to cut deadwood or to pick up the squaw wood you can find on the ground. Camp stoves are, of course, usable at any time. As for supplies, these are available at numerous campgrounds and at nearby villages. Safe drinking water is found at established campgrounds.

Pets are allowed in national forests if you keep them under physical restraint or control. Some states require that they be kept on a leash in picnic areas or campgrounds. If yours is a city pup, it's especially important for his own safety to keep him under physical control in wilderness regions.

Firearms can be carried in the national forests and used in line with state laws for hunting and target practice, but they may not be discharged on or near camp and recreation areas. The local ranger will tell you where they may or may not be fired. Also check open seasons and game and varmint-hunting regulations. In most regions you'll find you can hunt something the year around.

For those interested in photography, camera subjects in the national forests are nearly limitless. They range from seldom viewed canyons and gorges to tremendous expanses of timberlands, hidden lakes, bright waterfalls, and wild cliffs and glaciers. Let's consider a few.

In Pisgah National Forest in North Carolina near Linville Gorge, a canyon of wild beauty, there is a waterfall 90 feet high reputedly visited by Hernando de Soto back in 1539. There, too, you can sometimes see the mysterious so-called Brown Mountain lights that seem to rise like skyrockets, glowing brightly, then fade and disappear, occasionally to reappear higher up.

Do you like mountain climbing? Then try George Washington National Forest in Virginia, where man-made lights relayed Civil War messages to Confederate troops threatening our national capital. Signal Knob is the name of the vantage point from which the signals were flashed.

For more strenuous hiking, go to the graceful White Mountain National Forest, which straddles the New Hampshire-Maine border, or take the rugged Appalachian Trail. This 1,995-mile footpath, with its chain of free lean-tos and fireplaces, twists from Mount Katahdin in Maine to Springer Mountain in Georgia, crossing eight national forests on the way.

Hikers and climbers in the West can find wild grandeur along the Pacific Crest Trail, which extends 2,156 miles in a country-long slash from near mount Baker in Washington to Campo in San Diego County—from the tree-clad skyline of the northern Cascades in Washington and Oregon and down along the John Muir Trail in the Sierras—virtually from Canada to Mexico.

Both these great trails are enlivened by hundreds of miles of secondary trails that invite side excursions. In fact, within the 154 national forests in 39 states and Puerto Rico are over 181,000,000 acres and more than 105,000 miles of trails, all open to backpacking.

Campsites range from the wild and primitive areas, such as those in the Cherokee National Forest of Tennessee, to splendidly planned and equipped facilities where there are washing machines, electric lights, hot and cold showers, and good restaurants. When we camped in the Cherokee National Forest wilderness, a bear blundered into the side of our tent one night. On the other hand, at Lake Arrowhead Campground in South Carolina we found just about every luxury a family camper could ask for, from soft drinks and drugstore items to ice and camping gear, city water, showers, automatic washers, fine rest rooms, and a beautiful grove in which to pitch the canvas.

Adventurous souls with a yen for the past can pan for gold, and find it, in German Gulch at Deerlodge National Forest in Montana, or go canoeing in Minnesota's brawling Superior National Forest. In Oregon and Idaho, in Payette, Nezperce, and Wallowa-Whitman national forests, the Snake River has carved a canyon more than a breathtaking mile deep. Or for entertaining contrast, visit the spongy bogs of Monongahela National Forest in West Virginia where, by jumping up and down, you can bounce a companion standing 150 feet away.

For those looking for antiques in nature, Inyo National Forest in California is the place to visit. Here is found the oldest known living thing, the bristlecone pine called Methuselah, more than 4,600 years old. For older things yet, you can visit a part of this wilderness in which fossil graptolites are found. These are the remains of sea creatures, estimated to be some 400 million years old, relics of the age in which this area was covered by a prehistoric sea. Up in Ashley National Forest in Utah, near Sheep Creek Canyon and the notable Flaming Gorge, are exposed geologic formations believed to be a billion years old.

For a tropical atmosphere, try Ocala National Forest in Florida, where you can swim in Alexander Springs, from which 78 million gallons of pure water flow each day, or paddle down jungle-rimmed streams and listen to eerie bird calls. If in abrupt contrast you like chilly and rugged camping, trek to Alaska's great Tongass National Forest, where you can drive to the largest glacier in the world that's accessible by road—imposing Mendenhall Glacier, a glittering two miles wide and up to 200 feet high.

If you prefer backcountry camping, the national-forest wilderness areas are made for that. They're little traveled by sportsmen and seldom visited, even by rangers. You must plan for such a wilderness trip with great care for safety. Select your gear with an eye for any emergency. Carry a map and compass and know how to use both expertly. Carry a first aid kit and know how to employ that effectively. There will be no one to help you but the members of your own party.

Incidentally, the Forest Service officially frowns on the individualist who ventures into the wilderness alone, although we've both been doing it for years. But you'd better know what you're doing. Too much can happen to a lone traveler that might result in endangering the lives of many others who'd have to go and search for him at considerable expense and hazard. In any event, it's only sensible to let someone responsible know where you're going, where you'll camp, and when you'll return. Then stick to these plans.

The U.S. Forest Service publishes numerous excellent and exciting booklets about the national forests. Three especially will be of interest: (1) *National Forest Vacations*, \$.30; (2) *Camping* (U.S. Department of Agriculture, Forest Service, PA-459), \$.20; (3) *Wilderness* (U.S. Department of Agriculture, Forest Service, PA-459), \$.20.

For other information about specific national forests, write to: Regional Forester, U.S. Forest Service, at the appropriate following addresses:

Federal Building
Missoula, Montana 59801

Federal Center
Building 85
Denver, Colorado 80202

New Federal Building
517 Gold Street, S.W.
Albuquerque, New Mexico 87101

Forest Office Building
Ogden, Utah 84401

630 Sansome Street
San Francisco, California 94111

319 S.W. Pine Street
Box 3623
Portland, Oregon 97208

50 Seventh Street, N.E.
Atlanta, Georgia 30323

Carpenter Building
710 N. Sixth Street
Milwaukee, Wisconsin 53203

Federal Office Building
Juneau, Alaska 99801

If you're seeking a wider choice of campgrounds, want some real wilderness camping, or wish to hunt or fish while camping, don't miss our national forests.

21

Snowbird Camping

EVEN WHEN THE WHITE SNOW IS DEEP AND YOU HAVE TO BACKPACK your outfit to a tent site on snowshoes or skis, or drive in on a snowmobile, camping can be a good way to spend a vacation or even a weekend. In fact, many campers who ordinarily put away their gear come Labor Day have discovered that taking to the woods in winter has its particular attractions.

In regions where winter brings really blustering weather, there are no insects, no snakes, no hurricanes, and usually no thunderstorms. There's little competition for campsites and not much danger of forest fires.

Even the sleeping is better. It's usually easier to keep warm, or get warmer, in winter camping than it is to keep cool during the hot months. Now, with the foliage off the deciduous trees and underbrush, the views are more spectacular. And if there's any snow in the woods, you can have the incomparable fun of tracking wild neighbors, sometimes right to the tent door.

Keeping food fresh is considerably less of a problem. About the only food worry in the whitened wilderness, in weather so cold that breath makes a continual fog, is freezing. We've both camped out during subzero weeks, and cooked when the temperature was as low as 60 degrees below and the campfire sprayed forth smoke that flattened against the ghostlike radiance of a frost ceiling. While we had to make a few adjustments, such as cooking with our mitts on, even these can be fun. You cut your steak with a saw, for instance, or break it over a handy ledge.

These minor changes in meal-getting techniques are compensated for by the magnificence all about you. Firewood snaps, while ice of a nearby lake cannonades, the ground cracks noisily, and trees bang with the intensity of detonating cartridges. Your breath freezes about you with a crackling noise reminiscent of crisp paper being crumbled. The Aurora Borealis, a prodding battery of icy searchlights, sweeps the night sky. All this is extreme, but even on a day when the temperature is well above zero there'll be the sudden thunder of snow falling from tall spruce and much more that you'll discover for yourself. Interesting? It is.

As far as personal comfort is concerned, many like snowbird camping better than hot-weather tenting. In the heat, there is only so much clothing to shed. In cold weather, you can always add more, exercise harder, or if it gets still more rugged, build a roaring fire and enjoy the supreme luxury of basking between that and a heat-reflecting ledge.

Of course, getting into the woods is more difficult, but with care you can make it. Many campgrounds are closed, but there are state and national forests open for campers, as is much private land if permission is obtained to use it. A check with your state conservation department, at the state capital, will reveal plenty of land open to winter camping even when the public campgrounds are shut down.

Once having located a place, you will have to find a way to get to it from your car. Incidentally, it's an excellent idea to head the car outward when you park it. If more snow falls before you get back, it will be a lot easier to start for home.

Experts on skis may want to ride them while packing their outfit in to their site. Unless you are an expert, though, it will pay to stick to a good pair of high boots or snowshoes. Snowshoes are simple to use, permit traveling in deep snow, and can get you to spots where skis would be useless or even dangerous to a beginner. When wearing webs, remember to walk with your feet fairly far apart to avoid hitting your ankles with the edges of the shoes. Dig your toes through the top holes when going up a steep grade and lean back slightly when coming down a sharp incline.

Even a tyro on snowshoes can work through brush, up and down wooded slopes, and through blown-down areas where a man on skis would be helpless and a man afoot would soon be bogged down. There are three basic types of snowshoes. There's the tailless, oval, bearpaw type, ideal for thick brush and rough terrain; the Maine or Michigan type, a bit longer, and with a short tail, best for all-around work; and the long, slender pickerel variety, more like skis than snowshoes, with sharply turned-up toes and long tails, for use in open country with a minimum of bush.

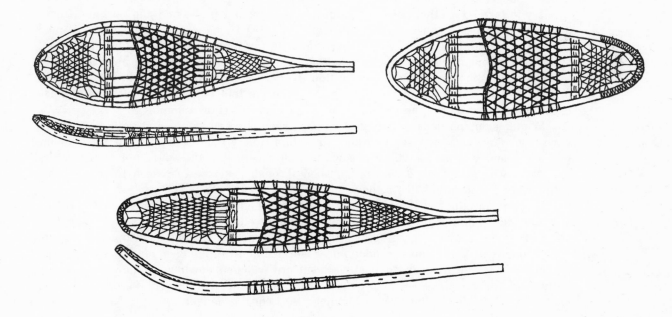

Types of Snowshoes
Top left: Maine. Top right: Bearpaw. Bottom: Pickerel.

The colder snowshoes are, the better they will support you. Warm webbing may sag. So keep your webs stored outside where it's colder. If porcupines are about, though, hang them out of reach since porkies have a hankering for rawhide and leather straps.

If the snow is not deep and you use boots, it's best to take it easy so as not to perspire while packing in. Peel down so that the exercise will keep you warm without sweating. Perspiration inside clothing can chill you badly, and in subzero weather, even dangerously. When resting, don a jacket to hold in body heat, but remove it when you move on. If snow is deep, the Maine type of rubber-and-leather shoepacs, also excellent for snowshoeing, are good. If you use skis, take along another pair of boots for camp use. Ski boots are too stiff and unyielding.

Never dry wet boots of any type too quickly or close by the fire. Even the upper realms of a heated tent, as mentioned before, can be too hot. Invert over stakes, perhaps, or fill with hot paper wads or warm pebbles, or let them dry naturally. Never oil or grease any sort of rubber. Work any kind of good grade of boot grease into the leather, on the other hand, paying special attention to seams. Incidentally, soles with a good tread are best on any type of boot and a real must in snow.

One of the handiest ways to pack gear into a winter camp is with a toboggan. If you can't get close with an automobile and chains, you'll either have to backpack the gear, use a snowmobile, or drag it behind you. A small toboggan is ideal, particularly if fitted with a simple wooden chest with a lid that can be fastened down. It holds gear together, keeps it dry, and makes a fine storage bin or woodbox in camp. The back of the chest is handy for pushing when you come to an upgrade. Use the top for a table.

Tie as many pull ropes to the front as there are campers. Knot a large loop in the end of each line so that you can pull with your shoulders and keep both hands free. An extra rope and loop affixed to the back of the toboggan will be handy as a brake when proceeding downgrade. Take it easy, and be especially careful not to be run over by a heavily loaded toboggan on a steep downgrade.

Try to take a tent that does not require a heavy metal frame and can be hung from a line between trees or on an easily fabricated wooden frame made on the spot. If much snow is expected, use a tent with a sharp pitch to the roof so that the load will slide off. Otherwise, too much weight might break the suspension lines. Stakes are hard to drive in frozen ground, but tent corners can be tied to trees or rocks or hitched to logs. If you're unable to do any of these, place heavy gear inside the tent corners to hold them out. The igloo-type tents requiring no guys or stakes are ideal for snow camping.

Winter camping does not require screened windows or doors, but your tent should have a sewn-in floor for insulation and protection from ground dampness. If the tent has no floor, a heavy tarpaulin will do almost as well except that the space between tarp and tent sides will permit some cold air to seep through. Very few modern tents are made without good waterproof floors, however.

If it has an attached floor, the tent can be pitched on the snow provided the bottom is waterproof. Snowshoes make fine shovels for leveling the tent area. If you can find adequate space in an evergreen grove, the snow will not be as deep as in open areas, and the needles will help keep the floor fairly warm. Before erecting a tent in such a spot, though, look to see if the branches overhead are weighed down with snow. If they are, better find another place—or shake the snow down before you level the ground. A heavy load of snow suddenly dumped on a canvas tent can be dangerous.

If you'd like to buy a tent that's especially good when the ground is frozen too hard for stake driving or there's snow on it, consider the types that need no stakes at all. These

**Using
Snowshoe
as
Shovel**

have built-in fiber glass or aluminum frames or are hung from external frames. Such tents have been used with great success in the Arctic, where staking is impossible.

If you have a tent that normally requires staking yet doesn't need a center pole—such as those hung from an overhead branch, suspended from a tripod, held erect with an internal frame as in the umbrella types, or kept upright with inflated air tubes—you can still use it. Cut four poles long enough so that you can nail, notch, or lash them into a rectangle to go around the outside base of the tent. Then tie the stake loops to this frame. If the tent has a sewn-in floor, you may prefer to arrange this frame inside, along the bottom of the walls where they join the floor. Either way will do a substantial job of anchoring the tent without stakes.

**Tent Anchored by
Rectangular Frame**

If there are likely to be high winds and your tent has stake loops, better try to stake it down if possible. Use steel stakes as they drive better into frozen ground. A well-pegged tent will ride out a considerable blow, so don't be stingy with the stakes if they can be used. If not, either utilize the frame-around-the-base idea, or tie down to low bushes, trees, or logs buried in packed-down snow. Carry extra rope for this.

If the ground is not level, it can be built up with snow or boughs. On the other hand, if it is perfectly level, maybe you should be suspicious. As a youngster, one of us found such a locality and built a fire for his lunch only to have it suddenly drop, frying pan and all, into a small pond.

A few boughs under a tent floor or tarp will prevent it from freezing to the ground and make it easier to take up when you break camp. Too, the canvas floor will be drier for packing out to the car.

For a stay of several days, it's a good idea to use a tent large enough for you and all your gear plus a small heater or tent stove. The smaller the tent the easier it will be to heat. On the other hand, don't use one so small that it would be unsafe to use a heater inside. A 2- or 3-man tent is easy to pack but is really too small for both men and heater. A larger tent, say one 9 by 9 feet, would be fine if several men were going along, and there'd be enough room for a small heater.

Open-front tents of the Whelen or Baker design can be heated with an open fire in front, especially if a reflector tarp is used behind the blaze, in the absence of a natural reflector, to beat back and help contain the heat. Just don't hang the reflector too near the fire. Open-front tents are easy to heat with wood fires, but they cool off quickly as the fire dies down. For really cold weather, especially if plenty of wood is not easily available, a closed tent with a heater inside is much better.

If you decide to use one of the wood- or charcoal-burning heaters, an opening in the tent must be provided for a stovepipe. One way is to buy an asbestos stovepipe hole which can be set into the wall or roof of the tent to handle such a pipe. The hole can be covered during warm weather with the piece of canvas you remove to make room for it.

Many tent heaters are fueled by propane, liquid petroleum, gas, alcohol, kerosene, and even gasoline. All heaters, including those burning wood and charcoal, must have adequate ventilation to offset the carbon monoxide they give off. This is all-important, always. At the very least, leave a window halfway open. Even a small lantern will do much to keep the chill off in a small tent.

Little or no danger is involved if a well-designed heater is used according to the manufacturer's directions. It's not a bad idea to keep the heater off the ground with a couple of sticks, split so that they will not roll. Also, keep it away from all walls and equipment and in a safe spot, too, so that in case of an accident everyone can get out the door without going past or over a flaming heater. To be fully prepared, buy a small pressure fire extinguisher that can be used and reused until empty. It will be handy for camp, car, or cabin and is inexpensive.

If your tent becomes plastered with snow, it will help to keep you warm. But remember that if a heater is used, the snow will melt and run down and may freeze along the bottom of the tent, making it difficult to strike camp when you are ready to leave. If this happens, don't try to chop the fabric loose. Instead, melt it with hot water. Incidentally, snow makes ventilation all the more necessary when you are using a heater.

In locating a tent, try to place it where there will be a minimum of wind. Put it under trees, in the lee of a ridge, or in a ravine, and you'll be warmer. If a sleet storm develops, keep an eye out for ice-laden branches overhead which may come down. A bank of snow, brush, evergreens, or a well-hung tarpaulin can do much to shelter your tent from the wind.

Food for winter camping is easy to take care of. If the weather is very cold, though, it is wise to cut meat into eatable portions before taking it to camp. This includes bacon, which may also be partly cooked beforehand. The slices, in either event, can be frozen separately and carried this way until needed, or buy some of the canned bacon.

Potatoes freeze into something resembling marble, so if you wish to pack along some of these, boil them until they are a bit on the hard side. Slice thinly and put out to freeze in individual pieces. Carry the frozen chips in a cotton food sack. They will go well heated in the fat from fried bacon.

Eggs will be hard to keep below freezing. If you take them, twist them individually in metal wrap so that if they freeze and crack, they'll still be together. You can peel a frozen egg just like a hard-boiled one, then either fry or poach it. Eggs keep well down to freezing if protected by papers or carried in a wide-mouthed vacuum jug.

Frozen bread will be fine. In fact, this is one way we keep it fresh in the Far North.

Canned goods may freeze solid in extreme weather, but they can still be used. Open the top as usual, and then split the can down the side with an old knife or sharp ax so the metal can be peeled away from the contents which can then be thawed in pot or pan.

If the snow is quite deep, you can sometimes keep food from freezing by placing it in a container and burying it in the snow. The temperature beneath the snow may be higher than it is in the air above. Just be sure to mark the location of such a cache with something such as a long stick so you can locate it the next morning even though heavy snow falls during the night.

The new freeze-dried foods are no problem inasmuch as no moisture remains in them to freeze. Of course, ordinary refrigerators work both ways in very cold surroundings. If foods are put into them warm, they will keep pretty well but will not freeze solid.

Remember that in cold weather everything you cook will seem hot long before it really is. Foods and drinks, barely warm, will steam. Be sure they're really hot before taking them from the fire. Foods cook more slowly in cold weather, but many kinds can be hurried by covering them with aluminum foil to keep the top hot while the underside is cooking. Don't set hot pans and dishes in the snow, as they'll melt down into it, perhaps tipping over. Put them on flat stones, level logs, or across two logs or sticks that are level.

When melting snow for drinking water, be sure you put in only a little at a time until some water forms in the bottom of the container. Otherwise, the receptacle may be damaged. Crust or ice, in that order, will give more water for the effort involved. If snow is soiled, scrape away the top layer and use the pure, white snow beneath. Use only clear, colorless ice for melting. Amber-colored ice may be safe enough, but it may have a weird flavor from sap, bark, or other impurities. Icicles from snow ridges, dead branches, and ledges are usually clear.

Sleeping in a snowbird camp can be just as comfortably warm as in a summer camp if you have a good sleeping bag. If the tent is heated, problems are even less. It is almost impossible to suggest a particular sleeping bag since everyone has a different tolerance for cold. Some can get along with a bag filled with two pounds of insulation, while others shiver in a four-pound bag wearing everything they have with them. But a four-pound bag plus regular clothes should provide enough warmth for almost anyone, especially if the tent is heated.

Insulation under you is just as important, if not more so, than covering over you. To be effective, this must be directly beneath you, something to remember if a cot or air mattress is used.

Whether to sleep in or out of your clothes is a subject for argument among campers. Why not try it both ways and decide for yourself? To be scientific about it, because of the way an unimpeded bag breathes and rids itself of body moisture, you'll be most comfortable sleeping in a warm enough bag with no more than skivvies on.

Keep your tent's interior as dry as possible. Wipe your boots clean on a scrap of old rug, boughs, or a burlap bag before you enter. Brush clothing as free as possible of snow to keep it dry, for if the tent is warm, any snow will melt and make your clothes damp. An extra piece of material or plastic over the tent floor will help keep it dry.

A fly pitched over the entrance will enable you to shake off a heavy layer of snow before going inside, even when snow is falling. Keep heavy snow off such a fly, as well as off the tent roof. Snow banked about the lower part of a tent is good, on the other hand, as it will keep the interior warmer.

When heating an open-front tent with an open fire, you can save time in the morning by banking it well before turning in, unless, of course, you plan to keep it going all night. To bank a fire, merely cover the live coals with ashes. In the morning, just scrape away the ashes, add some light fuel, and you're in business. Get a little snow on your outfit. You'll both enjoy it.

You're apt to do your cooking on a stove. Stoves are convenient, highly efficient, and their use saves scrounging around under the snow for firewood at odd hours. There are several combination stove-heaters which are especially handy for winter camping.

Snowbird camping is a fine challenge for those who have never tried it, and we can recommend it wholeheartedly as an interesting change from summer camping.

22

Camping
on Rock and Sand

WHEN YOU TAKE TO THE WILDERNESS, PERHAPS YOU'LL RIDE OR HIKE up from the burning plains to where a canyon's rising tangents lift into broken masses of ravine and butte and the deep green sweeps of pine, to camp far up where peaks rear their stony shoulders. Or perhaps you'll pitch a tent on sand, either where deserts spill their tawny flatness across the earth or below the smoky heat haze of a beach. Camping on such rocky or sandy terrain is not the easiest pastime, but it offers unique pleasures if you go about it with the proper know-how and the correct equipment.

The coolness and isolation of a mountain can be a wonderful place to camp, so long as a few simple facts are borne in mind. For a backpacking camper, an outfit naturally should be as light as possible. Those who camp alone or with one other outdoorsman may not care to bother with a tent.

It is strongly suggested, however, that you carry at least a lightweight tarpaulin to shelter the sleeping bags when clouds sweep damply about and to provide shade in exposed areas. However, just a sheet of transparent plastic suspended over your camping bags will help to keep them dry. A poncho will serve as both raingear and as a cover for the other equipment. An extra poncho, which need weigh only a few ounces, is a handy thing to have about such a camp in case of heavy rain.

If you're thinking of camping on the summit of a high mountain, try to pitch your tent a bit below the exposed peak on the side away from the prevailing winds. Above the sheltering treeline, try to find a reasonably flat place among the rocks where there is at least two-sided protection for your sleeping bags or small tent.

It's especially unwise to make camp on an exposed mountaintop in regions where thunderstorms are common. You'd be an invitation to lightning. For the same reason, don't set up near lone trees or a fire tower. They're often struck during such a storm.

If high winds are common in the area, tie your tent down in every way possible. On a rocky mountaintop it's often impossible to stake down a tent in the usual way, but you may be able to tie it to bushes, clumps of vegetation, or small boulders. Failing that, drive a stake in a ledge crack and rope off to that, or jam the guys into such cracks, or use heavy slabs to weigh down the tent corners.

Ideal Tentsite for Mountain Camping Should Have Shelter from Wind

**Stakes Driven into
Ledge Cracks**
(Note: Steel stakes are
best for this trick.)

A mountain tent, desirable for its lightness, is generally small, making it comparatively easy to erect. Several types of such tents are supported by inside or outside frames of fiber glass rods, which can be carried with little difficulty. These tents can be lifted about even when fully pitched and make ideal shelters where staking is difficult. However, if you can lift such a tent, so can a strong wind. Flat rocks inside, or outside on the corners, may solve the problem.

If a bad storm is on the way, it may be advisable to drop your tent flat to save it from possible wind damage. It's amazing, however, how a well-pitched tent can ride out a gale with little if any damage. We've both camped extensively in the windy White Mountains, including the upper slopes of Mount Washington, where some of the fastest winds ever clocked have been recorded. Even here, a small tent, pitched low to the ground and anchored solidly, will ride out all but the highest gales.

Cooking at high altitudes is not much different from cooking in the valleys, although in such rarefied chill a small campfire will feel even more welcome as it strikes up a responding flash in your eyes. At higher altitudes, however, water must boil longer to cook properly. This is because liquid, as a result of reduced atmospheric pressure, boils

128

at lower and lower temperatures as altitude increases. Your stove, if, as is very possible above treeline, you're using one, may need more air, but most modern stoves have adjustments for this.

Keep campfires small and sheltered from high winds. Gusts have a habit of blowing sparks that can lodge in ledge cracks and start a blaze after you've left. Mountain gusts can be astonishingly strong. When one of us was camped on Panther Mountain in New York State, such a gust actually blew the beans out of the frypan, then tipped over the coffeepot and put out the fire. Much the same thing happened to the other one of us on Mt. Selwyn in the Canadian Rockies, where, because of the turmoil, we'd built a small trench fire.

Fuel may be difficult to locate above timberline, but look about the ledges or between the rocks where wind-strewn branches from below may have lodged. Too, there is dried brush and vegetation. Any live trees found near the peak of a mountain, if you're allowed to cut them, may be tough to chop because of their stunted, twisted grain. It's better to scout around for fallen dead stuff. This, too, may be hard to sever. Probably the best bet is to try breaking it by jamming one edge into a crack and putting your weight on the other end.

There are many tiny lightweight gasoline and alcohol stoves that, weighing but ounces, are easy to carry, and which above treeline and in wet weather are worth their extra weight. You can even buy pocket stoves that weigh only a few ounces and do a fine job of cooking for several pennies' worth of fuel.

When taking to the mountains, be sure your sleeping bag will keep you warm down close to freezing temperatures. Even in summer, mountain nights can be mighty chilly. A short air mattress will be well worth its weight if you sleep on sandy or rocky soil. Even an inexpensive beach float of plastic will be of great value under the bag even if it supports you only down to the knees. Longer mattresses are more comfortable, but this must be balanced against the weight they put on sagging shoulders. Many camping-goods dealers carry short mattresses especially for mountain campers, and they are obtainable by mail from one of the big catalog-issuing concerns.

Every summer you read of inexperienced hikers and campers who are caught on a summit or high trail by sudden cold, sleet, or snow. This often results in rescuers being called out at great personal risk. So even if you feel positive that the skies will remain clear, carry adequate clothing for cold weather and at least a lightweight tarpaulin for emergency shelter. The experienced mountaineer watches the weather continually and is seldom caught unready. To venture into high country unprepared is not only a mark of the rankest greenhorn, but it's downright dangerous.

On such a camping trip, unless you're an old-timer bent on exploring or perhaps prospecting, stick to marked trails as much as possible. The walking will be easier. There will be a better chance of finding water, shelter, and emergency help. And you'll run little risk of getting lost.

Do not camp on, near, or under what might be a slide area—slopes of loose rock slabs or round stones that could easily start dusting downgrade. Such traps can be especially perilous during a thaw or prolonged rain.

Keep your pack light, rest often while climbing and descending, and mountain camping will be an exciting adventure. The clear air, the pulsating immensities, and the smoldering solitude of the sunrise alone are worth the effort.

Those who partake of desert camping will find it an engrossing challenge. You'll discover a multitude of new sights and sounds, as well as a few special problems. For example, staking a tent may present a fresh hurdle. The ground may be too soft to hold ordinary stakes securely. If the sand is really fine, anchor shields may be needed on your stakes. These are broad metal disks that slip over metal and plastic stakes to present a wider surface to the ground, thus reducing the proclivity of a stake to pull loose.

If you don't care to buy shields, try longer stakes. Or hitch the guy ropes to logs or crossed sticks buried in the sand. Some campers on desert and beach have found that cheap tin plates make good anchors. Just punch a hole in the center of the plate, run a rope through, anchor it with a large knot or a cross stick, and then bury the plate a foot

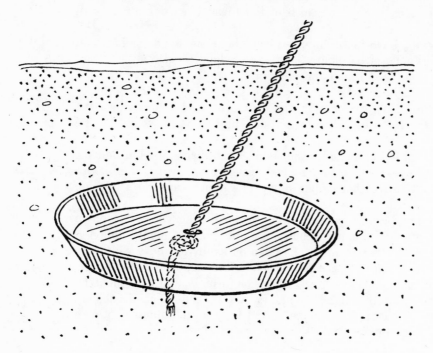

**Tent Anchor Made
from Tin Plate
Buried in Ground**

or so beneath the sand. If your tent guys have slides, it will be wise to rig each plate with a short piece of rope and a hook to catch the loop that's normally thrown around a peg. A practical substitute for a tin-plate anchor is a short length of wide board having a hole in the middle. When camping in the desert, even close to the civilized bustle of a highway, do not make the mistake of pitching your tent on the luringly level bottom of a dry gulch or riverbed. A faraway storm, of which you may not even be aware, can send a flash flood roaring down such a declivity with hardly a moment's warning, sweeping everything in front of it. Just keep to high ground and you'll be safe, but make certain that the area is on the same side of the gulch or dry river as your car is parked. High ground will afford a better possibility of an energizing breeze, too. But beware of high winds that may mean sand and dust storms.

In sandy country all such precision equipment as cameras, firearms, and binoculars should be kept in their cases when not in use. A sudden whirlwind or dust devil may spring up to fill your tent with swirling clouds of abrasive clutter. This can penetrate all but the tightest cases. A tarpaulin thrown over such gear when a dust cloud approaches may be of some help. If your car is nearby, this equipment will be safe inside with the windows rolled up tight.

There may be plenty of fuel in desert country. Sagebrush builds a hot fire, and there may be other kinds of dry growth about your site. Dried cattle refuse, akin to the buffalo chips of the pioneers, makes a low hot fire. When poking about low brush, though, keep your eyes alert. It's unlikely, but you might spot a lizard or snake.

One feminine reader of our books recently wrote to ask if the old story is true that a horsehair rope around your bed will keep rattlers away. A snake will slither over such a rope as readily as over a rope made of hemp, nylon, or ermine. The best defense against snakes is to avoid known snake country and to use a tight tent with a sewn-in floor; that or sleep in a car or station wagon.

Of far greater potential peril to desert campers, though, is scarcity of water. Keep to well-known roads or trails, and never enter desert country without plenty of water, far more than it seems likely you'll ever need. Never wander off into the open desert without ample water and a compass, and then only if you've had considerable desert experience. The wind-rippled sands can be dangerous. Be careful of any water you find, incidentally, even if it's fresh, unless you treat it with halazone or the newer Globaline tablets (see Chapter 32).

Don't be misled by hot days. The chill of desert nights can cut through to your bones. Have warm duds along for donning after sundown. An eiderdown jacket or woolen sweater will be most welcome, and your sleeping bag should be heavy enough to keep you warm down around the forties or lower.

Camping in the desert can be thrilling for those who are prepared. One of us tried it for a few nights and moved out there to live for awhile. Just keep to the roads, until you know your way around, camp on high ground away from the hazards of flash floods, and have plenty of water along. You'll get a bounce out of desert camping, even without meeting up with that snake you're sure you'll see.

Beach camping is one of our favorite kinds of outdoor living, too, and there's often the bonus of water sports and fishing. Nearly always there is a fine breeze to discourage the winged biters. All in all, a beach is an ideal camping spot, whether along salt or fresh water. Such a spot, incidentally, generally abounds with wild edibles for those interested in such bounties.

A shoreline will offer either sandy or rocky soil for pitching a tent, so you can use some of the tips already considered for staking a tent on mountain or desert. Just be sure that the tent is well staked down. Sudden squalls can blow in from the sea or lake to test your tent-pitching ability.

If your shelter faces the shore, a squall may drive in through the door and really give the canvas a workout. Many beach campers face the door away from the shore, or at right angles to it, especially if the tent is pitched on an unsheltered height. Others prefer their tents back from the beach in the shelter of trees or dunes.

When camping along a tidal beach, be sure to pitch your tent well above the high-water mark. And if you choose a site on a point, with low land between you and the road, keep an eye out for extra-high tides that might cut you off.

Check metal equipment regularly for signs of rust and corrosion from damp salt air. Keep such belongings as camera, guns, and tools in cases when they're not in use. A light coating of rust inhibitor, oil, or light grease will protect metal against all but the worst conditions. In an exceptionally damp area, check leather goods for signs of mildew and air them frequently in the hot sun.

For beach campfires, there will likely be plenty of driftwood. This burns magnificently and often with unexpected colors from the salts impregnated in the wood. Of course, in the improbable instance that no driftwood can be found, a camp stove can always be used for cooking.

If you are the adventurous type and would like to camp along the beach by yourself, that's fine. But be careful when driving. Sandy beaches can swiftly bog down a car unless it's equipped with extralarge tires and is lightly loaded.

If you do get stuck in the sand, don't spin the wheels. This will only get you in deeper. The correct procedure is to dig sand from behind the wheels, prior to backing out, and slope it up to level again. Fill in the troughs with grass, leaves, sticks, or small stones— anything to give traction and to prevent the car's sinking in deeper. Use boards if you can find them, or driftwood, and then start backing slowly. You may have to let some of the air out of the tires to present a wider area of rubber to the sand.

Habitual beach drivers carry pieces of plywood, old sacks, and assorted other items to use for traction if they get stuck. Beware of driving onto a beach at low tide. You may become mired and an easy target for the next incoming tide.

Try mountain, desert, or beach camping for a change. It will be enjoyable and perhaps exciting. It's not a bad idea to talk first with others who've camped on rock and sand, and you may want to write to the conservation or recreation commissions of states in which you'd like to try these kinds of wilderness living. Who knows? You may find that taking to the woods in this fashion will be your favorite camping adventure from now on.

PART THREE
LEARNING THE TRICKS
OF THE CAMPING CRAFT

23

That First Night
in Camp

AFTER YOU HAVE TAKEN TO THE WOODS FOR THAT FIRST DAY, YOU want to rest. Anything that remains between yourself and that repose you disencumber yourself of as swiftly and as easily as possible. The ends in view are a relaxing meal and a dry, comfortable place to sleep. The straighter the line is to those two points, the happier you'll be.

The first night of any camping trip can be one of the most memorable experiences if you'll do a bit of planning beforehand. Advance preparations, in other words, can make all the difference between a pleasant, bracing milestone in your life and a miserable prelude to the morning after. Here are a few suggestions whose adoption should make that first night in the woods an event which will leave you yearning for more.

First, you'll need some sort of protection from the elements. The choice of a tent, sleeping bag, or blankets from home will depend on your preference and pocketbook. However, you should have the protection of shelter of some sort, even in warm weather. You'll likely wish to start camping with a tent, but even without one, camping will be almost as enjoyable as long as the weather holds warm and clear.

If you stop over at a public campsite, level spots will already have been arranged, and there will be water. Either there will be wood for a campfire, or you'll be required to use a camp stove.

When not staying at a public camp, pick the tent or bed area with considerable care, for you'll get to know it intimately during the night. Clear the ground of all sticks, rocks, loose debris, and protruding roots. Smooth it as much as possible with the side of your boot sole or with a flat stick. Even if the tent you'll be using has a floor, the ground beneath should be leveled to make walking about easier and to protect the fabric. If the terrain slants, place the head of your bed at the highest part.

An air mattress will do away with concern about uneven ground, but check for anything sharp beneath it such as pointed sticks or jagged stones. For added comfort, don't pump your mattress too full of air. Just enough to let you barely feel the ground when you're lying on your side will be fine.

If you have no pneumatic mattress, cover the bed area with fresh boughs, leaves, conifer needles, wild hay, or any other native soft material. Use plenty, for it will pack down during the night. Spread a moistureproof tarp, shower curtain, or piece of plastic over the ground cover before putting down your sleeping bag or blankets. This will keep out ground dampness, make your sleep warmer, and serve to keep your bedding clean.

In the absence of an air mattress, some outdoorsmen advocate scooping depressions in the ground for hips and shoulders. These hip holes sound fine, but in reality they are not too comfortable, just better. Besides, you're moving all night, anyway. It will be more restful just to use more padding over the entire bed area.

Sleeping Bag Cushioned by Conifer Boughs

If weight and bulk are no problem, camp cots in addition to sleeping bags and air mattresses are well worth the trouble. A small air pillow is another little extra that pays off in extra rest.

Summer camping without tents can mean mosquito problems. If these whining biters bother you as much as they do most, you'll require some extra protection at night. You can either use plenty of dope on face, neck, hands, and wrists, probably rousing at least once during the night to replenish it, or thwart them with netting. Most find such a mosquito bar preferable, even indoors on occasion, unless they are in a tight tent with adequately screened door and windows.

An effective mosquito defense for tentless sleeping can be fashioned from a few yards of preferably black or other dark mosquito netting. Dark, rather than light, netting is suggested for two reasons. It's easier to see through from the inside. The darker colors attract fewer insects than, for example, white.

Use the finest net you can find, and sew it into a sort of pup-tent shape long enough to drape loosely over the bed once it is in place. Hang this canopy over your bed, using something such as a tripod or two of light sticks or string suspended from overhead branches. Too, mosquito bars as such can be purchased from some outfitters.

Be sure there is ample netting to cover your hands and shoulders so that they won't rest against it during the night. If they do, every blood-imbibing insect in the woods will seem to find that spot, and you'll be miserable. To be doubly safe, use dope on at least your hands. If you have a bug spray, use that on the canopy to help keep the whiners away and to eradicate that one insect that always seems to get inside the net.

If you are sleeping without a tent, it is a sound idea to pick the site with an eye to some sort of protection overhead in case of an unexpected shower. But beware of camping under a lone tree with thunderstorms in the offing.

Half the fun of an overnight camp, no matter what the season, is a small cheery blaze that is kept flickering as long as possible. If you've never done it before, you'll be amazed at how much wood can burn between turn-in time and that first steaming cup of

coffee the next morning. If the fire is kindled against a ledge, it will not only reflect better, but it will burn slower than if in the open where oxygen can reach the fuel from all sides. Don't build a fire against a down log, for you may find it difficult to extinguish.

If you are out where the weather is apt to turn frosty, leave some of your all-night logs long enough so that you can just hunch up in bed and shove them further into the fire as they burn down. A stout forked stick will extend your reach.

Keep any all-night fire small. The more conservative the blaze, the nearer you'll be able to sleep to it safely, and the less fuel it will consume. Some dry kindling is a good thing to keep handy during the night in case some more light is needed in a hurry, as in the case of four-footed prowlers. Too, it can enable you to enjoy coffee and hot cereal in bed if you have everything ready. Pile this kindling under cover to keep off the dew.

When you're ready to crawl between the covers, the most relaxing procedure is to clean up and put on fresh dry shorts, long underwear, or pajamas. Some individuals consider the latter a luxury, but if weight is no problem, they're worth taking along for the extra rest they'll assure you.

If you don't change clothes, at least remove your trousers. A functional place for them, after pockets have been emptied, is under the sleeping bag or blankets where they'll both stay dry and provide additional insulation from ground cold and dampness. Keep your shirt on if you like, after first removing the contents of the pockets, but of course take off footwear. A pair of dry woolen socks will keep your feet warm if the night is chilly.

Our wives, both enthusiastic campers, both recommend pajamas as night wear for the ladies, and they suggest slacks for camp comfort.

There may be some very cold nights when you'll elect to sleep in your trousers. Then loosen your belt, empty the pockets, and keep the legs down where they belong by tucking them inside your socks, perhaps adding rubber bands around your ankles just above where the trousers end.

Place your boots, shoes, or moccasins in a sheltered place. If you decide to keep pocket items in them, set them under a corner of the ground cloth or sleeping bag corner. Transparent plastic bags also make excellent storage places. If your boots are empty all night and on the ground, shake them out in the morning before you put either your hand or foot into them. Over the years campers have shaken quite an assortment of livestock out of theirs, including scorpions, mice, and even foraging packrats.

Each member of the party should have his own flashlight, loaded with fresh batteries. If you're going to be in camp more than a few days, take along some extra batteries. You'll be surprised at how much you'll use a flashlight in the dark out of doors, although you can preserve the power to a large extent by utilizing the lights only in short spurts.

If you have rifles or shotguns with you, keep them covered at night because of dampness. Put them in scabbards, plastic cases, or under a tarp or other cover. A good place for a rifle in game country is lengthwise between the outside edges of your air mattress and sleeping bag. Be sure the weapons are unloaded, although if you're alone deep in a hunting area where a trophy may walk through camp at any time, you may elect just to empty the barrel and to keep the magazine filled. The same goes for handguns, and when at a public campsite, check local regulations regarding firearms. They are prohibited in many public camping areas.

Axes and hunting knives may be kept handy. However, make sure they are sheathed or covered, not only for safety but for protection against the night's dampness.

If the night is cold, you can warm your sleeping bag or blankets ahead of time by turning them inside out and spreading them in the heat from the campfire. You can also place clean, warm stones inside, especially down where your feet will be. Don't heat the stones too hot, though, or they may damage the material. Those little lighter-fluid hand-warmers will do a great deal to warm up your sleeping gear, and they can be left in all night if it's really nippy. A close-fitting knitted toque on your head is good if it's really cold. Strangely enough, it will help you to keep warm feet.

Numerous campers prefer sleeping in a tent, but those who choose not to invest in one right away can do very well under the stars, and it's often a lot more interesting, especially if the night is clear—a good argument for an open-faced shelter, such as a Baker tent, later on. Try counting the shooting stars before you're lulled off to sleep, and watch for nightbirds and flying squirrels.

A faint, pervasive forest perfume of dampness greets your nostrils. The forces of the world seem to be in suspense. Then an owl who-ho-hoos. A whippoorwill cries, like a moonbeam turned to silver. In the following silence, there is no stillness at all.

A twig snaps beneath the cautious feet of some night creature—deer, field mouse, skunk, raccoon, or porcupine. Or this time maybe it's just a falling cone. Before turning in for the night, it's always a good idea to store food in the car, knapsack, or in a net bag hung high in a tree. This is good insurance against prowlers. If you're really in the wilderness, or much more likely in one of the great national parks, you may actually hear a bear, but if your food is out of the way, don't worry about it.

The first night in camp will be an interesting one, and you may be surprised at how long and pleasantly it'll last. After you've been in bed for what may seem like hours, you may awaken to find it's not yet midnight, and the fire has burned to chilly embers. You shove the ends of the logs well into them and watch the flames licking up. A night wind is blowing across your face, and you snuggle deeper within the welcome warmth of your sleeping bag. Instantly, it is morning.

Keeping a vacuum bottle or canteen of drinking water handy by the bed is a good idea, especially if there are youngsters in the party. Or you may want it to keep the mouth from getting too dry in high altitudes. If you like, have it full of coffee for a quick pickup before bacon and eggs are sputtering.

Have fun your first night in camp. Plan it well, and you'll be back for many more. And the next day you'll be refreshed, clear-headed, and there will be a spring in your step.

24

Those One-Night Stands

THERE ARE TIMES WHEN YOU CAN TAKE TO THE WOODS ONLY ONE night at a time. Done right, such excursions into the wilderness can be very much worthwhile in addition to being definite moneysavers. But you have to go at them right.

A couple of years ago, as one of us relaxed with his wife after supper in a wilderness campground in Canada, a load of campers drove up to the next site. We assumed from their actions that they were going to stay for at least a week.

Members of the party unloaded a tent big enough for a small revival meeting and enough outdoor gear for an entire Boy Scout troop. With the aid of flashlights, not having a camp lantern, and with much stake whacking and pole rattling, they finally got the tent up, after vociferous arguments about where to locate it and how to erect it.

We lounged and watched, amused and amazed, as the men split gigantic piles of firewood and the women started to ready supper over an open fire. The usually prevailing wind wasn't blowing, so one of the men rebuilt the site's stone fireplace so as to get a better draft.

It was well beyond midnight by the time this group's supper was cooked and the dishes washed. By that time not only our noisy neighbors, but also the rest of the campers in the area, were fed up with the woodchopping and clatter. Eventually the chopping stopped, and the group finally took to their sleeping bags. But not for long, unfortunately.

The sky was just quickening in the east when this inept bunch started hacking away at more wood for the breakfast fire, kicking pegs loose, and tossing tent-frame sections into the car's trunk. Eventually, the party had breakfast and drove off, no doubt planning to go through the whole dusk-to-midnight performance again.

The following night at about the same time, another car drove up, and two couples got out. We groaned, anticipating another sleepless evening and early morning.

The two men pitched a compact tent and inflated the air mattresses. The women lighted the stove and started supper. The campers together unloaded a compact camp kitchen and struck a match to a good lantern.

After the meal one of the men unloaded a half-dozen split logs from the well of the station wagon and started a fine, little campfire. The women gathered up the supper dishes and heated water in which to wash them. It wasn't more than an hour from when these campers arrived to the time they had everything put away and were enjoying the flickering flames and the night sounds.

The two couples turned in early, and when we opened our eyes the next morning they were gone—tent, wagon, bag, and baggage. We surely wished them a pleasant trip, which they doubtless had, for they knew just how to make travel-camping a pleasure for themselves and for everyone near them.

Many a would-be camper-tourist, after considering the problems involved and perhaps assaying such camping once or twice, has come to the conclusion that it is more bother than it's worth. However, with a bit of forethought and imagination, plus the right equipment, you can make these one-night stands comfortable, pleasant, and emphatically economical. Here are a few suggestions that can replace the franticness with fun.

The major thing is to make certain that pitching and striking camp will be rapid and simple. Your planning should include the erecting of some sort of shelter either to sleep in or, if you plan to bed down in the vehicle, for protection of gear. Other points to be weighed include the cooking of meals, the cleaning up afterwards, and those quick getaways from camp in the morning.

These activities can be facilitated by selecting compact, well-designed equipment of the ideal size for your purposes, packing intelligently, and, finally, assigning chores to be carried out individually by each member of the party.

The tent should be of a type that is compact and yet big enough for the party it must accommodate, and it should take a minimum of frame assembly and guying. Small two-man tents are fine for one-nighters, as are some of the larger models that can be put up quickly.

Those easily erected igloo-shaped tents are ideal for travel campers. They come in sizes that vary from a small two-man affair up to one that is spacious enough for the entire family. The smallest model is ideal for the storage of displaced baggage outside the car.

When we use one of those igloo-shaped tents, we don't bother to take apart the sectional fiber glass ribs when we strike camp. We just release the top unit so that the tent ribs collapse. Then we stow the tent, with the ribs still assembled, in our station wagon.

The new inflatable one-man tents, supported by an air rib over the entrance and held forward by a rib tied to a stake or a tree or such, can be pitched within minutes. Many other mountain-type and backpacker tents are also excellent for one-night stands.

If you expect to sleep in your sedan or station wagon, as numerous campers do, a quantity of luggage and other gear that must be removed from the car will need protection by some sort of a tent or tarpaulin. A handy way to protect such duffle is by piling it on a picnic table and then roping a tarp over it.

Some travel-campers pack the luggage under a table for added protection. Others transfer it to one of those play tents designed for backyard campers. Such tents, if really waterproof, are excellent for this purpose and can be purchased for just a few dollars.

If you're sleeping in the car and desire ventilation without bugs, screen your windows. It's actually simple. Try using 3 by 3-foot squares of fine screening material, preferably some such color as dark green or black for better looking out. Drape the netting over the outside of the open car door. Fold the top of the material over the top of the door so that it will be held fast when the door is closed. Tape the bottom of the material to the door below the window.

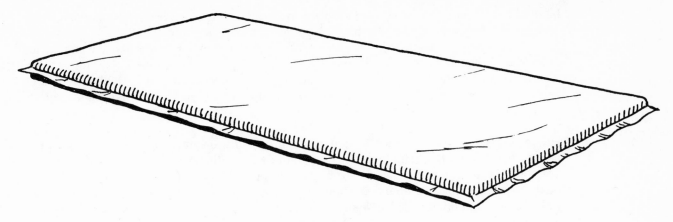

Foam-Plastic Mattress

By utilizing a foam-plastic mattress, you can save the time you'd otherwise spend in inflating an air mattress. These foam mattresses do the job in either car or tent. If you prefer air mattresses, however, why not either buy a small electric pump that will inflate them while you go about other chores or, especially if you are traveling light and have plenty of time, leave them inflated throughout your vacation?

One additional advantage of traveling in a station wagon is that its tailgate can serve as a work table, dining table, or camp-stove stand. If you are using a sedan and plan to stop where there won't be picnic tables, stow a small folding table and enough camp stools or folding chairs in the roof rack.

A small bright campfire seems to strike deep at the heart of adventure. Color, mystery, and the vastnesses of unexplored forests are there in the flickering flames, symbolized compactly for the nourishment of the imagination. Nearly every camper likes to cook over, lounge around, and wonder at a campfire. But for quick-stop cooking, the fact remains that you can't beat a small two-burner stove. Even a compact one-burner can speed the evening meal and breakfast coffee, and it can do away with the often difficult chore of locating firewood after dark.

A stove is almost a must for the traveling camper, since open fires are illegal in some areas at all times and in other regions under fire-hazard conditions occasionally. Nevertheless, if you'll be stopping when and where open fires are permissible, you might take along at least a few dry sticks so that you can have that campfire with a minimum of scrounging. A handy practice is packing along a few sticks of really dry, split kindling in a paper bag, which may be used as a unit to start a blaze.

There is a special angle to all this, however, that you may care to consider. The oftener you take to the woods, the more it will become evident that the ability to build a campfire under any and all conditions may one day mean survival itself. For this reason, we recommend that you get all possible practice in building campfires along the way, without paper and other manufactured starters.

The problem is getting them going, and this is more satisfactory when you use natural rather than man-made materials. If you have dry kindling, there's nothing difficult about it. Just take your knife and make three or four fuzz sticks by shaving the preferably straight-grained sticks again and again, not detaching any of the thin, curling strips. If there are softwoods nearby, you needn't even go to that much trouble. A small compact handful of resinous dead twigs found in the bottoms of all conifers will quickly start your blaze with, if you've practiced a bit, seldom more than one match.

You may find it reassuring to carry an adequate supply of pure drinking water. Some roadside campsites have picnic tables and even a privy, but few have any water supply. A vacuum jug of the 1-gallon size is handy. On the market, too, is a folding plastic 5-gallon carrier with a spout that'll keep a good supply of water handy for drinking, washing and fire extinguishing.

Never take a chance with any untested water near your camp. You can seldom be sure that lake or stream water is free of impurities. If you have to use such water, boil it hard for at least five minutes at sea level and an additional minute for each additional 1,000 feet of elevation. Or use halazone tablets or other water purifiers. If you're south of the border, iodine water purification tablets, available in drugstores, are a good idea, as chlorine is not effective against all the germs found in Mexico and elsewhere in southern areas.

If you expect to prepare most of your meals while on the road, a compact camp kitchen will be a great help. In one container, perhaps a plywood box made for the purpose, you can stow plates, cooking utensils, and even some food. This container can be moved quickly and easily to a table, to a wagon's tailgate, or to a folding stand. There's nothing to prevent your having the ingredients for a quick lunch in a separate bag, either.

Meals can be further speeded by using some of the many varieties of instant coffee, tea, cocoa, and fruit drinks, as well as the dry and the instant hot cereals. If you tote along a small icebox, you can have a bracing variety of sandwich spreads ready for quick snacks. Many experienced traveling campers have their big meal at midday, often at a restaurant, and then enjoy rapidly assembled suppers of soups, canned stews, sandwiches, and the like. If you'd like to get a really quick start in the morning, brew a large pot of coffee the night before and keep it steaming hot in a vacuum container near your sleeping bag.

Plan your route so that it leads past as many campgrounds as possible, and try to reach each night's destination before darkness sets in. The earlier you stop, the better will be the chances of finding a site and getting set up before dark. The various state and provincial guidebooks and maps, all free for the asking at the government travel bureaus in the respective capital cities, will help you to plan your trip.

If you'll be journeying in a region having only a few designated campgrounds, it will be a good idea to start looking for an overnight spot by the middle of the afternoon at the latest. Pick a location that's off the road and away from low and swampy land. The location should have some sort of a windbreak such as a grove, a hillside, or a picturesque ledge.

Never camp in the dry bed of a river or brook, particularly in open country. A flash flood might swamp you during the night in such a spot, even if the storm that caused it was miles away. Some find it advantageous to check with local inhabitants about possible floods and other hazards, fire regulations, and potential camping spots.

It seems a shame to have to mention this, but it would be wise for you to keep all your valuables in a safe place. Such items as binoculars, radios, cameras, and firearms have been known to disappear right off a picnic table while the owners were sleeping only a few feet away. Lock such possessions in your car or luggage, or, if you are tenting, hide them out of sight in the tent.

When you move out of your camp after breakfast, make sure that you have repacked everything. Check the ground, picnic table and benches, nearby rocks, and the area where you pitched your tent. Look under the car, too. If you've enjoyed a campfire, make certain it is dead out no matter if you built it in a fireplace rather than on the mineral earth. Soak the ashes, stir them, and then soak again.

All you actually need for a bountiful travel-camping trip are the urge to go, a bit of planning, a little cooperation from the rest of the clan, and an outfit tailored to the proposition of pitching and striking camp with a minimum of motion. Too, practice makes perfect. After a few nights on the road, with adequate equipment, you'll be able to set up a comfortable camp in no more time than you'd need to check into a motel and get your bags unpacked. Best of all, think of the room and board money saved.

25

Campsite Layout

A FEW YEARS AGO, WHILE CAMPING IN UPSTATE NEW YORK, WE WERE awakened in the middle of the night by the racket of a car starting by a tent site nearby. The headlights shone back and forth and this way and that. The driver just couldn't seem to get the automobile out of where it was parked. Finally, he stopped the engine and turned off the lights.

The next morning we went over to see what had been the trouble. The camper, who had arrived after dark, had parked his station wagon where he could easily unload it from the tailgate and then pitched his tent behind it, figuring to drive out another way. In the darkness of early morning his youngster had developed a stomachache, and the father had decided to drive to town for a doctor. But in spite of all the maneuvering we'd seen, he couldn't move his car without taking down the tent. Fortunately, the stomachache departed amid all the confusion, but it could have been serious.

Another time, in Nova Scotia, we glimpsed a sudden big blaze from a nearby tent site. It turned out that the chap had stacked a fine big pile of dry kindling close to his fire ring so as to have it handy. The wind shifted suddenly, as it does in the Maritimes, and he found the kindling was too handy to the fire.

Over a lot of miles and years of camping, we've come across some camp arrangements and layouts that caused considerable inconvenience, and others that were outright dangerous to campers and their outfits. A handful of suggestions about laying out your camp may make it safer and additionally convenient for the entire family.

Upon arriving at the tent site, park the automobile where it can be driven out without your having to move tents, flies, guy ropes, or equipment. You'd be surprised how many times this precaution is neglected, even by experienced campers. It's a good idea to turn the car around so that you can easily unload from trunk or tailgate, then easily drive out if need be. The location of the car can also afford some protection and privacy.

No matter where you take to the woods, never park so that you block a road, even though it's a woods road that seems to be seldom used. Check first for solid ground. Then back off the road, facing it but not blocking it. Many backwoods roads are used by fire patrols, game wardens, and other outdoorsmen. Blocking such a thoroughfare can be not only inconsiderate but dangerous.

Before starting to put up your tent, scan the site carefully. Even a brief survey can save a lot of inconvenience later. Turning your tent a trifle one way or the other will often do much to make the whole site better for your purposes. If you have extra flies, a screened dining canopy, tents for the youngsters, and such, give some advance thought to where they'll be most convenient.

If you have the type of tent that attaches to the back of a station wagon, enabling you to go from wagon to tent under cover, don't tie any unnecessary or tricky knots when joining them. Knots can tighten, especially in damp weather, and turn out to be frustrating when you want to get them loose in a hurry. A small stick inserted in each knot while tying it, then left there, will help you untie it even when everything is dripping wet. Just pull out the stick or break it at the knot, and the resulting slack will make everything easy to undo.

Campers who like to sleep in a wagon bed should try to park their automobiles as level as possible. A slight slant downhill from head to foot can be tolerated. If your head is much lower than your feet, however, you'll have a rough night. If the wagon tilts sideways, you'll be fighting gravity from the moment you turn in.

A car not used as part of the camp itself should be turned so that it faces out of camp, parked where it will be convenient for storing things, and locked when you're away. Cache an extra set of keys nearby.

If it is possible, pitch your tent so that it will stand in the shade at least part of the day. The ideal arrangement is to wake up to the stimulation of rising sun and scenery, then to have the sun for several hours to dry off dew, condensation, and any night rain. Shade is appreciated when the afternoon sun is hot. In any event, do the best you can with the shade available. And keep an eye out for trees that lean dangerously, are dead, or which have broken or drooping branches that might fall into the campsite.

No matter what sort of tent you're using, be wary of hitching your guy ropes to branches or young trees that might whip around in a high wind. Once during a line squall, we saw a small pyramid tent that was suspended from a leafy overhead branch lifted right off the ground with all the gear inside.

The tent will be the center of your camping home in all likelihood. The rest of the units—fireplace, dining area, woodpile, and waste-disposal areas—should be arranged about it for the utmost in convenience.

The campfire, the cynosure of all campers, should be downwind of your tent so that smoke and sparks will be carried away from the fabric. Some outdoorsmen prefer to have their fire to one side of the tent front so that traffic won't have to detour around the blaze or go through smoke. No matter what your preference may be, keep the fire at least ten feet from the tent, and make sure that the area between is well cleared of flammable materials.

If you cook on a camp stove, keep that away from the tent, too, and on a steady table or stand. Make sure that such things as airing sleeping bags, laundry, and towels will not blow across it or, of course, across a campfire in a wind that may come up. When you pitch a shelter fly or windbreaks, be sure that everything is secure and that nothing will go up in flames if a line gives away.

Privacy screens are handy to have in some camps. They can also be used to furnish a better draft for the campfire, a sunbathing area, shade for the small fry, or to shut out blowing sand or cold winds. Some camps use plastic sheeting, painters' drop cloths, or

Privacy Screens

shower curtains. Others invest in lightweight camp tarpaulins. Often a crowded camp-ground can be made much more pleasant by the use of a few well-placed opaque screens. Incidentally, in the wilderness screens will often keep out wild animals. They hesitate to enter any type of man-made enclosure for fear of being trapped. If it looks as if a storm is on the way, all such screens should be taken down.

Store the fuel, be it wood or liquid, a safe distance from open flames. If you burn gasoline, kerosene, or alcohol, a good place for those reserve cans is in the car. Your woodpile should be convenient to the fire but not too close. Keep a small box or bundle of dry kindling in the tent so that you can always get a fire going in a hurry in any kind of weather.

Your icebox should be close to where you cook and serve meals, provided it's in some sort of shade. Otherwise, position it somewhere else in the shade so as to conserve ice. This can be shade from a dining fly, vegetation, your car, a bank, or a boulder. Most tents are hot inside, so don't put your icebox there. If there is no shady spot near where you'd like the container, pitch a small fly over it. Remember that the pattern of shade will change throughout the day.

Any food not stowed in the icebox should be kept near your cooking or eating area except when you're away from camp. A rugged wooden box or chest will keep away small animals such as mice, raccoons, and skunks. But nothing short of a portable steel safe will bar scrounging bears who'll demolish almost anything to get at grub. If you've a hunch that there may be bears about, keep your food in the car trunk with the lid locked. Bears have been known to break car windows, climb in, and make off with food left on seats.

If you sleep in the back of your station wagon in bear country, don't keep your victuals there. Tie them in a sack and hoist this at least ten feet up a tree, suspending it from a branch out from the trunk. If you're in a bear area where there are no large trees, an all-night fire will help keep bruin away.

Keep water buckets and canteens in the shade near the icebox. Even if there's plenty of water at hand, it's not a bad idea to keep a bucket full by the fire in case a campfire gets out of control.

The ax and shovel should be kept together in one place, along with any other tools such as a hatchet, and returned there after use. The best spot is usually by a woodpile, with the blades safely out of the way. Many like to drive ax and hatchet into dry wood, with the handles vertical for easy spotting. A band or two of bright color around the handles will help you see tools in the bush.

Your garbage pit should be downwind of the tenting area and well away from any source of water. Burn all dry garbage. Tin cans should be rinsed and burned to kill any odors, then flattened and buried with whatever else you can't burn. Don't leave any empty bottles loose around the area. They can act as magnifying glasses and start fires, especially if they collect water. Dig your garbage pit two or three feet deep and cover each deposit with a layer of well-tamped earth. Before heading back to civilization, fill the hole entirely.

A camp latrine should also be some distance downwind from the tent site. Public campgrounds, of course, usually have toilet facilities. But if you have to dig your own, it should be marked so that it can be located after dark. It should not be near, nor uphill from, any source of water. The earth should be heaped to one side and some thrown in after every use. If you utilize a toilet tent, this also should be well away from any water source, even though portable toilets are used. Any disposable waste containers should be buried deep and away from any water.

Such things as clotheslines and guy ropes tied to trees should be placed where they will not be hazards. If they cannot be located above head height, even in horse country when you're mounted, mark them with bits of white cloth. Keep such camp accessories at a minimum, and plan your site so that getting around it will be as easy and safe as possible.

A bit of planning before you make camp can do much to save time and trouble later. It's often helpful to sketch a layout to scale, showing the various pieces of equipment, before starting on the trip, then try to come close to it upon arrival. Terrain and vegetation may alter the way you spread out the outfit. But if you have a functional plan in mind, you at least will have something sound to aim at. It might make a lot of difference when you take to the woods.

26

Emergency Bivouacs

THE FORMULA FOR AN EMERGENCY SHELTER IS SIMPLE: WHERE YOU are, with what you have, right now! When we were youngsters, a small lean-to handily thatched with evergreen boughs was a popular one-night stand. Today one is often frowned upon by conservationists even in wilderness where there is plenty of coniferous growth, but in an emergency nothing is wasted that can give you protection or comfort. Anytime you need shelter, use whatever is handy. Conservation of life and health is important, too.

In earlier days and still in the more primitive reaches of the continent, most sportsmen expected to spend some nights in the woods without tents. They frequently were caught away from their cabins by storm, darkness, or by having ventured too far away tracking down game. Or, as some trappers do today, they may have deliberately headed into the wilds on a hunting or exploration trip without carrying any shelter.

They either slept in the open or, if the weather called for one, hastily threw up a shelter from the materials at hand. They were expert at erecting such bivouacs in minutes, using only a sheath knife, belt ax, and perhaps a few feet of rawhide thong.

Tents today are inexpensive, easy to pack and pitch, and come in almost any size and design to meet a variety of weather conditions. However, knowing how to make a snug, quick shelter in an emergency can still be important, perhaps even a matter of life or death. A camper can become lost or stranded, or his regular shelter may be destroyed by fire. But even without such emergencies, it can be fun to see what you can build for a night of sleeping in the woods from the materials at hand.

For the sheer aroma of camping, there's little to compare with sleeping under a bough lean-to on a spruce-tip bed, with a long overnight fire crumbling to coals in front. Here's one way to go about it, and you can improvise a dozen others. Select two trees about eight to ten feet apart, and place a ridgepole horizontally between them about seven feet high. Crotches can generally be found for this, or in a pinch you can lash the ridgepole in place. Dimensions, of course, are up to you. The smaller the shelter, within reason, the more comfortably warm it will be.

From the ridgepole of this particular lean-to, slant a series of light poles about eight feet back, making a shelter deep enough to accommodate a small party sleeping with their heads to the fire. The lower ends of these poles can be sharpened and rammed into soft ground or held down with flat rocks. The poles should be about six inches apart for a stout roof. Hold the horizontal sticks in place by weaving them in and out among the slanting poles or, of course, by lashing them. All openings to the resulting latticework should be roughly six inches square.

The sides of the lean-to can be filled with similar latticework. Stick the lower ends of the side poles into the ground. Lash or wedge the tops into the roof framework.

Now collect a pile of balsam, hemlock, or spruce tips. Begin at the bottom of the roof and hang these tips on the latticework, each row overlapping the one beneath it like shingles. Make the roof thick. Thatch the side frames similarly, and you're in business. A good lean-to frame can be thatched again and again upon return visits. Some of ours are still standing after a decade and more of use.

Carpet the interior of your shelter with more evergreen tips, with aromatic needles, or with dry leaves and grass. Then you'll have a snug retreat against wind, snow, and light rain. Speaking of rain, there's a modern gimmick whereby you can waterproof such a shelter for any kind of weather. Just carry a rectangle of thin, light plastic, maybe six by eight feet, in your breast pocket whenever you go outdoors. It won't take up any more space than an ordinary handkerchief, and it's always coming in handy if only as a means for carrying that heart, kidneys, and liver, or for quickly roofing a luncheon niche in a downpour.

If possible, build your lean-to so that the open side faces downwind. Kindle a long

Bough Lean-to

fire in front of it. A bank, ledge, or man-piled wall of green logs behind this fire will increase the heat reflection. Facing the shelter downwind not only makes it warmer, but it also helps prevent sparks from blowing into it.

If you'd care to go a step beyond just carpeting the floor, make a framework of small logs, held in place by notches or stakes, and fill it several inches deep with dry forest litter. Remove any stiff or sharp twigs, of course, for they have a way of finding the tender spots in your hide.

Lean-to Floor with Log Framework Filled with Evergreen Tips

Just sleeping on the ground can be fairly comfortable if you scoop out hip and shoulder holes. However, a layer of leaves, grass, or evergreen tips beneath you will help keep out the dampness. Keep at least your feet and head covered if possible. This will do much to keep the rest of you warm, a point to consider when dressing for the bush. In bitter cold weather, use leaves or needles up to your neck over whatever else is available for insulation. Even snow will help, believe it or not.

Every time we think of trying to sleep warm in freezing weather we recall the fantastic but apparently true story we found in an old town history some years ago. A couple of New England moose hunters had killed and skinned a huge moose when a blizzard overtook them. They had only one blanket apiece, so one hunter gave the other his blanket and rolled himself up in the green moose hide with the warm, grayish black hair next to him. When dawn broke he tried to move but found himself frozen solidly into the hide, unable to extricate even an arm. Fortunately, the other fellow had a hatchet and chopped him out.

There are shelters, too, that use slash, saplings, leaves, rocks, grass, and similar odds and ends which can be constructed with no special tools, although a sharp sheath knife or a small belt ax will make the work easier and faster. A few feet of strong cord, such as a hank of parachute line, will also help, although you can get along without it. In fact, you can do very well with just bare hands. For the sake of illustration, though, let's assume that you have at least a sheath knife on your belt.

To begin with, you'll need a framework. This can be started with a small tree or sapling. Select a fairly straight one, about an inch or an inch and a half in diameter and some ten feet tall. Trim off the branches about an inch from the trunk. Cut off the top some nine feet from the ground and sharpen it.

Now bend this sapling to form an arch about three feet high at the center and four feet wide at ground level. Ram the sharpened top of the tree into the ground several inches deep, until the arch stays in place. If it won't stick in this particular ground, leave the top of the tree on and hold it down by the weight of a rock, log, or such, or tie it with cord or vine to the bottom of a nearby tree. This will form the doorway of your shelter.

If the sapling is too springy to stay in position with any facility, just change the doorway to an inverted "V" by cutting through bark and cambium so that the stick partially breaks at the center. This will take most of the spring out of it, as well as leave a spot for the ridgepole, your next step, which can then be wedged in the cut so that it's centered in position.

The ridgepole will be a similar sapling, cut and trimmed about eight feet long. It's placed from the top of the doorway arch to a point on the ground behind the arch. If the ground slopes, face the framework of the shelter so that the doorway is higher than the foot of the shelter, in order to sleep with your head both nearer the opening and higher than your feet, as is desirable.

If more than one individual is to be accommodated, of course, the size of the doorway and the final shelter will have to be proportionately larger. In any event, once the doorway and the ridgepole are in position, prop short branches against the ridge to close in the sides. Or you can form more arches of saplings and make the sides of the hut rounded, adding smaller and smaller arches as you proceed down the ridgepole.

Now add smaller sticks and entwine everything with leafy branches, evergreen boughs, and odds and ends. If there's a field nearby where long wild grass grows, that, too, may be thatched into the sticks of the framework. Cover the ground inside with leaves, grass, needles, or more boughs, and you'll have a snug little bivouac that, with practice, can be built in minutes.

A large fallen tree will provide a wall for a simple one- or two-man shelter. Simply lean short branches against the trunk, wide enough for a man underneath, cover it with leaves, and add sticks to hold these in place. For two men, just make the tunnel longer and sleep one behind the other. This is a good shelter if there's no time to build a better one.

Make it on the lee side of the log so that the latter's bulk will serve as a windbreak as well as protection from possible falling branches of other trees in case there should be a high wind or storm coming up. If there is, put more sticks or even flat stones on the roof to hold it in place. Fill in the floor with leaves, needles, or grass, or even small sticks and twigs if there is nothing softer to hold you off wet ground.

The low branches of evergreen trees often provide almost perfect ready-made shelters.

Shelter Made from Fallen Tree

If their branches don't already touch the ground, they may be held down with rocks, logs, or other branches. Or just trim a niche in one side of the bottom of a thick fir or spruce and use the branches to thatch the sides. Under such evergreens you'll usually find a bed of needles several inches thick, all ready to use. These are usually nearly dry on top even after a rain, since water quickly drains down through them.

Caves and overhanging ledges also provide shelter in emergencies, but you should inspect the former first for skunks, bobcats, other animals, or snakes. One way is to poke

Niche Trimmed in Evergreen Tree

as far as possible inside with a long stick. As for overhanging ledges, check these for stones or loose sections which might roll off onto you. Lean poles against the overhang and use whatever materials are handy for thatching. If no boughs, grass, or leafy branches are available, use stones, shale, or even earth if it's loose and workable.

Two boulders sufficiently near together to allow roofing with branches, saplings, or boughs will form a hut. Fill in the upwind end with more sticks, rocks, or brush. Floor with plenty of leaves or such. Even a wide crack in a ledge can serve as a shelter, with brush added as a windbreak or roof. It's interesting, satisfying one of our basic instincts, to try to spot possible shelters while walking in the woods, even if you don't plan to build any.

A fallen tree that has raised a great fan of earth at its roots may serve as a starting point for one of the most rugged emergency shelters. A couple of decades ago one of us

Fallen Tree Shelter, Using Roots and Earth as Wall

and another hunter used such a toppled tree for an emergency bivouac, regarding the roots and earth as one wall and adding poles and brush to enclose it. We spent many a night there, and a year ago we found the shelter was still in fair condition. Some "temporary" shelters are pretty long-lived.

If the fallen tree is held up from the ground, it may be possible to build a shelter in the tangle of branches themselves, particularly if they are leaved or if you are working with a conifer. But be sure to test it for rigidity to make sure it is in no danger of falling any farther, especially if the trunk is a heavy one. If there is an adequate opening among the branches, add limbs and brush to form the shelter. You may even be able to add flooring.

How about winter? All these various types of bivouacs will serve well in the cold season, too. As a matter of fact, adding snow to roofs and walls will help to insulate them. It's actually easier to bivouac in winter. Even in deep snow, all you have to do is

153

stamp out a wedgelike trench, partially roof it with evergreen boughs, put a thick matting of boughs on the floor, and enjoy a small fire in the narrow end.

If you should plan to use such shelters as these on a forthcoming trip to the woods— and who can tell when you may need one—a rugged knife, several feet of nylon cord for lashing poles together, and a piece of waterproof material to use over the frame will speed the building.

It's important enough to repeat that the latter can be a rectangle of light plastic sheeting which is available for about a dollar from many outfitters and which may be a permanent bulge in a breast pocket. It's tough enough for fairly rough use. Hold this in place by sandwiching it between branches or boughs. To tie part of it, so as to form a fire-reflecting canopy in front, just knot the cord around a small rock bunched in the material.

Such waterproof material may also be wrapped around a tripod of forked sticks tepee style, draped over a slanting pole, or just put over your head poncho style for sitting out a sudden storm. One will roof the cosiest of noontime niches, made by cutting a few boughs from a thickly needled small fir or spruce, using these boughs to sit on, and building a small gleaming fire in front.

It pays to be careful with fires, of course. Be sure not to build them too close to any such shelters, which because of their materials are apt to be particularly flammable. Make them on bare ground rather than on humus. Watch out for sparks that might touch off the thatch.

Keep your fire small, feeding it with small pieces of fuel, and it will still give off plenty of heat. If you're sleeping broadside to it, a small fire will ordinarily suffice, but make it long. Mixing green wood with dry will make it burn longer. A handy index to the heat-giving qualities of firewood, by the way, is its weight.

Kindle the fire against a rock or ledge if possible, so that it reflects heat into your shelter. On the other hand, don't build it against a big log, for it will be difficult to extinguish later. Such a fire may smolder inside the log for months, even all fall and winter, and break out in flames long afterward. If darkness is falling, get a high fire going and plenty of fuel handy before starting your shelter. The cheery companionship of the flames will help you see.

If a fire is impossible or unwise for any reason, here are a few tips for conserving body heat. Lie with your back against a log if it is part of your shelter. Unless heat is being reflected from it, an expert survival trick, don't lie with your back against a cave wall or ledge, for it will cool off long before you can warm it. If there are plenty of dry leaves about, spread your coat on the ground, pile plenty of them inside the back, lie down on it, and slip it on. Then put some more of the leaves inside the coat front, too, and you'll have insulation.

Turn up your coat and shirt collars. Unfasten enough of the front of your outer coat to permit sleeping with your hands inside, next to your chest. If you have on long trousers, tuck the bottoms inside your socks or boots to exclude cold air. Keep on your hat or cap, for the bare head is one of the major places where the entire body loses heat. If you wake up shivering during the night, get up and exercise. Then hunch together again and relax with some more sleep.

Remember that a large shelter isn't needed, just one big enough for you and any companion. A space seven feet long by three feet wide will usually do. This will mean both less time and care in preparation and more ease in heating.

There is a marked difference of opinion as to whether or not such emergency shelters should be removed. Many feel strongly that they should be eradicated, with any poles laid flat where they won't show and where they'll eventually rot back into the forest floor. Others feel that they should be left as conveniences to other sportsmen. We like to leave the woods as we find them, but it's a personal matter. If the shelter is in deep wilderness where it will not be offensive to the sight, and where other outdoorsmen may one day need it, we see no harm in leaving it.

If you are strayed or stranded and it's a tossup whether to keep going or spend the night in the woods, for safety's sake start an emergency shelter and do it before darkness has taken over the forest. With very rare exceptions, never try travel by night. Making a shelter will help keep the mind occupied and perhaps, especially in the case of newcomers to the wilderness, prevent panic. And it's considerably safer to be inside, even if cold, than stumbling about outside.

You'll be surprised at how snug an emergency shelter can be built. Although most campers prefer a tent for a long stay, when one isn't too hard to transport, knowing how to make a snug sanctuary from materials at hand will give you a real sense of security in the farther places even if you never have to fall back on the knowledge.

Trying to get along with a minimum of equipment is quite a challenge to even an experienced camper. And while we don't go along with the idea of inflicting survival camping on your family for fun, a lot of primitive camping can be exciting and a pleasant change for anyone who's game to try it. And you can travel lighter and go farther, back to where the big ones are hanging out.

27

Good Camp Keeping

THE SUN HAS NOW LOST ALL BUT THE TIP OF THE TALLEST PINE. THE long aromatic shadows of the wilderness are sifting across the aisles of the forest. You recline on a log, poking the remnants of your small cooking fire prior to laying on the heavy night logs. Your sleeping bag, air mattress soft, awaits you within a snug tent. Everything else is in its place. Nothing can bother you now. The forest is yours, for you have taken from it the essentials of primitive civilization—shelter, warmth, and food. You are at home.

Good camp keeping is far less work in the long run than slovenly camp keeping. Mostly it's a matter of common sense, mixed with a little know-how. You make no move until you know it follows the line of greatest economy. To putter, or to put off, is to wallow in ceaseless sloppiness. It takes a bit more know-how to have an orderly camp in the wilderness than in a public campground, but it's not hard either place. And it means full enjoyment.

Did you ever notice how much you can tell about an outdoorsman by the camp he keeps? Watch a veteran camper in action, and you'll notice that he's usually as neat in camp as at home. He's not trying to impress anyone. He's camping to enjoy himself. He simply knows that a camp in good shape pays off in convenience, fewer bugs, better health, more self-respect, and more friends.

A slovenly camper, on the other hand, invites flies and other pests, runs the risk of contaminated food and water, is likely to damage tents and other available gear, and annoys fellow campers. In extreme cases, he may even lock horns with the local lawmen. Mostly, he'll never have the deep-down satisfaction of doing well for himself.

To begin with, a well-kept campsite looks good. It's free of scrap paper and cigarette butts. There's nothing to trip over, run into, or sit on that could damage hide or pride. All edged tools are safely sheathed or placed handily so that they won't cause any trouble. Firewood is neatly stacked so it's convenient to the fire. Incidentally, it's smart camping to keep some extra kindling covered with an old piece of oilcloth, tarp, or under a tent fly or overhanging ledge in case of rain.

Inside and outside the tent, good camp keeping is extremely important. The tent should be well pitched and kept that way—no sagging walls, leaning poles, loose stakes, or slack

156

guy ropes. Brush off dirt and leaves. Bird droppings, unless left too long, are easily removed with fresh water and a rag. Before pitching your tent, as far as that goes, look over the ground for excessive droppings that may indicate a roosting tree overhead.

If you get pitch on the tent or other gear, gasoline from the stove or lantern, or nail-polish remover, will take it off, but it will possibly remove the waterproofing, too. It's best to let the pitch dry, then to scrape it carefully off with a dull knife. The same applies to cooking grease, although many such stains can be removed with soapy water or by gentle rubbing with a hard-fiber soap pad.

After a downpour, the bottom of your tent will probably be spattered with mud. This may be flushed off with clear water before it dries. Or, if water is scarce, let the mud dry and whisk it off with a stiff brush. Some campers carry a small broom for such uses.

Any dirt in the tent should be swept out daily. If your trousers have cuffs, and in the woods it's better that they don't, you'll be bound to bring in a fine assortment of twigs, leaf bits, small pebbles, and other forest debris to be spilled out when you shuck off your clothes at night.

Mud should be kept out, especially if the tent has a sewn-in floor. A mat of evergreen boughs outside the door can do much to keep the floor clean if all members of the party remember to scrape their boots before venturing inside. Another trick is to put an old blanket inside the tent where you walk most. This can be carefully borne out and shaken free of dirt each day, thus saving the floor from stains and wear. If the tent has a floor and can be easily dismantled and erected again, it's often not a bad idea to strike it every few days, turn it inside out, and shake and brush it clear. You'll be amazed at the amount of twigs, leaves, and other accumulated rubbish unloaded.

If the weather is continually damp, keep an old pair of boots or moccasins just inside the door to change into before entering, or leave your rubbers outside when you come in. Few things can make a tent more uninviting than a wet, dirty floor in rainy weather.

The gear kept inside the tent should have specific places. Each member of a party should have a duffle bag or other container for his belongings. This is particularly important if there are small fry along. Don't just unzip the tent door and toss gear inside, figuring to put it away later. You may want it quickly. Community items such as first aid kit, ax, and lanterns should be in a handy spot where they can be reached and replaced easily and quickly.

One of the most glaring evidences of poor camp keeping is dirty dishes. While you're eating, be heating the water for dishwashing. Attend to this chore the minute the meal is finished, before lassitude sets in. Do not make the mistake of sitting down first for a little relaxation. Better complete the job while you're about it. You will appreciate leisure so much more afterward.

A bunch of tall grass bent double will make a swab, but hard-fiber soap pads will render the job easier. Scrape the dishes as clean as possible before washing them. That dirty frypan set on the heat with water and a few grease-cutting wood ashes will get the job started. Wash the cleanest pieces and the silverware first, saving the pots and pans for the last. Many campers prefer to keep part of the dishwater good and hot and to use it strictly for rinsing. That way drying chores are cut to a minimum. Once the dishes are washed and dried, get them under the cover of at least a mosquito netting to keep off flies and other insects.

Of course, paper plates and cups will save dishwashing, but you'll still have the pots and pans to contend with. Either way, there'll be garbage, grease, or greasy dishwater to dispose of. If you have lots of the latter two, dig a bucket-size pit and cover it with a

Grass Swab

screen of small branches over which grass, pine needles, or leaves are laid. Pour the grease into the hole through this filter. When the grease congeals, remove the whole top and burn it, replacing it with fresh material for the next pouring. Before you leave, fill the pit with dirt.

All refuse can be easily disposed of even when you're far away from a public campsite where trash is picked up regularly. If you'll be in camp for several days, prepare an adequate garbage and refuse pit (see Chapter 32 for tips on garbage disposal).

Assuming that you have a supply of pure drinking water (see Chapter 32 for instructions on purifying water), store it so that it will stay pure. Keep containers covered tightly, using either a fitted cover or netting attached with clips or weights. If there are pets in camp, keep your water containers where they can't reach them.

Personal camp hygiene also includes clothes, bedding, and laundry. Though your garb may be rough and ready, as well as somewhat old and worn, keep it clean, and you'll be a lot more agreeable to camp with. A small can of cleaning or lighting fluid will help get out grease and dirt spots. Shirts and undergarments should be changed regularly and the soiled ones rinsed out. If water is scarce, a good sunning and airing will help. After doing your laundry, don't leave it hanging out long after it is dry. One's washing is no great addition to nature's scenery.

By the way, there's a fairly simple gimmick that'll take the place of clothespins in the woods and still keep your stuff from blowing all over the place, as it can if you merely lay it over a line. Use a double clothesline. That is, fasten both lines between two supports, first twisting the ropes together, several times to each foot. Then merely slip corners of each garment between twists in the line.

The sleeping bag or blankets should be aired frequently over a line, bush, or rock when the sun is out and preferably a brisk, dry wind is blowing. Either open the sleeping bag flat or turn it inside out. If you use sheeting or a cotton-blanket liner, wash it at least once a week if possible or at least give it a good long airing then. When bedding is fluffed and dried by the open air, you'll sleep far more warmly and comfortably.

A veteran camper leaves his campsite at least as comely as it was when he came upon it. Fill any dug holes. If you've used boughs or leaves for bedding, scatter them so that they'll blend with the area and decay naturally. Be sure all clotheslines and other ropes are removed, even if you don't want to carry them out with you, and make certain that all scrap paper and rubbish is burned. Finally, be sure the fire is dead out, so that the ashes can be stirred deep down with your bare hands.

If you've brought along a checklist of your gear, as wise outdoorsmen do, check it carefully to make sure that you get everything you came with. It's only good woodsmanship to remove nails driven into trees when you leave. If they are left protruding, someone may be injured on them. If you merely pound them in, someone may wreck an ax or saw because of your thoughtlessness later on. The best procedure is to pull out such nails and then drive little wooden pegs in their places to prevent insects from entering the wood. Be sure, too, to remove any nails from your tent poles. To leave them invites holes in your canvas.

If you plan on returning to this woodland retreat sometime in the future, or if someone else may be along, it's conservative to stack leftover firewood, poles, and tent stakes made on the spot, so that they can dry out after rain and be easy to find. Otherwise, scatter them so that they'll decay naturally. Keep your site in a public camping area one neighbors can be pleased to camp next to, and with the above exception, your wilderness campsite one of those no one can find a few days after you've left.

28

Making Camp
Accident-proof

WHEN YOU TAKE TO THE WOODS, YOU'LL GENERALLY WANT DRINKING water and firewood within easy access of the chosen campsite. Next you'll likely look for pleasant surroundings. Parklike expanses, with plenty of scenery and not too much shade, are ideal. If it's mosquito season, camping by a stream or lake will provide the benefit of bug-lessening breezes. On the other hand, if the weather is cold, the warmest place will be a sunny bench halfway down the side of a sheltered hill.

When you've found a likely sanctuary in which to shrug off your packsack, unload your horse or car, or pull up a canoe, look around for nature's booby traps, triggered before your arrival. A conscientious check before unpacking your outfit can save a lot of trouble, not to mention possible danger, later on.

Not all campsites are booby-trapped, and surely no such retreat would have all the perils to be considered here. Matter of fact, camping is one of the safest recreational activities. It can be doubly secure if you are careful about picking and using a camping spot.

Beware of such things as threatening rocks on slopes and ledges above the site. Rain, a passing animal, or even wind could start things hurtling down toward your tent when least anticipated. A particular pitfall? Hitching tent or tarp to high loose rocks that the pressure of the night's air currents on the fabric could dislodge in the direction of your sleeping bag.

If trees are about, scan them carefully for any dead branches that could fall or be blown down. Particular offenders are the poplars, cottonwoods, aspens, and others of their ilk, as well as the butternut, silver maple, yellow locust, and Monterey pine. Dead standing trees, such fine sources of campfire materials, are especially hazardous. Everyone who has spent much time in the woods has heard them crashing down without even a breeze to give any warning. Dead birches, with waterproof bark holding moisture within their rotting cores, can be particularly dangerous.

A tent pitched under a lone tree can be in a dangerous place in an electrical storm, especially if the tree is tall and there is nothing higher in the area. If you are ever caught in such a circumstance in a sudden thunderstorm, the safest place will be within your vehicle, as safe a spot as anyone can be anywhere in an electrical storm.

Dangerous Place to Pitch a Tent

Have a look for hornet or yellow jacket nests. If either of these stinging colonists has established his buzzing abode nearby, better look for another place.

Not in the same class as insects, but still a small hazard, is the matter of poison ivy, poison oak, and poison sumac. These plants are imbued with an oily, highly poisonous substance that causes itching, blisters, and rash. Even the smoke resulting when such vegetation is thrown on a fire is infectious. In fact, if your pet wanders through such leaves and vines, its hair may pick up some of the oil and transfer it to your body. Learn to spot the smooth, waxy foliage of these bushes and vines and to avoid them.

If there are traces of other campers, keep a wary eye peeled for such debris as broken glass and tin cans that have not been properly burned, flattened, and buried. Be especially suspicious of any spot where there has been a logging, pulp, or mining camp in the past.

We once pitched our tent within the old log walls of what had been a logging operation in a remote section of New York State's Catskill Mountains. Like you, probably, we'd heard that in the woods spiders soon take care of any tiny inhabitants of such places. Yet before morning we were in misery, bitten nearly all over by fleas and bedbugs. What they had been feasting on before that night we'll never know, but from the way they chewed on our carcasses it couldn't have been much.

Camping by a brook or stream? Then be sure the bank is high enough to protect you from a flash flood upstream. The way to do this is to look around for the unmistakable signs of prior flooding. You can generally establish the high-water mark by finding the more or less continuous line of dead twigs, leaves, grass, and other flotsam deposited along the water's edge.

You can even have trouble in country not ordinarily subject to such flash flooding from cloudbursts. For that reason, it's best to think twice before pitching a tent on a sandbar or low island anywhere. We once sat down to eat lunch on a breeze-cooled sandbar in a New Hampshire trout stream, only to discover in the middle of our second sandwich that we were about to be marooned. The water was abruptly rising about our moccasined feet, and we had to grab our gear and splash to safety. It turned out that a farmer a couple miles upstream had decided it was a good day to drain his farm pond and fix the water gate.

Upon reaching camp, always park your trailer or other vehicle in a place where it cannot roll. If it must be left on a slope, make certain that wheels are well blocked and brakes are set. Cars have been known to roll into a campsite when improperly parked or when youngsters have released the brakes.

If everything about the prospective site passes the test so far, unpack your outfit and get a campfire going. Although unless you're in a spot where they are already built, fireplaces as such are apt to be no better than nuisances, a dry ledge that will both safely confine the blaze and reflect its heat is a fine thing against which to kindle a fire.

However, watch out for cracks that have become filled with moisture from rain or snow. Such a ledge can crack with a riflelike report and shed debris into what would have been a darn good stew. Heated shale, limestone, and slate ledges are particularly prone to do this. Too, it's best for this reason to avoid building a back wall of stream stones, no matter how smooth and intact they may appear to be.

The best idea anywhere in the bush, of course, is to get settled in camp well before dark. It's possible to cover just as much country that way, for it means that you'll be well rested and able to get away early in the morning. In any event, before twilight try to run a check of the after-dark hazards that are easily enough avoided in daylight.

Walk about as you may have to do in the darkness and look for loose stones that could cause a nasty spill and for root loops that might catch a foot when your hands are full of hot grub or firewood. If there are wet leaves or needles in your path, check to see there are no slippery sticks or stones beneath them. Chop free all root loops, and remove or brace loose stones. It's a good idea, too, to clear out any dead limbs that are underfoot in your path. Their damp wood will be just the thing to hold the fire if you are going to have a night blaze.

Individuals not used to the forest are often injured by walking into the lower branches of pines, spruce, and similar softwoods whose lower branches die but do not drop off. Getting about at night in unfamiliar woods makes such a menace an especial hazard to face and eyes, as branches are often pointed toward you at about eye level, and your flashlight is generally directed at the ground. Even in daylight, such snags blend with the brush and are hard to see. Before dark, stroll about your campsite and break off such branches where you see them. They make outstandingly good kindling for the campfire.

Then there's the matter of unintentionally building booby traps yourself at a campsite. We've all done it occasionally, but after learning the hard way we're a lot more careful than we were a half-century ago when we started camping. Leave axes in a handy spot but safe from careless feet and hands. If you have a hunting knife, keep it in its sheath when not in use.

Should you stick your hunting knife in a log—and this is ordinarily a poor idea, both because of what it can do to the edge and because it's a good way to lose a fine blade— insert it at a low angle so that if you unthinkingly place a hand there, stumble against it, or even sit in that spot, the blade will be safely down. Either set an unsheathed ax out of the way by the woodpile or sink it into a log where the cutting edge will be protected and the handle will be out of the way.

Safest Way to Stick a Hunting Knife in a Log

(Note: A sheath is a better place.)

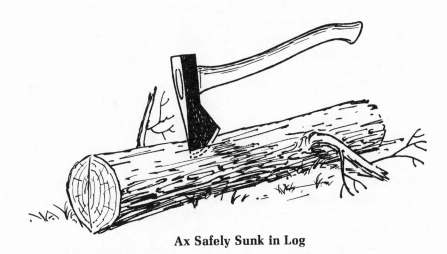

Ax Safely Sunk in Log

Incidentally, some loggers told us once that they never use a green log for this purpose, as it might draw the temper from the steel. Speaking of loggers, we once stopped to talk with a crew in the Adirondacks and noticed that every ax handle was painted with a bright light-orange stripe about six inches long. No matter where the loggers parked their axes, they could spot them. This is a good safety measure, but if you do the same thing to your ax, keep the paint away from where your hands grasp the wood. Otherwise, it may cause blisters.

While on the subject of edged tools, let's not bypass the dangers of the various kinds of saws. A lot of skin and clothing has been slashed on carelessly exposed saw teeth. The formidable crosscut should be placed either upright between two parallel logs with the teeth down between them and the handles upright, easy to see, or it may be laid flat on the dry ground with the teeth under the bottom curve of a log where they can't be tripped over. Smaller saws can be sheathed along the cutting edge with a section of leather or inner tube, or the entire saw blade can be inserted in the sleeve of a heavy old shirt or jacket and held with rubber bands.

There are several folding saws, with blades that jackknife into the handles, that are fine for camping. If you can find one with a handle substantial enough to hold up under the heavy pressure it'll get, you're in business. Too, one of us has a favorite roll-up, wire-strand saw which can be carried safely in a pocket. Used with a handle made from a limber branch, it does fine as a bucksaw for light wood, and yet two men can easily crosscut with it on heavier stuff.

The other of us swears by a light Swede saw. This has a tubular steel handle that comes handily apart for packing. The thin blade itself can be rolled into the diameter of a saucer, held in that small shape with a cord wound among the teeth, and wrapped for protection in a piece of canvas. The only time this needs more than ordinary protection is in brittle temperatures thirty or more degrees below zero. But even an ax blade can shatter in such cold if not warmed beforehand.

Always be careful where you stand, sit, or lie down in camp. Careless campers have relaxed on such things as red-ant hills, split logs which sag and pinch like the devil, poison oak and ivy, and even porcupine quills that have been lodged in bark. It's even a good idea to avoid brushing off a seat with your bare hands unless the spot is obviously safe. Use a bough instead. Never put your hands in openings in logs, stumps, or ledges without first probing well with a stick for snakes, hornets, and spiders.

It's always a good idea to inspect a campsite for concealed holes which might turn into ankle-twisters, greasy stones you could easily slip on, and sharp root stubs that could catch on trouser cuffs, shoelaces, or boot buckles.

Speaking of such things, trouser cuffs in the woods are nothing but dirt and spark catchers and grade A trippers. As a matter of fact, you'll generally do better in breeches, trousers with tight, perhaps knitted bottoms, or in stagged trousers whose legs have been cut off a few inches from the ground. Keep laces tightly tied, with the ends tucked inside the tops of the footwear. Hunting boots with ankle straps and buckles can also become a nuisance when you're working through a burn, blowdown, or heavy bush.

Other man-made booby traps include such things as hot dishes with nothing substantial to use as a holder, steaming utensils set on slippery or slanting rocks, that coffee-pot keeping hot by the edge of the campfire, and knives and forks left where they can be perilous.

One other hazard is the hot handle of a camp lantern which, perhaps because the light has been hung, is left over the top of the heat instead of being turned down. The same thing applies to tent heaters and to the bail handles on pots. Use gloves, a heavy handkerchief, or a forked stick if you think the metal is too hot to handle. If it is and you forget, you'll be more apt to remember next time.

Dry ice can also cause burns. This is great stuff, but for safety's sake keep it covered in newspapers, cloth, or foil. Never touch it or handle it with the bare hands. Such contact, even for an instant, can result in a serious burn from the extreme, dehydrating cold. Children are generally fascinated by the coldness and the smokelike vapor and should be particularly cautioned against touching it. Burns from dry ice can be very painful and prone to become infected.

A number of camp lanterns and stoves efficiently use small pressure cans of liquefied petroleum gas. These devices are safe and easy to use, light readily, and operate smoothly. However, you cannot safely remove one of these cans from the appliance until the contents have been entirely exhausted. Once a container has been put in the appliance, there is no way to shut off the flow of gas if the can is removed. Therefore, take it out only after the flame or mantle has gone out completely.

Beware of storing unpunctured liquid propane (L/P) cans in a hot place, such as near a campfire or heater or on the rear shelf of a car where the sun can heat them. They might explode. Never put one of these "empty" cans in a campfire or incinerator. Follow the warnings and directions printed on these cans, and they will give safe and fine service.

All flammable liquids, as for lamps and outboard motors, should be carried in sturdy metal, never glass, containers with screw tops and tightly sealing gaskets. Incidentally, their use for igniting campfires should be reserved for extreme emergencies. Even a can of lighter fluid can become a roaring Molotov cocktail under certain conditions. Never use gasoline for campfires unless under survival exigencies; then only in small amounts, lit by standing a safe distance away and tossing a lighted match or other substance at the pile.

Even your tent can lie in wait for you after dark, although most experienced campers learn to bypass its bulk safely at night. In the meantime, use white guy ropes and paint the tops of pegs white for easier spotting after dusk. Another angle is to take along strips of white cloth to drape over the guys at night. The main thing, though, is to steer wide, not so hard to do even without a flashlight if you wait until your eyes become accustomed to the darkness.

A man-made hazard that is not so obvious, but which has cost lives, is a sleeping bag that has been inadequately aired after certain types of cleaning. The best thing to do is to play safe and carefully and completely air the bag after any dry cleaning, preferably by hanging it outdoors on a clear, windy day. Do this before storing it and again before using it.

If you're going to be in camp long enough to use a clothesline, place this high enough so that the tallest camper can pass beneath it without hanging himself, and don't string it across paths. A slap from a pair of wet socks is a lot less startling than a rope burn across face or throat. If you have to put it where it might be a hazard, perhaps in horse country, attach strips of white cloth or paper to it for after-dark visibility.

Naturally, a flashlight is a necessity unless, perhaps, you're backpacking. Even then, a small one comes in mighty handy. One of us hunts and fishes with a small backpack, this being the most painless way to carry a lunch and those few odds and ends such as an extra shirt, binoculars, and camera. On those days when we may not be hitting camp again until late, we pack along a two-cell flashlight with a spare bulb in back. The other of us has a favorite luminous, white, shockproof, waterproof light which glows reassuringly all night and which goes everywhere with him. He takes along a second light for safety and to reactivate the luminous one if it's been packed away from the sunlight too long.

Guns are a personal matter. If there are children along or if you are camping near civilization, magazines should be emptied and any clips removed. Deep wilderness is another matter. There, game may walk through camp at any time, and you may want loaded rifles readily accessible but with cartridges always removed from the chamber.

All fishhooks should be in a safe place to avoid snagging. Don't leave them swinging from a rigged pole where they may catch you or your clothing, or where some little four-footed visitor to camp may investigate the fly or drying bait with disastrous results.

As a final thought about man-made booby traps, have an unbreakable waterproof match case for carrying strike-anywhere matches. If you need matches frequently, either use safety matches or distribute the kitchen variety one to a pocket. Carrying them bunched in a hip pocket is the worst place of all. A camper friend used to do this, slid from a rock to turn in one night, and his frantic efforts for the next few seconds were about what might have been expected.

Don't fall for a booby-trapped campsite. By keeping an eye out for trouble, you'll have a safer, happier, more comfortable outing when you take to the woods.

29

Easy Steps to Pitching Tents

EVERY WESTERN THRILLER HAS ITS GOOD GUYS AND BAD GUYS. SO does the art and science of taking to the woods. Here, though, they can't be identified by white or black hats. Camping's good guys are recognized by the wrinkleless tents and flies they help to support, and by straight and rigid poles. Its bad guys go off in ineffectual directions and result in some pretty droopy-looking tents and shelters.

Camping's guys, of course, are ropes. If you appreciate the proper use of guys and stakes, and how to create reliable substitutes for the latter, your excursions into the farther places will be more fun and less apt to build up frustrations.

Back nearer the turn of the century, when taking to the woods was on the rugged side, most tents were held erect by a heavy ridgepole, supported by heavier door poles or shears, with a frantic conglomeration of guy ropes angling off in all directions. Staking and guying such a shelter proved a real test of muscle.

With many of the modern tents, only the door awning requires guying. However, most campers and tent-trailer users employ windbreaks, privacy tarps, and dining flies. All these require some sort of dependable support against wind and perhaps even animal intruders. So pegs, guys, and poles are all still extremely important camping necessities.

In the old days, campers used sturdy wooden stakes which were whacked resoundingly into the ground with the flat side of a heavy ax. Today, unless weight is a factor to be considered in your camping outfit, there is a wide variety of metal and plastic stakes that are far more functional. Incidentally, if you carry stakes, fit them into a separate canvas bag so as to keep the tentage clean and intact.

Early stakes were generally about a foot, or sometimes two feet long, and made of hardwood. They were roughly square and had a deep notch near the top to hold the guy. These stakes, which frequently required resharpening, weren't the easiest things in the world to drive into rocky or even hard ground. Their heads, weakened by the notch, often split. In fact, if you're making your own tent pegs on the spot today, perhaps from split firewood, it's generally better not to bother with a notch, letting the angle of the driven stake hold the rope instead.

Many of the modern pegs are made of heavy-gauge aluminum or angle steel. A few are round. Others are in the shape of an elongated angle. The open face of this particular peg proffers a "V" to the ground for easier driving and a better hold. There are also tough, light, shatterproof, rustproof, brilliantly colored plastic tent stakes.

Stakes should be placed deep and at nearly right angles to the tension of the guy rope. All the pull concentrates at the point where the stake goes into the ground. The farther the peg is set in the earth, the stauncher it becomes. The closer the guy rope is to the ground, the less leverage it will exert on that portion of the peg beneath the surface.

Letters occasionally come in from correspondents who assert that stakes should be muscled in so that their heads are pointing toward the line of strain, rather than at right angles to the tent or tarp. Well, science and a combined century of peg driving and pulling have educated the two of us to the fact that the right-angle method is best.

**Correct Way
to Sink
a Stake**

It so happens that when boys we both had summer jobs pitching the huge Chautauqua tents for plays and other entertainments. If the canvas boss had ever caught us putting in a stake that was leaning toward the tent, we'd have been skinned, frozen, and used as a peg driven in the right direction—away from the big top.

Guys should be looped over the peg and set securely in the notch; then the stake should be driven down until the rope is practically in the ground. Such procedure not only affords maximum holding power, but it also leaves fewer exposed surfaces for someone to trip over.

On those occasions when the camping ground is hard or stony, a slender metal stake is better than a thick one of wood, plastic, or metal. The reasons are that it will both dodge underground stones better and pull out with less effort. If your tent is one of the two-man lightweight mountain-type units, 6-inch or 8-inch spikes, or some of the longer aluminum skewer-type stakes, will hold it staunchly.

What about guys? These are commonly made of such materials as hemp, manila, sisal, braided cotton, and nylon. Others are plastic, often braided for additional strength.

When wet, ropes manufactured with natural materials will shrink and exert an incredible force, enough either to yank stakes out of the ground or tear the support from the tent or fly. Some sort of slides or other adjustment should, for this reason, be used so that the tension on the guys can be slacked off during wet or damp weather.

The most common slide is merely a short piece of dowel or rectangular section of wood with holes bored through it near each end. The guy passes through one of the holes,

**Guy Rope Passing
Through Slide**

around the stake, and then back through the hole in the other end of the slide, where it is stopped by a knot. By sliding this device up and down the guy, you make the loop around the peg larger or smaller, thus tightening or loosening the rope. Other slides, especially those made for small-diameter nylon rope, are metal and have smaller or more numerous holes for a better grip on the slick synthetic material.

Storms sometimes blow up unexpectedly in the wilderness. If there is the likelihood of wet weather during the night or while you're all away from camp, slack up on the guy ropes so that shrinkage won't pull them loose. Even if the ropes are synthetic and so will not contract, a canvas fly or tent may shrink, so such precautions may still be necessary.

A built-in defense against shrinkage is to insert a section of shock cord into each guy rope. This insert will stretch a bit and yet hold securely. We have slept during driving rains in a tent that had heavy strips of inner tube set in the guys, and they worked fine.

To save weight, leave the slides at home and use guyline hitches in the ropes to adjust tautness. Such a hitch is simple and will secure all but the largest tents. Just make a simple overhand knot in the guy rope some distance above the end. Pass the end around the stake and back through this knot. Then, using the end, tie another overhand knot about the standing part of the rope. By sliding this knot up and down the guy rope, you can adjust tautness. Secure this hitch by tightening the original knot.

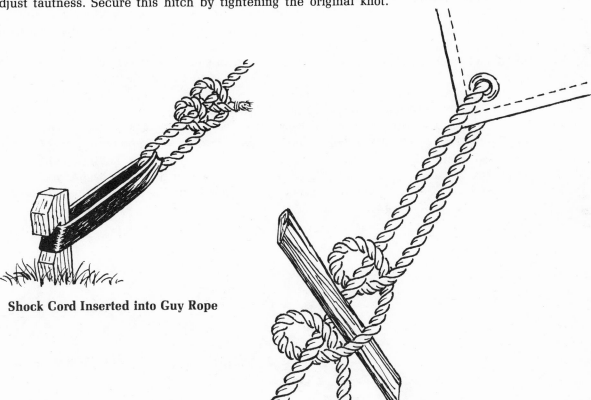

Shock Cord Inserted into Guy Rope

Easy Way to Loosen a Knot in a Guy Rope

Tie a small stick into the knot.
When you want to loosen it, just break out the stick.

If you take to the woods often, you'll be tenting one day where there is no suitable surface in which to drive stakes. Trees are often handy, though, around which you can loop your lines. Even heavy clumps will often suffice. Too, the guys can be tied to a sapling that has been lashed or locked between trees or rocks. For this purpose, use a clove hitch or a timber hitch (see Chapter 30). Either will hold without jamming.

If the ground is extremely sandy, or there is heavy snow, tie the guy ropes to short logs. Buried beneath the surface, these "dead men" hold quite well. You can also anchor the guys with rocks or jam them into cracks in nearby ledges, perhaps using cross sticks to hold them in place.

When regular staking is possible, place the pegs so that they provide the staunchest possible bracing against high winds and other strains. A well-pitched and -guyed shelter of any kind will shed moisture better than a sagging and wrinkled contraption and will mark you as a knowledgeable bushman.

The pull of almost any guy rope should be diagonally across the surface it braces and in line with a guy rope and stake on the opposite side. This setup helps to keep the material taut with a minimum of strain. In the case of the center poles which support the ridgepole, and with dining flies and the vertical screens that are put up to provide privacy or protection from the wind, double guying is advisable.

The majority of modern tents and tent trailers stand well enough without guying, but the time often comes when you'd like to attach a fly or awning. A substantial way to do this is to run light but strong lines from the fly's corners back across the tent roof, anchoring them to pegs on the opposite side of the tent. In stormy weather, this system, supplemented by sapling poles cut on the spot, can be used to extend shelters across the space between dining fly and tent.

If you make up your own guy ropes, or have a choice of lines when purchasing a tent or fly, be sure they are extralong, at least three feet more than is usual. A long guy can always be shortened with a sheepshank knot, but one that won't reach is useless.

Incidentally, the sheepshank can be tied in after the guy rope is stretched in place, thus removing any guesswork. Just lay three loops, one atop the other, where you want to take up slack. Then, with your two hands, pull both sides of the middle loop back through

Sheepshank

the first and third loops respectively. The resulting sheepshank can be adjusted as desired, and it is easily untied.

It's a good idea to carry one very long guy with you in case rocks or something else prevent sinking one of the stakes at the regular distance. With a long rope you can always move the stake farther from the canvas, where the ground may be soft, or knot the guy around a tree or boulder. It's also sound practice to pack an extra stake or two and a spare slide.

When packing gear, it will save time and confusion later if the ropes and slides are made so that you'll know which canvas they go with and whether the lines are long or short. Too, bundle the ropes together with the proper stakes.

Speaking of stakes, it pays to keep them clean. By painting them some such hue as bright yellow or white, as with outside enamel, you will both lose fewer in the leaves and grass and reduce the risk of stumbling over them when the light is bad.

Stakes can be driven with an ax, hatchet, or rubber mallet. A hatchet is usually handiest. When using one to drive metal stakes, it's a good idea to protect their tops, as well as the hatchet's head, by using a piece of wood as a buffer.

An easy way to remove most stakes is to loosen them with several sideways blows, then hook them out with the back bottom edge of an ax. Too, for a few cents you can purchase a stake puller—a strong metal hook on a wooden handle which yanks stakes out in a hurry. Or just take a loop of rope, hook it in the notch, and pull without prior loosening at the same angle at which the peg was driven in.

By bringing along some extra rope and a few spare stakes on trips to the woods, plus some tarps and plastic sheeting, you'll be able to improvise all sorts of temporary shelters and windbreaks. Poles can be fashioned of saplings, although this may be frowned upon in some spots where you'll be camping.

If you've been troubled in the past with tipsy tents or frowsy flies, try these tips. You'll discover that camping's good guys can make life a lot more easy.

30

Knots and Lashings

TAKING TO THE WOODS MAY SEEM TO HAVE NOTHING TO DO WITH the old saying that "for want of a nail a shoe was lost; for want of a shoe a horse was lost," etc. Many a camper, however, has painfully discovered that for want of a good knot or lashing a temper was lost, and along with it a tarpaulin, canoe, or valued pet.

Knots and lashings correctly and easily tied are a mark of the experienced outdoorsman. They can prevent a lot of trouble. Learning to tie a few basic knots and lashings is a fine way to pass an off-season evening in front of the fireplace. You may be surprised at how interesting such simple outdoor skills can become. The next time you take to the woods you'll be tickled with your new know-how.

Hundreds of knots have been devised over the centuries. You can get by very nicely, however, with just a few basic ones. In fact, with a square knot, a bowline, and two or three others you can do very well in the bush. All good knots have three things in common: (1) they're easy to tie, (2) they hold securely or slip if required, (3) they are easy to untie.

Even if you learned your knots as a Boy Scout years ago, a brushup won't hurt a bit and will be fun. A little time spent with a hank of clothesline will refresh your memory, and you'll be delighted at how much you recall.

Over the years we've seen some wild, complicated snarls serving campers in place of good, simple knots. We've also seen campers hacking away at such snarls when breaking camp rather than take any more time in trying to solve them. As a matter of fact, a sharp knife is often the only solution to such a tangle. Knowledge of a few basic principles would have saved time and rope.

Speaking of rope, ends should be whipped to prevent both fraying and untwisting. Whipping makes a rope easier to handle, longer-lasting, and more professional-looking. It helps most on ropes that have to be threaded through grommets, guy rope keys, and other openings. Whipping should be applied to any rope, however. There's nothing to it.

Whipping is done with strong string, either waxed or plain. There are several functional methods. The one we find easiest and most effective is simply enough done. Make a short loop in one end of the string and lay this loop along the top of the rope end. Then tightly wind the free end of the string several times about both loop and rope.

Finally, firmly grasp the other end of the string and pull it. This works the loop under the coils, and with it the free end that has been passed through it. Cut off the string ends, and you have a simple and secure whipping. To implant this in your mind, why not whip both ends of your practice rope?

Steps in Whipping a Rope End

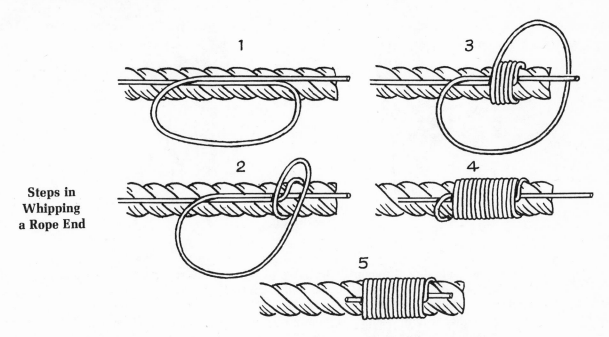

For such functions as mooring a boat, attaching a guy rope to a peg, or even tying a clothesline to a tree, use either a clove hitch or two half hitches. The clove hitch is a simple knot, yet few campers know how to tie it. All it is, however, is two loops going in opposite directions, around an object, with the free ends under the rope in both instances. These loops bind each other so that the hitch cannot slip.

The clove hitch, which of course can be used on either a horizontal or a vertical, can be untied in a twinkling. Slack, in the meantime, can be taken up easily. Merely loosen the first loop, take up the slack, and retighten the second loop. Keep the loops together so that they bind on each other.

The details of tying two half hitches are also simple to learn and use. Just pass the rope around something such as a chair arm, bring the end back and around the standing part (long portion of line), and then down through the loop thus formed. Make another loop around the standing rope and again pass the end down through it, this time in the opposite direction.

If you plan to keep these two half hitches tied only a few minutes, or if you wish to be able to free them quickly, leave the working end of the rope long and bend it back on itself when inserting it in the second loop. Then when you wish to loosen the knot, just yank this doubled-back end and it will be free. This same quick-loosening trick, by the way, can be used on nearly all knots.

Here's another gimmick. If the knot end is difficult to work back through the last loop of a knot, twist the rope to tighten the braiding or twisting as you push it back. This not only makes this section of the rope smaller, but it also gives it stiffness. Some campers

Clove Hitch   **Two Half Hitches**

insert a small stick through the last loop along with the rope end. Then when they wish to free the knot, they first break or pull out this little stick, leaving a handily large hole through which to return the rope end.

Another way to fasten a rope to a pole is with a timber hitch, although this is neither a permanent knot, nor secure when left slack. Just pass the end of a rope, preferably an old one in this case, around the pole. Make a half hitch around the standing part. Then take several more turns under and around the loop thus formed. Draw tight and maintain a steady pressure. A pull on the loop will quickly loosen this knot when you're ready.

If you need at the end of a rope a loop that will not slip and yet will be easy to free, the bowline will be perfect. It can be successfully tied in anything from light string to heavy line and will hold perfectly. Whoever invented this knot centuries ago was a genius.

Make a small loop in the standing part of a rope. Bring the end up through it, leaving a loop of the desired size. Now pass the end around the standing part of the rope and back down through the small loop. The resulting no-slip loop can be made as large as necessary and is a functional choice for rescue work. At the other extreme, a small bowline makes a good loop through which to slide the running noose of a lasso.

For tying a bundle, a pack, or a broken shoelace, the knot for you is the square knot. This basic knot is simple to tie, holds dependably, and yet can be untied easily, provided both ropes are about the same size. It is prone to turn on itself if tied to join a heavy rope with a considerably lighter one. For such a union, use the sheet bend. For the square knot, just cross the two ends, pass the first under the second, reverse the directions of the two ends, and cross the first over the second and down through the loop thus formed.

Square knots are used for numerous purposes and can be tied in anything from straw, to rope, to bandages. Even when tied in soft bandage material, a square knot can be untied by pushing the halves of the knot together.

For joining two ends of rope, especially when they are wet, frozen, or of different sizes or materials, no knot is more efficient than the sheet bend. It is simple to tie, never slips, doesn't require much rope, and can be speedily unknotted. Make a bight in the larger

Timber Hitch

Bowline

Square Knot

Sheet Bend

rope. Bring the end of the other rope up through the bight and around the standing parts. Then pass the end of this rope under itself where it comes up through the bight, so that when tightened it is held against the outside of the bight.

As for lashings, two are of major importance to the average individual who takes to the woods. They can be used for making camp chairs, stools, tables, washstands, shears to support a ridgepole, and numerous other projects. Twine and even string can be used for small things, while rope 5/16- or 1/2-inch thick will do for the larger enterprises.

The square lashing is the easiest of the bunch. A square lash will hold poles together for all sorts of construction from lean-to shelters to simple bridges. Position your poles. Then affix one end of the rope to one of the poles with a clove hitch. Wrap the joint, going around all the arms three times and ending with frapping turns. This frapping is accomplished by winding the rope between the poles two or three times, tightening the lashing. Finish the square lashing with another clove hitch around one of the poles.

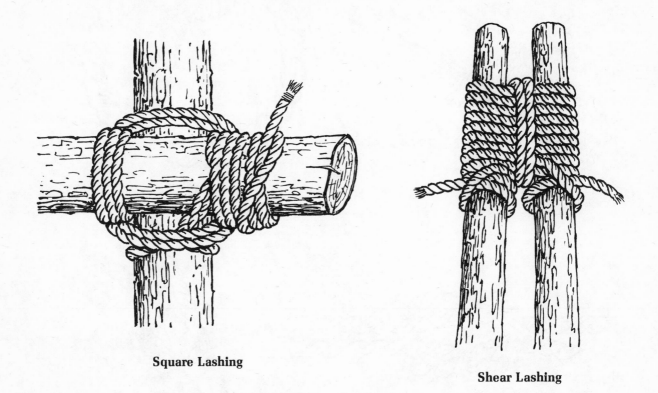

Square Lashing

Shear Lashing

When making a rectangle by fastening four poles together with square lashings, its rigidity will be increased by lashing a longer pole diagonally from corner to corner.

The other type of lashing that's primarily useful to campers is the shear lashing. This is just the ticket for fastening two or three poles together at one end. Place these poles side by side. Start with a clove hitch. Then wrap the rope around the poles. After several winds, frap between the poles for a tighter bind. Finish with another clove hitch.

Once you become adept with these few basic knots and two simple lashings, you'll wonder how you ever managed to take to the woods without them.

31

That Small Emergency

SOME SMALL EMERGENCY MAY ARISE ON ALMOST ANY TRIP TO THE woods. It may be no more than a screwtop jar or bottle you can't open, or running plumb out of matches, but it can be mighty frustrating.

If a screw-top container is stubborn because of sticky contents dried in the threads, put the can or jar upside down in a pan of warm water for a few moments. If this treatment doesn't loosen the top, dent its center with a stone, wrap a wet cloth around it for a firmer grip, and try again.

If you have lightweight rubber boots, wrapping the container top in the rubber gives a very firm grip. Rubber bands can be used the same way; anything to keep your hands from slipping. If none of these methods works, rap the top sharply with a stone all around the edge to loosen the threads or immerse the top of the container in very hot water for several minutes. Besides loosening sticky material in the threads, the hot water will cause the metal top to expand.

The easiest way to start a campfire or ignite a gas stove without conventional matches is with one of the little metal rods that, impervious to moisture and safe to carry, can be used for this purpose. Its inventor discovered a few years ago that by combining certain rare earths he could produce a solid stick that could be safely scraped to produce sparks that burn with considerable heat.

First use a knife, a sharp piece of metal, a bit of broken glass, or a sharp stone to scrape a few fine particles of metal from the rod into dry leaves, shredded cedar bark, dry moss, an old bird's nest, or some other tinder. Then, with sharp, glancing blows of the same sharp object, drive a shower of sparks onto the particles. They will ignite and burn with a very hot flame, kindling the surrounding dry material.

Sparks alone from the rod will ignite camp stoves and lanterns even in a high wind. To light a camp stove, have your little rod and sharp edge ready, turn on the fuel, and scrape a shower of sparks directly at the burner. To light a camp lantern, just remove the globe, turn on the fuel, and aim the sparks at the mantle. The little rod cannot start a fire by itself, is not penetrable by weather or water, and will not melt under normal conditions.

Many modern tents have door and window zippers. Occasionally a zipper will open behind the slide, leaving the door or window open. You can't close it again because the slide won't pick up the teeth in reverse. This happened with our tent's door zipper a few years ago, and we had to do something about it because we planned a long stay in insect-filled woods.

First, we removed the metal clip at the lower end of the zipper and took the slide completely off the teeth. At the top of the zipper, we cut out half an inch of teeth on both sides. Then we eased the slide into the opening and fed the teeth into its open ends. Once the teeth were engaged, we pulled the slide down a few inches and used a safety pin as a stop. We pinned this through the material behind the slide so that the slide could not move back into the opening cut for it. At the lower end of the zipper, we used another safety pin to prevent the slide from coming off the bottom.

Later, we replaced the pins with rugged thread and darned the small hole at the upper end of the zipper to keep out no-see-ums and other tiny insects. That zipper is still okay. Incidentally, if zipper trouble is caused by a defective slide, there's an inexpensive repair kit on the market that could be useful. The kits we have each consist of two slides, a repair tool, and a tube of zipper lubricant.

It is difficult and dangerous to sculpture ice to fit a chest with your hunting knife, to say nothing of what this does to a good point and blade. Such emergencies can be avoided by buying an ice pick designed for camping. For less than $2 you can get a proper one with a strong steel point, a comfortable solid handle of colored plastic that can be easily seen, and a strong and safe sheath to cover the sharp point, protecting both it and yourself.

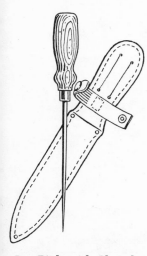

Ice Pick with Sheath

(Note: A metal tube longer than the pick point may replace the sheath.)

If you have one of those always popular gasoline pressure stoves and discover that the pump no longer functions, the leather washer on the piston may be dry or glazed. It's simple to repair and can be fixed in a few minutes. First, remove the wire bail in the collar of the pump. This unlocks the collar so that you can extract the rod and piston in one unit.

Work a little bacon fat, oil, or boot grease into the leather or use a drop or two from the dripstick of your car. Do not use much, just enough to soften the leather. Once this is done, replace it in the piston tube and put back the wire through the cap and tube neck holes to secure it in place. The pump, which operates on the same principle as a tire pump, should perform excellently after this rejuvenation.

If flashlight or other dry-cell batteries become weak and you have no replacements, they can sometimes be pepped up by baking them for an hour or so. Try setting them on a stone near the fringes of a small campfire. When we're enjoying log cabin living, we regularly replenish radio batteries by leaving them all afternoon in an oven at low heat. The trick can be used several times with weak batteries, perhaps giving you time to replace them.

A small item that can see you through more than one emergency is a rubber or plastic fuel-transfer pump which, selling inexpensively, consists of a squeeze bulb with tubing at both ends. It can be used to transfer fuel from car to appliance, boat to appliance, fuel can to appliance, or from one appliance to another. If you ever run out of gas on the way to or from the woods, it will transfer enough fuel from the tank of a friendly motorist to get you going again. This handy little pump, whose intake must always be higher than its outlet to continue working automatically, can also be used to bail a small boat or suck up water from the floor of a tent.

It seems unlikely that any camper would arrive at his campsite without the frame for

How to Refreshen Batteries by Baking Them

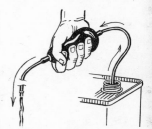

Fuel-Transfer Pump

his tent, but it happened to a friend of ours. He thought his son had packed the frame, and his boy opined his father had taken care of that detail. They arrived at the end of a logging road in Maine with no frame for their umbrella tent. Their tent had holes in the peak and eaves' corners for the tips of an interior frame.

What to do, go home or improvise? They cut four 12-foot saplings, lashed them into tepee shape, and hung the tent beneath it. They shoved a loop of stout line through each hole from the outside, then rammed a short piece of wood through each loop to anchor these inside the tent. Then they tied the lines to the peak of the tepee frame and a pole at each corner. The tapes at the bottom corners of the tent were affixed to these poles with longer lines. One sapling, which proved to be too limber, had to be replaced, but otherwise the improvised frame worked fine.

Another common camping mishap is to bog down on logging roads. If holes and ruts are dark with water, use a pole to determine how deep they are before you venture over them. If they are too deep, fill them with dirt, rocks, or brush. If you get into soft sand, deflate your tires a bit to get better traction, or go very slowly and be careful not to spin the wheels.

If your rear wheels do sink in, jack up the rear of the car, fill the holes with brush or gravel, let the car down carefully, and drive out. If the wheels are too deep, jack up the back and, releasing the brake, let the car slide forward off the jack to get the wheels out of the holes. After experiencing this nuisance once or twice, you'll test more surfaces before driving on them.

It's amazing how often the can opener is forgotten. At least half the people we've talked with admit they left it behind at least once. There are various solutions for this omission involving knives and axes. More careful campers tuck an opener inside the icebox lid, leave one in the glove compartment, or, as we do, hang one from the key chain. There are little G.I. openers that are great for this latter use and cost about $.20. They'll open good-sized cans in a jiffy.

Improvised Sapling Frame for Tent

Forgetting to pack spare lantern mantles can be frustrating, too. The campers who've done this now carry a couple of extras wrapped in cellophane, either taped in the bottom of the lantern, in a wallet, or even in the sweatband of a hat. One fellow has his inside his razor box. If they can help it, these individuals don't intend to sit in the dark again.

Have you ever reached camp and found your flashlight, walkie-talkie, or electric razor with dead batteries, or during the night noticed a faint glow inside your duffle bag? Well, you're not alone. The answer? Simply tape the switches in the off position before packing. Reversing the batteries can be even surer. Either method not only saves batteries but also preserves good dispositions.

Those who wear glasses will be well advised to take a spare pair. Otherwise, breaking either lens or frames can make a camper pretty miserable until he gets them repaired. It is also not a bad idea to carry a small repair kit with small, replacement screws and a miniature screwdriver. Incidentally, a piece of broken safety razor blade will serve for the latter in a pinch.

You can also repair broken glasses with transparent tape, copper wire, thread, elastic bands, and other assorted items. If a lens is broken so that the pieces can be fitted together, regular transparent tape may hold them in the frame so that you can at least read the road map.

Several years ago we were experimenting with Eskimo glare glasses. These consist of small strips of bone or bark with very tiny slits cut in them, through which the wearer peers out. The smallness of the slits enables the Eskimo to see without injury to his vision in the terrible glare of arctic snow and ice. One of us could not wear his ordinary glasses

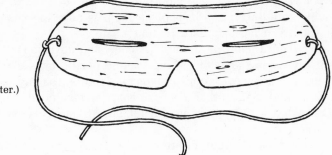

Eskimo Glare Glasses

(Note: The finer the slits the better.)

while testing these gadgets, easily made of birch bark, but he was surprised to find that he could see quite well through the small slits without his glasses.

This intrigued him, so he experimented with holes he made in paper and cardboard. He found that he could read the small print without any lens at all when he looked at it through a small hole held close to the eye. The smaller the hole, the better it worked. He made a row of tiny holes in a piece of paper and held it close across his eyes. He found he could easily read the small print of maps, compass bearings, and directions for operating appliances.

An oculist gave a simplified explanation for this. He said that when an individual's eye lens is imperfect, rays which do not enter the exact center of the eyeball are distorted unless corrected by glasses. By peeping through a pinhole, you reduce the rays entering the eye to those in the very center of the eye lens. If you lose or break your glasses, then, make a substitute pair by punching tiny holes in paper or birch bark with a needle or pointed stick.

When camping in a very rocky area, take along a few mountain climbers' pitons. Pitons are flat, pointed, inexpensive steel pins with a hole or ring at the blunt end. Drive the pitons into cracks in the rock and tie your guy ropes to the rings. With pitons, you can often avoid lugging heavy rocks and logs.

If you are short of wooden stakes or break those you have been trying to drive into hard ground, more can be made from saplings about an inch thick. Chop or saw a sapling off just below a branch and then cut it again about a foot above the branch. Trim off the branch about two inches from the trunk and sharpen the other end of the sapling. After driving this peg, loop the guy rope under the downward-pointed branch stub.

When you are fixing a small hole in an air mattress and you've no repair kit, pitch from a conifer will serve in a pinch.

How many times have you grabbed, usually too late, at a tablecloth that's taking off in a sudden breeze? Now you can lick that problem with some little plastic spring clamps that hold the cloth to the edge of the table. No matter whether the tablecloth is plastic, cloth, or paper, these inexpensive clips will hold it securely.

This reminds us of a trick we learned a few summers ago while camping beside a lake where the onshore breezes kept us busy chasing empty paper plates around the table. We bought a roll of plastic tape manufactured with two sticky sides, and the next time it was breezy we made a cross of it on the bottom of each paper plate before setting it out. It worked. Incidentally, a loop of paper masking tape will work just as well.

Accidental fires in a campground can be frightening, but an extinguisher can make the difference between a small accident and a real tragedy, particularly when a tent and its contents are involved. Small, reliable extinguishers, containing either liquid or foam, cost from $1 to $5 or so. It's important to keep such a fire extinguisher out where it can be reached in a hurry. The best place for it is near the camp stove or campfire, or in the tent if you are using a lantern or tent heater.

Ever raced around in a storm? If you have any amount of camp gear that should be covered, try buying some of the big opaque plastic bags. Grocery stores carry them. They make fine weather covers for appliances, food, garbage, laundry, tape recorders, camera equipment, and many other necessities. The opaque material camouflages the contents enough so that a petty thief might not be attracted. They can be used many times and take up little room.

Trouble packing your car-top rack? Those who use these racks without enclosed carriers will find elastic shock-cord rigs for luggage a blessing. A tie-down rig consists of a metal ring from which radiate as many as a dozen elastic cords, each with a stout metal hook.

Place the ring over the center of the load, stretch the hooked cords in all directions, and fasten each end to the rack frame. The tension is great, so be sure that each hook is securely anchored before letting go its cord. Otherwise, a cord can snap back dangerously. If there are luggage handles handy, pass the cords through them as well as through straps, duffle-bag handles, and package bindings.

Small fry along? Infants in a camping party sometimes require warm drinks in a hurry. You can plug a little drink-heater right into your car's cigarette lighter socket and warm liquid quickly. The heater sells for about $3 and will warm milk, coffee, tea, or cocoa in a cup or glass. For doing this some distance from your vehicle, there is a 25-foot extension cord for cigarette-lighter sockets that sells for about $4 and can be used on any appliance that is designed to operate from a vehicle dashboard. It is particularly fine for fluorescent tent lamps, which require little power and give a fine light.

If your tent has wooden slides for the guy ropes and you have wondered what you would do if one should break or split, take along a couple of the little metal slides that can be installed in less than a minute. These sell for about $.15 apiece and can be carried in a small space in your pack or car.

No place to hang anything? For the tent camper there are many little gadgets that can be attached to tent poles, fly poles, and ridgepoles. For example, there is a bar containing a set of hooks for clothing and other gear that can be attached to the ridgepole. There are separate hooks that clamp to tent or fly poles for clothing, etc., and also such accessories as clamp-on mirrors, soap dishes, and shelves. For years we've used hanging sets of canvas pockets, each with its snap-fastened flap, for small articles.

Most male campers feel better if they have tools along for repairing appliances and other gear. There is a handy little combination wrench, pliers, wire cutter, and screwdriver that sells for about $5. This tool was originally designed for ski troops in World War II, but it has become so popular that it has now been brought out in hardened, chrome-plated steel. Small and light, it fills many a need for the tinkerer in camp.

There are also many small, inexpensive items available from the local hardware store that are often handy in camp. Take along a small coil of copper wire, a few 3-inch nails, assorted safety pins, tweezers, about 50 feet of strong nylon line, a few assorted web straps with rustproof buckles, and even a box of toothpicks. The latter are fine for picking out clogged stove-burner openings and lamp tubes. Pipe cleaners are handy for getting oil into difficult places and for holding plastic bags closed. You can even use them as emergency shoelaces.

32

Camp Sanitation

NOT MANY YEARS AGO, WHEN CAMPING EXCEPT FOR THE WAGON trains was almost 100 percent a man's sport, camp sanitation was as rare as a razor in the wilderness. The rougher campers lived, the better the men thought it was, up to a point. Beyond that, even their own lack of sanitation began to get them.

They soon found that cleaning game and fish in camp and failing to clean up afterward brought flies by the thousands, that failure to build and use a latrine was a sad mistake, and that garbage and dirty clothes left unattended took the pleasure out of their surroundings. Small cuts and blisters became infected, and dirty underwear started to chafe and irritate. Perhaps a little sanitation wasn't such a sissy idea after all.

Today, with women and youngsters going along on a majority of camping trips, camp sanitation is a must rather than a whim, for it can make the difference between a pleasant time and a sad occasion. Not that it's necessary to go to extremes; you can maintain a clean camp by observing a few simple rules.

Personal sanitation can prevent chafing, blisters, and infections through small cuts and scrapes. Clean hands and face greatly help to keep infection to a minimum, and clean socks and feet will almost eliminate sore extremities and blisters on a backpacking journey. Washing clothing, especially underwear, is important even in the absence of modern laundry appliances.

As a matter of fact, family campers can buy a small, hand-operated, camp washing machine that does a fine job for small loads. One sells for under $25, weighs less than nine pounds, and is only a trifle more than a foot square. It will handle up to seven pounds of laundry at a time and can use cold water as well as hot. It's fine for camping mothers who have small fry to keep clean.

Even without machines, a dunking in water with a little soap or detergent and drying in the bright sun will keep clothes clean. Don't worry about wrinkles. If you insist, though, you can hang clothes on a line and snap them flat while they are still wet, so they will dry smooth. We've often done this sort of snap pressing in Alaska and British Columbia with khaki shirts and trousers, and they come out fine. Blue jeans can also be pressed this way. Just be sure the inside of shirt collars are smooth so as to prevent chafing, but if they do come out rough, a soft handkerchief worn about the neck will solve the problem.

Bright sunlight is a fine fumigator, and even soiled clothing turned inside out and aired in the sun for a few hours will be pleasanter to put back on. Socks aired and sunned this way, even without washing, will keep your feet in sounder shape.

Keeping the interior of your tent clean will help keep your clothing clean. This can be accomplished several ways. Either use a sheet of plastic film or a lightweight tarp over the tent floor so that it can be removed and shaken clean when dirty, or use a small

Tent with Doormat

scrap of old carpet or canvas as a mat outside the tent door for wiping shoes and boots on before entering.

If the area around the campsite becomes muddy, keep a pair of dry shoes or slippers inside the tent door so you can shed muddy footwear outside and change before entering the living quarters. This will help keep the tent floor drier, too.

If your tent has no floor, try to keep it as free of leaves and ground rubbish as possible since these may harbor small animals while you are out of the tent and also promote dampness. A tarpaulin spread over the interior ground of the tent will help keep it drier and more sanitary.

Many campers carry a child's play broom. One takes up little room in the car or station wagon and is a great convenience in keeping a tent floor clean. We've even seen some long-term campers carry a rake to keep their tent area spic-and-span.

Sanitation in regards to food and water is most important. Unless you are at a public campground where water is piped in from a pure source, or camped high in true wilderness at a spring, there is a possibility of contaminated drinking water. If you are tenting near civilization in a rural area where there are septic tanks or outhouses, be especially wary of any water, running or not. It may be contaminated by either human or animal waste.

Boil any suspicious drinking water at a fast, rolling boil for a full five minutes at sea level and an extra minute for each additional 1,000 feet of elevation. Then cool it before drinking it. If such water tastes flat, pour it back and forth between two clean containers to aerate it.

Another way to purify water is to add a halazone or Globaline (iodine-releasing) tablet to every pint you use per instructions on the labels of the small bottles in which these are obtainable at drug stores. If the water is especially suspicious, use two tablets per pint. Then wait thirty minutes. It's a good idea to make up your drinking, cooking, and washing water for dishes and teeth ahead of time for this reason. It takes only a moment to drop the pills into a canteen or waterbag.

Open food should be protected with netting held away from it to prevent flies from landing on it. These pests in particular carry germs, and in country near habitations such flies may come directly to your table from a neighboring outhouse or barnyard. Keep opened cans covered with metal foil, waxed paper, or plastic, or put them in the icebox. Keep food on the table covered as much as possible to keep it uncontaminated by flies and insects and to prevent its odors from attracting hornets and wasps.

As much as we all dislike dishwashing, it's best to get it done as soon as possible after eating if only to prevent insects from collecting. We put the dishwater on to heat when we begin dining so that it's hot when we're finished. Do not empty your dishwater near the tent, for it is bound to attract flies. Dig a small hole, pour it in, and cover it with dirt at once.

Garbage disposal in camp can be simple and effective if you prepare for it. Dig a garbage pit, at least 100 feet downwind of your tent and downhill from any water source, about two feet deep. This is for the residue. First, scrape anything burnable into your campfire. All relatively dry refuse such as paper plates, corn husks, and grocery wrappers can be burned. Even remainders such as meat scraps, fruit rinds, coffee grounds, and egg shells can be dried and then burned. Spread these soggy leftovers on a piece of metal foil, wire screening, an old grill, or a green-branch grill over the coals to dry for later burning, or dry them to combustible condition on hot stones close to the fire. What won't

Steps in Garbage Disposal
Left: Burning refuse. Right: Covering garbage pit with dirt.

eventually burn can be dropped into the garbage hole and covered with dirt. Then it isn't a bad idea, depending on the season, to spray the spot with insect repellent.

Tin cans should be rinsed, opened at both ends, burned out in a fire, flattened, and buried away from the camp area. Pour the rinsing water on the ground and cover it with dirt to kill food odors. The burning of the rinsed cans not only eliminates food smells that attract animals, but it removes the lacquer or tinning so that the cans will rust away

Disposing of Tin Cans

easier. The flattening will make them simpler to bury. Wash out and bury glass food containers, too. If the ground where you are camped is too rocky to permit the burying of empty cans, leave them in an exposed place away from camp and they will soon rust away, but be sure to flatten them so that no small animals will be trapped in them and so that they won't hold water to breed mosquitoes. This presupposes that for some reason you are not able to take them out with you when you go and dispose of them in regular trash cans, always the recommended procedure.

Burn any cardboard food packages as well as tin ones, and also candy wrappers, especially chocolate papers for they attract insects in a hurry. Chocolate odor is especially attractive to some bears, so if you are in one of the parks where bears are an attraction, get these wrappings burned as soon as possible.

Keep scouring pads for cleaning pots and pans wrapped in metal foil or store them in a covered plastic dish, or they too will attract insects because of the particles of food and grease trapped in them. Wash off grease or food spilled about the fireplace or tent area with hot water or cover it with dirt. Keep cooking appliances free from grease.

If despite these precautions animals are still digging about your garbage pit, build a small fire over it after filling it with dirt. This helps kill the smells.

When dressing fish or game in camp, keep the refuse in as small an area as possible, and then bury and cover it. Rinse off any blood or liquids from such refuse and cover it with dirt. Better do such work away from the tent area, but never dispose of such refuse in a stream or lake. If you use a nearby flat stone or log for such cleaning, pour boiling water over it afterward.

Never throw tin cans or bottles in any stream or lake, and don't break bottles against rocks or use them for target practice. The pieces may not only cut some animal's feet, but those of another camper or his tires. Sections of glass bottles or containers may collect water, converting them into magnifying glasses that can start forest fires long after you've departed. This has happened time and time again, so bury all glass and metal containers.

The disposal of human waste is one of the world's most pressing sanitation problems, and it's certainly a serious one for the camper. He is often far from medical aid, and careless camp sanitation can contaminate drinking water over a surprisingly extensive area.

The indiscriminate use of the woods for a toilet is not only poor camping manners, but it is dangerous to health. If you plan to camp for any length of time in one spot where there are no facilities for disposal, you must get rid of the waste in one definite area in such a way that it is no hazard to water supplies.

A latrine should be located at least fifty yards downwind from the tent area, preferably farther, and as distant as possible from any usable water. The latrine pit should be dug in a low spot so it will not drain away from the area and so that all liquids will sink into the ground immediately below the pit.

The depth of this pit will be determined by the length of your stay and the number in the party, but it should be at least two feet deep. Save the removed dirt for filling after each use, and it is not a bad idea to add a bit of chloride of lime on each occasion from a handy, inexpensive can. A small trench shovel or clean tin can can be used for moving the dirt.

Poles lashed between trees can serve as a seat, and a roll of tissue on a stick or branch can be covered with a large inverted can, such as a four pound jam tin, to protect it from squirrels and the weather.

With modern portable toilets now available, there is really no need for the ladies in the party to worry about camping conveniences if you're car-camping. These toilets can be bought from around $6 up to $350 or so. The former are the most popular and consist of a standard seat top mounted upon folding legs. Disposable, opaque plastic bags clip under the seat for later removal and disposal in a pit or at a public toilet of the privy type.

The expensive model is ideal for permanent camps, cabins, trailers, boats, and so on. It operates automatically after each use, consuming every particle of waste in a flame of 2,100 degrees and converting everything either to harmless carbon dioxide or water vapor in seconds. No plumbing, no chemicals, no cleaning, and no odor or flushing are required. All that is needed is a small vent pipe to the outside.

Many experienced campers take along a small inexpensive tent to shelter the toilet, whether a dug latrine or a portable seat type. These can be bought for under $15.

Camping sanitation may seem almost more bother than it's worth. However, rest assured that you will soon realize what a difference it can make. It marks the considerate and veteran camper and is a public indication of just what sort of housekeeper you are at home. You are sure to find it well worthwhile.

33

Getting the Best of Pests

OFTEN INDIVIDUALS HAVE COMPLAINED THAT THEY ARE ESPECIALLY good mosquito bait and that the pesky insects will seek them out in preference to other people nearby. U.S. Department of Agriculture scientists have determined that this may be true.

The human skin produces lactic acid and carbon dioxide which in combination is an effective mosquito attraction. Some individuals' skins produce more of this acid than others, and they are those who have the greatest bite-and-itch problem. However, now that the chemical nature of human attraction for skeeters has been determined after a concentrated ten-year search, it is hoped that the information can be used to develop effective mosquito traps. A summer without mosquito bites may yet become a reality.

In the meantime, many would-be campers hesitate to take to the woods for fear of running into a wide variety of so-called camping pests. This is especially true of city inhabitants and women. While you're bound to meet some camp pests sooner or later, chances are that it won't be too often. Don't let them keep you at home.

The most obvious pests are the insects, with mosquitoes heading the list. These are usually only temporarily bothersome, though, except in some southern camping areas where they might carry malaria or other disease. Check this with local health or conservation people in areas where you plan to camp, and take the steps they advise.

The best way to dodge mosquitoes anywhere is to camp where they're scarce. Avoid pitching a tent near stagnant water or in damp areas with thick vegetation. Mosquitoes usually haunt brooks, lakes, and rivers, but if you camp on ground high above the water, breezes will help keep them away.

Too, there are now many types of good mosquito repellents on the market, led by those in which diethyl toluamide, a U.S. Department of Agriculture development, is an active ingredient. The stronger of these are particularly effective, not only on skeeters but also on ticks, chiggers, gnats, fleas, and other biting insects. They come in various forms, including sprays which can be safely applied to skin, boots, clothing, and hats, as well as to tent and cabin screening.

The best nighttime protection against mosquitoes is a tent with a sewn-in floor, plus well-screened windows and door. The floor keeps them from sneaking in under the sides through the grass. With such an arrangement, and with a good repellent for the daytime, you needn't fear any country.

Such insects as chiggers and ticks can be more than just a bother. Ticks, particularly, can be downright dangerous, as they've been known to carry tularemia as well as Rocky Mountain spotted fever.

Chiggers are tiny, red, and nearly invisible. They are found in the South, where they are commonly known as red bugs. They swarm among thick vegetation by trails and game runs, eager to hitch a ride on your clothing. There they soon move to burrow into your skin and bite, causing acute irritation. Spraying clothing, especially shoes and socks, with diethyl toluamide compound will keep them away. Use it also on collars, sleeves, and head-gear when traveling through thick bush in known chigger country. Old remedies weren't nearly as effective.

If you should get some chiggers on yourself, use strong ammonia water, a paste of baking soda and water, or calamine lotion to control the itching. As with all bites, do not scratch with dirty fingernails and thus risk the added chance of infection. If you're suspicious of the region, keep away from high grass, brush, and other places where chiggers may lurk and perhaps move on to a better campsite. Check with local conservation or health agencies before going into an area where there may be either chiggers or ticks, and be armed against them.

Ticks are 8-legged, about 3/16-inch long, and hang out in grass and brush along trails. There are several species of tick, and they are fairly widely distributed. Sprays and lotions containing the same diethyl toluamide are effective against these critters. When in tick country, be sure to tuck your trousers into your boots and to wear smoothly finished clothing to help prevent ticks from catching hold as you pass. Ticks will even travel some distance to get to individuals sitting on the ground or to clothing left in the open. You'll probably never see a tick, but it is just as well to know what to do just in case.

When a tick reaches the warmth of a human body, it will painlessly embed its head in the skin and begin to draw blood, swelling grotesquely as it does so. If you find one, remove it at once, grasping it as close to the head as possible with the fingers or prefer-ably by tweezers, being careful not to burst the tick and so spread its possible contagion. A covering of thick oil or grease, preventing the tick from breathing, may also cause its withdrawal. Heat from a match or lighter will often cause it to let go. Just be sure to remove all the tick, especially the head. If that remains, dig it out immediately and apply an antiseptic to the wound.

In tick country inspect yourself and your clothing from time to time to make sure you haven't become a host. Removal of a tick within five hours after its attachment will probably prevent transmission of any disease.

In high country and particularly in the northern coniferous forests in the spring the black flies swarm. Many enter sleeves, collars, ears, and trouser bottoms. They are partic-ularly apt to settle behind ears and along your temples, where they bite viciously enough to cause blood to flow. Then there are beach flies—also called midges, punkies, and no-see-ums—so tiny that only the finest screening will deter them. Use repellents liberally, particularly on face, neck, and ankles, to discourage these pests. Keep repellents away from eyes, of course. If the beach flies are too bad, use a head net.

Public camping areas, because of enforced sanitation and spraying, are usually free of most insect pests. It is mostly only back of beyond that such pests become a problem.

If you camp in such backcountry, keep all foods covered, fill in or drain any small puddles about the camp, and burn or bury all garbage at the earliest possible moment.

In the absence of a tent with screened windows and door, a few yards of fine-mesh bobbinet from a dry goods store can be draped into an effective cover over your sleeping bag, or even just over your head, on a simple frame of sticks. Keep face and hands away from the mesh as you sleep to avoid being bitten right through the material.

Fine-Mesh Bobbinet Insect Cover

Wasps and hornets are occasionally camp pests. Hornets, especially the yellow jackets, sometimes nest in the ground and can be a hazard to anyone allergic to their sting. If you see them going in and out of a hole near camp, wait until the cool of the evening when all are inside. Then pour boiling water down the opening. Follow up by stamping it closed and then adding a flat rock. This should reduce the hornet population for the remainder of your stay. Another trick is to hang a small skinned fish over a pan of water. The hornets will feed on it until they cannot fly away, then fall into the water and drown. If you are extremely allergic to stings, check with your doctor as to what medication to carry with you.

Next to insects—and today's repellents will really tame these—snakes seem to be the main bugaboo to some campers, especially the girls, even though your chances of seeing a snake, let alone a dangerous one, are thin. One of us lives less than fifty miles from New York City, and he has seen more snakes in his backyard than he has during a half-century of camping and wandering about the woods and fields. In fact, he can't recall ever seeing one in camp, not even in the Florida swamps, where his party were looking for them as part of survival training.

Snakes like to be left alone, so they shun camping areas. Out West you might find a rattler in known snake country, and in the East you might spot a copperhead or rattler even close to New York City if you knew where to look. But about all the average individual will ever see of a snake will be the last few inches of him as he hurries to get away. As snakes subsist on live food, they're not interested in whatever you've brought along. A tent with a sewn-in floor and screens will certainly be snakeproof, or get one of those jungle hammocks and sleep between two trees.

We had a letter from one reader whose wife spent most of a camping trip snoozing in the car while the rest of the family was comfortable in a good tent. She thought she'd seen a snake the day they arrived. After several days, one of her youngsters found the "snake"—a green-and-white striped belt minus the buckle.

Not a few women also worry about mice. Certainly there are some scampering through the woods, but chances are you'll never see one except by accident. The little white-footed deer mice, which look like refugees from a Walt Disney picture, love to get into any food that's left open. They especially dote on peanut butter, apples, and sweet repasts like molasses. Incidentally, the best bait to use for trapping them in a country home, such as one encountered on your camping travels, is peanut butter mixed with molasses and a whisper of salt.

These are the little chaps with white bellies and feet who take over birds' nests for their homes, as they can climb trees almost as well as squirrels. So if you spot a little mouse with big ears and jewellike black eyes scampering up a pine, don't think you've been too long in the sun.

The other mice of the woods are the little voles, generally called meadow or field mice. Smaller than the deer mice, they are gray and have short tails. They live on grasses, so they have no interest in your food box. You might spot one along a wall or ledge, or perhaps skittering about the roots of a tree, but you'll almost never find one in the vicinity of your tent. A sewn-in floor will assure safety from these creatures.

Other possible camp visitors are raccoons, skunks, and porcupines. Raccoons will amble into camp occasionally to see what's been left out of the food box. They'll try almost anything edible and are partial to eggs. On one trip when we found that our eggs had passed the point of no return, we put out one each night just to see the coons come out and get them. They put on quite a drama.

Coons will dig up garbage unless it's buried too deep for them to smell, and they're apt to pry open anything that's not securely fastened. Even sliding bolts and stout hasps won't always stop them, since they are especially clever about solving such gadgets. If coons are about, keep your food securely locked up, suspended from an overhead branch on an unchewable wire, or safe inside the closed tent or car. Raccoons won't bother it in any of these places. They'll never molest an individual, and a yell or flashlight beam will send them scurrying.

Skunks, too, may visit camp, but ordinarily they'll leave with dignity when you yell, rattle some pans, or turn a light on them.

Porcupines, on the other hand, may not leave unless you toss sticks at them or chase them out of camp with stones. Don't get too close in case a porky takes a swipe at you with its flailing tail. They can't, of course, throw their quills, but that appendage may swipe anyone who comes too close. The main danger from porkies, however, is to equipment, for they dote on gnawing such belongings as ax handles, saddles, and canoe paddles for the salt left from sweaty hands.

Porcupines can ruin any of these in minutes, so keep such gear out of their reach or safely in a closed tent or car. If you have to leave such belongings outside, they can be protected by treatment with a wood preservative and stain containing copper naphthenate. This comes in either brown or green. There's also a functional colorless preservative containing zinc naphthenate.

Another chap we know of, who had a sort of permanent camp in the woods, saved his outfit by heaping a couple of handfuls of rock salt on a stump 100 yards from camp. The porcupines gathered there instead of around his favorite ax.

Antlered and horned animals seldom enter a camping area, but occasionally one just passes through or becomes curious and gets close enough to become entangled with a clothesline or guy rope during the night. In that case, it's best to let nature take its course and allow the animal to work out his own problem while you watch from the sidelines.

Incidentally, the best defense against an aroused animal, if you are unarmed, is to stand still and talk in a low, calm tone. The quiet human voice has a soothing effect on a wild animal. Don't run. Then the immediate instinct of the animal will be to pursue. But as soon as things ease down, retreat without showing any haste or excitement.

Wolves and coyotes are exciting to spot in the wilderness, and they offer no danger to the camper. Unless they are startled, cornered, or sick, they are as harmless as your pup, and even under those circumstances they would rather run than fight if given half a chance. There has been no authenticated case of a wolf attacking a human being anywhere in North America.

We've both traveled many miles with professional wolf trappers in country where timber wolves run in packs, while armed with nothing more lethal than cameras and a battered hatchet for cutting trap stakes. Too, we've slept out many a night with wolves howling close by, and never thought a thing about it except always to thrill at the savage symphony. You'll never find a wolf or coyote within eyesight of a camp if the animal can help it.

Mountain lions occasionally visit a camp, but it happens so rarely you can safely dismiss the possibility. Noise and lights will keep them at a distance, and even a small poodle will send them racing away. It's difficult enough to find a mountain lion even when hunting them in lion country, so don't worry about one's bothering you.

Bobcats and lynx are so rare that campers seldom see them. They generally avoid camps and other places where man has left his scent, although for several years recently in the Far North they followed the varying hares south and became common about one of our northern British Columbia cabins. They taste like chicken, incidentally.

Javelinas, small wild members of the swine family found in our Southwest, are occasionally seen near camps. However, even where they are plentiful, they rarely come close unless fleeing from an enemy and the camp happens to be in their path. They are certainly no danger to campers.

Small predators such as weasels are rarely seen near camps, although a few years ago one raced through our campsite in Maine, carrying a dead mouse in its teeth. This was most unusual, and except in the Far North, where they are common, we've rarely seen others even long distances from habitation. This also goes for other members of the Mustelidae family including mink, fisher, marten, and otter.

Muskrats and beavers never bother campers, although they occasionally saunter through camp on the way to water or a feeding area. Two sociable muskrats walked through our camps in different extremities of Canada looking for scraps, but both were entirely friendly. Amiable beavers have also visited our canoe camps.

Various kinds of squirrels and chipmunks are almost certain to come into camp. In Utah's Bryce Canyon National Park, the Rockies, and other areas, ground squirrels are very tame, but a serious word of caution about feeding them is in order. Park personnel warn that it is dangerous to let them approach too closely or to try to touch them. They may be covered with fleas, lice, and other parasites carrying diseases. They may also nip deeply if you attempt to touch them. Photograph them all you want, but toss food to them instead of attempting to lure them onto a hand or knee.

The interesting wood rats may sneak into your camp looking for food, but they are ordinarily clean and harmless. Screened doors and windows and a sewn-in floor will keep them outside your tent.

Out West, the so-called pack rat has a habit which can be annoying if not dangerous. He's a real kleptomaniac and will carry off anything that is bright, small, and eye-catching; car keys, cartridges, jewelry, wads of tinfoil, and almost anything he has no use for, including one of your socks. He often leaves a small payment in its place such as a pebble, a bit of bone, a leaf, or a pinecone. For this reason, he is called the trade rat. It's small consolation, however, to find a pinecone in place of your car keys, so keep small, important objects in a safe place if you think pack rats may be around.

Bats are never a peril to campers except when rabid. Rabid bats are about as rare as rabid foxes and really present no danger to the average outdoorsman. True, bats may fly about at night near your camp, but they are merely picking up insects attracted by your campfire or lantern. They make your camp a better place to live. They will never run into you or your tent, thanks to built-in radar.

Tarantulas, desert scorpions, black widow spiders, brown spiders, and centipedes are poisonous to some degree, to be sure, but they are far less hazardous than wasps, hornets, and our good friends the bumblebees. Keep an eye out for them, and if they are in the area, shake out your bedding, boots, and hats (if left on the ground) before getting into them.

Right off the bat, let's dispose of the bear menace. It's almost unheard of for the average camper to meet bruin except in such places as Yellowstone National Park and a few similar areas where bears are tourist attractions. In numerous areas there are bears and plenty of them, but if you keep at a distance, never feed them, keep victuals safely locked in the car trunk, and avoid cornering them or separating them from their young, they will be far less dangerous than the cattle you'll encounter while crossing pastures. The ordinary farm bull is said to be the most dangerous animal in the world.

Bears in some areas have learned that campers mean food, especially sweet and salty items, and they go to almost any lengths to get it, climbing on cars and testing windows, trunk lids, and iceboxes. Don't have a crack open where they can get a claw hold. If you keep food in it, be sure the trunk of your car is locked when leaving camp or bedding down for the night.

Bears especially like chocolate, ham, bacon, and honey, so keep these items at a minimum in your larder or safely stored either in the car or suspended high above the ground, but never in your tent if in brown bear country. Leaving the grub outside in an icebox is not a good idea, for a bear may carry it off and smash it at his leisure, or he may break into it right there as easily as a boy opens a box of cookies.

If there is a dump near your campground where bears come to feed, by all means watch them at their meals, but approach the area with caution if you are alone and make some sort of noise so as not to surprise them. Keep back 50 to 100 yards and make no sudden moves. If a bear starts toward you or makes threatening noises, retreat at once. Such bears are not tame. They are wild animals merely tolerating your presence. Never throw anything at them. Never try to get a little closer and, certainly, never try to have your picture taken with such a beast unless it is well in the background.

If bears come around your camp at night, bright lights, noise, and poking up the fire will usually send them away. In the case of a stubborn visitor, it will be best to retreat until he leaves. Never rush him or sic a pet dog on him. You could change an interesting evening into a tragedy.

Outside of insect and animal pests, there are such annoyances as poison ivy, poison oak, poison sumac, and minor menaces such as nettles. The best defense against such vexations is to know what they look like and to stay away. It's easy to learn to recognize them, both from books and from natives. Most public campsites are fortunately free of such nuisances. If you live or are going to country like California where poison oak is thick, it's not a bad idea to make yourself immune if possible by taking pills or drops, available at the drugstore, before exposure.

Upon accidentally coming in contact with any of these plants, wash yourself well with several soapy solutions of a strong soap such as the yellow laundry variety. Use calamine lotion, or one of the newer applications which your doctor or druggist knows about, on poison oak, ivy, or sumac rash. Parts of the body stung by nettles, which incidentally are good eating when young, may be washed in ammonia water to stop itching or stinging.

If you are worried about any of the pests here discussed, we still recommend that you go camping. Outside of the flies and mosquitoes, the chance that you will encounter any of them is small. The chance that you will meet many of them is practically nil. It is ridiculous to think that you will see all of them on a single camping trip.

34

Stay Healthy in Camp

ALTHOUGH SERIOUS ILLNESS SELDOM STRIKES DURING A SOJOURN IN the woods, it's wise to know how to try to prevent it and what to do if it occurs anyway.

Aside from including in your outfit a well-stocked medicine kit and the knowledge of how to use it—such as is contained in the compact, easily portable *Being Your Own Wilderness Doctor* by E. Russel Kodet, M.D., and Bradford Angier—one of the soundest ways to assure your enjoyment of a camping trip is to maintain the good general health of every member of your party.

If, for instance, you plan a canoe, bicycle, or backpack journey back of beyond, don't plunge right in after eleven months of sedentary work. Get in some advance toughening if at all possible. Without the benefit of some serious practice in paddling, pedaling, or climbing beforehand, at least take it easy the first few days. If you are middle-aged or have any signs of heart or any other sort of trouble, check with your doctor on how much wilderness activity you should undertake.

If you're overweight, some dieting and exercise will help, provided it's done gradually and intelligently. Don't forget that anyone who's overweight is carrying extra poundage even before slipping into pack straps or picking up a duffle bag.

Be particularly careful if plans call for hiking or camping at high altitudes even if you consider yourself already in pretty good shape. If you normally tend to become short of breath, it might be wise in the mountains to take along one of the small oxygen inhalers. These are also good for treating motion sickness, fainting, and nausea. Ask your personal physician about the advisability of having one along.

If anyone in your party is undergoing medication, be sure he takes along enough of whatever capsules, pills, or liquid is necessary. Also have him ask his doctor for written prescriptions in case the original supply is lost or ruined. If the medication needs refrigeration, be sure ice is available unless the party's equipment includes one of those propane-powered refrigerators or there is a filling station, farmhouse, or store nearby to keep the medication cold for you. If your written prescriptions become lost, a local druggist will probably be able to refill them by phoning your home pharmacist and giving him the numbers of the prescriptions on the empty containers or by calling the doctor directly.

People especially allergic to certain foods, plants such as poison oak, insect bites such as bee stings, or anything else, should carefully avoid them and carry remedies for additional protection.

For those who need glasses, it is a good idea to take an extra pair. Before an extended camping trip in backcountry, these should be made up with unbreakable lenses. Another tip, this for those who wear glasses just for reading and close work? Why not invest $3 or $4 or so in a pair of those so-called reading glasses advertised in many magazines and newspapers. These aren't perfect for long use, but for scanning maps, tying flies, or sewing up a seam, they'll do fine.

Take along a good pair of regular sunglasses or a pair of those clip-on lenses that convert ordinary glasses into sunglasses. Sun lenses are a must for eye comfort if you plan canoeing, boating, sunning on beach or rocks, long spells of fishing on glaring water, or a camp in snow country.

Experienced outdoorsmen know that the sun's rays can cause trouble even on an overcast day. To avoid sunburn, unless you already have a good tan, use sunburn lotion or cream for protection. Sunburn can be serious. Don't try to get your vacation tan all the first day.

Expose youngsters to the sun gradually until they have started a tan. They should wear light-colored clothing to turn away the rays, and broad-brimmed hats if they burn easily. These suggestions also hold for adults. About the worst and most unexpected burn can be picked up on a windy, overcast day with no sun visible.

If you buy milk, be sure it's fresh and pasteurized. Canned milk will be far better and safer than raw milk purchased in the field. So will reconstituted powdered milk.

If there's any question about meat's being tainted, bury it. Adequate refrigeration is required for such food, as well as for fish and milk. But if such things as bread, cheese, and bacon develop spots of mold, these can be removed, leaving the rest edible.

If the camp menu includes dehydrated foods or other items to which you're not accustomed, it's wise to try them before setting out on your camping safari.

Vegetables can be fresh or canned instead, if weight and space aren't problems. Vary meals so that they don't always include fried foods. It has been said that the white man's frypan has killed more Indians than firewater. Try to include broiled, baked, and boiled grub.

Have plenty of liquids, including fresh juices and whatever fresh fruit you can come by. If the climate is hot, ample liquids are a must, particularly for people who perspire greatly. This not only takes moisture from the body, but also salt and other chemicals essential to physical well-being.

Salt is especially important and must be replaced. When perspiring is profuse, the taking of a level teaspoon of salt with water twice a day is recommended by the American National Red Cross as a preventative for heat exhaustion. Or if you prefer, you can buy salt tablets.

When paddling, fishing, or hiking for long periods in the hot sun, keep your head covered, use salt tablets, and wear light-colored clothing to reflect the sun's rays. Remember to take it easy the first few days. If you start to feel dizzy or faint and are perspiring heavily, stop at once, seek shade, and relax. Pale, clammy skin and sudden weakness are signs of approaching heat exhaustion.

The body temperature is normal or subnormal with heat exhaustion. If you are cold, use hot packs. Recovery is the rule. Rest in a cooler location is the treatment. Salt is not especially indicated, but it does no harm along with copious fluids.

Heat cramps are the result of too much sun and too little salt. They are generally aggravated by drinking excessive amounts of water, as it's very easy to do, without sufficient salt. Heat cramps, which can be painful if not serious, can affect arms, legs, and abdominal muscles. Their onset may be marked by muscular twitching and a feeling of nausea. There is dizziness, and the skin is wet. Treatment consists of rest in a cool area and the taking of sufficient salt. For immediate relief, cover the affected area with a warm wet towel and apply pressure.

Heat stroke is a far more serious condition and one that frequently hits older folk overdoing it in the sun. A heat-stroke victim must have medical aid as soon as possible. The symptoms are a hot, dry skin and high temperature, often as high as 112 degrees. It is vital that this temperature be immediately lowered. Treatment consists of removal to a cool spot and, if possible, cool baths or rubdowns.

One aspect of camping health that it's easy to forget in the bush is personal cleanliness. Yet this can do much to keep you hale and hearty, ward off infection, and make camping generally more pleasant for both yourself and the rest of the party. Keep your hands clean, particularly when handling food. Change at least daily to clean underwear to prevent chafing and infection. Especially while doing a lot of hiking, keep your feet and socks clean. If blisters should develop despite these precautions, clean socks and feet will reduce the possibility of infection.

Camping should not be an excuse to let yourself become slovenly. Camping health and cleanliness go hand in hand. Camping health is just a matter of common sense in eating, drinking, exercising, and dressing away from home. There's every reason why campers should enjoy the best of health and come back haler than when they left. After all, that's a major reason why so many millions go camping.

35

Keeping Cool in Camp

REMEMBER THAT DUSTY, FLY-INFESTED DAY WHEN THE MERCURY sweltered above the hundred-degree mark and the entire forest smelled as if it were baking? Great drops of sweat gathered on your face, and it became even too much effort to lift the back of a hand to wipe them off. Even at night there was no wind, and the campfire, throwing its glow into the dark, seemed almost too much to sit beside. In other words, it can get hot even in the woods.

The difficulties of keeping warm while camping during really frigid weather can be considerable, but keeping cool during hot weather is an even greater problem. However, there are a few things a camper can do, even in extremely hot weather, to make life a bit more bearable.

One thing we learned years ago, while flying gliders, has helped keep us cooler in the woods. Motorless aircraft depend upon rising currents of warm air for their flight, and knowledge of what causes these eddies can help in locating a breezy area in which to pitch a tent. Veteran hunters, accustomed to watch every vagrant change of air during the day, accumulate much the same experience.

During a hot day, bodies of water of any size are slow to heat. Land areas, on the other hand—woods, fields, and rocks—heat more quickly. As a result, warm air over land rises and cool air flows horizontally toward these areas from the water to fill in below it. The rising warm air mass is called a thermal column.

At night, the land cools off much more quickly than the water, which is now warmed, so the flow of air is reversed. Then thermal currents rise over the water, and the air flows from the land to refill the area unless strong surface winds or a change in the weather disrupts the cycle. That's why in fair weather you hunt up in the morning and down during the late afternoon. That's also why, in the mountains, it's a sign of continued fair weather if mists waft down ravines in the morning and back up in the evening.

Camping on a slight rise near a pond or lake, particularly if there are open fields beyond your tent, will enable you to take advantage of these ground currents. If the ground breezes are slight, situate the tent so that its openings permit air to flow through. Use of lightweight tarps to funnel the air will help to increase the flow.

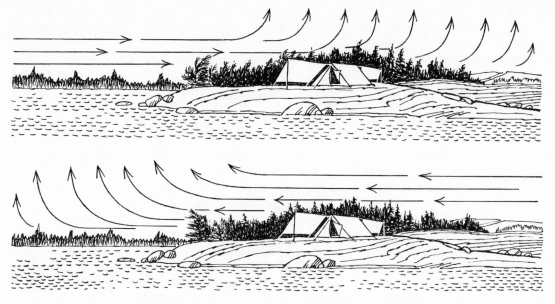

Tentsite Taking Advantage of Cooling Air Currents

Top: During day, cool air from nearby water area flows over land to fill space under warm air rising from vegetation. Bottom: At night, cool air flows from land to fill space under warm air rising above water.

Any tent becomes unbearable in warm weather unless it's in some sort of shade. Tall trees are better than low, thick ones, since the former not only afford shade, but they permit air to move through them and into the tent. Low, thick trees may give shade, but they also act as windbreaks, keeping cool breezes away. A fly or large tarp pitched over the top of the tent, with several inches of air space between the roof and the fly, will provide functional shade as well.

Tents with aluminized tops have become popular with those who camp on deserts and beaches or where shade is impossible to find or provide. The tops keep the interiors several degrees cooler. Some tents are painted white instead of aluminum on top. Either is fine. Desert nomads have used white robes, tents, and headgear for centuries to reflect the sun's rays. Certainly, light-colored tents are always cooler than dark ones because the material in the latter absorbs the sun's rays, while light colors turn much of them away.

If your tent doesn't already have an aluminized or white top, it may be a good idea to paint it this summer. A quart of good canvas paint will be sufficient for a small tent top, while a gallon will do for larger models. The paint may stiffen the material a bit, but this should be no problem if only the roof is treated. The paint will not harm the fabric and should give it increased waterproofing.

If there is plenty of water available at your hot-weather campsite, try wetting down the tent from time to time so that the interior will be cooled by evaporation. Desert water bags work on the same principle, although their material is generally more porous than tent canvas so water can seep through.

Sleeping in a hot tent can be oppressing, but once the sun has gone down and the outside air has cooled off, the inside can be ventilated by opening all the doors and windows and fanning the interior with a big towel or jacket. Exchanging the hot trapped air for the cooler outside air will make sleeping more comfortable. If it is still hot and you normally sleep on an air mattress and cot, give up the cot for the night and snooze on the ground or tent floor where the air will be cooler. Sometimes just a couple of feet can make a noticeable difference.

Don't use a sleeping bag if the weather is hot, of course, but keep it handy, or at least have a light blanket available, so that if it turns chilly during the night, you can keep warm. The softer and more form-fitting the sleeping bag's material is, the warmer it will be. So on hot nights, remove your bag and sleep directly on the air mattress. The latter can be made even cooler by blowing it up hard. Then the grooves will permit air to flow under you.

A little gasoline generator (there are several on the market) is handy for plugging in a small fan to cool off your tent or at least to keep the air circulating. If you have a fan, a small converter can be purchased that will enable you to run a 110-volt fan from the car battery. These converters are also handy for electric razors. A lot of old-time campers will snort at such a luxury, but if you have youngsters who mind the heat, such a converter-fan combination can be pleasant on a hot, muggy night.

During the day, keep in the shade and drink plenty of cool water. If you perspire a lot, take salt tablets occasionally. But remember that cool water is often hard to come by except at campsites by a running stream, shady lake, or deep natural spring. If none of these is nearby, however, any water that you may have can be cooled as much as twenty degrees by using a desert bag.

Such bags are simple, efficient, and long-lasting. They are made from flax or similar material and hold anywhere from two to five gallons. Soak the fabric well, fill the bag, and hang it where the wet material can evaporate. Water from the inside seeps through

Desert Bag

to continue the evaporation cycle, and this process cools the water inside. The bags are inexpensive. Out West you often see them on the bumpers of automobiles, the cooling process being speeded as the car moves. Some Western camper cars are fitted with special homemade bumper hooks from which the larger water bags can easily be hung.

Larger sizes of these bags can be used to take showers in camp, a fine way to cool off if there is no swimming available. Even a camper with only a small camp shower can precool the water in one or several of these bags.

Keeping your head cool will keep the rest of you cooler, just as warming the head is the way to help warm cold feet in the winter. One way to accomplish the former feat, if you're exposed to the sun, is to wear a high-crowned western-type hat. Originally, these hats were all worn with a high crown, and even today the real herders wear them high when the sun is blazing. The dead air inside acts as insulation from the heat and reduces the danger from sunstroke. The fancy and multi-creased western hats that dudes often affect are nowhere nearly as cool as the high-crowned headgear of the old-timers. Light-colored hats are cooler than dark ones.

Bathing the wrists, ankles, neck, and face with cool water will do much to keep you cooler, for in these areas the veins are closer to the surface, where the cool water can reduce the temperatures of the blood. Perhaps you've seen cowboys or others who have to work in high temperatures wet kerchiefs and tie them around their necks. They've learned this will help them to keep cool.

During torrid weather, try not to eat meals that are too heavy. Stick to sandwiches, salads if you can get them, and keep away from hot meat dishes with potatoes and gravy.

If it's only possible to pitch a tent so you'll have shade part of each day, try to arrange it so that it will be shaded in the afternoon rather than during the morning. This will give the interior an opportunity to cool off during the shaded portion of the day, before you enter for sleeping. The morning sun is cooler, and if your tent has to be in the sun part of the time, it might as well be there when the sun is not quite so hot. Early morning, when it's cooler, is also a fine time to do any camp chores.

Keeping cool in camp is a challenge for even the veteran camper. But with a minimum of activity, a reduction in meals, and the use of some of the preceding suggestions you'll feel you are giving the sun a bit of a battle.

36

The Bedtime Story

WHEN YOU TAKE TO THE WOODS NOTHING CAN SPOIL YOUR FUN more completely or faster than bad nights, and all the good days won't make up for them. Bad nights are almost a certainty if your camp bed is cold, hard, or damp. The problem, then, is to acquire outdoor sleeping gear that's warm, soft, dry, and easily transported.

First, let's consider warmth. Blankets are comfortable enough during the summer, provided the weather is mild and the coverings are nearly 100 percent wool. Cotton blankets are never very satisfactory, absorbing moisture easily and not retaining body heat nearly as well as woolen blankets do. If you own good woolen blankets and don't mind taking them on a camping trip, they can be used with a fair amount of comfort by folding and pinning them into a sort of sleeping bag. Two lightweight blankets are better for this purpose than a single heavy one. If possible, take along three lightweights, just in case.

Any number of blankets, however, will be chilly on a cold night unless they're made into a bag. This can be done with or without pins, although horse blanket pins are best, and with one or more blankets. Chances are that you'll sleep a lot more snugly if the blankets are pinned so that you won't be kicking and twisting your way out of them about two o'clock some breezy morning.

Various self-evident techniques can be used for folding and pinning blankets. Whatever method you favor, however, there's one basic requirement to keep in mind. Have at least as many layers of blanket under you as there are over you. For a pillow, use a jacket, saddle, or knapsack, or get one of those little inflatable rubber entities for a dollar or so.

Regardless of your fortitude or skill at blanket rolling, nothing can take the place of a good sleeping bag. Such a bag will be warmer than wool blankets of similar weight and bulk, cheaper to replace, and a lot easier to pack.

One thing is certain. It pays to buy as good a sleeping bag as your budget will permit, for it will be a long-term investment in comfort. There are bags for one individual, double bags for a couple, and single bags that can be zipped together to make a double bag. Some sleeping bags have several separate layers of insulation for use under various weather conditions. Some have shoulder flaps to form a sort of cape around the neck and shoulders, most important in really frigid climes. Some are made of foam rubber.

The two basic sleeping-bag shapes are the mummy and the rectangle. The mummy type usually covers the neck, fits snugly about the shoulders, and then tapers down toward the feet. Frankly, we find this type too confining. People who normally sleep on their back may like the mummy type. But if you roll about, slumber on your stomach, or like to have your arms free, a mummy bag can be maddening.

The one-man rectangular sleeping bags, popular with a majority of campers, come in sizes from the usual 34 x 76 inches up to 45 x 90 inches. They may weigh from less than four pounds to more than twenty, depending on size and insulation. Some have a flap that forms a carrying reinforcement for the rolled sleeping bag. A few have a flap that converts by zipper into a carrying sack. Some models have carrying straps on the flap.

Types of Sleeping Bags

Top: Mummy type. Bottom: Rectangle.

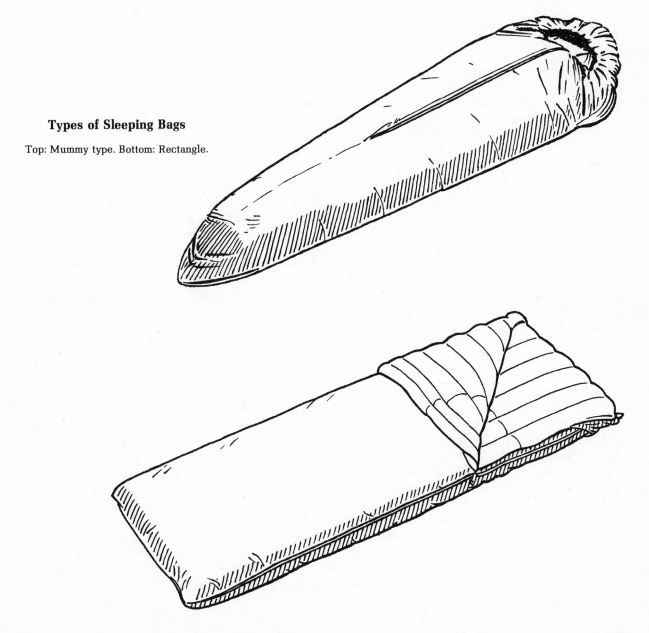

The insulating materials used in sleeping bags vary widely. There is cotton batting, kapok, wool, synthetic down, combinations of synthetics and waterfowl feathers, and on up to 100 percent goose down. The amount of insulation will determine how warm you'll be, everything coming down to the thickness of the insulation and therefore the amount of air it can deaden. A good bag with up to five inches of waterfowl down will keep you lightly warm in temperatures as low as fifty degrees below zero. The cost, however, may be well over $100. Such a bag is required only for arctic conditions. Most can do very well with gear that costs considerably less.

Good new goosedown is about one-fourth the weight of wool. Yet it's four times as warm. Down also has the advantage of being considerably more comfortable than wool at relatively high temperatures. Such fillers as reprocessed down, or combinations of down and feathers or down and synthetics, can't compare with 100 percent new down.

The superbuoyant new down is warmer for its weight to begin with and, because it allows a great deal of the body moisture to pass right through it to the open air, doesn't have to be aired as frequently as some other materials in order to retain its insulative qualities. Speaking of airing, be sure that your bag has a zipper or snaps across the bottom so it can be opened fully for sunning and airing.

Next to new waterfowl down, the most satisfactory insulation is one of the new synthetic downs made especially for sleeping bags, Dacron 88. This is far lighter than wool and at least twice as warm. It is soft, fluffy, and doesn't mat or retain an excess of moisture. It springs back after compression, thereby still retaining its insulative characteristics after long use. In addition to all this, it is nonallergenic and moth-, vermin-, and mildewproof. The best buying approach is to talk with other campers who have used such bags. In any event, read labels carefully and consider the reputation of the manufacturer of the insulating material, generally a different concern from the maker of the bag itself.

Except in extremely cold weather, these new synthetics will give satisfaction at far less cost than genuine waterfowl down. The favorite bag of one of us has four pounds of Dacron 88 and will keep him warm down close to zero or below. The other of us has long used a 16-pounder, bulky with goosedown, and it keeps him warm down to sixty degrees below.

It's important to remember, however, that everyone has his own tolerance for cold. A bag that's warm enough for one camper may not suit another. Also remember that sleeping comfort is affected by the wind, your shelter, and what you wear to bed.

A sleeping bag's outer covering should be tough and water-repellent, never completely waterproof. Fine-count poplin, duck, or sail silk are good choices of material. This should never be rubberized, as such treatment causes excess condensation of body moisture inside the bag, making it clammy and cold. Some bags are made with a rubberized bottom. This will protect you from ground dampness, but such a bag is nearly impossible to dry-clean satisfactorily. This problem is solved, however, if the rubber bottom is removable. Most campers prefer to use a waterproof tarpaulin or air mattress.

Best of all is a sleeping bag with no rubber at all. You can use such a bag on a cot, with or without an air mattress. And for sleeping on terra firma, the best of all combinations is a tough waterproof ground cloth, then an air mattress, and finally the sleeping bag itself. The ground cloth will separate you and your bedding from ground dampness, as well as protect it and the air mattress from the scraping and puncturing of twigs and rocks. A good ground cloth can be made from a light tarp, rubber-coated cloth, oilcloth, heavy plastic, or even muslin into which all the paraffin it will hold has been rubbed and ironed.

As might be expected, any sleeping bag will last longer and give better service if you take reasonable care of it and keep it clean. A liner of sheeting or flannel will help to keep the interior tidy. Protect the outside from sparks, grease, and oil. Take care not to catch the material in the zipper. During use, air a sleeping bag at least once a week, or more often if convenient, opening it wide and shaking and brushing out any twigs, dirt, and leaves.

Sleeping attire is a matter of personal preference. Many campers like pajamas, and some enjoy sweat pants and sweat shirts. Others prefer to sleep in their underwear, changing every evening rather than in the morning to gain the extra warmth of clean, dry materials. Still others just empty their pockets, shuck off their boots, loosen their belts, and crawl in.

If the stay is to be a long one, however, some sort of change from your daylight duds is both healthy and comfortable. Many veteran campers, by the way, swear by the wearing of a fresh pair of woolen socks on especially cold nights. For the warmest sleeping? Believe it or not, because of the matter of perspiration, it's a sufficiently heavy sleeping bag and no clothes at all.

Warmth, however, is only one factor in comfortable camp bedding. Softness is nearly as important. That's why we're all in favor of the air mattress. Since trying them years ago, we wonder why any camper ever tried to sleep without one, unless of course he prefers the newer solid ones of foam rubber or plastic. With either variety, you can sleep on a mountain ledge or hard station-wagon floor as comfortably as you do at home.

Air mattresses are generally made of plastic or of rubberized cloth. The latter are more durable and somewhat more expensive. Air mattresses are obtainable in numerous colors and in various types of tufted or tube construction. They're available with or without attached pillows.

Standard air mattresses run about 25 x 72 inches when inflated. They may be several inches wider and an inch or so longer when not blown up, so select your air mattress by the inflated size. They weigh about 5 pounds in the rubberized materials and about 3 1/2 pounds in plastic. For lighter traveling, you can buy a short mattress that'll just support your head, shoulders, and hips, as outlined in the chapter on backpacking.

Air mattresses are inflated with either your breath, the dampness of which doesn't hurt them any, or with a pump. Various pumps can be operated by foot pressure, by a handle, or even by an automobile's exhaust. There's even an electric pump that plugs into a car's lighter socket.

It's important not to make the common mistake of inflating an air mattress too much. Blow it up so that when you sit on it, you can just feel the ground. Then when you lie down, your hips won't touch the earth. If the mattress is much harder than that, it will be uncomfortable, and you may strain the seams. Too, you'll have a tendency to roll off a mattress that's too hard.

To deflate an air mattress, merely open the valve and roll the mattress toward you. Between camping trips, store the mattress at least partially inflated, or roll it loosely rather than folding it tightly, to help prevent any cracking of the material.

The question is always coming up as to whether air mattresses can be used as fun floats during camping sojourns by the water. The answer is in the affirmative, but we don't recommend the practice. Rubberized fabric is not improved by repeated soaking and drying, and rough beaches can easily puncture plastic mattresses. We'd suggest that you use your main mattresses just for sleeping, for which good ones will be functional for years, and get other and cheaper floats for water sport. Then if a float gets wrecked, you're not out much money, and will still get that good night's sleep.

Leaks in mattresses can usually be repaired quickly with a patching kit, and you should pick up one of these when buying the mattress. To find an evasive leak, inflate the mattress hard and dip it in still water.

Some campers, remembering their veteran camping experiences, still like to carry along a bed-size cloth bag which they can fill with leaves, wild hay, or evergreen needles. This makes a pretty good mattress, and an aromatic one, but you'll need a lot more forest litter than you'd suppose.

In past years campers slept on the ground and made do with either hip holes or a bough bed. To make hip holes, an outdoorsman simply scooped out depressions in the earth to fit his hips and shoulders. The bough bed was, and is, a great improvement over hip holes. Its use depends upon the availability of material and upon whether the camper has the half-hour or so of time needed to make one before turning in.

With today's emphasis on conservation, the making of a bough bed is frowned upon. However, light trimming of lower branches in a real evergreen forest does little harm to the trees. These branches generally die off eventually, anyway, and meantime the clipped ends sprout new tips the following year. So you might well enjoy such an aromatic mattress, but be sure beforehand that such construction is permitted where you're camping.

A bough bed is easy to make but takes a fair amount of time. Place the first row of evergreen tips at the bottom of the sleeping area, with the stub ends pointed toward the ground. Place the next row, and as many additional rows as are needed to cover the bed area, the same way, with the soft tips overlapping each other like shingling. Add layers until the bed is about eight inches thick.

Some campers put a frame of small logs around the bough bed. The logs may be pegged in position to keep them from rolling. Other campers span such logs with limber saplings

**Bough
Bed**

and then thatch these with the evergreen tips to add to the bed's springiness. In any event, be sure to spread a tarp or ground cloth over the coniferous covering to protect blankets or sleeping bag from pitch.

After a few nights of use, the evergreen tips will pack down or shed so many needles that you'll have to add a fresh layer. In trail huts, we've come upon such replenished bough beds that were over a foot thick. Unfortunately, by then they were shared by chipmunks, field mice, and assorted wildlife, and sleeping in them made our nights pretty interesting.

There's also a primitive camp bed, actually a sort of trapper's cot, which consists of a canvas strip about eight feet long and four feet wide, with a four-inch tubular seam running along each long side. You just cut and smooth two poles to insert in these tubes. Then rest the pole ends on a log or stone at each end of the bed to keep the bedding off the ground.

Notch the logs to hold the pole ends apart, and you're in business in any area where poles and logs may be cut. For slightly over $3 you can buy a canvas army-cot replacement to use as a trapper's bed. This has side tubes all sewn, plus end tubes in which to insert cross sticks.

If transportation is no problem, though, you may appreciate the convenience of regular army cots. The newer camp cots are generally better, though, than the familiar old articles. Most of the newer ones are made of aluminum tubing and weigh as little as seven pounds, compared with twice as much or more for the old type.

The best cots in the opinion of many are those with flat spring, metal legs. If a cot with stick legs is being used in a tent with a sewn-in floor, place flat stones or boards under the legs to avoid poking holes in the canvas floor. If you use cots for seats as well as for beds, sit in the middle to avoid breaking the seams along the frame.

For camping in mosquito country in a tent without screens, buy a mosquito bar to put over your bed. Or if mosquitoes surprise you in the backwoods where such conveniences are not available, get a few yards of the finest netting available and fix it over your bed with a roughly improvised pole frame.

It's much easier than it ever was before to sleep comfortably when you take to the woods, and the days are a lot more fun when you snooze soundly at night.

37

Stoves, Lanterns, Iceboxes

AMONG TODAY'S MOST POPULAR ITEMS OF CAMP EQUIPMENT ARE stoves, lanterns, and iceboxes. This popularity is easy to explain, for when such gear is functioning properly, it makes taking to the woods a lot more pleasant. When it's not functioning right, however, it can be more trouble than it's worth.

Sometimes, certainly, there's something haywire with the gear to begin with. But as we watch campers in action, we find that troublesome camp appliances are generally the fault of improper care or the failure to follow the operating instructions. We'd like to offer a few suggestions that may be helpful.

A camp stove preferably should be operated in a sheltered place, away from gusts and drafts. Both rob it of heat, thereby boosting the time needed to cook everything.

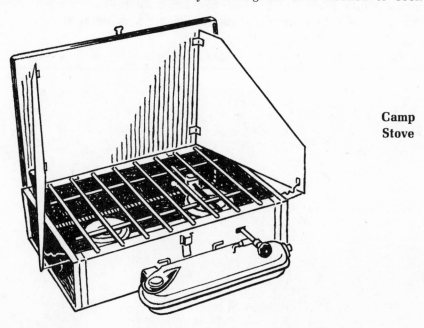

**Camp
Stove**

Strong gusts can even blow out a burner's flame. Many stoves are designed with a lid that provides a rear windscreen when opened. Sides may spread apart to form additional protection. Incidentally, it's a time-saving idea to spread a sheet of aluminum foil under the burners to catch drippings. Then just whisk out the foil to get rid of the grease.

Keep your camp stove at the right height to make it more convenient and comfortable to work with. Folding stands, particularly designed for camp stoves, are on the market. Or you can use a ledge, a box, the tailgate of your station wagon, or one end of a camp table. Just be sure the stand is level and steady to keep hot pans and pots from teetering and sliding, and grease or fat from flowing to one side of the pan.

The gasoline, alcohol, or kerosene you pour into a stove must be converted into a gas in a so-called generator unit, which is part of the stove. After its conversion into gas, the fuel burns with a hot blue flame. Such conversion requires both plenty of air about the stove and proper pressure inside the fuel tank. It's this pressure, of course, that impels the liquid fuel into the generator.

With the tiny pocket stoves, this pressure is produced by heating the tank in your hand, thus expanding the air inside. This expansion forces a few drops of fuel out of a

**Pocket
Stove**

minute hole in the burner unit, where it is lighted with a match. Once lighted, the burner continues to draw fuel from the font and so keeps burning.

If such a stove has been used and then extinguished, you may have trouble building up enough pressure with your body heat to restart it. In this case, apply a lighted match to the bottom of the font until the first drops of fuel appear for lighting. Ignite these first drops at once, and, importantly, heat the tank no more. By the way, when filling small, hand-warmed tanks of pocket stoves, do not fill the font completely. Leave a little air space so that hand heat can expand this air for compression.

Pressure in the larger stoves must be maintained another way all during the burning process to keep fuel fed into the burners. This is achieved with a built-in hand pump. When the roar of the blue flames starts to lessen, pump more air into the fuel tank. For efficient compression, follow the manufacturer's directions precisely.

Turn the pump's plunger knob to the left to unlock it. Place your thumb over the hole in the center of the plunger to hold in the air, and work the plunger up and down until you feel pressure solidly resisting your stroke. This may require about three dozen strokes or so, and don't forget to keep the thumb firmly over that little hole in the knob while working the plunger. When back pressure makes pumping hard, turn the plunger knob to the right at the bottom of a stroke to lock in the compression. As the fuel in the tank is used up, the amount of pumping required to keep up the air pressure must increase, for there's more air space in the tank.

To keep your pump in the best working order, put a drop or two of light oil into the hole of the cylinder can where it says "oil" once or twice during a season, depending upon how much the stove is used. This softens the leather part of the plunger, insuring that it will fit the inside of the cylinder more tightly.

Difficulty in lighting a gasoline stove may be caused by forgetting to turn the wire of the lighting valve to the "up" position when you open the stove valve to ignite the burner. This wire must be turned up when you light the stove and then, after one minute, turned down for best burning efficiency. It's not a bad idea to affix the manufacturer's instructions inside the lid of the stove with transparent tape as a reminder. Most beginning campers forget to perform this operation in sequence, then wonder why their stove doesn't operate properly.

If you ever find it difficult or inconvenient to pump up your stove or lantern, you may be interested in a little gadget that will do it for you with the help of a carbon dioxide cartridge.

Another unit enables you to convert a gasoline stove into one that burns canned gas. This gimmick weighs only a few ounces, replaces the liquid-fuel tank, and will accept L/P gas cans instead.

If you are using gasoline, it will be a good idea to flush out the fuel tank once or twice during the season with a little gasoline. To do this, release the pressure in the tank by turning back the filler cap. This exhausts the gasoline vapor along with the pressurized air, so be sure there's no open flame, spark, or burning tobacco nearby to touch off this explosive mixture. After the pressure is safely released, slosh the remaining fuel back and forth and then dump it out in some safe place.

When using one of the tiny pocket stoves, release the pressure as soon as you blow out the gasoline flame. On the other hand, if your little stove burns alcohol and is pressure-fed from a miniature font above the burner, remember to open the filler cap on the tank before trying to light the burner. Otherwise, the alcohol won't run down into the burner unit. Each camp stove has its own standard operational procedure which must be followed for top performance.

If food spills onto burners, clean it off as soon as convenient to prevent clogged openings. Remove any excess spilled grease, this being a fire hazard. Keep any stove a safe distance from burnable materials such as tents, flies, dry leaves, and extra fuel. The latter should be transported in sealable metal cans, never in bottles or glass jugs.

If your stove burns propane gas, make sure it is adequately shielded from the wind. Some of the older propane stoves had no shields, and they required an improvised windshield for most effective performance. The modern ones have shields and are advantageously designed. When you're cooking with them on windy days, however, it's still a good idea to check occasionally to see if the flame is still burning.

When affixing gas cylinders to stoves, do not tighten the connections with pliers or wrench. Hand-tightened fittings are sufficient at all couplings. If you suspect leaks, by the way, do not test with a lighted match. Use your nose, or apply soapy water and watch for bubbles. Be wary of crossing threads at any coupling. If a connection turns hard, stop and check for cross threading. If that proves to be the difficulty, reset the two pieces and turn firmly and slowly to recut the original threads.

At high altitudes gas stoves may not burn well because of a sparsity of oxygen. However, most gas appliances designed for camping have an altitude adjustment by the valve knob where the tube tank joins the device. Open this air aperture wide if your stove does not seem to be burning well.

In extremely cold weather, propane and L/P gas stoves may not work too well. Warming the cans or cylinders may help to start them, but never put them over an open flame. Hand warmth may be enough to do the trick, or set the containers near a heat source such as a car's engine. If you place them by a campfire, set them only near enough to be warmed.

Before leaving on a trip, check manufacturers' operating instructions and test out all new gear to make sure you know how to operate it correctly. This advice applies to lanterns as well as stoves. Lighting a lantern generally takes place after dark when it's difficult to read instructions or, for that matter, to see what you're doing. Bungling even one step can make the difference between efficient and faulty operation.

For instance, on many fine gasoline lanterns the instructions say to open the operating valve wide, as far as the knob can be turned, as soon as the mantle ignites. This step is important, as it works a mechanism that stops pressure from escaping. Outdoorsmen who fail to do this must pump repeatedly to maintain pressure. Others using these excellent lanterns fail to open the valve only one-quarter of a turn before lighting the mantle, another important move.

If a mantle burns yellow or if black spots appear on it, the air supply is clogged. Shut off the light, remove the mantle, and with something such as an old toothbrush brush the screen in the burner and above the mantle. Fine pine needles held together like a paint brush, with the tips even, make another good emergency brush. While you're at it, also check the lamp's air intake opening. Now install a new mantle, and the lantern should burn well. We find it extremely reassuring to have a few extra mantles along. Wrap them in metal foil and tape the packet beneath the fuel font, where it will be easily accessible in an emergency.

Before storing a lantern, rinse out the font with a little clean gasoline to remove any stale gasoline. This treatment prevents old fuel from souring and forming gum. Then leave the cap off until all gasoline evaporates.

If your lantern is burning properly but the pressure keeps dropping, necessitating a great deal of pumping, the pump may be leaking. Turn off the lantern and permit it to cool. Then, with pressure still in the tank, set the lantern on its side with the end of the pump in a dish of water. If bubbles dance to the surface, you've found your trouble. The best bet then is to take the lamp to a manufacturer's service dealer.

If it's possible to pinpoint the leak, however, emergency repairs can sometimes be made with adhesive tape or with plastic cement, a small tube of which is always handy in camp. Before attempting such emergency repairs, release the pressure. Give the repair a chance to seal the hole without pressure working against it.

Lanterns burning gas instead of gasoline are not very tricky to use. Just be sure that valves and connections are right. Never throw "empty" cylinders or cans into the campfire. On all lanterns, keep globes and hoods clean and reflectors bright.

Camp lanterns except for electric models give off a great deal of heat, so never suspend them near canvas or cloth. Don't hang them close to evergreen boughs, either. Another thing to keep in mind? The handle can get very hot.

Since heat from the lantern rises, you can safely use a lantern on the tent floor or on a low box, but beware of suspending it from a pole too close to the tent fabric. A lantern will warm a tent by many degrees, but be sure to watch the ventilation when using one. Where light is not objectionable, a lantern will do a fine job as a small heater.

One camper we saw made a sheet-metal cover for his lantern. It completely covered the lantern and had air holes near the bottom of the sides, as well as some small ones in the flat top to let out the accumulating heat. It had a wire handle, and the whole thing folded flat for carrying. For a homemade affair it was a dandy.

This bushman could leave the lantern burning in the box all night for heat. The small amount of light escaping from the cover wasn't enough to bother him. He set a piece of asbestos under lantern and box to protect the tent floor, and of course he allowed for adequate tent ventilation. He said the only bad part of the arrangement was that the lantern handle got very hot.

Along with the camp stove and lantern, the camp icebox also deserves a certain amount of consideration. Open it as infrequently as possible, and then close it as quickly as you

**Camp
Icebox**

reasonably can. A few moments with the top left open can make a great deal of difference in the temperature inside a small icebox. Keep the box in the shade as much as possible and away from any heat source.

Some campers tilt the contrivance slightly and leave the draincock open so that the melting ice water will run off. Personally, we're of the opinion that anything cold, including water, adds to the icebox's efficiency. Besides, warm air can seep in through a draincock. If water becomes too deep, the food can be raised on a metal shelf. Or you can avoid the problem by using one of the commercial freeze liquids that are packaged in cans and can't leak as they melt. Beware of these liquids in plastic sacks, however, as wood mice like to gnaw on them.

You can also avoid trouble by freezing water in milk cartons. The commercial cans of liquids may last longer, but water in cartons does very well. Too, some campers distribute cake ice among plastic bags that contain the water as the solid gradually melts.

Keep your icebox's interior clean and spotless. Rinse it and air it occasionally, particularly after food has been spilled. To save ice, be sure not to place any cooked leftovers in the refrigerator until they are as cool as you can get them.

Don't wait until the ice is all gone before getting more. Chilling an icebox, once it has warmed up, takes plenty of ice in itself. Obtaining a new stock of ice before the old has entirely melted keeps the icebox cold. If there isn't room for all the new supply, place the extra in a basin or pail, cover it with a wet cloth, and set it in the shade. Wet papers will also protect this surplus until it can be fitted into the icebox.

Covered containers in an icebox will help keep food in good shape, for they are resistant to the temperature changes encountered when the box is open.

Keep foods that spoil most easily close to the ice or at the bottom of the box. This includes butter, uncooked meats, and opened jars of such perishables as salad dressing. Foods such as cold cuts, eggs, bacon, and freshly caught fish will keep pretty well on top.

As you use the camp stove, lantern, and icebox a few times on journeys to the woods, you'll learn many additional ways to get the most out of them. Above all, follow the manufacturer's instructions exactly for top operation. For more information, write to the manufacturer's customer-service department. All such camp gear is designed for good service. Give it a chance, and it will deliver.

38

Axes and Saws

A CRUDE STONE AX WAS DOUBTLESS ONE OF THE FIRST WEAPONS made by man. Perhaps some caveman, after fastening a stone to the end of a stick to produce a club, found that the rock's sharp edge could be effectively used to gash a tree—or another troglodyte.

American Indians used stone axes to help fell trees, not by cutting the trees down but by burning them and then knocking out the charred wood with a stone ax as the fire progressed. Later, when the redmen were offered steel trade axes, they abandoned the crude stone affairs.

These early steel axes were frightfully efficient battle weapons. In fact, white men used them against the Indians, as well as vice versa.

C. B. Colby's seventh great-grandmother, Hannah Duston, was captured by Indians back in 1697, taken 100 miles on foot in winter, and held captive until she got up one night and killed 10 Indians with one of their own tomahawks. She then scalped the lot and later collected the bounty on the scalps. Many New Englanders know the story of Hannah Duston and her tomahawk. One of her several statues, complete with tomahawk and scalps, stands on Penacook Island, near Concord, New Hampshire, where she killed and scalped her captors.

Today, however, axes are put to more mundane uses. A skilled axman can cut fuel, build a cabin or other shelter, construct bridges, make camp furniture, open a can of beans, and even shave with one.

If we ever get stranded on a desert island or in the wilderness with just a single tool, we hope that tool is a sharp ax or hatchet. An ax can do anything that a knife can do and a lot more, from cleaning a trout to dressing out a half-ton moose. If you run out of food, an ax can help you fashion deadfalls and traps with which to get nourishment. With an ax you can fashion spears or a bow and arrows, blaze a trail, or make splints for a broken arm or leg.

Determining what sort of an ax or hatchet to invest in is simple, even for a newcomer to camping. If you are interested merely in splitting kindling or driving tent stakes, a good hatchet will do very well. If you plan a long stay in the woods or are venturing into the wilderness and will have to cut a lot of firewood, take along an ax rather than a hatchet.

For general camping use, a hatchet is handy, even if your outfit already includes an ax, saw, or both. There are several kinds of hatchets, including a folding model. Be sure

Hatchet

that the one selected is of good-quality steel and has a perfectly fitting handle. Or get an all-steel model in which the head and handle are in one piece.

Some of the so-called "army surplus" hatchets are worse than no hatchet at all, being of extremely inferior quality. These hatchets have heads made of cast iron and poorly fitted handles that are painted khaki color. Stick to reputable makes, and buy from reliable stores or outfitters. Most hardware stores carry high-quality tools.

Many woodsmen prefer a hatchet with a good wooden handle because of the tool's feel and balance. However, many metal-handled hatchets are well-balanced, and with such a tool there is no need to worry about the head flying off or the handle breaking. All-metal hatchets, which weigh some 2 1/2 pounds and come with a leather sheath, cost less than $3. Better grades cost as much as $7 or more. These are lighter in weight and do a superior cutting job because of better steel and balance.

Back in Colonial times, woodsmen carried a hand ax designed not only for camp chores but also for throwing. These tools were known as belt axes since they were carried, sheathless, in a man's belt or sash. The handle of a belt ax was tapered, with the butt end being the smaller, so that the ax could be pulled from the belt without catching. The straight handle was designed so that the ax, when thrown, would revolve in the air and strike blade-first. A good frontiersman could split a twig, or a skull, at a right smart distance.

Today there's little need for ax throwing, except in friendly target competition, so all axes and hatchets should be safely sheathed when not in use. If not sheathed, the blade should be driven into a log or stump so that it is not exposed.

For many who take to the woods the best all-around camp ax is the type called the Hudson Bay or Old Montreal ax. This tool has a head weighing about 2 1/2 pounds and a 26- or 28-inch handle. Usually sold with a good leather sheath, this ax is well-balanced and, in the hands of an expert, will do the work of a heavier ax.

Another fine cutting tool, called a cabin ax, has a head weighing 3 or 3 1/2 pounds and a straighter handle than the Hudson Bay. The cabin ax is certainly as heavy an ax as almost any camper will need. We recommend either it or the Hudson Bay over the hatchet. Either will do more work than the smaller, but not much lighter, hatchet.

Also on the market is a fine all-metal camp ax with a 4-inch cutting blade and a steel handle with a nylon-vinyl grip. Total weight is only three pounds. This ax has good balance, sells for less than $10, and comes with a leather sheath. It is basically an all-metal Hudson Bay-type ax.

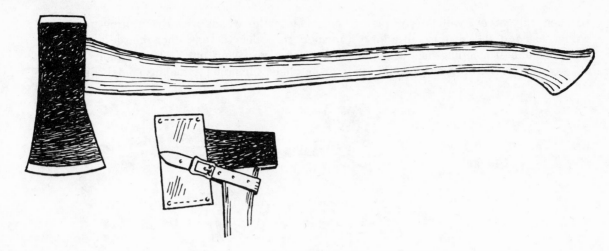

Hudson Bay Ax

Whatever type of hatchet or ax you buy and use, keep it sharp. A really sharp tool is far less dangerous than a dull blade, which is apt to glance from a log or bounce from a block instead of biting in.

Keep your tool's cutting edge sharp with a file and a whetstone. Use the file to remove small nicks and to do the primary sharpening. Then put a keen edge on the blade with the stone.

When using the file, hold the head of the ax or hatchet securely. Apply pressure only on the forward stroke of the file, thus saving the file's cutting ridges. File both sides of the blade, evenly, and when it is as sharp as you can get it with the file, finish the job with the whetstone, using a circular motion along the cutting edge from one end to the other. A bit of water or a drop of oil on the stone will help with the final sharpening.

Don't produce what is called a feather edge—an edge so thin that it will crumble or bend when hit against wood. On the other hand, an edge that's too thick will not cut well.

Do not use an electric grindstone to sharpen your cutting tool, for the heat from such high-speed abrasion may ruin the temper of the blade. The old-fashioned hand- or foot-powered grindstone is fine for this purpose since it does not generate enough heat to damage a blade.

Extreme cold is also bad for a blade made of hard-tempered steel. If it is very cold out, warm the blade somewhat before using it, or the steel may shatter like glass. One way is to hold the blade over the fringes of a campfire or near the camp stove until it is warm, not hot, to the touch. Once you begin to use the tool, the friction from the cutting process will keep the blade warm.

Anyone using an ax or hatchet should follow a few simple safety rules:

(1) Keep the tool really sharp.

(2) Be sure that the chopping area contains no obstacles that might get in the way of either your backswing or your downswing. Such obstacles can be branches, clotheslines, guy ropes, or even people.

(3) Make sure that the wood to be cut is placed so that it will not roll, tilt, bounce, or flip when hit, and so that any chips will not fly dangerously in the direction of any nearby campers.

(4) Be sure that your footing is secure and that your feet, legs, and hands are out of the line of fire. Spread your feet well apart, and if new at this chore, stand on the side of the log opposite from the one you're cutting.

Don't waste your time felling a dead tree for firewood that will provide more fuel than you need or one that will be too big to handle when felled. If possible, select a standing dead tree, the wood of which will be seasoned and dry. Two 4-inch-thick trees are easier to fell and cut up than one 8-inch-thick tree, and felling the former is a snap with a sharp ax or even with a hatchet.

If the tree has been dead for a long time, a condition indicated by barkless patches or by the complete absence of bark, give it a good shake or whack it a few times with the ax head, watching out above you all the while. Such a test, if the tree is small enough, will help remove any dead branches that might otherwise come crashing down while you chop. And get out of the way when it's coming down lest the standing trees break off some part and send it smashing back down in your direction.

All of us have seen some campers worry down a small tree like a beaver with a loose upper plate. They waste wood, work up a tremendous sweat, and generally embarrass every axman within sight and sound. Felling a small tree is really a simple chore, and when done correctly it can be fun.

First, select an aiming point on the tree. To provide as much wood as possible and to help eliminate a hazard to future pedestrians and horsemen in the area, this point should be as close to the ground as reasonable.

The initial cut should be at right angles to the trunk and on the side toward which you want the tree to drop. The next cut should be down into the trunk above the first gash so that it meets the horizontal cut and pops out a nice triangular chip. Maintain this in-and-then-down process until you have cut a bit more than halfway through the trunk.

Now move to the other side of the tree and repeat the process, starting a couple of inches above the first cut. Again, cut the tree a bit more than halfway through. Unless the tree has fallen already, you can now push it over toward the first, or lower, cut.

When the tree begins to crack and fall, keep well clear. Never stand directly behind a falling tree because the trunk may jump back when it separates. Keep other campers clear of the falling tree.

When stripping branches from the felled tree, cut them from the underside. That is, chop from the butt toward the top of the tree. This approach prevents the blade from getting jammed in a crotch where a branch and the trunk meet.

To chop the trunk into sections, cut diagonally into the wood, first from the right and then from the left, thus opening a good-size V. When the log is cut halfway through, move to the other side and repeat the process until the log is severed. The two V's, of course, meet at their tips. Be careful with the last few strokes, as the ax may come clear through.

Do not try to cut all the way down through a log from its uppermost side. The job will take much longer, and the V-notch will have to be twice as wide. Then your ax may cut deeply into the ground at the end of the process, thereby dulling the blade.

When sharpening stakes or splitting kindling, place the wood on a stump or log, never on a rock or on the ground, in order not to damage the blade.

To split a short piece when you are beginning, place it on a log or stump, set the ax blade into the wood with an easy stroke, raise the piece of wood and the ax together, and

Felling a Tree the Correct Way

Right Way to Strip Branches from a Felled Tree

(Note: Always cut with slant of branch.)

Chopping a Trunk into Sections

Easy Way to Split Kindling

bring them down smartly on the log or stump. The piece will split without your having to hold it with your fingers.

Another way to do this is hold the near end of the piece, held horizontally, and split the far end with the blade. Then set the blade into the split. Hit stick and blade together on the stump. The blade will work down into the split and separate the piece safely.

In order to take pieces from a big stump, never try to split the stump in half, or you may bury the blade deep and, trying to work it free, snap the ax handle. Instead, split pieces from the sides until the stump is small enough to split as a whole. Beware of a stump full of twisted grain or knots, as it may bind the blade, deflect it, and at the least require a lot of extra perspiration.

To split a good-size piece of wood, lean it on the far side of a felled log so that only its top is above the level of the log. Then, while standing on the side of the log opposite the leaning wood, hit the piece near the end that's on the ground. This is important. Hit it low. If you strike it too far above the ground end, the piece may bounce up or, worse, catapult over the log in your direction.

Take good care of your axes and hatchets. Check each one often to see whether the head is still secure and well wedged. If you find that a wedge is missing, don't chop with that tool again until it is rewedged. It pays to take an extra wedge or two of suitable size along on camping trips.

If you lose a wedge in camp, whittle a replacement from hardwood such as oak or birch. Make it longer than necessary and drive it in as far as possible. Then break it off and trim smooth with a knife.

To tighten a loose ax head, hold the tool near the end of the handle, raise it in the air with the head down, and whack the butt with a rock. The handle ends of most axes have a shaped and pointed butt known as a "fawn foot." This looks pretty but is a handicap when you wish to use the head-tightening method suggested above. Many axmen cut off this fawn foot, or at least part of it, so that there is a flat area upon which to hammer with a rock.

To determine whether or not an ax head is working loose, check the area of the handle just behind the head. If the head seems to be coming loose and yet the wedges seem well set, drive the handle back into the head, redrive the wedges, and then soak the head overnight in water. This stratagem will cause the wood in the head to swell and thus tighten everything. To keep the steel from rusting in the water, wipe it with some sort of grease such as bacon fat, oleomargarine, gun oil, or such.

Axmen do not like painted or varnished ax handles, for several reasons. Such a handle may raise blisters on the hands after prolonged use, and the covering may conceal flaws in the wood. However, many woodsmen do put red or yellow paint on the heads of their tools, or on the last three or four inches of the handle, so that the axes are easy to spot in the woods.

If you paint the head of an ax, also paint the handle end that shows in the eye of the head. Then if the ax head begins working loose, the paint at that point will crack and reveal the potential danger.

It's a good idea to steel-wool or sandpaper ax and hatchet handles until they are smooth, then to rub in a little linseed oil to preserve them. From that point on, natural oil from your hands will help to keep the wood smooth.

Camp saws are becoming more and more popular, and for good reasons. It is far easier to work wood into proper lengths with a saw than with an ax. We both have a couple of folding saws that save wood and time when we're rustling fuel for the fire. A hatchet for splitting kindling and a folding camp saw make a fine team when you're travel-ing light. On the other hand, campers who plan an extended stay with plenty of camp-fires to build will do well to invest in a stouter camp saw such as the versatile Swede saw.

What about engine-driven chain saws? Tree lovers and the parents of small children may view such machines with misgivings, but times have changed since the first chain saws were introduced. These, used almost exclusively by lumbermen, weighed about fifty pounds and cost around $400. Today, however, these units are much smaller, weigh far less, and sell for less than $170. If you'll be swamping trails, building a cabin, getting in firewood for the winter, or doing any other heavy cutting chores, consider a power saw.

We have a little chain saw that weighs less than 10 pounds and yet can cut through an 8-inch-thick tree in as many seconds. We also have a still smaller saw that weighs 6 1/2 pounds and can be used with one hand. This saw has only a 12-inch guide bar, but it can fell trees 2 feet in diameter.

Such power saws, which can be carried in a saddlebag or even a rucksack, can be a godsend to the packtripper, campground operator, long-stay camper, outfitter, or wilderness dweller. They are as safe as an ax, if used with caution, and will do a lot more work quicker and easier.

39

Camping Tricks and Gadgets

THAT OLD BROMIDE, "IT'S THE LITTLE THINGS THAT COUNT," MAY very well be applied to small camping gadgets and tricks. Some of the smallest items that can be tucked into a duffle bag will solve a lot of problems on stays in the woods.

Years ago one of us was trying to locate a tiny thorn in a young camper's hand. It was so all-fired minute that we just couldn't spot it. Another camper saw our plight and asked if we had a pair of binoculars. He showed us how to use them as a magnifying glass by reversing them, holding the eyepiece about half an inch above the place under observation, and then looking through the large end of the glass. This works fine not only for locating slivers and thorns, but also for looking at insects, minerals, fungi formations, etc.

Aluminum foil, that jack-of-all-trades about a campsite, is boundless in its uses. On a recent trip to the Jackson Hole area of Wyoming, we saw two new uses in one boat during a rain. One chap, without a hat, had made himself a neat one of foil, complete with brim. The other fisherman was bailing the boat with a foil cup he'd formed by pressing a sheet about his clenched fist.

A roll of foil, or one of those flat-folded sportsman packets of the stuff, will help solve many camp problems. For instance, a pickup we carry in the bush is composed of a teaspoon apiece of instant coffee, powdered cream, and sugar, wrapped together in a foil packet. Anytime you need a bit of stimulation, just pop the contents in your mouth without even the preliminaries of boiling the kettle.

Another little western trick for wet weather was shown us by the horse wrangler in charge of our mounts. In a downpour he poked the crown of his Stetson into a high, rounded dome and turned the broad brim down all around. He explained that the rounded dome sheds a real storm for hours, and the turned-down brim keeps the rain out of eyes and ears while letting the torrents from the crown run off in any direction but not down the neck. Spraying the crown and brim with water repellent, some evening back around the campfire, will make the headpiece even more stormproof.

Many small, easy-to-carry items can make taking to the woods more fun. Bring along a small thermometer to answer that familiar question, "How cold did it get last night?" To find out what may happen in the way of weather while you're away from newspapers and radios, tote a small barometer to warn you of storms or reassure you about better weather to come.

A pedometer, too, can be fun. It gives an idea of how far you walk while exploring the area around camp. Used with a compass, one can help you follow maps.

A fine pair of tweezers, obtainable in any drugstore, is good for such jobs as removing splinters and thorns. Too, one blade of the tweezers makes an excellent small screwdriver for tightening camera, sights, binoculars, fishing reels, glasses, and so on.

Enjoying the refreshment of a drink is often more convenient with the use of a small collapsing or folding cup. There are other uses for it, too. When nothing handier is available, one can even be used to bail a boat.

One of the handiest small items around camp is the safety pin. A functional collection of assorted sizes can be carried on one large pin. These can be used to pin laundry to a line on a windy day; temporarily mend tents and clothing; clean out clogged burner orifices on stoves and lanterns; pin on a watch, compass, or paper money in pockets; or to pin pockets themselves closed. They can also be formed into a reasonably strong metal chain.

Spring-type clothespins have numerous camp uses. They will clip materials to clotheslines to form sun- or windscreens, hold tarps over food on tables, affix rain curtains to mesh-screened porches, keep open doors and windows, or hold awnings in any position. They can be used to make a boxlike enclosure out of a tarp inside the tent to protect gear from damp floors or from the ground if it's that sort of a tent. They can also be used to reclose bread wrappers and other food packages. Some campers drill a small hole in one of the clothespin arms so that they can hang small items from lines.

Transparent plastic bags which let you see what's inside come in a handy assortment of sizes and are inexpensive in the extreme. They can be used as emergency rain hats or protection for food. They're fine coverings for cameras, encased or otherwise, binoculars, pistols, and all sorts of personal belongings affected by dampness, blowing sand, or driving rain. They'll hold ice, and they will protect fresh-caught fish. Large enough plastic bags will serve as rubbers over shoes if held about the ankles with rubber bands.

Speaking of rubber bands, a little bunch of assorted sizes is always proving useful in many unexpected ways. They'll keep foil or waxed paper over opened cans of food, hold coiled rope, keep sections of a dismantled fishing rod together, retain a loosely fitting handgun in a holster, hold trouser legs snug about the ankles in chigger country, keep several exposed films together so one won't be mislaid, and seal items in plastic bags.

Clothesline or braided nylon cord will have many uses. Utilize it for a laundry line, of course, or maybe even for lifesaving. Haul your grub up above the reach of animals, stretch shade tarpaulins between trees, or make a swing for the youngsters. Rope is also handy for lashing tarps over your outfit in storms, for the reinforced guying of tents in high winds, lashing firewood for easier carrying, or dragging large logs to a campfire.

A tiny tube of zipper lubricant may eliminate some high-powered annoyances. And if you have many zipper-equipped items, take along a zipper repair kit just in case. One costs about a dollar and includes the lubricant, which may also be purchased separately.

Candles are always coming in handy. Or take along a stick of wax or block of paraffin with which to seal leaking seams on tents and tarpaulins. You can also get a push-up stick of wax and use it on everything that's made of canvas, even to the small fry's sneakers. A spray can of waterproofing will also come in handy.

A pencil and small pad of paper, or the loose-leaf notebook like that which one of us always carries, will come in handy for jotting down addresses of new friends, leaving notes for others when you are away from the tent, and for making records of observations.

Other items of great convenience include clamp-on clothes hooks for your tent. Selling about two for a dollar, these have two hooks apiece and can be used for camera, binoculars, clothing, and fishing tackle. Other models, costing a bit more than twice as much, have as many as eight hooks. Still others, made of leather, are designed to go around larger poles and have four hooks.

To ward off insects that interfere with your relaxation, why not take along a mosquito bar or screen? These will cover a cot or air mattress completely, with plenty of room inside to sprawl and relax. At night, too, they can make all the difference. Another use? To keep insects away from food.

Head nets for protection from small biting insects take up little room; yet if insects are especially bad, they can spell the difference between a fine trip and a miserable one. They enclose head, hat, and neck. If insects are especially small, be sure the netting has very fine mesh.

For the relaxing camper, a hammock provides instant comfort. Swung between trees, it gets you up off the ground, protects you from ground insects and dampness, and makes a mighty comfortable vantage point for lounging. The surplus hammocks, if you can still find one, are excellent in this department. Too, the ordinary canvas hammocks have many uses. For example, one will hold equipment off the ground, can with the ends joined be used as a sling to hoist food up away from night visitors, and can be thrown over firewood and equipment as an emergency tarp. Spraying such a canvas hammock with water-repellent liquid will make it doubly handy and efficient.

Another convenient little gadget with some king-size uses is elastic shock cord with a hook at each end. It comes in various lengths and can hold a tarp over gear piled on a table, lash things to the top of a car, hold the trunk lid snugly down, lash fishing rods and firearms to a duffle bag, serve as a clothesline, retain lids snugly on grub and pack boxes, and even serve as an emergency belt or suspenders. You can purchase this shock cord in long hanks if you want and make a handful of units of any lengths desired.

Waxed milk containers make pretty good table lights in a pinch. Set one on a non-inflammable metal plate or pile of sand and put pebbles or dirt in the bottom to keep it from blowing over. Then light the top. The container will burn for about ten minutes and give off a pretty fair light even in a drizzle or rain.

The next time you take to the woods, tuck a few of these little gadgets away in your gear and dig some of the tricks out of your memory. You'll enjoy more fun and convenience in the farther places. It's not always the big things that make camping a success.

40

Bucking the Elements in the Woods

RAIN, HAIL, SNOW, GALES, AND EXTREME TEMPERATURES MAY BE minor discomforts near to home. But they suddenly loom important when you find yourself pitted against them in camp. Successfully combating the elements can mean the difference between a pleasant camping trip and a grueling experience.

The main source of protection from weather in the woods is usually your tent, so do your best to keep it shipshape. In rainy weather, both ropes and fabrics are likely to shrink, often to a surprising degree. To neglect this fact of woods life can mean uprooted stakes, split seams, and possibly a collapsed shelter.

When rain strikes, slacken the guy ropes and sink the stakes deeper, if necessary, or double them. If your tent poles are adjustable, shorten them an inch or two to allow for canvas shrinkage. With nonadjustable poles, a good trick is to dig a hole a couple of inches deep beside where each normally stands. Then during wet weather just set the poles lower.

If the wet weather continues, check your ropes and tent fabric occasionally to make sure that the rig has not tightened too much for safety. Some outdoorsmen insert a short section of elastic shock cord or a short spring between the tent and each guy rope to take care of this problem.

Unless your tent is of heavy and well-waterproofed material, try to keep from hitting it on the underside, and see that nothing touches it, as this may encourage a leak at the contact point. Where any part of a roof or door awning is horizontal, rain may gather in the sag and eventually leak through. Before water collects, prop up such surfaces to take any sag out of them. Use any handy pole or stick, but cover the end so that it doesn't poke through the fabric.

The openings where the spikes of tent poles protrude through the grommets are a possible source of leaks. These spots can be sealed in several ways. One practical method is to cover both spike and opening with metal foil, held in place with elastic bands. Waxed paper will do as well for short periods. Another procedure is to cut 6-inch disks of inner tube and to poke a small hole in the middle of each. Stretch this hole over the spike, and the disk will protect the aperture.

When your tent has a screened porch, a neat trick to keep out driving rain is the use of spring-type clothespins to hold waterproof material to the eaves, closing in the sides of the section. This will afford the added advantage of more living space in wet weather. A tip? Be sure to clip the plastic sheeting, oilcloth, old shower curtain, or whatever else it is you're using under the edge of the roof and not over it. Otherwise, when you eventually dump the water from the awning roof, it is apt all to come down inside the curtain.

In a tent with a sound sewn-in floor, you'll stay dry even during a heavy rain that soaks the ground. But even without a floor, it's still possible to keep your outfit dry by raising it off the ground on brush, poles, or boughs. Another procedure is to use a tarp on the ground with its edges turned up in box fashion, the corners fastened together with clothespins.

Such an arrangement will prevent water from getting to your gear from below, although in a real cloudburst you'll have to protect it from spray coming through the tentage by covering it with ponchos or other waterproof material. Then when the shower is over, sun and air everything. If the dampness keeps up for several days, watch for signs of mildew on leather equipment, and keep it saddle-soaped and oiled if necessary.

Snow, hail, and sleet, not as likely to soak through a tent as rain is, may sweep into or under a shelter in the accompanying wind. Keep them out of a floorless tent by banking the walls; just lay poles, brush, leaves, or the like outside against the bottom. Hail will ordinarily bounce harmlessly off taut canvas, but on those sudden dramatic occasions when the stones approach the size of golf balls, slacken off on the guy ropes to soften the impacts. Keep snow brushed off the tent roof to reduce the load and to help prevent melting and freezing on ropes and sides. In brushing snow from canvas, use a soft bough to prevent damage to frozen or stiff fabric.

During really cold weather, snow banked against the sides of the tent will help keep it warm just as it did the log cabins of our pioneer ancestors. But when you're outside, be careful not to walk too close lest your additional weight split the material. For this reason, boughs piled against the sides of the tent and then covered with snow are even

Snow Banked against Tent for Warmth

better for keeping it safely warm, the combination serving as a very functional insulation because of the large amount of inert air it traps.

With sleet and freezing rain, watch out for ice forming on your tent roof, dining fly, and even on a station-wagon boot top. Ice can build up a heavy load in a hurry. When you crack off the excess, take care not to damage the fabric.

When cold weather settles in, a tent can be warmed by one of several kinds of heaters, or use a lantern with a shield around it to block off most of the light during sleeping hours. Many like to have a bit of light in a tent at night. No matter how you warm your tent, though, always be sure that it is adequately ventilated. Even in fair weather the fabric will not breathe sufficiently to assure this. Openings and circulation are needed.

In contrast to cold, extremely hot weather can make a tent close to unbearable. If at all possible, pitch your tent where there's some shade and a breeze. If there are too many trees, there may be too little air movement. On the other hand, the presence of water encourages air currents.

Pitching a large fly over your tent, with an air space between fly and tent, will protect the latter from the direct rays of the sun. Too, a fly set up in front of the tent will provide welcome shade for eating and lounging.

In a tent with windows, open them so that any breezes can waft through. If the tent has no floor, lift the side of the shady section so that cooler air can enter there to replace the hot air leaving through the windows. Inexpensive mosquito netting can be used to bar insects if they seem bent on entering under a raised side.

When ample water is at hand, hang one of those flax desert bags full of water from

Fly Pitched over Tent for Protection against Sun

the center of the ridge, with a pan under it to catch the drippings. These bags keep cold water cold by evaporation, and they will cool warm water the same way. Such a bag in your tent will also help a little to reduce the inside temperature.

Then there's wind. In a high wind, the important thing is to prevent the wind from blowing inside. If the door faces the wind, drop the awning and tie it down, or cover the doorway with any handy material. Pile heavy gear along the windward side of the floor to keep blasts from sweeping under it. In a tent with no floor, heap poles or stones along the outside ends and sink the stakes deeper. If it's obvious a storm is coming, tighten the ropes and if possible double the stakes.

When wind becomes really violent, you may have to remove the interior poles and drop the tent to save it, collapsing it atop the gear inside. This is especially true of open-end tents. It is an inconvenience at best, but it's better to yank out the poles and drop a tent rather than risk losing it plus some of the gear inside.

Thunderstorms pose no real danger other than high winds unless your tent is pitched under a lone tree that might attract lightning. However, if you're in water, come out of it when a storm is approaching, and don't get back into it until you're sure the lightning has passed.

Into the life of each outdoorsman some rain and samples of many other elements are bound to fall. But a bit of preparation will do much to help you make the best of it.

41

Fires for Camp

YOU'VE COOKED OVER YOUR SMALL GLOWING FIRE, AND THEN YOU lay on a few logs to ward off the pleasant chill from the eternal snows. You exchange tales of other trails. Then someone tosses a handful of pinecones on the fire. These flare up, throwing their light about the camp. Drowsily you prepare for bed.

Sometime late at night you come awake, shivering in your light sleeping bag. You open one eyelid. Several ruddy coals mark where the campfire has been. The snow-whitened mountains seem to have drawn closer, and the moon is drifting high among them. With a sigh, you reach out enough to toss a few dry sticks onto the embers. Flames begin curling up, sending an aura of warmth through the camp. You draw the jersey flap back over your ears, and soon it is morning.

Among the pleasantest aspects of any camping trip are the campfires. They are the center of most camping activities, especially after dark, and on a cold or gloomy day there's nothing cheerier than a good, brisk blaze. If you're a confirmed campfire cook, those few resulting coals become an even more important part of your trip.

Unfortunately, not enough of those who take to the woods know as much about wood, draft, and fire as is necessary to assure that their campfires will always be good ones.

Many campers have the opinion that any wood is good for burning. That's right under some circumstances, especially when fuel is difficult to locate near camp, or only one kind is available. But if several types of wood are close at hand, it will be to everyone's advantage if you use what's best for the type of fire you plan to kindle.

Fires are started and kept going by three factors: heat, fuel, and oxygen. Remove any one, and the fire refuses to burn. If heat is taken away by dousing with water so that the fuel cools below the ignition point, the fire will go out. It will also be extinguished if dirt, chemical foam, or some other such material is applied to cut off the oxygen supply. If you remove the fuel, it will die as quickly.

A good fire must have adequate amounts of all three essentials at the same time. The heat is supplied by the match used to start it and by the burning of the fuel as the blaze continues. The oxygen is from the air, and the fuel is wood. The only one of these three elements with any variance in quality is the wood.

If what you're seeking is a quick fire, use such fast-starting woods as spruce, pine, cedar, balsam, alder, or basswood. All start easily and burn quickly. On the other hand, they don't last long without replenishment and will not provide good embers for cooking.

Hickory is the finest of all woods for a slow-burning, long-lasting fire with excellent coals for cooking. Not far behind are oak, apple, maple, hornbeam, birch, locust, elm, cherry, and ash.

The woods that spark the least, also burning with a minimum of smoke along with a maximum of heat, include hickory, oak, maple, beech, white ash, holly, birch, Osage orange, and elm. It can be fun to learn how to identify all these woods from a good book on trees, such as William Carey Grimm's *The Book of Trees* (The Stackpole Co.), or from an experienced bushman.

When seeking firewood near your campsite, look for dead trees that are either standing or are lying with their trunks held off the ground. Such trees make the best firewood, although birch, whose tight, oily bark retains this tree's abundant moisture which in turn rots the wood, is an exception.

In many regions it is unlawful to cut live trees. However, if you are in an area where the woods are thick, and it is permitted to chop some live ones, remember that there are a few green woods that burn pretty well. These include birch, white ash, beech, maple, and hickory. Splitting or making fuzz sticks of such green wood makes it easier to burn. For a hot fire, mix such split green wood with seasoned sticks.

If the forest is buried in deep snow or soaked from a prolonged rain, consider yourself lucky to find an old rotten pine log or stump. Using the back of your ax, knock out the stubs of branches sticking out of the stump. The knots at the bases of these, rich in resin, will burn fiercely even in the soggiest weather.

Make sure that the site of your fire is first scraped clear of all ground debris, right down to the mineral earth. Also be sure to clear away all inflammable substances for at least three feet on all sides of the fire, no matter how small it is to be. The blaze should be based on dirt or rock. Otherwise, embers can burn along underground roots and rubbish to break out some distance away, perhaps months after you've left. Too, if you build your campfire on a ledge, be sure that there are no cracks down which live coals can tumble into inflammable material.

If all that's needed is a tiny fire for a quick lunch, simply use three stones or three stout green pegs to support a pan or kettle, and build your little fire among these. Or, better, suspend the receptacle from a slanting green stick.

If there are no stones, use logs instead and make a hunter's fire. This is simply two logs laid on the ground a few inches apart, with the fire between them and the pots resting on top of the logs. Just be sure that before leaving you douse not only the cooking fire but also the sides of the logs. When rocks are available, make two parallel rows of small stones and set the utensils across them.

If neither logs nor stones can be located and your pots have no bails, dig a trench parallel to the prevailing wind with the upwind end open for a better draft. If the trench is narrow, set the pots across the open top. If the trench is too wide for this, use green sticks to support the utensils.

If there is considerable wind blowing, consider the sort of Indian fireplace we've used in the treeless belt of Labrador and in the Barren Lands. There the natives dig a hole slightly larger than their kettle, build a small fire in the bottom, and then hang the kettle on a stick across the mouth of the hole. In addition to saving scarce fuel, this also prevents the terrible winds from blowing all the heat away from the kettle.

Tiny Fire for a Quick Lunch

Two Types of Hunter's Fire

Trench Fire

Indian Fireplace

The pot itself, if more fuel is available, can be set in the actual hole. Just be sure there's space around the pot's bottom for air to circulate. A variation of this Indian firepit is called the Dakota fireplace. Upwind of the main pit is a second hole, which leads to the bottom of the main pit, to bring oxygen to the base of the blaze.

One of the popular fireplaces in the West is the keyhole fireplace in which the main fire is in a ring, and the cooking fire is built in a slight extension to one side of that ring. The fire is built in the large round part of the keyhole. Then embers are raked into the smaller portion where they are covered by a grate, grill, or metal rods. The cooking is done over these coals. Just be sure that the keyhole fireplace is planned so that the smoke from the main fire wafts away from where you'll be cooking over the embers. Such a fireplace not only permits smokeless cooking over coals. It also provides a place for the evening campfire.

When camping by a loose ledge or in a region where there are plenty of stones of assorted shapes, you can build as elaborate a fireplace as the stone, time, and your ambition permit. Make the back of any fireplace high for better draft, or place it against a flat-sided boulder or ledge. Make the sides fairly high and flat-topped to hold extra pots, pans, and other kitchen equipment. Use a ring of low stones across the front to hold in the fire. Do not build a fireplace against a big down log unless it's petrified, as otherwise it'll be hard to extinguish when you leave.

You can do away with all such contrivances, and build your fire atop the ground where it will have by far the best draft, with the use of some such device as a rugged wire grid. This will hold pots and pans above an unfettered wood fire, or you can broil meat and fish on it directly.

Some of these grates have sharpened legs, which, stuck into the ground, will support the device at the proper height above the coals. These sharp extremities, however, can be somewhat of a menace to man, beast, and outfit, especially when you're on the move. We take them off for this reason and also to save weight. The grill can be laid almost as handily across stones or sticks, and it will be more stable. In both soft and stony terrain, you often have to do this, anyway.

An older arrangement, less bulky to pack, consists of two iron rods about half an inch in diameter and some four feet long, which are handy to place across almost any kind of campfire. Flat or angle irons of similar stiffness are also used. Support any of these above the fire with logs or rocks at each end, separating the rods just enough so that the smallest pan won't slip down between them. If transportation is no problem, as on many canoe trips, a sheet of metal spread across these will provide much of the convenience of a stove. Caution: let the rods cool before picking them up.

Once you're ready to lay the fire, try to get it started with one match. The practice may stand you in good stead if lucifers are ever short. The formula for such a fire is simple: (1) plenty of dry tinder, (2) ample dry kindling, and (3) a sufficiency of dry fuel. The emphasis is on the kindling, for while almost anything fine and dry will serve as tinder, there is often too much of a gap between this and the logs for the fire.

Birch bark, which contains enough oil to burn even in dripping weather, comprises one of the best tinders. A few loose shreds, not enough to deface a tree, will do the job. Old birds' nests will also work. So will cedar bark rubbed almost into fuzz, one of the best tinders of all. A fairly tight handful of dead evergreen twigs will start a fire blazing in a hurry.

Man-made fire sticks are also fine. Whittle them in moments by shaving long splinters from a soft dry stick and leaving as many of them as possible attached. Continue this

**Fire Stick,
or Fuzz Stick**

shaving until you have what looks like a little pine tree. Prop this fire stick upright in the ground and stack small stuff around it like a tiny tepee before setting a flame to the lower slivers.

An easy, rapid way to get a fire going is to lay a short stick across two other sticks a bit larger so that the first is three or four inches off the ground. Place dry tinder under this ridge. Then use small, dry kindling to make a little lean-to on the downwind side. With the wind blowing into the open front of this miniature lean-to, the tinder will light quickly, and the flames will be carried back and up through the kindling. Add heavier stuff when the kindling catches.

Of course, always carry an unbreakable, waterproof match case. It's also simple to waterproof wooden matches by dipping the heads individually into melted paraffin or into nail polish, and these can be distributed among your pockets. The wooden or so-called kitchen matches are best in any event as they can be struck on anything, and you can hold them under tinder longer. They'll also stay lit better in a wind. Again, make it a challenging habit to build most of your fires with only one match, or at the most two, for the day may come when this skill can save your life.

To transfer the flames from the tinder to the main logs, you'll need lots of kindling of a suitable type. This can be any kind of dry sticks about half an inch or less in diameter. If the wood is larger, split it down to about this size, a practice which has the added advantage of making wood burn more readily.

The dead lower branches of the pines, spruces, cedars, and other evergreens make some of the best kindling of all. This is known as squaw wood because Indian women used to gather it. The finer branches make ideal kindling, and the larger branches can be added later. This wood is usually so dry that it snaps off readily.

Once the kindling is burning well, larger sticks can be added in a pyramid for a hot fire or in a crisscross layup to produce hearty coals for broiling and roasting, assuming as previously discussed, the wood is right. Then at night start a couple of long logs burning at their ends so that, without getting out of your sleeping bag, you can push them farther into the fire as they are consumed.

When a fire seems to be dying, perhaps the wind has shifted and the fire needs more draft. If it is a hunter's fire, raise one of the side logs with a small stone or stick. If it's a fire in a stone fireplace, perhaps moving the stones apart a bit will do the job. In any event, you'll learn something from every fire you build. And as you get to know the woods better, each sojourn in the farther places will be a warmer, brighter, and more cheery stay.

Since the introduction of modern camp stoves and accessories, too many have forgotten the fun of campfire cooking. Such pioneer methods may not be as quick or as antiseptic as cooking on a camp stove, but there are plenty of outdoor veterans who assert with considerable conviction that nothing compares with the smell of a batch of hot biscuits that wafts out of a reflector baker in front of an open fire, or the soul-stirring aroma of a brace of trout or quail skewered on a couple of green sticks over a glowing bed of hot coals.

To begin with, you'll need a good cooking fire, not a bonfire. Make it of the previously discussed hardwoods if possible instead of such soft species as spruce, which leaves poor coals for cooking. Coals are the secret of successfully cooking almost everything, except foods that require quick boiling or which are baked in a reflector baker.

A reflector baker is an ingenious portable device that turns out many delectable camp dishes that otherwise would be impractical. To use it, unfold the sheet-metal contraption which resembles a book with the usual two covers but only one page. The oven is set up on its side, about eight inches from the blaze, with the shelf or page horizontal and with one of the covers opening above it and the other opening below. On this shelf the food is placed.

Heat from the fire reflects down on the shelf from above and up against the shelf from below. The resulting concentration of dry heat will cook all sorts of bread, pie, cakes, biscuits, and the like if the fire is kept going steadily. This is one kind of outdoor cooking in which flames are better than coals. The blaze should be approximately the same height and width as the oven itself.

There's one other primitive cooking device that you may be called upon to fire during stays in the woods, and that's the venerable Dutch oven. This ancient oven, awkward and

 Dutch Oven

heavy to carry unless the camping party is lodged in a cabin for good or traveling with canoe or pack animal, is nevertheless the ideal receptacle for baking such standbys as bread. With it, too, you can prepare a complete one-dish meal such as a giant mulligan in the morning, go hunting or fishing all day, and have it all steaming and savory when you arrive back at camp in the evening.

Dutch ovens are inexpensive. If your dealer doesn't have one, write the Lodge Manufacturing Company in South Pittsburg, Tennessee. A good model for use with small parties is 12 inches in diameter, 4 inches deep, and 17 pounds in weight. Models are also available in diameters of 8, 10, 14, and 16 inches.

You need a heavy, thick, preferably cast iron pot with a similarly rugged lid, stoutly lipped to hold a ruddy bed of coals. The Dutch oven selected should also have squat legs to keep the pot anchored firmly and levelly. It will also require a convenient handle by which the hot top can be lifted and an easily manipulated bail by which the entire contrivance can be moved.

Both these latter jobs can be performed with the help of a forked stick cut on the spot. When shifting the ember-heaped lid, though, use a second stick to keep it better balanced. You'll also need a shovel, one of the folding models being convenient to carry.

Dutch ovens are used both above and below the ground. The easiest way to get things going for the latter, more typical use is to build up your overnight fire with hardwood and let this burn to coals. Move these to one side. Scoop a hole large enough for the oven in the warm earth. Line this with some of the ruddy embers, put in the receptacle, heap the remaining coals over its lipped top, and cover the entire mass with earth.

It takes experience to learn how to use a Dutch oven most advantageously, especially when baking such comparatively critical dishes as bread. But it'll be safe to assume that a hearty vegetable and game meat stew readied in the morning before leaving for the day will be ready by the time you get back to camp, weary and ravenous for supper. And there may be enough hot coals left to start the evening fire.

Cooking over the campfire may not be as simple as using a camp stove, but it can be an interesting change and a challenge to those who have never tried it. Many ordinary foods take on an added deliciousness when flavored by the glowing, seething coals.

Just remember to cook from the upwind side, and use coals instead of high flames except for baking in the reflector baker and for fast boiling. Of course, a few bits of hardwood coals adhering to a steak will make it all the more authentic, and most outdoorsmen are willing to overlook some shortcomings on the part of an open-fire chef that they wouldn't tolerate in the home dining room.

Taking Your Kitchen to the Woods

IT DOESN'T MATTER WHETHER YOU AND THE FAMILY TAKE TO THE woods to keep expenses within bounds or, like so many others, because you don't really start living until you're outdoors. Somebody has to do the cooking. The way you put together, then set up, a camp kitchen can go a long way towards making the preparation of meals simpler, more comfortable, and safer.

Much has been accomplished during recent years to make camp cookery more convenient. In former days almost every woods chef did his work over an open fire. He fought smoke, skittering embers, and unsteady rocks, logs or grills on which he tried valiantly to balance his pots. Many a rousing meal was readied despite such handicaps. Today, though, unless you're backpacking and sometimes even then, better methods are at hand. Modern outdoor kitchen contrivances make camp cooking as easy and handy as meal-preparing at home.

Gasoline, kerosene, and gas stoves are available in numerous varieties. There are also jellied-fuel stoves, liquid alcohol stoves, and others that burn anything from bone-white driftwood to powdery muskeg peat. These stoves range from those that will fit handily into a pocket to the bulky sheepherder type that's just the thing for a packhorse journey. In many camping areas, where open fires are forbidden, a stove of some sort is the only device that can be used for cooking.

No matter what type you buy, there is one axiom to follow. Get the best you can afford for the cooking you want to do. A tiny pocket-size stove will do for the backpacker who wants quick meals in high country, breezily above the treeline. Both the pocket and the single-burner types are ideal for taking the chill off a tent and for starting a can of soup steaming. The larger units are better for families and for more elaborate repasts.

Many outdoorsmen use a single burner along with a double burner. A two-element stove lets one start vegetables simmering and steaks sizzling at the same time. An additional small stove is then excellent for toast and for brewing coffee right at the table.

You can even bake in camp, of course. Today there are three basic types of manufactured camp ovens: the folding-box variety that's used atop the heat, the reflector oven

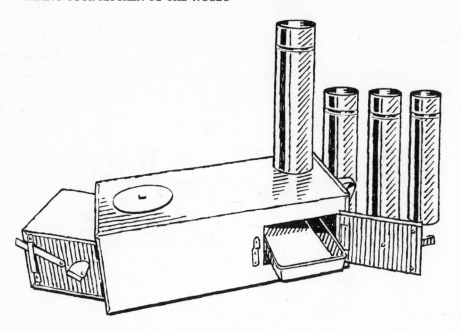

Sheepherder-Type Stove

that deflects warmth from usually a high open fire into and around food on its shelf, and the Dutch oven that was long proved even before it accompanied voracious gold stampeders of the last century.

The better of the folding-box ovens have functional temperature gauges in their doors. Really expert baking can be done in this type of oven or in an oven with a separate, inexpensive gauge. The only secret is to keep an eye on the gauge, for when doing any sort of cooking outdoors you have to be watchful for changes in temperature brought on by wind, changing shade, and the varying splashes of sunlight that sometimes fall as heavily as metal through the yielding screens of boughs.

The reflector oven, which generally folds flat for transporting, works as well today as it did for your pioneer ancestors, though building the high heat it requires still takes a little getting used to. The Dutch oven, in essence, is just a large metal kettle with a heavy lid. When one is used for baking out of doors, it is buried in hot ashes and coals, and the lid is heaped with additional embers. Dutch ovens have long been made of heavy cast iron, but today they are also available in aluminum. With care the latter do about as good a job as the heavyweight models, although they don't hold heat as evenly or as long. But they heat faster.

New bakers may be purchased that perch over ruddy coals, or fit snugly inside the hood of a barbeque cooker, and are effective for cooking potatoes or delicious sweet corn. New bread toasters make it easy to toast right at the table or over a campfire. Several varieties of wire grills, either with or without legs, will do good service in cooking over embers raked to one side of a campfire. Or you can do the same thing with two flat iron bars, each perhaps a convenient two feet long. There are also sheet-metal griddles for cooks who prefer to start their bacon, eggs, and ham sputtering on a flat sheet instead of in the oft-abused frypan.

Long-handled wire broilers to fit almost every requirement are available for grilling hamburgers and frankfurters over the campfire. Sizes obtainable range from one that will

**Reflector
Oven**

accommodate a single hamburger or three weenies to those that will take a 9- by 12-inch porterhouse a succulent three inches thick. Families can even obtain a broiler with six wire compartments for grilling a half-dozen hamburgers at once without the danger of their slipping out when being turned.

Frypans, round or square, can be found as big as nearly two feet across. When you're readying a meal for a large family or group, the oversize skillets make it possible to cook for everyone at once without having to attend to several smaller frypans at once.

When it comes to pots and pans, there are numerous nested sets on the market from which to make your selections. These range all the way from neat one-man outfits to remarkably complete, compact serving and cooking sets for eight. These nested sets are far handier to pack and carry than a conglomeration of off-size pots, pans, cups, and plates. Some of the components turn out to be so handy, in fact, that unless you pack everything conscientiously away, they're apt to be used in the home kitchen.

For cutting down on washing and scouring, paper dishware can be one answer. Modern paperware availabilities have come a long way from the sodden items one used to have to do with. Many are now sheathed with plastic which prevents dampness from soaking in. There are now cold or hot cups and even insulated ones. Even if you prefer to drink from regular cups, a store of paper plates will save a lot of dishwashing. Today, paper cereal bowls, dessert dishes, hot-dog containers, hamburger receptacles, and a variety of other items are worth considering.

It's hard to beat camp coffee made by using anything from a pot to an open can, perhaps with a wire bail attached through nail holes near the rim for convenience, and started by putting a rather coarse grind into fresh cold water, using two level tablespoons for every cup of water. Hang or set this over the heat. Immediately after it's boiled up once, lift it to a warm spot to take on strength for five minutes. Then settle the grounds with a couple of tablespoons of cold water and start serving. On the other hand, many prefer to merely heat water and pour it into a cup with a teaspoon of powdered coffee.

There are those who hate to turn from their percolated coffee, even in the woods, and large groups can get percolaters big enough to brew twenty 5-ounce cups at once. For campers traveling with a car, hot liquids are even less of a problem. Small plug-in heaters for the automobile's cigarette-lighter socket will bring a glass of milk, bouillon, or soup to a simmer in about four minutes.

Several varieties of tongs and detachable handles are available that simplify the moving of hot pans and pots. A pair of lightweight asbestos gloves will make life a lot easier for the city cook not accustomed to the outdoors. Or, of course, you can use ordinary, preferably leather gloves or mitts or a thick kitchen holder. Heavy-duty asbestos gloves will make it possible to extract roasted corn and potatoes directly from the coals and to shift hot pots and pans without bothering with holders or handles.

A table of some kind is needed for efficient camp-kitchen effort. Most public campgrounds provide these, as well as benches. Campers who aren't apt to be where such conveniences exist and who are traveling by car should take along a folding table. Incidentally, the lowered tailgate of a station wagon makes a handy place for a camp stove. There are also compactly folding camp-stove stands that hold stoves at convenient working heights. Folding tables with seats attached are available that, with perhaps a second small table for odds and ends, will provide the needed working space. By the way, it's a good idea to provide a safe place to stand or hang a lantern for cooking after the sun has gone down. You can buy a tall stand for your lantern.

By using some line carried for the purpose, it's a simple enough matter to build your own table in the bush. Just select two adjacent trees near where you plan to light the fire and lash two rugged poles across them. Then cut short pieces to length from smaller poles. Tie these close together across the two main poles. If you are actually going to cook on such a table, make extra sure it is strong and stable, for tilting hot liquids can be perilous.

**Improvised
Camp-Kitchen
Table**

If cooking is done over a campfire, locate the table and other appliances upwind of the blaze so as to avoid sparks and smoke. Keep your icebox handy but not near enough to be affected by the heat of the stove or campfire. Try to locate it in the shade all the time. Unless you expect to sit around the kitchen table to eat, a good spot for the icebox is under the table. Some campers prefer to keep their iceboxes in their tents. The drawback to this is that the interior of a tent is usually warmer than it is outside; also, a bear may track down the icebox and ruin your tent to reach it, even with you sleeping beside it. It has happened.

When traveling with an icebox, keep it in the shadiest part of the car or station wagon. Putting it on the right side of the vehicle when heading west, on the left if driving east, will help to keep it cool and will conserve ice.

A shelter over the cooking area is a very practical arrangement, not only for shade on hot, sunny days but for cover when it rains or drizzles. If such a shelter is high enough, you will be able to cook under it on a camp stove with perfect safety. But don't try to pitch a fly over a campfire. The whole works is apt to go up in flames.

Food and utensils may well be stored in boxes handy to stove or campfire. So should spare tanks of gas or spare gasoline, but always keep these at a safe distance. An old metal icebox is a fine, safe place for food unless big bears are around. If they are, you'll do better to lock the food in your car trunk or station wagon unless it will interfere with sleeping arrangements. In that expediency, suspend the food high enough from a branch so that the animals can't reach it. In bear country never keep food in your tent. It may attract keen-scented, undesirable visitors.

If you don't have an old metal box for grub, all is not lost. Make a few from exterior-grade plywood, designing them to fit your particular requirements. Good for the purpose is 5/6-inch exterior-grade plywood, with brass screws and hinges to prevent rusting. Some outdoorsmen construct compartmented kitchen boxes with a place for everything. Others just build a simple container. Paint such boxes with outside paint for protection.

To build a compartmented box, assemble what you need to carry in as compact an arrangement as possible. Then design a container to fit. It's a sound idea to make a dummy box out of cardboard first, sticking the partitions and shelves in with tape until you get them properly spaced, then duplicate everything in plywood. Use thinner plywood for the interior, and don't forget to allow for the fact that even then it is likely to be thicker than the cardboard. The cover can best be attached with piano hinges, which make a strong connection. Use brass chain to hold the cover in open position.

Keep all the most used items close together, within easy reach, when setting up a camp kitchen. Table knives, forks, and spoons should not be scattered among cutting and slicing knives and sharp-tined cooking forks. Potentially dangerous equipage such as these should be kept in a special compartment of your kitchen box or, at least, covered with some type of guard. Large corks stuck on sharp fork tines will keep you from being jabbed. Corks will also remove much of the danger from ice picks and similar devices.

If you have long, slender carving knives, it will be a simple matter to make functional wooden cases for them. Just take a piece of wood as long as each blade, or blade and handle if you prefer. Using a rip saw, cut a slot lengthwise in the piece deep enough to hold the blade completely. Cover the top of this slot with a thin strip of wood, and there you are. Leave a strip under the handle if you prefer, or just cover the blade.

Make certain that the point of the knife is safely within the slot. Such cases can be fashioned for all types of carving, steak, and vegetable knives. Some campers fasten such wooden cases to the interiors of their kitchen boxes. Then when they are ready to set out, they can tell if any knives are missing just by checking the cases.

If there is much slicing or chopping to do, carry along a clean square of soft pine on which to do it instead of using a dulling plate or flat stone. Such a chopping block can be made to slide into one of the cabinet compartments, and the soft pine will protect the knife blade. Rinse and scour it after every use to eliminate odors.

Keep your pots and pans as completely nested as possible to conserve space. When they are not in use, cover them with fine meshed netting to keep insects off. Make it a habit never to put utensils away dirty.

When taking to the woods, keep the kitchen equipment, stove, utensil containers, food boxes, and camp lantern together so that all can be located quickly on arriving at the destination at mealtime or after dark. We carry ours within the tailgates of our wagons where we can quickly shift them to the lowered tailgates. If it storms, we move at least our lunch items to the front part of the wagon's rear so that we can reach a snack over the back of the seats without getting out in the weather.

To the woman in camp, or the experienced male camp chef, arranging the kitchen can be a pleasant chore if the cook has a reasonable choice of modern kitchen items to use, a few stout boxes to keep things where they belong, and a table to work on.

43

Food in the Farther Places

APPETITE IS A CONSTANT COMPANION IN THE WOODS. IN FACT, THE way you begin looking forward to even the simplest meals is something wondrous. Nor does all this eating seem to put on poundage. You work off the calories and smell each campfire smoke with a special zest, hankering for more. One of the pleasantest parts of camping is the robust outdoor eating that goes with it. As far as we're concerned, unless these meals are interesting and worth looking forward to, taking to the bush won't be half the fun it should be.

Camp meals should be extranourishing, for you'll burn up more healthy energy in the woods than you generally do in town. They should also be varied. The pioneer's old reliable three B's—beans, bacon, and bannock—can get all-fired monotonous after the first few days. And if you're packing in your chow, it should be low in carrying weight.

More sugar than usual will be needed to help provide all the energy you'll be expending. Sugar substitutes, such as the chemical sweeteners, aren't worth a whoop in this department. So if you still insist on them for drinks, be sure to include plenty of natural sugar in the form of jams, jellies, and such to provide all the pep you'll require.

The foods most suitable for camping are easy to carry, compact for the amount of nourishment they contain, slow to spoil, and quick and easy to cook. When backpacking or portaging, don't take foods that are either heavy, bulky, quick to deteriorate, low in nourishment, or difficult to cook. When camping by car or near an outfitter's you can enjoy a wider variety all the way.

Dry cereals, bulky in ratio to the actual nourishment they provide, are generally ruled out for trips where there is extensive packing. Canned goods are both heavy and bulky, and the emptied containers must be burned, flattened, and buried. Fresh fruits produce relatively little nourishment, especially when you consider the weight of skins and pits. Eggs, as well as foods in glass containers, are heavy and likely to smash. Frozen foods will, of course, rapidly thaw and spoil. Even fresh meat won't keep long and may be messy to pack.

The elimination of these foods from the menu may seem to the inexperienced camper to limit hopelessly the chance for good wilderness meals. Seasoned outdoorsmen are aware, however, that grub that packs well affords nearly endless possibilities for deliciously nourishing camp meals. Modern processing, helped along to some extent by functional packaging, makes it a simple matter to ready some mighty fine meals without the handicap of excessive weight on your back.

Everyone is already familiar with some of the quick-fix beverages, soups, and milks. Instant tea and coffee now compare favorably to the regularly brewed drinks, and there's also cocoa and malted milk. Almost every kind of soup you can think of now comes in packages that will serve up to four with just the addition of a little hot water or, at most, a few minutes of simmering. There is a choice of instant milks, totally different from those old-fashioned powders that used to take endless mixing. There are tasty instant puddings with which to blend it.

Other lightweight, easily prepared foods requiring only the addition of water include many vegetables. For instance, you can buy instant mashed potatoes which need only to be stirred with a small amount of boiling water, a bit of salt, and perhaps a little cream for that final touch. If the potatoes come in a foil package, the whole process can take place in the container itself, and that extra embellishment of cream can come from powdered products.

If you'd like rice instead, you're all set. The new noncooking instant rice needs nothing but a little boiling water to make it nourishing, snow white, and delicious. Want a quick dessert? Then stir in a few seedless raisins.

In fact, the new dehydrated, time-saving foods are coming out fast and furiously these days. Before planning meals for camp, do a little exploring in your local markets and camp-supply stores. Ask for suggestions, as new grub, ideal for taking on trips to the woods, is appearing almost every month. For example, one manufacturer now offers concentrated nourishment for one meal in a space only a trifle bigger than a 12-gauge shell.

Fruit tastes especially good in backcountry, and tremendous strides have been taken in the dried fruit industry. From the earliest days we've always taken such dried food with us into the wilderness, but now it's closer to the fresh delicacies than ever, with repasts that are lighter and far easier to prepare. Whereas even the best dried fruits used to require overnight soaking to be halfway palatable, you can now buy dried fruits, either separately or in deliciously blended mixtures, that can be prepared on the spot as needed for breakfast, supper, or even noonday lunch. These are also excellent for snacking on raw while on the trail.

Many camp foods can be removed from outside boxes, making them lighter and more compact. The inside envelopes are often sufficient protection. Repack the more fragile units in plastic envelopes or bags, or in the small, soft plastic jars that are available from outfitters.

The smells of frying bacon and ham are just the thing to get them clambering out of their sleeping bags in the morning. Sliced bacon is easy to handle, but slab bacon will keep far better, and you'll have the rind for greasing pans. Before leaving on your trip, a good trick is to wet a cloth with vinegar and wipe the bacon with this. It will remove any traces of mold and prevent more from forming for many days, yet won't affect the taste. On long expeditions, repeat this process as often as necessary. As most people like bacon, especially in the bush, better figure on about 2 1/2 pounds of it per person per week, particularly if you'll be cooking fish.

Sliced ham will keep well if there is some way to keep it reasonably cool and can be used either for sandwiches or grilled for breakfast. It now comes sealed in plastic to make it keep longer. However, just as slab bacon is preferable to the sliced meat when you're going to be back of beyond for more than a few days, so will a whole ham keep better.

Eggs become precious commodities in the bush and, especially if they are kept in a cool place, will stay good for several weeks. They, along with butter or margarine in watertight containers, will do well in a spring or cool brook. Backpacking eggs is touchy, but it can be done if you're careful. Pack in an egg box, one of those stout cartons made of heavy pressed paper pulp being best, and then enclose everything in a plastic bag in case of breakage.

If you'll settle for scrambled eggs anyway, just break your eggs in a rugged plastic bag for easy carrying. Or use the present whole egg powders, which can be welcome in the silent spaces, especially when the taste is touched up with delectable slices of ham or bacon. What wouldn't interest city-bound appetites, dulled by smog, stress, and sedentary living, can be ambrosia when served to rejuvenated taste buds and ravenous hungers under the star-scouring pines.

Other good foods for breakfast include oatmeal, toast, and pancakes. The first now arrives in instant form with the added encouragement of dried fruit, needing only boiling water and a couple of stirs in the bowl itself. All three staples are easy to prepare, especially with the help of a practical cookbook written expressly for the woods, such as Bradford Angier's *Wilderness Cookery*. They'll stick by you for a morning of hunting or fishing.

Fruit juices will round off the meal, and these can be carried in powdered form or concentrated in small containers which will make plenty of juice to compensate for the weight of the cans.

As for meats other than breakfast bacon or cooked ham, few will keep well unless on ice. Some hard sausages like salami will do all right for a few days. Of course, canned meats, canned fish, and canned chicken are fine if you can carry the weight. Such fare can be mixed up for a hearty hash, used in bubbling stews, sliced cold for sandwiches, or grilled, perhaps on individual forked green sticks, for a hot meal. Frankfurters and pork sausages will not keep more than a day or two away from ice. If you wish to take a few along, eat them first, saving the unopened canned fare for later.

The same thing goes for fish. Eat any freshly caught fish, saving the canned fish for later. For days when you're too taken up with other woodland activities to fish, canned fish cakes are a good food around which to construct a meal. Take along a little flour to roll them in before sautéing them in bacon fat. A small, flat can of sardines will also provide a nice change from luncheon sandwiches. By the way, don't forget a safe can and bottle opener, plus a key to handle each of the various types of metal containers.

One fine argument that precedes most camping trips is whether to carry bread or make it in camp. If you're not going to be in the bush too long, the former will save a lot of time. Bread will keep upwards of two weeks under ordinary conditions, particularly if it is bought unsliced.

Even if it gets really dry, toast it and then break it into pieces for use in steaming, appetite-arousing soups. Or cut a hole in the middle of as many slices as necessary, relegate the slices to a hot buttered frypan, and drop an egg into each hole. The bread will toast and the eggs fry. Toast the "hole," too.

If you don't carry bread, just make bannock. Or settle for flapjacks or dumplings, both prepared from the same basic recipe. To make enough bannock for one meal for one hungry outdoorsman, just mix dry 1 cup flour, 1 teaspoon baking powder, and 1/4 teaspoon salt, taking all the time you need to do this thoroughly. Then, working swiftly, stir in enough

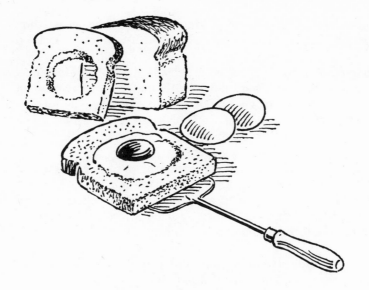

**Easy Way to
Toast Bread
and Fry Eggs
at the Same Time**

cold water to make a firm dough. Shape this, with as little handling as possible, into a cake about an inch thick. Dust this lightly with flour, so it will handle easier.

Lay the bannock in a warm, greased frypan. Hold it over the heat until a bottom crust forms, rotating the pan a little so that the loaf will shift and not become stuck. Then turn, cook the other side, and you're in business. The whole affair will take about fifteen minutes. Bannock is best broken, not cut, into serving sizes and enjoyed steaming, dripping with melting yellow butter or, if you have room to take it along, maple syrup.

For venturing into sheer wilderness that is days away from any supplies except for what you can get by living off the country, it will be sound procedure to take along a few units of emergency rations just in case something happens to your grub through storms, flood, or even loss overboard from a canoe. Such emergency rations aren't fancy, but will provide the energy to keep you going under full steam in case of trouble.

If transportation is no problem and there is even a small icebox along, you can have a field day, limited only by preferences and budget. Therein lies a major advantage of camping at a public campsite where fresh meats and vegetables are readily available. A small icebox alone opens up a whole new area in camp grub, for it will store such pleasant

**Cooking
Bannock**

foods as fresh butter, cheeses, cold drinks, and meat. Fruit can be kept cold, and salad dressings can be added to your menu.

Car camping permits taking along canned foods, which means you'll be able to enjoy just about everything you sit down to at home—steaks, roasts, stroganoffs, soufflés, and what have you. There is almost no limit to what you can take along in cans when bulk and weight are no worry. If there is the possibility that your canned goods may be exposed to rain or water, and camping sometimes can be a damp affair, mark the contents on the end of the cans in case the labels come off.

For backpacking, portages, and other occasions when light weight is desirable, there are some remarkable new food products that will interest you. One of the more revolutionary new types is the freeze-dried foods. It includes numerous kinds of meats that have been frozen stiff and then had about 99 percent of the moisture removed.

Once the food has been quick-frozen, it is placed in a cabinet where a nearly perfect vacuum is created. Then heat is transferred to the top and bottom of the meat. The temperature is so minutely controlled that the food does not thaw. Instead, all the ice crystals are transformed directly into vapor instead of liquid, much as dry ice vaporizes instead of melting. This leaves all the soluble salts, proteins, and sugars dried in their natural locations. There is little shrinkage, a disadvantage as far as packing is concerned, and there's no hard crust.

Freeze-dried food keeps indefinitely without refrigeration, for there can be no bacterial or enzymatic action. The weight saved with these foods is fantastic. For example, a half-pound steak weighs about two ounces after processing and looks something like a thin, porous, very dry, light brown cooky. Simply soak it in cool water for a few minutes, and it becomes a juicy steak.

Among other freeze-dried camp foods are scrambled eggs that can be ready in less than a minute, chops, chicken and beef stews, shrimp creole, and even complete breakfasts with eggs, pork-sausage patties, and potatoes all in one unit.

There is a wide choice of foods dehydrated in more conventional ways. Some of the earlier types of dehydrated foods for campers made for pretty rugged eating. Starting with World War II, though, great strides were made in the industry, and the new types are far better and afford much greater variety. They're packed in heat-sealed packages and require no refrigeration. There are many reliable brands, but the best procedure is to try a few different kinds at home before making a final decision.

Take cookies and crackers, as well as candies and jams for the youngsters. Hard or wrapped candies are best. If you buy chocolate bars, either keep them in a cool place or choose the semisweet kind that's sometimes called sportsman's chocolate. It's a harder variety and will keep better in warm weather. Should candy become soft, put it in a watertight container or wrap it well in foil and put it in a cool brook until it hardens.

Planning the camp grub list can be fun if the whole group gets together and helps out, each putting down what he or she would prefer and then comparing the lists. The few items that only one or two seem to care for can be eliminated and the final menu arranged from what is requested most.

Campers who've been camping before will remember what tasted particularly good beneath the pines or what they forgot on their last trip. For a first trip, a good rule of thumb is to take along plenty of whatever everyone likes at home and that can be easily prepared in camp, then fill in with other items that will occur as you make up the menus. Whatever you bring, take enough. Even the simplest fare tastes magnificent in the open.

The actual planning of meals is best done on paper, well in advance of the journey.

Figure on more sugar than you'd use at home, and don't forget salt, pepper, and any special condiments you may feel necessary. If you're going to be gone for, say, four days, plan the whole dozen meals. Be as lavish as you like at first. Then go over them and see what can be omitted to save weight or can be carried in powdered or dehydrated form. If you're packing into camp, you'll have to pare even more.

Once the menu is cut to where it seems both practical and appealing, work out on paper how much of each food you'll need for the entire trip. Then total up the weight of the whole business. Be sure to figure in the margarine, spices, and so on used in cooking.

For a rule of thumb, each camper should have a minimum of 2 1/4 pounds of reasonably water-free foods each day. If you've cut to less than that, it will be a good idea to put back a few items. On the other hand, if your compilations work out to three or four pounds per man each day, you're either planning to lug a lot of unnecessary stuff or you have a preponderance of extraheavy items. Perhaps some of the latter can be carried in dehydrated form to save weight, yet still afford as much variety and nourishment.

There's no really magic formula for making up the menu, but you'll soon learn what to leave behind and what to take. No matter how painstaking the planning, there will almost inevitably be too much of one thing and not enough of another. But don't worry. Veteran campers are still finding this out on almost every trip. Without planning, you'd be far off the mark.

Don't forget those extra few small items which help to make camping meals mighty pleasant. Take along that ketchup, the onions, and the special sauce if you can, for the trifling added weight will pay off in the extra pleasure of having camp food the way you like it. Incidentally, ketchup, jams, and jellies are available in plastic envelopes. Of course, car-camping travelers or those near supplies as at a public site can forget practically all restrictions and plan their meals as they like, buying ahead only as they need to.

In packing food for camp, use plastic bags and containers whenever possible to prevent the breaking of jars and bottles. However, don't empty into such containers any hermetically sealed foods that will spoil during the trip. Ice cream containers are convenient. Too, you can do wonders with aluminum foil and waxed paper to reseal or cover opened and partially used foods.

To seal punctured cans of milk and juices, whittle wooden plugs or cover the top of

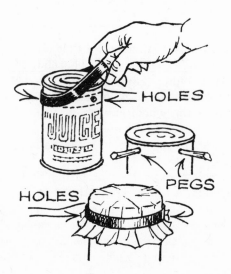

**How to Seal Punctured Cans
of Milk and Juices**

the can with foil and seal with rubber bands. A gimmick is to puncture such cans just below the rim on the side, then cover the holes with a wide elastic band. A few plastic bowl covers in assorted sizes are always coming in handy.

If you're taking along frozen foods for the first day or so, wrap them in several layers of newspapers, then in a plastic bag in case they thaw and leak. When packing meat for first-day use, remove any heavy bones or excess fat, leaving enough of the latter for flavor, of course. Want a gimmick for carrying fresh eggs? Break them into narrow olive jars. Then screw the tops on tightly. When you need eggs, you can pour them out one at a time.

It may be possible to supplement camp meals with wild fruits and vegetables. Just a word of caution: don't eat anything you're not sure of. Carry along books such as Bradford Angier's *Free for the Eating* and *More Free-for-the-Eating Wild Foods,* both of which picture and describe different edible wild plants in detail.

Planning meals is a fine way to spend time before you leave for camp, not after you get there.

44

Know Your Woodcraft

ANYONE WHO TRAVELS TO A FOREIGN COUNTRY WITHOUT FIRST finding out something about it generally has a far less enjoyable time than those who have taken time to become well grounded in the background. The same thing holds with taking to the woods. To know your woodcraft is to have a better time from the first.

Knowledge of woodcraft makes it possible to select a tent site that the morning sun will cheerily dry but which will be shaded from the hot afternoon rays. It will help in picking such a location free from the dangers of leaning trees, dead overhead branches, possible falling rocks, and potential floods.

Woodcraft knowledge includes lore about insects. Knowing this will enable a camper to recognize buggy regions and to pitch his tent as far from them as possible, especially from lowlands, marshes, muskegs, and dense ground vegetation. The woodsman will raise his canvas on high ground, away from damp areas and where an energizing breeze will keep insects in check. A knowledge of this subject will also make it easy to stay clear of hornet and wasp nests, anthills, and areas where black flies are especially thick.

The outdoorsman's grasp of woodcraft will keep him from pitching his tent and making camp in or near poison oak, or poison ivy or sumac, or where nettles are prevalent.

Woodcraft includes knowledge about wood for various types of campfires. It will enable you to build a fire quickly, even when a cold rain is freezing on the trees, and to end up with either high flame for light and heat, coals for cooking, or both. You learn that such woods as pine, spruce, cedar, alder, balsam, and basswood are about the best for a quick, hot blaze. On the other hand, all-night companionship is best gained from hickory, oak, maple, birch, ash, and the sweet-burning apple. The latter woods make for long-lasting heat with a minimum of dangerous sparks and annoying smoke.

Apple is our favorite, closely followed by green birch. An abandoned orchard with some down trees, so good for hunting, is a fireplace to enjoy some exceptionally rousing campfires. A good book will enable you to identify all these trees by such characteristics as leaves, needles, and bark. In winter, the debris under the snow at the base of the tree will help you substantiate your identification.

Poison Sumac

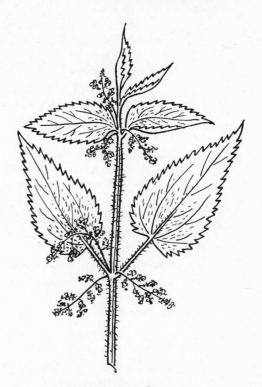

Stinging Nettle

Poison Ivy

Poison Oak

Experience will tell you where to find dry tinder even in wet going: wisps of birch bark which can be pulled off without damaging the trees, old birds' nests, and the pitch-enriched knots of rotted pine logs. The dead, dry twigs found in the bottoms of all evergreens will start a fire directly from the match. Bark from a cedar makes fine tinder, especially if split and rolled between palms into a soft cottonlike ball.

Safe and skillful use of ax, hatchet, and knife is a trademark of one who knows what he's about when he takes to the woods. It will pay you to read about and practice with these tools until you can handle them proficiently. Care of such tools is also the mark of a good camper.

Knowledge of woodcraft will enable you to find water. You'll automatically note where slopes and ravines direct the water to low spots where it will come to the surface in rivulets and springs. Such lore will also reveal where to find delicious fruits, nuts, and edible bulbs should you become lost. Under such circumstances, a knowledge of such woodcraft learned at leisure with some good books can make the difference between panic and calm.

One reason a lot of people don't get enthusiastic about taking to the woods for recreation is that they don't know what to expect. The unknown makes them ill at ease. This is especially true when they have been afraid of meeting wild animals. But in reading up on woodcraft and camping, they quite often get the urge to go out and try it.

Most city folks, and not a few country residents, have never come into close contact with wild animals. One of us well recalls a city family who moved near him a few years ago. One day the husband phoned in great excitement to say there were three deer in the backyard. He wondered if it would antagonize them if the youngsters went out on the porch to see them better. He fully expected the does to attack the moment the family showed up on the veranda. Later he called with the invite to come over and see a "black snake's nest with eggs" that his children had found in the backyard near the woods. This turned out to be a neat pile of fresh black and round droppings from the same does.

Most supposed perils will simply fade as you gain a knowledge of woodcraft. For example, you'll learn that the interesting skunks, a common visitor to many campsites for late-night snacks, are entirely harmless unless threatened or cornered. If they are left alone and watched quietly, they will prove to be entirely engrossing and harmless visitors. Even should they enter your tent, as has happened to us, they will patter off inoffensively if you just sit tight and leave them alone.

One tip? It is best to keep away from any animal, no matter how small, that appears injured, sick, confused, or overly tame.

The most common animal visitors in camp, in addition to skunks, will be rabbits, squirrels, chipmunks, possums, raccoons, foxes, badgers, and deer. Bears or bobcats are rarely encountered, even in primitive wilderness. None of these is really dangerous if you leave them alone and give them plenty of room. Even the bruin much prefers to go the other way unless surprised or cornered. For additional enjoyment, take along a well-illustrated guidebook.

Find out what the various animals in your vicinity eat. Then use these edibles to attract them if you wish to meet them for observation. If you don't, keep such appealing foods well covered in camp. Chicken, eggs, fish, and bread are favorites of the raccoons that, at different sides of the continent, we feed at our back doors regularly, although they will tackle almost anything edible if nothing else is about.

Skunks and opossums will try anything once and seem to have no particular favorites. Most animals will arrive only during the darkness, but a bear may saunter into a wilderness camp during the daylight if its residents are away. When you return to camp in some regions after anything but the briefest of absences, it's not a bad idea to announce your arrival with singing or whistling, just so as not to surprise a bear.

An added word of caution? In Yellowstone Park, where bears are as much a part of the scenery as the campers, the bruins behave unlike wild bears and have no fear of man. This setup can be perilous. Leave bears, wild or tame, strictly alone, and watch from a distance.

Woodcraft learned from books or from experience will afford protection from poisonous snakes, at the same time letting you enjoy watching the harmless ones at close range. The average campground is free of snakes, for they dislike human company as much as people disrelish theirs. But by knowing where snakes are found and what they eat, you'll be able either to find them for observation or to avoid them.

Unlikely as it seems to some individuals, snakes are fascinating critters. Some of the more deadly looking are entirely harmless. One in particular, the puff adder or hog-nose snake, is a real hammy actor. He looks tough and acts it when you first meet him. He swells up like a cobra, hisses, strikes like mad, but never bites. If you threaten or touch him, he'll play dead, rolling over on his back with his forked tongue hanging out. The difficulty is, he doesn't know enough to stay dead. Roll him over on his belly again, and he'll probably roll over on his back to look expired, which gives the whole thing away.

Knowledge of woods lore will explode such reptile myths as: (1) horsehair ropes will keep snakes out of camp, (2) some snakes swallow their young in time of danger, (3) when a poisonous snake bites himself, his flesh is unfit to eat, and (4) snakes won't die until sundown.

What is more, an understanding of woodcraft will enable you to prophesy with reasonable accuracy what the weather is going to be. You will learn that a red sunset with a clear sky means a fine tomorrow, and a red but hazy sun means hot weather ahead. You will learn that dew and cobwebs on the grass indicate a fine day to come, and that high clouds never rain on you.

On the other hand, you'll soon discover that a gray sunset and a red morning mean rain, and that when lots of birds are perching instead of flying, and when ground odors are strong, there's wet weather ahead. So is there when the forests murmur and the mountains roar.

Mountain climbers and high-altitude campers know that height means cold and dress accordingly. Woodcraft experts are aware, too, that wind greatly increases cold's penetration. Wind is partly responsible for numerous cases of frostbite. For instance, a 45 m.p.h. wind at 20 degrees is as chilling as 45 degrees below zero with only a 2 m.p.h. wind blowing.

Knowledge of various birds, animals, flowers, and insects will make taking to the woods more satisfying for the whole family. Get all the woodcraft information you can. Carry appropriate guidebooks. How much more satisfying it is to be able to say, "Watch out for that big bed of poison ivy!" instead of, "Let's take some of those shiny red (or green) leaves home to grandma."

Wood lore, ranging from how to identify wild foods, to sharpening and using knife and ax, pitching a tent, and finding fresh water can do much to make the next camping session memorable. It's never too late to store up a lot of woodcraft. Pretend it's as essential to each new season as your campfire and tent, and you'll soon discover it really is.

45

Compass and the Camper

TOO MANY INDIVIDUALS SET OFF INTO THE WILDS, OR STRAY A BIT from camp, with absolutely no idea of the terrain, how to read landmarks, or how to use a compass. Far too many don't even carry a compass. So it is small wonder that the year around newspapers are dotted with reports of lost campers, hikers, fishermen, and hunters.

The preponderant majority of such misfortunes are completely needless, for it is easy to learn how to use the little spinning needle—in fact, it can be fun—and compasses themselves are inexpensive.

An understanding of and confidence in the compass make getting about in totally strange woods as easy as anywhere else. Everyone who takes to the woods should know how to use the device, if for no other reason than that it is an old outdoorsman's skill and a trick of the camping trade of which anyone can be proud.

A compass is merely a little steel needle or disc magnetized so that one end of the pointer always indicates the earth's magnetic pole.

The magnetic north pole is not at the geographical North Pole but rather 1,000 miles south of it in the Viscount Melville Sound about 600 miles north of the Arctic Circle and just west of the 100-degree meridian. In Labrador, for example, a compass points about 40 degrees west of true north, while in Alaska it points about the same amount east of the geographical North Pole. Every year this declination varies slightly.

In most areas of the contiguous United States this declination is only a few degrees. You might check with local surveyors, or write to the Government Printing Office, Washington, D. C., 20525, for a copy of *Map of the Compass Declination in the United States.* Or mark the direction of the North Star some night and the next day check it with a compass. The difference will be the reasonably accurate declination. This information is not needed for merely using a compass for heading to easy-to-find landmarks, but for orienting a compass with a map it is essential. Incidentally, declination is shown on many maps.

Hand-held Compass

There are various types of compasses, but the only ones with which campers are concerned are the small, hand-held types that employ a swinging needle or a rotating dial.

The simplest of these is a sheet-steel needle, without case or dial, that can be set upon a sharp sliver of fingernail, a wooden splinter, or the tip of a pine needle. There is also a tiny cased compass measuring less than 1/4-inch across its glass face, originally designed to help war prisoners escape but now in the stock of some knife makers. At the other end of the spectrum are the highly accurate, sight-equipped engineers' compasses.

Between these extremes are many kinds of compasses. Some have fine, watchlike cases. Others have plastic or brass cases. Some have needles or dials that float in liquid, dampening their swinging. Some are equipped with more or less complex dials marked off in all 360 degrees and even fractions thereof, while others just indicate north, east, south, and west.

Compasses for campers range in prices from a few cents to about $15. The cheapest compass will help you get back to camp provided you know how to use it. The more complicated types will enable you to travel easily across country and back again and to make side trips to points of interest, all by compass headings or azimuths as they are called. There are small compasses designed to be set into rifle stocks and knife hilts. Another model, one of the more popular, is an official Boy and Girl Scout compass. This one has a lever that lets you stop the needle when the compass is not in actual use, thus reducing wear on the pivot.

All magnetic compasses should be kept away from iron and steel objects, other magnets, including each other, and electrical devices, so that the magnetized pointer is not affected. If such objects are nearby, the sensitive needle is apt to point promptly to them rather than to the magnetic north pole, which it should indicate to be of any use. If you're in doubt, move the compass well away from any such object and see whether the needle swings in a new direction. If it does, chances are that this heading is the correct one.

If you are carrying or wearing something that you suspect might affect the pointer— such as a rifle, handgun, or steel belt buckle—the best thing to do is to set your compass on a stump, walk away, and then come back for a look. If the needle swings toward you as you approach, then you'd better get rid of the questionable item before using the compass.

Small radios of any type also affect the heading of a compass, so keep these items away when taking a reading. Even a tiny second compass, if close enough, will affect the needle. Try putting two compasses together sometime; if you've never observed this before, you'll be surprised at just how violent the reaction can be.

Once you have a compass you're in business. Then by timing yourself or by otherwise measuring distances, and by making either a written or mental record of all angles of travel, it becomes easy to know always just about how far away in what direction lies the spot from which you started.

Even the most experienced frontiersman does well to carry a compass whenever in the bush, if only to save time and energy. For instance, we're on a Gaspé Peninsula knoll. The sun has set. We can glimpse smoke curling up a mile away from the tents where all day our wives have had a mulligan simmering. Heading directly there in the straightest possible line can mean the difference between arriving easily and safely during the remaining daylight and taking the needless chance of getting a dead branch in the eye.

So we sight over a compass. The tents lie exactly south by the needle. Once we've dropped down to the flat, we're in small thick spruce so dense that some of the time we have to get down and crawl. We cannot see far enough ahead to line up a straight route without a lot of time-consuming care, but checking the compass occasionally assures our keeping headed in the shortest direction.

Or we're on the other side of the continent, atop a Yukon mountain. A cloud swirls about us, blotting out all landmarks. Camp, we've ascertained during the climb, lies east down what is the only safe slope. The weather is thick by now. Which way is east? If we have a compass, we neither have to wait on this exposed peak for the atmosphere to clear, nor need we risk any undue or unnecessarily dangerous scrambling.

If camp lies against some long and easily followed landmark, such as a subarctic river with a smooth, hard shore, returning there after a day afield can be practically foolproof. It is in such a place that an experienced man will whenever possible be careful to locate his camp, for he will still be able to find it although the weather becomes stormy and the night black.

Where Bradford Angier has lived for some years in the largely unmapped and unexplored primitiveness of northern British Columbia, becoming lost could be serious in the extreme. We could walk from our homesite for veritable hundreds of miles and never cross a road nor see the most meager sign of habitation. It would very likely be weeks, furthermore, before anyone even realized we were missing.

That would have concerned us a lot more than it actually did, particularly at first, if it were not for the fact that the Peace River cuts from west to east through these mountains and foothills. Our home in the woods is on the sunny north bank. Any time we keep on traveling south while on the north side, we're bound to reach the great waterway. If we happen to be on the south shore instead, it's merely a matter of reversing the direction and heading north.

After even the roughest general reckoning, therefore, we'd be halted by the Peace River and guided by it to our log home. The country alters sufficiently, becoming more precipitous upstream and leveling to eventual plains toward the east, so that at worst we'd then have no excuse for proceeding in the wrong direction very far.

The preceding is admittedly a broad example, for all of us will generally want to keep sufficient track of our whereabouts to be able to intersect a broadside such as a road or river within a reasonable distance of the spot desired. The question of which way then to turn should not ordinarily be left to chance, however.

Coming upon an unmarked destination directly involves such a disproportionate percentage of chance that rarely is it wise even to attempt it. Unless there are guiding factors such as reliable landmarks, the most expert technique by far is to bear definitely to one particular side of the target. Then upon reaching the trail, shore, or whatever the lateral may be, we will know at once which way to follow it—knowledge that can save time, energy, and therefore one day perhaps life itself.

Somewhat more difficult is picking up a dead-end trail that somewhere ahead comes into being by running directly away from us. By adapting the lore we have just been considering, however, we can also solve this problem handily and certainly.

Let us assume for the sake of interest that we are in a level pine forest. Earlier we came to the end of a long fire lane that slashes north and south. For three hours since then we've continued to hike northward by compass, the day being cloudy and the country more enhanced by animals and singing birds than by landmarks.

We have boiled the noonday kettle, and now it is the halfway time when we should return to camp. We would prefer because of distance to return there by the faster going of the fire lane. How should we proceed?

Do we hike back southward by compass at the same pace with the idea of rejoining the trail in about the same three hours? The flaw in that procedure, we realize, is that straight lines are only a matter of speaking in ordinary bush travel. The most that we will be able to count on in that respect is that variations will roughly balance one another if by mark or compass we compensate for drift and keep headed in the same general direction.

But suppose we do travel south for three hours, and then for one more hour, at the same pace we've been walking all day? Unless we have already encountered the lane by that time, we may be as sure as one is of anything that the lane now lies either west or east of us.

What at that hypothetical point would be the desirable procedure? To try going due west, say, for up to fifteen minutes, with the knowledge that if we haven't cut the lane by that time, we should cross it within a half-hour by hiking back due east? Or to begin zigzagging methodically southeast and southwest, increasing these lines until the lane is reached?

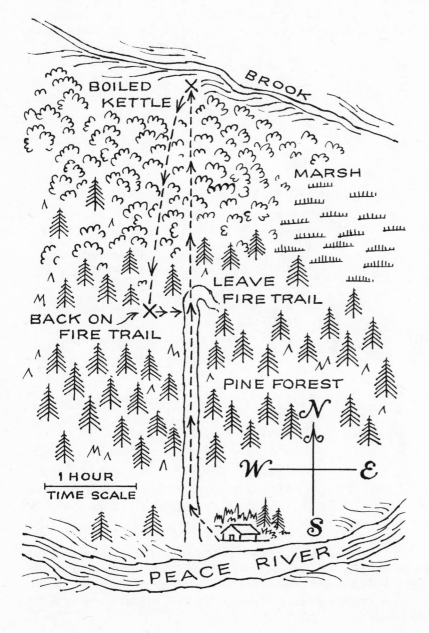

How to Pick Up a Dead-End Trail That Lies Ahead

All such approaches, you rightly decide, leave a great deal unnecessarily to chance. Percentages favor our reaching the trail with less time and bother by aiming at it from one definite side. So, from the very beginning, we don't proceed south at all. Instead, because the going is somewhat more open that way, we choose to bear slightly west of due south. Then after traveling for the same safe four hours, we can swing east with the assurance that the fire lane lies broadside a short way off in that direction.

Now let us suppose that a small party of us has pitched our tents beside a spring in flat dense wilderness where there are no roads or landmarks. Everyone has to leave camp separately each day to carry on prospecting operations. How do we all find our respective ways back each evening?

The reasonable solution will be to make a mark at which to aim. One way to do this is by blazing four lines, each perhaps a mile long, depending on the circumstances, north,

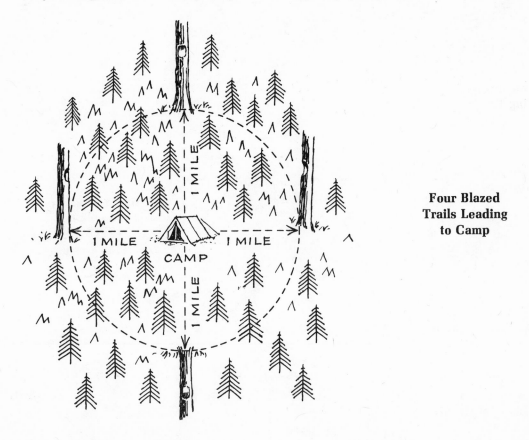

**Four Blazed
Trails Leading
to Camp**

east, south, and west from camp. To save time that would later be wasted in following any of these radii in the wrong direction, some informative system can be used such as cutting the higher blaze on each tree on the side nearer camp.

That's all there is to staying found.

Anyone who's fond of the outdoors should know how to get around in strange wilderness as well as he does in his own familiar patch of woods. Learning how to use the compass can be fun, and the skill itself is the mark of a good camper and woodsman. Camping will be safer and a lot more enjoyable if every member of your party or family has his own compass and knows how to use it.

46

Foiling Petty Thieves in Camp

SOURDOUGHS IN SOME OF THE MINING CAMPS IN THE FAR NORTH HAD an effective way of dealing with a thief back during gold-stampede days at the turn of the century. They escorted him at gunpoint to the edge of a river, tied him on a raft, and set him adrift.

Today there are often four-legged vandals sneaking into camps sometime after dark for a free snack. Mice, raccoons, skunks, opossums, porcupines, deer, and an occasional bear have been an understandable part of camping's night life and usually a welcome part. Unfortunately, the scene is now beginning to change.

Until recently, the two-legged intruder has been a blessed rarity among modern campers. Occasionally a local character, envious of good outdoor equipment, has been unable to resist temptation and has made off with campers' property. But among the campers themselves, vandalism and theft have been virtually unknown. We never had anything stolen or our camps molested until a recent Labor Day weekend in the Catskill Mountains of New York.

We'd had torrential rain for a day or two, and one night it rained so hard that the Colbys couldn't take the food box to the station wagon as usual. They left it under the dining fly on the table, covered with a heavy tarpaulin all neatly tucked in. The next morning it looked just the same. When a box of doughnuts was opened, however, it proved to be empty. The cover had been neatly replaced. Also missing was a loaf of bread, two packages of cheese crackers, and a package of hamburger rolls. The tarp was still tucked in, and not a trace of torn paper or box could be found. No four-legged sneak thief did this.

We've talked with rangers, equipment manufacturers, outfitters, and other campers since this incident, and we have been astonished at the sudden increase in such petty thievery that they report. Here a lantern, there a camera, some fishing tackle, a gasoline stove, or a loaded icebox have been stolen. More than once even a tent has been entered and pilfered. This represents a tragic change in camping honesty and a lack of respect for the property of other campers. Apparently you may no longer assume that all other campers are honest and will leave your unattended equipment alone.

Of course, most campers are honest. It only takes one or two bad potatoes to ruin a whole bin. But as camping increases in popularity, petty thievery grows also. These petty criminals may be young, old, poorly equipped, or camping in style. Much of the theft may be on-the-spot impulse. However, some of it is rather professional.

Stealing from a camper is a low form of pilfery, for it too often means the end of a long-planned vacation for a whole family. Equipment many times proves impossible to replace in the wilderness.

If a camp thief is deliberate and seriously intent on stealing, there's very little you can do to deter him other than to keep anything of real value locked in the car. Even there it may not be safe. These thefts are committed by people who go into campgrounds deliberately for that purpose. With them, camping is a means to an end. A solution? Insuring your outfit and possessions under the special policies inexpensively available.

On the other hand, too, something can be done to prevent thievery done on impulse by other campers or juveniles unable to resist the lure of small items, new appliances, and assorted gear at a tent site.

To be successful, camp thieves must have opportunity to steal and enough time to complete the act. The thief's greatest fear is being caught by either his intended victim or another camper. Unless he can do the job quickly, he'll hesitate or even abandon a chance for theft. He can't risk having to spend any time making the theft or walking away with anything obviously not his own. Here are a few practical suggestions to foil camp thievery.

First, don't display expensive equipment openly, particularly if groups of young campers are roaming about or eyeing your outfit with more than casual interest.

Using a small chain and padlock to link several bits of equipment together is another way to discourage a thief. The items can be moved close together on the ground or picnic table and held by a small chain passed through the handles, frames, hasps, or bails and locked at the ends with a padlock. Unless a would-be thief has a heavy-duty wire cutter, he won't be able to open, with the exception of the icebox, or to carry away one of the pieces without taking the rest. No thief would walk away dragging such a collection behind him, and even in the wilderness he'd hesitate to hang around long enough to try.

Some outfitters sell a cable padlock. This cable coils up inside the lock and can be adjusted to the required length. A cable lock can link such items as stove, stove stand, and lantern. But be sure to have along an extra key for any lock so used, or you may have to go hungry. For this reason, combination locks where available are a good idea.

While such devices won't long deter the determined thief, they'll keep the casual criminal from making a quick snatch. Even a professional thief hates to take the time to fool around with padlocks, rattling chains, and clanking appliances in a public campground.

Keep all small, easily picked-up articles locked in chests or boxes out of sight or in the automobile, where they can be locked up at night. If you leave them on a table, cover them with an opaque tarp so that they won't tempt passers-by.

A photographic record of equipment is a very good method of insuring it against permanent loss. Photograph your whole outfit. Then type identifying facts such as make, model, and serial number on the back of the print or, if you prefer, on the negative before it is printed. Catalog these photos, and keep the entire record at home in a safe place or in a bank safety deposit box with your other valuable documents. Whenever a positive identification of the equipment is necessary, you'll have the best proof there is.

Keep a list of the serial numbers with you. Place identifying marks on items that might be stolen. These can be either initials scratched into paint or burned into wood.

Or it may simply be a private mark known only to you. Properly photographed, it will provide you with proof of ownership.

One individual we know paints all his gear a bright orange, not only so he can spot it in his campsite but also to make it mighty conspicuous in another's camp. If the hinges on a chest or appliance have plenty of screws, removing a certain one and filling the hole with paint or putty makes an almost positive identification mark. Huge monograms painted on an appliance are so hard for a thief to cover up that they'll often discourage him.

It's obvious that valuable items such as firearms and cameras should never be left unattended in camp but should be locked up in your vehicle whenever you leave for any length of time. If they're stowed in the glove compartment—an obvious place, incidentally, for thieves to ransack—be sure at least to lock the compartment as well as the vehicle itself.

When you expect to be away from the campsite for some time, put all your gear in the tent, zip the door shut, and drop the storm flaps over door and windows. This keeps out the rain and prevents snoopers from seeing what's inside. If the door's storm flap is used as an awning, cover the door opening with an opaque tarp.

Zippers are a poor substitute for a closed and locked house door, but they often keep casual snoopers from entering. Solder brass rings into the small pull tabs of the zippers and run a padlock through them where they meet. One company makes a special lock for securing zippers. It sells for about $2.50. With this in place, the zipper tabs can't be reached to pull the zipper open.

According to some lawyers we've talked to, if anyone enters a zippered and secured tent, it is equivalent to breaking and entering a house and a far more serious offense than merely picking up a lantern from a picnic table.

Keeping possessions such as axes, boxes, and lanterns in specific places about your camp makes it easy to tell if something is missing. A checkoff list will prevent leaving anything behind accidentally, as well as reveal what may have been taken and not missed.

Such items as sleeping bags, iceboxes, and air mattresses aren't often taken. They're too bulky to remove without being spotted by another camper. It's the small items that are generally stolen, and these are the hardest to spot as missing.

If you suspect that another camper has taken some of your equipment, it's pretty tricky business to accuse him of such a theft unless he's caught in the act. If there is a ranger at the campground or if the owner of a privately operated campground is available, report the suspicion to him and give him a complete description of the item you suspect is stolen. Then let that individual take it from there. This will prevent the suspicious camper from claiming he put your identifying marks there himself.

Usually a petty thief will move out of a campground after stealing something, but he may claim that he found the item. In this case, just identify it and thank him for "finding" it and let it go at that. Trying to press the matter might turn the incident into something more serious. Recovery of such an item is certainly not worth a suit for false arrest and a court appearance. Serious altercations have been caused over accusations of stolen property.

A check with your insurance agent will probably reveal that a low-cost temporary policy will cover all your equipment from loss of any kind for a vacation period. It's worth investigating such a policy if there is costly equipment that needs protection. In the case of valuable pieces such as guns and camera, coverage can be inexpensively bought that will even pay for repairs in case of accident.

Thieves in the night can be discouraged by the chain or cable lock. The rattle and clank of either will sound particularly loud in the darkness. Because sneak thieves hesitate to use flashlights, it can frustrate them to encounter a chained collection of gear so near sleeping owners.

Another suggestion is to hang a stout black thread, such as heavy carpet thread, about your tent site and, with sticky tape, suspend a collection of cans, aluminum plates, or similar noisy objects so that when the string is hit by an intruder the hardware will bang together. If the thread is placed about ankle high, it will warn you of both two- and four-legged visitors.

A few years ago we bought some little "booby traps" from a joke store. These would have been fine for such a trip-line barrier. Each consisted of a small explosive in the center of about a foot of stout string. When the ends of the string were pulled, much like party favors, the device went off with a heck of a bang. A couple of these would be quite effective.

If these are hard to come by, you can make an excellent substitute with a mousetrap. Just screw a little trap to the top of a stout stake and attach the ends of the string to a set trigger. Place a big, loud, cap-pistol cap where the descending trap loop will hit it when the string is touched, and no one will get into your camp unannounced. Stick the cap on with a touch of glue or rubber cement and let the loop down on it gently for carrying. A couple of these set into the string barrier, then placed where anything six inches or less in height will hit it, will help keep grub safe.

If there's no food in your duffle bags, keep them in the tent with you. Too, take in anything of value around camp when you go to bed: canteens, packs, laundry, or anything that might attract sneak thieves. Keep all suitcases, duffle bags, and backpacks zippered and, if possible, locked. When going swimming, even within sight of camp, be sure valuables such as billfolds and watches are well hidden or locked in the car.

A little preparation and imagination will generally discourage sneak thieves and prevent loss of valuable gear. And in the wilderness, about the only thief encountered will be the furry, four-legged type. All but the boldest are night marauders, and many of the same gadgets and mousetrap rigs work very well.

It's a shame that human vandals and sneak thieves are beginning to move into campgrounds. Up until very recently, camp has been a place where another's property, no matter what, has been respected even when left alone and in the open. It's some consolation that the vast majority of campers are still honest and trustworthy.

47

Camp Entertainment

MANY PARENTS SHY AWAY FROM TAKING TO THE WOODS WITH THEIR children because they're not sure how the youngsters will react to the great outdoors. Of especial concern to some parents is the question of what the kids will find to do with all that time on their hands.

To start with, practically all children, even the very young ones, enjoy camping when they're with their families. However, let their instincts have their sway. If you take the youngsters camping, don't make the mistake of asking them if they'll be afraid to sleep in a tent in the woods. Few children are afraid of new situations unless somebody gives them that idea.

The great majority of youngsters take instinctively to camping, like young otters to a mudbank slide. In fact, they adapt to the woods a lot easier and quicker than most adults. To kids everything about camping is fun, even rainy days, leaky tents, and odd-hour meals. Just taking to the woods, living in a tent, and seeing new unspoiled sights will keep them contented much of the time.

Children's natural curiosity will generally provide them with plenty of things to do in camp. Even so, it's wise to be prepared when they occasionally ask, "What can we do now?" A few simple pastimes planned beforehand will take care of these rare interludes. More about these items in a moment.

It has always seemed a pity to us that so many campers ignore their surroundings. To us, that's even more deplorable than going to an interesting city and never getting outside your hotel.

Cameras, of course, are standard equipment these days for camping expeditions, but have you ever tried your hand at wildlife photography? With a little care, even a beginner can have pretty good luck. Most wildlife is best pictured at night with a flash camera. Even inexpensive cameras today, though, are designed to accept flash attachments.

To attract animals, bait and patience are needed. To take some interesting pictures, place the bait on a rock or stump so that the quarry has to stand or climb to reach it. Measure off the distance to where you're either going to sit and wait, or, more professionally, leave the camera trained on the bait. Focus the camera for that distance. If the camera is to be left alone, prop it between stones or set it securely on a tripod.

Now either lurk in the dark until you hear something at the bait and snap a picture yourself, or rig a tripper to set off the flashgun while you're snoozing in the sleeping bag. In the latter event, leave the camera in the dark with the shutter wide open. When the animal touches the trigger, he'll set off the flash and take his own picture.

If you see the flash go off, you can make your way to the camera in the dark, close the shutter, then put your flashlight on and advance the film, install a new flashbulb, turn off the flashlight, and once more open the shutter. Of course, be sure to set the alarm clock so that you can close the shutter before dawn. Otherwise, daylight will darken the portion of the negative that's exposed.

We've both had very good luck with this system, placing the flashgun above the bait and to one side, but aimed directly at the bait. We use two soft copper wires set so that the slightest movement of the bait causes them to touch, thus triggering the flash.

Another system is to stretch thread from the shutter across the path or to run it directly from shutter to bait. Make sure, however, that the camera is well anchored and that the thread is fragile enough to break after the shutter has been tripped. Otherwise, the camera may be dragged over or even pulled away. This is especially true if the thread is placed across a runway where a passing animal will simply blunder into it and set off the flash.

All sorts of animals—raccoons, skunks, porcupines, deer, mink, fishers, and even bears—will take their own picture if they're hungry, and they usually are. You're nearly certain to attract some kind of subject if you bait with salt, odds and ends of meat, fish scraps, bread, bacon rind, jam, or peanut butter. Some wildlife photographers put out bait for a few nights before setting up their camera, to get critters accustomed to visiting the spot.

Once the flash flares and you wish to reset the camera, use caution in approaching the bait. For one thing, the animal may still be there. And the use of a flashlight is apt to ruin the picture. Keep all light away from the camera until you have closed the shutter. Some animals patter away as soon as the flash illuminates the countryside. Others pay little or no attention and may still be on the spot. So check an area before approaching.

Occasionally, you can get two or three photos in a single night, either of different animals or of an especially persistent and hungry one. The youngsters will enjoy this sort of photo project.

An inexpensive camera, too, will enable young campers to picture their camp favorites, whether people or wildlife. Jays, for example, will soon deign to come close enough for pictures if food scraps are placed where good snaps can be taken. Squirrels can't resist tidbits, and neither can chipmunks. Porcupines will often sit for their portraits if you approach slowly. Caution: don't let the youngsters climb a tree to get closer pictures because porkies can back down a tree surprisingly fast, leading with their quill-ladened tails.

Although national and state parks, as well as numerous privately owned campgrounds, do not permit firearms of any kind, campers in the wilderness can enjoy target practice with BB guns, carbon dioxide weapons, and 22's. If your youngsters are responsible enough to handle such weapons, target practice can become an interesting adjunct to camp life. Be sure your bullet backstop is safe and that no member of your party shoots at anything under or floating in water, as bullets can ricochet dangerously from such a surface. It's a good idea to check with local rangers or peace officers, if you can contact them, before shooting.

For some quiet camp fun, bring along a good magnifying glass for each youngster old enough to enjoy using one. They'll find numerous new things to examine, including insects, flowers, logs, shells, and rocks. A glass of swamp water full of water insects will prove to be a zoo of considerable interest to a young camper.

Binoculars for outdoorsmen of any age can do much to bring wildlife closer. They also bring faraway mountains within inspection distance. We met a camper a couple of years ago who had a high-power telescope on a tripod. He used it to "climb" remote mountains right from his comfortable camp chair. He said he often found surprising things such as an eagle's nest. He told of just watching a pair of climbers for an hour until they vanished over a cornice. From time to time he had spotted large game and small, and he felt that his scope was just about the most enjoyable part of his camping outfit.

A few inexpensive pocket books on animals, birds, trees, shells, minerals, and flowers will add greatly to a youngster's and everyone else's interest in the outdoors. If you're not in a restricted area, a collection of wild flowers can be made by pressing these between book pages for later display. Leaves, bits of bark, and evergreen needles can also be made into a collection for later study. Insects, including butterflies, can be collected and kept in jars.

If the children are really interested in small wildlife, you may care to obtain one of those wire animal traps that catch small animals unharmed. Use the very small size for such wildfolk as field mice, ground squirrels, and moles. A larger trap may capture a skunk. Warn the young trappers not to shake the cage, poke the little captive, or try to handle him. Let him free after a short inspection and see what you can catch next. Seeing small animals really close is a big thrill for youngsters. The best all-around bait is a mixture of peanut butter, molasses, and salt. Apple and cheese are also good.

Armed with an explicit, well-illustrated book on the subject, adding from season to season the recognition of a few more edible wild plants can be a fascinating and practical hobby, as well as a thrifty and healthful way of pleasantly introducing new delicacies to your table. Such acquired knowledge can even mean, in some unforeseen emergency, the difference between eating bountifully and starving.

One of the more challenging of collections is that of animal tracks cast in plaster. They are simple to make. All that's needed is an inexpensive bag of plaster of Paris, a few inch-wide strips of cardboard or thin aluminum, some paper clips, and a little water. You can find animal tracks along almost any brook or lake shore and in damp places along forest trails. It's fun, too, to make a track trap near camp by loosening and smoothing the earth around a stump or stone where food scraps are left. The smoother and finer the surface, the more distinct will be the imprints.

Casting a track is easy in the extreme. First, make a loop of the cardboard or aluminum strip, and hold the ends together with a paper clip. Press this loop gently into the ground around a track. Now into this loop and the track itself pour a thin mixture of the plaster and water.

Let it stand until it's really hard to a fingernail or knife point. This may take half an hour or so. When the plaster is hard, lift it from the ground and remove the paper or metal ring. If you turn the plaster over, you'll find a negative of the track sticking up out of the material. Brush the loose dirt and twigs from the plaster, and there you are.

Now to make the track look as it did in the ground, cast a positive. Cover the entire negative surface of the first cast with grease, such as petroleum jelly from the first-aid kit. Put the flat back of the cast down and surround it snugly with a wider strip of cardboard or metal, the ends fastened again with a ubiquitous paper clip. Now pour the thin plaster about an inch deep into the ring, covering the inverted track. The mix will not stick in the greasy surface.

When the plaster is really hard, remove the ring and pry the casts apart. When the halves separate, you'll have a perfect replica of the track as it appeared in the ground, plus the negative from which other casts can be made.

If the halves stick, you can either break the negative and save the positive, or break the positive and try to cast another one. Sticking is caused by either not having enough grease between the casts or by some projection on the negative that is locking it to the positive. Mark each cast with the name of the animal, the place, and the date. If you like, paint the cast brown to match the earth. In any event, you'll have the start of what can grow into a really spectacular collection.

There are useful books for beginners about animal tracks and animal homes. In fact, C. B. Colby has written a couple himself, including *The First Book of Animal Signs* (Franklin Watts Inc.). Another helpful book is *Pocket Guide to Animal Tracks* (The Stackpole Co.).

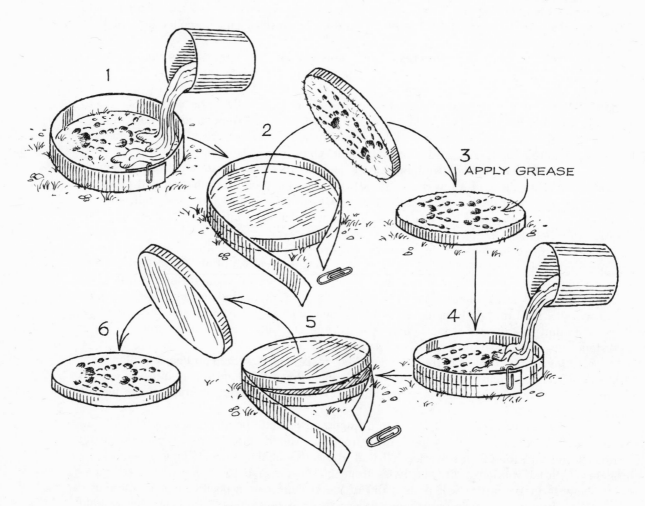

How to Cast an Animal Track in Plaster

You'll be amazed at how many different tracks, nests, burrows, and dens may be found close to your tent.

Another thing that even many veteran campers seem to enjoy is whittling. A great many campgrounds have their displays of whittled canes, walking sticks, and fancy name signs. Whittling is a good outdoor pastime, and you can always use the shavings to start campfires. Youngsters old enough to use a jackknife safely can make any number of interesting gadgets. Just don't let them get in the habit of carving their initials in living trees, benches, tables, or any other wooden structure.

What you do on sojourns in the woods is up to you. You can be as lazy as all get-out, or you can try to learn more about the wilderness you've driven so far to become acquainted with. Chances are that if the small-fry campers get started on some of these projects, you'll soon join in.

PART FOUR

BEING SET FOR
THE NEXT TIME

Stow Your Gear Right

ONCE CAMPING IS OVER FOR THE SEASON, TAKE A LITTLE TIME OUT to make sure that your gear will be repaired, clean, and ready to go again the next time wanderlust strikes. This precaution will pay not only in convenience, but also in hard cash. Your outdoor equipment adds up to a considerable investment, and it's just good economy to take care of it.

Finding a rodent-free area large and dry enough for bulky camping equipment is sometimes a problem. Heat and cold generally don't affect the possessions, and a dry basement, attic, garage, or outbuilding can provide fine storage room so long as it's safe from mice and squirrels. Best, of course, is an approach-shielded, northern-type cache, protected from all the little four-footed critters.

A northern-style cache can be either up on four posts, each of which has a metal jacket for part of its length to prevent climbing by animals, or hung from a ceiling on four wires, when stored indoors. Outdoors the four-poster is used like a trapper's food cache, with a ladder for human access kept close by.

Seldom used closets, hanging shelves in attic or basement, the overhead in a garage, or boxes under a bed in a spare bedroom—all these make good storage places. Even a house without an attic as such generally has a crawl space under the eaves or roof where camping equipment can be safely put away.

In many attics the rafters are connected with small horizontal braces a few feet below the ridgepole. This is a good place for tent poles, and by adding a few boards you may be able to store all your gear here.

Tents, flies, tarps, and pole assemblies can be storage problems because of their bulk and length. Poles can be stacked in closet corners, put out under the eaves, slid under porch floors, or placed across pegs on attic rafters. The new telescoping tent poles are easy to store, compared to old-time poles sometimes ten to twelve feet long. These poles were generally left outdoors or in a garage or barn, where they warped.

It's a good idea to tie or tape tent poles together for each tent, eating fly, or screened area so that they won't become mixed with sections from another unit. This prevents confusion when you're assembling your gear for another camping trip, particularly if each set of poles is marked with the name of the shelter to which it belongs.

Before putting away the tent, perhaps the most expensive piece of camping gear, lay it out and brush it well on all sides, paying special attention to wrinkles, seams, and the part of the floor near the door where it is likely dirtiest. If there are spots of dried pitch or bird droppings on the canvas, work them loose and brush them away with a stiff brush. In scraping such spots, perhaps with a dull knife, be careful not to cut the fabric. Lighter fluid often removes such discolorations, but don't use it if the fabric has been treated with wax because it may dissolve this along with the foreign matter.

The new nylon tents can be cleaned with soap and water. If the tent has had much use, the seams may require sealing to close needle holes and prevent leaking. Cans of sealer are inexpensive. The sealer is brushed on with a soft brush and closes such holes quite effectively.

In any event, brush the bottom of the tent where rain has spattered mud, and clean out the grommet holes and stake loops. If there are small tears in seams or if the loops have begun to rip, sew them with heavy carpet thread well coated with beeswax for added strength. Any tears in the walls or roof should be patched as well as stitched. Doing this both inside and out, then spraying the area with waterproofing, will result in a stronger job.

Tent ropes, of course, should be cleaned of mud, pitch, and other foreign matter. Also clean out any bug nests from the holes of the rope keys or slides. Brush off wooden and metal tent pegs. It is also a good idea to give them a coat of white or yellow paint, not only to protect them, but also to make them easier to avoid in the dark at future camps. This also applies to tent poles of either wood or metal.

If window screens are torn, they can be repaired by either sewing a patch of netting over the tear or by reworking a web of stitches with fine thread. Generally, though, most insects can be kept out by just sewing the edges of the torn netting together with plenty of stitches.

When rolling or folding the tent for storage, be sure there are as few wrinkles as possible so as to prevent future damage. Rolling produces fewer creases which might weaken the fabric and cause leaking. If you'll roll the tent compactly—not straining the material, of course, to get it tight—there will be no openings to encourage mice to nest.

It's not a bad idea, though, to unroll the tent several times during the off season and check for mouse droppings, seeds, and other signs that something is camping in it. Some campers set mousetraps near stored tents. If the tent is to be stored in the cellar or attic, use old sheeting or newspapers to protect it from soot and dust.

Sleeping bags should be carefully prepared for storing. If a bag has been used extensively during the summer, especially if it has no liner, it might be a good idea to clean it. Dry cleaning, depending on the method, can remove too much of the natural oil from the down. Dacron fill, on the other hand, remains unaffected. So with down, we'd wash the bag (or garment) in tepid, soapy water, rinse it well, and then dry it thoroughly outdoors in fair weather or in a tumbler dryer at low heat.

The latter may redistribute the down some, making a much used bag warmer. On the other hand, the most satisfactory way of assuring even redistribution is to lay the bag flat on a clean, level piece of ground, inside out, and beat it methodically with a limber stick, starting at the bottom, where the down has accumulated most, and working your way up. You'll be able to see and feel the rate of progress.

If you do have any sort of bag dry-cleaned, air it well before storage and again before using it. Some of the compounds used in dry cleaning are killers.

Sleeping bags should not be rolled too tightly, and they should be covered with something to protect them from dust and dirt. If your bag has been used only a few times and isn't soiled, or if you have used a liner, prepare it for storage by merely turning it inside out and brushing it well to remove wilderness dirt that may have collected inside.

Check zippers and snap fasteners for signs of wear and loosening. If quilting seams are pulled loose or are raveling, replace them. Incidentally, protect your bag from dampness because the insulation may become soggy and matted. Sleeping bags need more careful treatment than tents because they are of more fragile materials.

Air mattresses should be stored away as loosely as possible. Sharp creases and folds may weaken the material and cause later blowouts and leaks. Air mattresses should be partially inflated for storage, but again there's the problem of space. The next best thing is to roll them from the bottom up. Rolling instead of folding does away with sharp creases and subsequent weak spots at the folds. Some outdoorsmen roll their air mattresses around their sleeping bags.

Check the air valves. If they are brass, wipe the threads with a bit of oil to make the valves easier to cap and uncap and to help prevent corrosion. If the valves are plastic, wipe them with a damp cloth to remove any grit that may be in the threads.

Cots should be brushed off and stored covered. Metal legs can be painted to prevent rust, and any seams that show signs of pulling apart should be resewn with strong thread as was the tent. Check cots while they are stored for signs of mice, too.

Camp lanterns and stoves should also be made ready for storage. Before putting them away, drain all fuel; then light each appliance and burn out any fuel remaining in the generator or the tubes leading to it. If gasoline is left, it will harden and form a sticky residue in the generator, possibly clogging it and requiring a great deal of work the next time you decide to take to the tall timber.

On the other hand, appliances fueled by propane gas are safe to store with the tanks attached. In fact, they may come in handy during a power failure. If the appliances are fueled with small cans of L/P gas, do not under any circumstances take off the fuel cans until they are completely empty.

An L/P gas can is fitted with a small, rubber nipple that is punctured when the tank is attached to the appliance. If the can is removed before it is empty, there is no way to shut off the flow of gas. Remove and clean lantern globes and covers, though. Pull a paper bag down over the lantern until it is used again.

Straighten any bent handles or frame members, and clean off food stains or grease before storing appliances near tents or sleeping bags. Oil any hinges on the stove or handles on lanterns if they are rusty. If lamp mantles are broken or torn, you might clean them off, all ready for new mantles, after draining the fonts.

Camp iceboxes should be well washed with soap and water, then thoroughly dried and stored with the drain cap removed and the cover propped open an inch or two to keep the inside fresh. Drop the drain cap inside the box, incidentally, so that you'll know where it is next season.

Touch up chipped paint or scratches with paint. Polish rusty metal areas with steel wool; then wipe them with an oiled rag to prevent more rust (perform the same touching up and polishing operations on all appliances). Oil the hinges and hasp. If there is a rubber gasket around the top, a bit of cornstarch or talcum powder will keep it from getting sticky

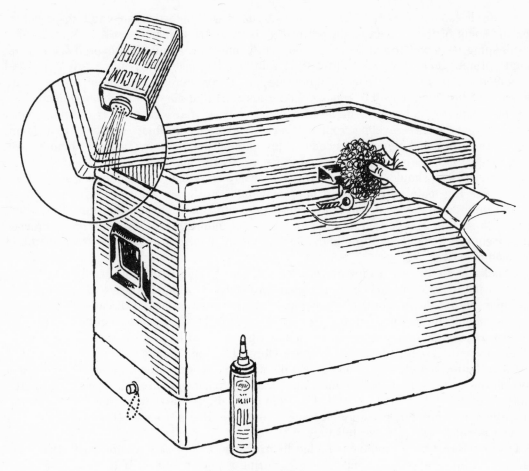

Good Icebox Maintenance

while in storage. Check everything occasionally during the winter. If the icebox is made of light plastic foam, do not store any heavy objects on it. Sharp objects easily puncture such boxes, too, so be careful what you place nearby.

Camp axes, hunting knives, and camp saws should be cleaned and sharpened before they are put away. Wipe off any dirt or rust, using steel wool if necessary. Lighter fluid or nail-polish remover will help to get rid of pitch. It is best to store these tools outside their sheaths, which may discolor or corrode them, and to coat the metal with a light film of oil. Sandpaper any rough places in the handles of your axes and set the wedges in the heads well in if they have loosened at all.

Sheaths should be kept rigid, so do not overoil them. Shoe polish makes a fine preservative. If an ax, hatchet, or knife sheath is ripped or has loose rivets, a cobbler can make it as good as new for a few cents. Or get rivets and do the job yourself, or resew the leather with heavy, waxed thread. This goes for gear with shoulder straps, except that here softness is a virtue, and you can safely oil such leather. Incidentally, clean out your pack basket or knapsack thoroughly before putting them away.

The cooking kit should be well cleaned, then covered to keep out dust. Canteens or vacuum containers will stay fresher if you leave caps off, corks out, and tops open. If

**Preservative for
Sheath Leather**

the corks are musty or broken, now is the time to buy new ones. Store these receptacles in a dry, well-aired place.

Any steel spoons, knives, and forks should be polished and packed where they'll be free from dirt and moisture. The same goes for other such gear. Wrapping them in metal foil or plastic is a good solution.

Many items of camping equipment such as flashlights, folding chairs, and tables will likely be used during the off season, so no storage precautions are needed. But if you do store a flashlight, remove the batteries and clean the inside before putting it away so as to prevent corrosion. Compasses shouldn't be stored next to metal objects, and such things as grills, clotheslines, camp mirrors, and other odds and ends should all be stowed where they can readily be found for your next trip.

As a matter of fact, keep all your gear together if at all possible with the exception, of course, of any items needed during the winter. That way, everything will be where you can locate it all again, and you'll be better able to check it occasionally for signs of mice, corrosion, mildew, and rust. Speaking of mice, don't pack any soap with your outfit as it's a favorite with the little rodents.

If you used wooden matches while camping and won't need them during the off season, store them in a screwtop jar, or deliberately use them up rather than risk storing them where they may cause fire. Such camp-use liquids as gasoline, kerosene, and alcohol should also be used up if possible or, otherwise, tightly and safely contained in well-marked metal cans and put away from any furnace or radiator. Apartment dwellers may be subject to strict laws against storing such liquids, so it's best to check.

Any food that's left over, whether canned or packaged, should preferably be used up. Canned goods, of course, may remain in good condition, but many campers like to start all fresh with their chow. If you decide to store canned goods with your camping gear, don't leave them near any source of heat such as radiators. It may be economical to hold over expensive dried foods, but be sure they're where no mice will be able to attack them and perhaps mess up everything else in so doing.

Towels, washcloths, blankets, and other such fabrics used on journeys back of beyond should be washed or cleaned before storage. And don't forget the mothballs or flakes and the tight plastic bags for storing wool. In fact, small plastic bags are excellent for protecting small items of nearly all types, and they are on sale in grocery and hardware stores.

When stowing things away, it's wise to follow the lead of numerous veteran campers and make a list of the items and their location. Then be sure you leave the list where you can locate it. From this all-important list you can see what new things will be needed for the upcoming season, and also check off those that can be left behind next time to save weight. Once you've decided what to add to your outfit, keep an eye out for pre-season sales. Many fine bargains in camping equipment can frequently be picked up during winter sales and even at auctions.

Do you own a tent trailer? If so, make everything shipshape inside before parking it for the winter. Many individuals raise the trailer on blocks to keep weight off the tires, or revolve the wheels a bit occasionally to keep the weight uniformly distributed around the tire treads.

If a tent trailer's canvas is stained, be sure it is cleaned as well as possible so as not to encourage squirrels and field mice to damage it, and check occasionally to see if any of the little animals have found a way inside for a cozy winter home. If the trailer must be parked under trees, a plastic tarp or other cover will protect the rig from droppings.

Remove trailer appliances, of course, and drain the fuel from the tanks. Small items should be stored inside the house or garage.

Wash any road dirt from the trailer's exterior and clean the wheels. Touch up scraped or flaked paint. Polish chrome trim and lightly oil it. If there are rust spots on the hitch, polish them off with steel wool and then oil the place to prevent more rust.

Check all cables for taillights and spotlights, and cover bare terminals with plastic held by plastic tape, or wrap them entirely with tape to prevent corrosion.

In metropolitan areas, check to see if it's permitted to park a trailer in a driveway or yard. You may have to arrange for dead storage in a garage.

Packing away camping gear for the winter may take a bit of time and thought, and you may even have to build a shelf or so. But working at storing the outfit brings back memories of the fun you've had with it, and future plans begin to germinate. The lady of the house will be a lot happier about taking to the woods next season if everything is cleaned, refurbished, either at the time of storage or later during the off months, and ready to use. So will you.

49

Homemade Gear

ONE OF THE PLEASANT PARTS OF SEEING THE CAMPING SEASON END is that you can start looking forward to the next one. Before you take to the woods again, there will be plenty of time to look over and work on your outfit, so that next season will be even more fun.

There are some things you never seem to have enough of around a campsite—tent pegs, for example. These can be made from a wide variety of materials. Pegs with rustic flavor can be fashioned from stout branches. Almost any type of wood will do so long as it's not brittle or rotten. We look for a branch with a side branch about the same size as the main limb. The side branch keeps the rope from sliding off the top of the stake.

These pegs can either be left natural or, for a plush effect, can be peeled, sanded smooth, and then varnished. Other stakes can be made from stout round sticks by cutting the head flat, sawing or whittling a notch below the head, and pointing the lower extremity. Make the rope notch at least two inches below the top to prevent the stake's splitting when you drive it. Other pegs can be made from 1 1/2-inch-square wooden pieces in much the same fashion. Buy good hard wood with a straight grain.

You can fashion some excellent pegs of aluminum corner-molding strips. Cut these sections ten inches long. Make the top cut straight across, but saw the bottoms at an angle so as to make points at the end of the stake. Next, using a round or rattail file, make a notch an inch or so below the square top. Be sure that this is smooth and there are no sharp edges remaining to cut the guy rope. Such aluminum stakes are light to carry, will nest inside each other for compactness, and will stand up well unless they are driven into rocky or extremely hard ground. For camping in that sort of terrain, you can make pegs from angle iron.

To add a pioneer touch to taking to the woods, why not try starting fires with flint and steel as our ancestors did? In the meantime you can make a leather pouch for the necessary items. All you need is a couple of pieces of soft leather about 8 inches square. The finished pouch can be either square or half-round. It should measure at least 6 by 8 inches to hold the items required for flint-and-steel fire lighting.

Homemade Tent Pegs

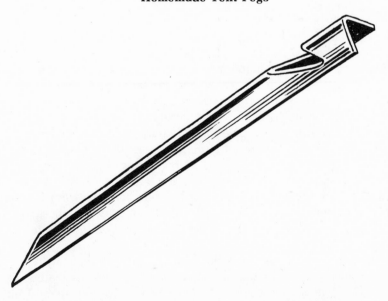

Stake Made from Aluminum Corner-Molding Strip

To make a square pouch, cut one piece of leather about 2 inches larger all around than the other. If the pouch is to be half-round, make one piece a half-pie shape and the other round, about 2 inches larger than the half-pie piece. Punch holes 1/2 inch back from the edge of the smaller piece and 1/2 inch apart around all sides but the top. Place this piece evenly on the larger piece and make companion holes in the larger leather. Now, with a thin thong, lace the top piece to the bottom piece, tieing the ends with a knot at the back side of the pouch.

Fringe the extra part of the larger piece up to the top corners; then trim the surplus to form a flap to fold down over the pouch. This flap can be fastened with a button attached by a leather thong. The button can be a disk of wood sawed from a stick, a bit of horn or antler, or anything else in keeping. A slit in the flap makes a buttonhole.

For the kit you'll need a piece of hard steel such as a bit of broken file, a piece of

**Making a
Leather Pouch
for Flint-and-Steel
Fire-lighting Kit**

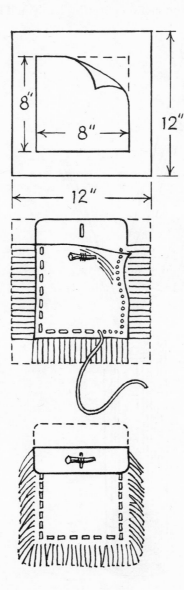

275

flint, and some charred wicking. Any lamp wicking will do if you first burn one edge of it. Charred cotton cloth works, too. You'll also need some shredded cedar bark.

To make the fire, place the charred wick or cloth on top of the flint, with the blackened edge close to the edge of the stone. With the steel, strike a hard, glancing blow down and across the edge of the flint, making sparks. These will be caught in the charred fabric where they will spread into a glowing line of fire. Place a ball of the shredded cedar bark around this and blow through it. When the bark ignites, toss it into some prepared light kindling. It's simple and fun to start a campfire this way.

Another worthwhile project is to ready waterproof matches for that emergency supply every camper should have. One easy way to go about this is to get some empty 12- and 16-gauge shells and dip them into melted paraffin. Fill the smaller shell with wooden kitchen matches and slip the 12-gauge shell over it to make a telescoped box. Now dip the closed package in more melted paraffin, and you'll have some really waterproof matches.

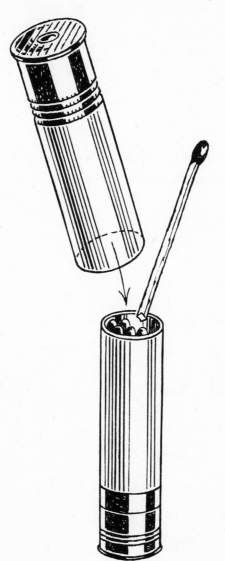

**Paraffin-coated
Waterproof
Match Case
Made from
12- and 16-Gauge Shells**

Some outdoorsmen fill ends of shells with small bits of cotton to prevent the matches from rattling, then seal the joint with tape before dipping it in wax the second time. For an added convenience, file some notches or ridges in the brass end of one of the shells to use as a striking surface when everything else is sleek and wet.

A waterproof matchbox that will float if dropped overboard can be fashioned from about four inches of aluminum tubing. Jam a cork into one end and cut it off flush with the edge of the tube. Fill the tube with wooden kitchen matches and fit another cork in the opposite end, but don't cut this one off. Now dip the whole business in melted paraffin, and you'll be sure of dry matches.

Another use for those empty paper shotgun shells is in making some handy little candles. Cut some cheap sash cord into pieces about 1/2 inch longer than the inside depth of the empty shells. Better still, buy some real wicking from a hobby shop. Insert a length in the center of a shell and pour in melted paraffin. These little candles will burn ardently, won't tip over easily, will not bend with hot weather, are easy to carry, and incidentally are fine for wet-weather fire starting.

Campers reasonably handy with hammer and saw can make a functional refrigerator for use at a brookside camp. This can be any size desired so long as the plans generally follow those here suggested. This spring box is made of lumber or waterproof plywood. A typical size is 15 inches wide, 18 inches deep, and 2 feet long.

It has a simple hinged top, held from falling back by a short piece of brass chain or leather thong. The shelves inside can be arranged any way you want, as long as all are about 8 inches above the bottom, or make a simple tray to lift out. In the ends of this container bore several holes about 2 inches in diameter to let the water flow in and out, cooling the food inside.

Place this refrigerator close to the bank right on the bottom, or set it on stones or

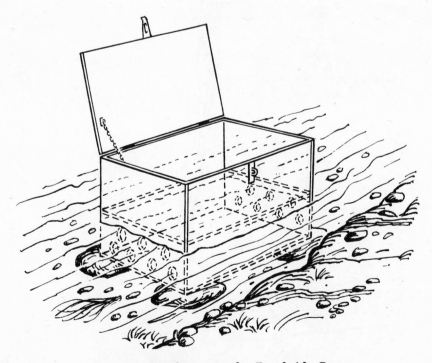

Improvised Refrigerator for Brookside Camp

slabs, so that the water level remains below the shelves or tray. Remove it from the wetness if a storm is expected that may raise the water level. If the current is strong, anchor the box to the shore with a short rope and stake.

Canned or bottled foods may be kept in the bottom, but mark the contents of each can on the end with nail polish, waterproof ink, crayon, or a sharp point, for the labels will soak off after a while. Such fodder as meat, butter, vegetables, and fruit can be kept on the shelves above the water.

Nails used in this homemade refrigerator should be galvanized, aluminum, or brass to prevent rusting. If strongly made, this box can be used to carry provisions to the campsite. It can even be used as a refrigerator before you get to the tenting spot if you wrap ice in plastic bags and put it in with the grub. For this use alone, cover the holes in the ends as with cardboard.

Another item of homemade camping gear is the desert cooler fashioned from an orange crate, some burlap sacking, and a shallow pan that will hold water. This contrivance works on the same principle as the water bags carried on car bumpers while crossing the desert—cooling by evaporation. This orange-crate cooler is suspended from a tree where a breeze will reach it to speed evaporation.

The crate is first covered with burlap, with a flap being left in the front that can be lifted to remove or replace food. Leave enough loose burlap at the top so that a pan of water can be placed on the top of the crate under this surplus, with the burlap resting in the water.

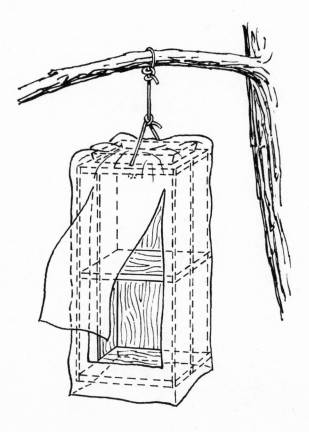

**Desert
Cooler**

Another pan can, if you want, be placed under the burlap empty and filled through the fabric. The water works its way by capillary attraction over the sides of the crate through the burlap, and as it evaporates it cools the interior. Keep the burlap well soaked for best results. Four ropes at the top corners can be tied to a single rope above the crate.

Other off-season projects include making saw and ax guards. A saw guard can be made from a suitable length of old garden hose, split lengthwise so that it can be pushed over the teeth of the blade. There it's fastened by short lengths of soft wire twisted around guard and blade.

An ax guard can be easily made from wood with a slot sawed in it. This can be held to the blade of the ax with a loop of inner tube about it and the ax head. Smaller rubber bands around the ends of the slotted wooden piece will keep it from changing position on the ax head.

Hanging toilet kits are always coming in handy. They can be made from heavy duck, unbleached muslin, or lightweight canvas. Make as many rows of pockets as you like. Start by laying out what you plan to use in the kit. Make the compartments to fit. Along the top edge make buttonholes, and on the back of the kit sew buttons so that the top can be buttoned back to form a tube.

This can be buttoned over a rope, tree limb, or other support when you want to hang the kit. Leave a flap at the bottom to serve as a cover when the kit is folded up, and attach tie tapes. If you're successful at this, you may want to make other similar kits to hang near the cooking fire to hold kitchen utensils.

Campers skillful with tin shears can produce some handy camp gadgets from large and small tin cans. For instance, half of a 5-gallon can cut diagonally from top to bottom makes a fine small reflector oven with the addition of a shelf or wire support to hold what you're cooking. These supports can be cut from wire coat hangers and inserted through holes punched in the middle, and a shelf can be made from the other half of the can.

With a little effort and some ingenuity, you can make your next camp more enjoyable and have fun making gear at the same time.

50

Next Season Starts Now

SOMETIME DURING THE DARK, WET DAYS OF WINTER, WHEN SNOW and sleet have closed out from the stultified mind even the memory of spring, the true outdoorsman usually catches his first renewed breath of the farther places. You may receive it from the note written with a stubby pencil on the back of a Christmas card, a glimpse of a photograph album, a faint recollection around the fireplace of a conversation while the flames of a campfire danced, or it may come over you with a glance at the way a sleeping bag bulges from a closet shelf.

The first vague thrill of discovery leaves you cool, but gradually, with increasing enthusiasm, you get out maps and catalogs and that fishing rod you've been promising yourself to rewind.

Making plans and getting gear in top shape are two of the biggest pleasures having to do with camping. Veteran sojourners in the silent places know these facts and take advantage of them. They use this preseason breathing spell not only to track down suitable camping spots, maybe at the head of those rapids through which they shot with such spray-drenching speed last summer, but also to make repairs and additions to their outfits, especially if put away hurriedly last fall.

A good way to start, once place names on the nearly roadless maps have begun to hop before your eyes, is by checking the tent, tarpaulin, and other canvas equipment. Spread them out on a clean, dry floor and check seams, corner reinforcements, grommets, and stake loops. Restitching any loose or torn ones will save more extensive repairs later on.

Such refurbishment can be easily done at home with a stout needle and waxed thread. Be sure to use a thimble to avoid injured fingers, plus perhaps a small pair of pliers. Or maybe Santa Claus has put in your stocking one of those inexpensive sewing awls that carries its own thread in the handle. These sewing awls have straight or curved handles for either canvas or leather and sew even heavy material easily and securely.

Check the seams of your tent, especially along the vulnerable ridge and at the corners. After any sewing, rub the new stitches with candle wax or with paraffin for additional waterproofing, or spray them with liquid waterproofing. Inspect the stitching, too, around sewn-in grommets where tent poles go through the roof or eaves. If these grommets are loose or pulling away from the material, strengthen them with more loops of thread.

If the loose grommets are the pinched-on type applied by machine, they can be replaced with an inexpensive, simple kit. It has a hole punch, a wooden block to back up the material while it is being cut, a die to set the new grommet into the hole, and usually several dozen grommets. Only one size of grommet can be attached with each outfit, so pick the size most used on your equipment. Incidentally, before installing such a grommet, you may have to set in a new bit of canvas.

If your tent has zippers needing repair, small kits for this purpose can be had inexpensively, including replacement zipper and lubricant. This special lubricant contains silicone and can be bought separately. As a matter of fact, while you're about it, check all zippers on sleeping bags, gun cases, jackets, packsacks, etc. On the latter, look also for signs of loosening stitching where shoulder straps are attached. If necessary, reinforce these strategic spots with new stitching or with rivets. Check, too, around buckles and D rings.

Check the seams of canvas cots to see if the material is still securely attached to the frame. A few new tacks, staples, or stitches in the right places now can avoid a collapsed cot later, perhaps at a time when you have no means of repair. Tighten any loose legs and touch up scraped or rusty spots on metal parts.

Leather equipment such as boots, binocular straps and cases, and rifle slings should be inspected for signs of cracking where the material is bent or folded about buckles or D rings or where there are other attachments. Treatment at such points with saddle soap or a good leather preservative will help keep the leather pliable and so extend its life. Work the soap or oil into the cracks and along the edges. You can also buy a little bottle of silicone leather preservative and waterproofing for about a dollar for touching up straps, boots, and other leather paraphernalia.

Such treatment will help protect leather from dampness and mildew. If mildew does form (and along the coast this may be a problem), wipe it off with a cloth and leather oil, then treat vigorously with saddle soap or the silicone liquid.

If you have edged tools that should have attention, now is a good time to give it to them. Sharpen the ax or hatchet with a good file, starting well back from the blade's edge and working carefully so as to retain the original contours while removing nicks and dulled expanses. Finish the sharpening with a whetstone. Then oil the ax lightly to deter rust.

If the sheath of an ax or hatchet is dried out, rub it with saddle soap to clean it. Then treat it with any of the good leather preservatives. This will darken it, keep it pliable, and help keep dampness from the blade. Go easy, though, when treating a knife sheath, as this should not be too pliable or it'll be apt to bend and give trouble when you're reinserting the blade after dressing out that bear. Shoe polish is a functional answer. With all these sheaths, check rivets and stitching and make any necessary repairs.

If the handle of an ax or hatchet has been badly roughened or cracked, it's better to replace it than to attempt repairs. If it has merely become slightly rough, smooth it with sandpaper but do not make the mistake of varnishing it. Varnish may cause later blisters on the hands, which should slide smoothly along an ax handle. Some axmen like to rub a small amount of linseed oil into the wood for smoothness without slipperiness.

Any wooden tent pegs that have split should be replaced. Either buy new ones or make your own from any tough, straight-grained wood. If you have metal pegs that have been bent in rocky ground, straighten them in a vise or with a hammer. If they're rusty, clean them with steel wool and then paint them, perhaps white to make them easier to see at night and to keep together when you're striking camp.

Check wooden tent poles for roughness, splitting, and for rust on the end spikes. Sandpaper away any roughness and varnish wood poles to help prevent splinters from forming. Remove any rust. Steel tent poles should be cleaned of rust and dirt, then painted. If they've been bent because of the rigors of past camps or transportation, straighten them in a vise or by pounding them straight on the ground.

Aluminum poles are tricky to straighten but can be corrected with care. One of the better ways to straighten an aluminum tent pole is to insert a smaller metal pole, pipe, or rod. If both ends of the bent pole are closed, remove an end cap if there is one, or saw off just enough of the end to expose the interior.

Another way is to fill a bent pole with sand and then proceed with the touchy job of straightening it. The sand will help prevent the pole from buckling. However, if the pole does buckle completely, you can still save it. Cut it in two at the buckle. Open the cut ends and insert a 2-foot wooden dowel, half on each side of the cut. Then drive small, rustproof nails through the hollow pole into the wooden support, and seal the cut with metal paste.

The tubes of liquid aluminum and liquid steel on the market are excellent for such mending. These can be used to repair almost any metal camping gear that's not subjected to extremely heavy strains. We've even successfully used it to fix the shoeing of an outboard motor. Such items as broken hinges can be tightened or fixed with this type of metal. Check your icebox and stove lid for such needs.

Repairs to such expensive gear as sleeping bags should be made with great care. Fix the zippers or grommets, check the seams, and inspect tie cords for wear and for frayed ends. The ends of all such ropes should be whipped (see Chapter 30). Check to see that no material is caught in the zipper when you put the bag away.

Packsacks and pack baskets, especially the pockets in such gear, should be emptied of any crumbs and accumulated woods litter. They make fine nesting places for field mice, as we've found out. You can fix split rims and broken strips on pack baskets with soft copper wire. Such repairs not only deter further splitting, but they also keep splinters from tearing other gear.

Check your guy ropes. Make sure the ends are whipped to prevent raveling. Untie any knots and check for weak spots. Worn and weakened places can be whipped with stout cord, a technique similar to that used by archers on their bowstrings to help prevent wearing from arrow nocks.

Preseason repair of an outdoor outfit is a pleasant and nostalgic project that will bring a lot of memories crowding back about where you've used it, besides assuring that it will be ready when you need it again.

Undoubtedly your thoughts will turn to the next trip into the outdoors, which can lead to some mighty fancy daydreaming. This year why not plan something fresh? You may discover that the new way of taking to the woods will be even more fun than what you've been doing.

Have you been travel-camping with one-night stops? Then why not try a longer stay at one spot? It'll mean less work, additional leisure, and even the meeting of more friends. You can make interesting side trips from base camp and thus get to know a great deal about the wilderness thereabouts.

If you have been hankering to see a certain part of the country, why not plan actually to go there and camp? Camping along the way, too, will cut travel expenses, and even a two-week vacation will provide time to see a lot of country. Write to the state travel bureaus in the capital cities of the states you might pass through and ask for lists of campgrounds on or near your route. Some of these grounds are at or near points of historical or natural interest.

On the other hand, you may come to wonder why so many tourists travel hundreds of miles to camp near your home. If you've never done so, why not sample some of the local camping areas? During these preseason months, try scouting out some of these regions.

If you've never tried backpack camping, exploring the backcountry on foot may be an engrossing experience. For tips on where to go, look around for a local hiking club or write to your state conservation department for information on state-maintained trails. Or borrow the previously suggested *Home in Your Pack* from the local library and write to some of the addresses detailed in it for maps and other information.

If you've been in the habit of camping inland, why not try a bit of seashore or sand dune camping? You'll find it different and relaxing. If you've been pitching your tent among the dunes, try some high-mountain camps. The change will be a test of skill, and you may like it even more than your favorite spot by the surf.

Maybe you've been camping in huge public campgrounds with most of the conveniences of home. Then try venturing off the heavily traveled roads to see if you can't be comfortable away from snack bars, regular ice deliveries, and flush toilets. With genuine camping skill, you can be. Variety is the spice of camping as well as of other phases of everyday living.

Happy camping!

Index